Beyond Monet

Dedicated to Michael Fullan, Bruce Joyce and Beverly Showers for encouraging us to explore and integrate the complexity of educational change with the intricacy of instructional design.

About the

Barrie Bennett is an associate professor at the Ontario Institute for Studies in Education of the University of Toronto, where he works with both graduate and undergraduate students. His teaching and research focus is instructional intelligence. Currently, he is working with several school districts in Canada, Australia and the United States on the integration of multiple instructional processes in the design of more powerful learning environments. Barrie has taught at the elementary, junior high, and high school levels. He was also a school district instructional consultant working with both exceptional and at risk teachers. He is the co-author of two other books: *Cooperative Learning: Where Heart Meets Mind* and *Classroom Management: A Thinking and Caring Approach*.

Carol Rolheiser is an associate dean at the Ontario Institute for Studies in Education of the University of Toronto. Carol is a leader in school district and university partnerships, concentrating on teacher education reform, teacher development, school improvement, and managing educational change. Her work as a teacher, researcher and international staff development consultant has emphasized instructional and assessment innovation, including portfolio assessment and student self-evaluation. Carol has been an elementary teacher, a district consultant and a school administrator. She is co-author of *Cooperative Learning: Where Heart Meets Mind*, *The Portfolio Organizer: Succeeding with Portfolios in Your Classroom* (available through ASCD) and the editor of *Self Evaluation: Helping Students Get Better At It!*

Copyright ©2001 by Barrie Bennett and Carol Rolheiser   ISBN 0-9695388-3-9

The authors have made every attempt to cite and credit sources. We welcome information to correct any oversights in subsequent editions. Also, the authors would appreciate suggestions for future editions of this book.

Published by Bookation Inc., Toronto, Ontario.
Designed by VISUTronX.
Distributed by Center for Development and Learning (CDL)
           208 S. Tyler Street, Covington, LA 70433
           Phone: (985) 893-7777   Fax: (985) 893-5443
           www.cdl.org   learn@cdl.org

Printed in Canada

Additional copies of this publication are available for purchase at www.cdl.org or by completing the order form at the end of the book.

Table of Contents

Chapter One

The Science Within the Art of Teaching

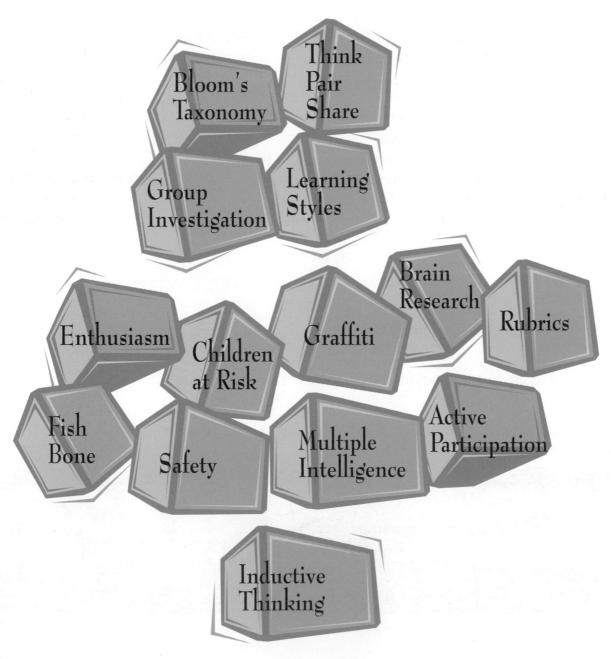

Bloom's Taxonomy

Think Pair Share

Group Investigation

Learning Styles

Brain Research

Rubrics

Enthusiasm

Children at Risk

Graffiti

Fish Bone

Safety

Multiple Intelligence

Active Participation

Inductive Thinking

Chapter One

The Science Within the Art of Teaching

Teachers are involved in one of the most complex, demanding and important professions in the world— a profession where changes emerge in the blink of an eye. One part of that complexity is that parents and students expect teachers to demonstrate expert behavior — a reasonable request.

In our experience, most teachers want to make a difference for students, but they often get too little time and support to work smart. So much comes at them so quickly, that just when they are emerging from what Michael Fullan labelled the "inevitable implementation dip", the next new idea comes along. If those ideas are not wisely woven over time, in an environment that values teachers as life-long learners, then the pressure to improve or add innovations is akin to throwing rocks to a drowning person. To respond to the ever-increasing demands and complexity, teachers must be aware of and act on the science within the art of teaching—a challenging task.

This chapter has five interconnected purposes:

1. To explain the focus of this book
2. To argue the importance of deep understanding
3. To clarify instructional creativity and expertise
4. To help readers understand the art and science in the teaching and learning process
5. To examine a sample lesson

Key Questions

1. How do teachers recognize the patterns that emerge "in the moment"?
2. How do teachers respond to those in-the-moment classroom demands?
3. What are the defining attributes of the concept teacher? In other words, why should a teacher be teaching rather than someone else who was not trained to be a teacher?

The Focus of the Book

From one perspective, the focus of this book is on how knowledge of instruction—as one component or thread in the teaching and learning process—can assist in responding to that never-ending press to create meaningful and powerful learning environments. This implies creative instruction; it implies intelligent instruction; it implies an ever-deepening understanding of subject knowledge. Most importantly, **it implies a collective expertise that assures that all teachers and students are actively engaged in challenging, relevant, and interesting learning situations—situations that connect to their past experiences and engage them in constructing new experiences.**

From another perspective, this book is a personal reflection—it reflects our own evolution and current understanding about creating meaningful learning environments. Our intention is a respectful integration of our ideas with the ideas of others through an understanding of the research on what makes a difference in student learning. It contains 25 years of personal thinking, experience, and research about the teaching and learning process. **More than ever before, we deeply acknowledge that a seemingly endless number of ways exist to be effective and ineffective**—and embedded within that acknowledgement is an appreciation that what is effective for one teacher and group of students may be ineffective for another.

Tangentially, just like violinists and knitters have to be careful not to blame the violin or knitting needles for not working effectively, perhaps we as teachers must also appreciate the skill needed to play with most educational innovations effectively.

The Importance of Deep Understanding

The more deeply teachers understand instructional organizers such as multiple intelligence, learning styles, ethnicity, gender, children at risk, learning disabilities, critical thinking, and brain research, the more precisely they will respond to the diverse needs of the learner. **The meaningless and superficial application of any instructional process does not do justice to that process nor does it value the learner.** As well, personal reflection and action by any teacher in the absence of an intense connection to the reflection and actions of other professionals would be indicative of 'weak-sense' thinking. Action without reflection and reflection without action are both unacceptable stances in education—students are too important.

Here is an example. A lot of educators think that because their students do group work, they are applying the strategy of Cooperative Learning. Having students work in groups without taking the time to inquire into the existing wisdom regarding effective group work is akin to thinking that any complex instrument will magically jump into your arms and start playing. The 'willy-nilly' application of group work is one of the least effective approaches to teaching. The various tactics and strategies that form part of the Cooperative Learning literature, on the other hand, work. We know of many elementary and secondary teachers who think deeply about the use of Cooperative Learning and employ it as one of many instructional options that make a difference in student learning. We also know of teachers who do not consciously employ aspects of Cooperative Learning and those teachers are also effective. They utilize other instructional options.

Instructional Repertoire: Creativity and Expertise

If we consider all of the existing instructional organizers, strategies, and content areas as part of the science of teaching, much like colours of paint are part of the science of painting, then we could argue that simply having an extensive collection of colours on the palette (the science) would not make one an artist. **There is no guarantee that a teacher who is knowledgeable, has an extensive repertoire of instructional practices, and is kind and caring will necessarily be an effective teacher.** That said, having all three would certainly increase the chances. This pushes the idea that art and science have a common ground—one informs the other. For us, teaching is an art informed by both science and an individual's personal experiences over time.

And if we are pushing for an "intelligence" in teaching, then it must be an applied and collective intelligence; one teacher working unconnected from others in the organization is not intelligent behavior when one considers how mastery evolves with effort over time. Pushing the art of teaching without being informed by the science of teaching, and pushing the science of teaching without attending to the creative/artistic demands of teaching are both unacceptable stances in the teaching and learning process.

We are not implying that a best way to teach or a best way to create learning environments exists. We are, however, responding to the ever-increasing pressure on teachers to create effective learning environments. When the pressure to learn and the amount to be learned increase, then the quality of what is selected and how it is implemented becomes increasingly critical.

Effective teaching is a creative act; so is *effective learning.* Of course, if you watch what effective teachers do day-in-and-day-out it may not appear that what they are doing is constantly creative.

At times it appears they are doing very little—perhaps they are simply scanning the class while the students are actively involved. **Nonetheless, if you observe effective teachers over time, you will see they are highly creative, weaving a variety of concepts and processes into a deep understanding of what is being learned.** If you asked them to discuss what was happening in their mind as the day unfolded, you would be impressed by the sophistication of their thinking. And, as you watched the students over time, from the first minute, the first day, the first month, until the end of the year, you would sense the result of their efforts. The teacher orchestrates, facilitates, encourages, and challenges — while the students engage in learning. The effective teacher's knowledge is obvious to the experienced eye.

Because teachers align their responsibilities with classroom action—action that continually reinvents itself as a by-product of diverse student needs—they **have no choice but to have many patterns memorized.** Those patterns are crucial to effectively respond to multiple demands and must be applied almost without thinking. This allows teachers to deal creatively with novel issues or concerns that constantly arise. In a way, this is similar to a chess player's memorization of patterns. (They say that chess grand masters have approximately 50 000 patterns in their repertoire.) The difference is that, in chess, only one player moves at a time and the pieces move only when the player

moves them. Teachers are not that lucky; their chess pieces think and move on their own.

The Expert—Mediocrity Tension

Becoming an expert (master) teacher involves continual practice and reflection over time. The literature on expertise argues that it takes at least 10 years to develop expertise in an area (Perkins, 1995). The research on the human brain reports that the brain's neurons become more efficient with practice (Diamond, 1998). Perkins, in his book, *Outsmarting IQ*, argues that the brain is a pattern maker. Those patterns are formed through the integration of three areas: (1) experience, (2) reflection, and (3) neuron development. The result of the ability to integrate these three is intelligent behaviour. Kounin (1970) labelled aspects of a teacher's intelligent behaviour over 30 years ago, one of which was overlappingness—the ability of the teacher to do two or more things simultaneously.

When the teacher cannot mentally apply existing patterns or create new ones when needed, then the teaching/learning process becomes less effective—more mundane and meaningless. This is when students sense classroom learning as a "hoop jumping" activity. And unfortunately, many **students who are unwilling or unable to jump through the hoop, passively buy out or actively misbehave, or some combination of the two.**

What makes the teaching and learning process so complex is its spontaneous nature. From our perspective, effective teaching has to be creative.

Ineffective teaching is not creative. When analyzing the literature on what happens instructionally, **we see that over time teachers are socialized towards mediocrity** (see Blase, 1985, *The Socialization of Teachers: An Ethnographic Study of Factors Contributing to the Rationalization of the Teacher's Instructional Perspective*). For the most part, teachers are caught in a conundrum—they work within a system that mitigates against creativity.

In the 1997 book that reports on his research into highly creative individuals, Czikszentmihalyi states that in order to attain and sustain creative behaviour, individuals need to attend to or experience a number of variables. Those variables or experiences include a deep understanding of a large amount of knowledge; time to experiment; access to information; and opportunity to work within a system that supports novelty and creativity. Unfortunately, **the organizations and systems responsible for the initial development and sustaining of teachers' professional growth often unwittingly urge teachers to work against what is in the best interests of students, teachers, and society.** That folly is observed in the low-quality professional development that serves to respond to the endless press of multiple innovations. In addition, there is greater responsibility to respond to increasing classroom diversity. All of this is nested within a professional culture that provides minimal time for teachers to reflect and connect.

The result is that most teachers are forced into replacing meaningful action with frenetic activity. That observation led Sizer to write *Horace's Compromise*—a story of how a highly moral teacher with the best intentions was, over time, socialized into mediocrity through a continual compromising of his values and beliefs. Tangentially, the current investment into extending teachers' instructional power easily meets the requirements of folly in Tuchman's (1984) book, *March of Folly*—folly referring to when we work or act in a way that is known to be against our own best interests. Saul's (1992) book, *Voltaire's Bastards: The Dictatorship of Reason in the West* presents this same idea:

"Thus, among the illusions which have invested our civilization is an absolute belief that the solution to our problems must be a more determined application of rationally organized expertise. The reality is that our problems are largely the product of that application. The illusion is that we have created the most sophisticated society in the history of man. The reality is that the division of knowledge into feudal fiefdoms of expertise has made general understanding and coordinated action not simply impossible but despised and distrusted" (p. 8).

Let's take the idea of creativity to another level. Why is effective teaching a creative process? ...Answer: No other option exists. First, step back and think of the complexity of teaching by considering the students who walk through the classroom door every day. Next, consider the variables over which the teacher has little or no control (gender, race, culture, divorce, drugs, alcohol, poverty, abuse in the home, multiple intelligence, learning styles, learning disabilities, etc.). Now consider the curriculum over which the teacher has little control, and juxtapose that with the time frame over which the teacher has little control. And last, consider the patterns that will "by default" and "in-the-moment" appear when the teacher spontaneously merges those variables. To respond to that complexity, teaching effectively has to be a creative process.

If you are reading this as a parent, think of the last time your son or daughter had a birthday party. How did you feel when it was over? Imagine having 190 birthdays, one after another. Imagine having only the weekends and evenings to prepare. Remember of course that you will have 30 at the party from 8:30 till 3:45; some will not speak English; some will not want to be at the party; some will have behaviour problems. The parents of some will tell you what to feed the kids at the party—of course what you feed them is math, reading, drama, music, art, history, French, etc. Oh yes, remember that one may be deaf, or have cerebral palsy; some will be isolates—others will tease them; and, 1 in 5 will have been abused or will have witnessed violence or will be living in poverty on public assistance in subsidized housing. Of course "the big birthday system" will test your birthday kids and compare them with other birthday kids from around the world. Don't worry though, you can plan each night after you have spent quality time with your family. One last thing— the statistics on this type of "partying" indicate that if you retire at 65, your life expectancy will be around 18 months—one of the lowest of all vocations and professions.

As a comparison to teaching, think of an operating room containing two surgeons, an anesthetist, and two nurses working as a team, with one patient—who is anesthetized. Class size of 5 to 1. Now, consider those variables mentioned above: multiple intelligences, learning styles, brain research, learning disabilities, gender etc. They are likely irrelevant to the surgeon when the patient is anesthetized.

Think of the plumber working one-on-one with the leaky faucet in your washroom; think of your hairstylist working one-on-one with you while you both drink tea. Now, position yourself as a teacher. Is there any doubt that teachers are involved in one of the most complex, important, and demanding professions?

The Art and Science in the Teaching and Learning Process

How hard was it to be A. Y. Jackson or Claude Monet? What did they need? A slice of cheese, a bottle of wine, and to be left alone in a field full of flowers or a forest full of silence with a canvas that did not move or talk back! The complexity of teaching is beyond the complexity of being Monet or Emily Carr. It is the artful integration of the science in teaching. It is about getting better, it is about being wiser, it is about making a difference.

Embedded in the development of this book, yet not dealt with directly, is the importance of **complexity theory—the idea that when certain forces come together, patterns will emerge**—much like a snow flake. The right temperature, pressure, moisture level, and—poof—billions of them —and every pattern predictably different. Fortunately for us the snowflake patterns are not inherently good or bad—they are not considered effective or ineffective—they are simply snowflakes.

Unfortunately, the innocuous nature of snowflakes does not hold for the teaching and learning process. In the classroom, patterns do instantly and ubiquitously emerge but how we respond before they emerge, as they are emerging, and after they have emerged does determine whether or not the pattern will be one that works or does not work. Complexity theory has a lot to say for teachers and the teaching/learning process. **Patterns emerge in the moment; the teacher must respond in that moment.** Pattern recognition and an extensive response repertoire are critical to success in the teaching profession.

Before dealing with the terms Art and Science, we will focus again on creativity. Our definition of creativity ties into the definition of intelligence, which is the ability to successfully respond to a situation or solve a problem when no set pattern for responding exists. The intelligent response results from the integration of what is known within a domain or between domains of knowledge, and is matched to a situation to solve a problem.

Hence the title of this book:
Beyond Monet:
The Artful Science of
Instructional Integration

Creativity depends on a number of factors: (1) having an in-depth understanding of the fundamental knowledge within a domain(s)—in this case the teaching and learning process; (2) having time to be creative; (3) working in an environment that values and demands creativity; (4) having access to knowledge within a domain; (5) having access to people in that domain; and (6) having the interest to continue pursuing knowledge in the field (Csikszentmihalyi, 1997). When these factors are not valued, creativity struggles to emerge. For us, Csikszentmihalyi's work implies that creative individuals are most likely experts; but it does not hold that experts are necessarily creative.

Northrop Frye Reflects on Art and Science...

In his book *The Educated Imagination*, Northrop Frye argues that although art and science meet somewhere in the middle, they start from different ends of a continuum. Art starts with the world we want to have; science starts with the world as we see it. Science learns more about the world as it goes on; it evolves and improves. An average physicist today knows more physics than did Newton. Art, on the other hand, does not improve over time. As Frye states: "...it does not follow that Whitman is a better poet than Dante: literature won't line up with that kind of improvement." (p. 7)

Although the idea of a principle of repetition or recurrence is important in art—i.e., to provide the rhythm in music and the pattern in painting—the principle or repetition or recurrence is not about one rhythm being more effective than another. The reason? Art is about identifying the human and natural world or identifying connections between them. Science, on the other hand, improves over time; if it does not, it is discarded.

So, how would Northrop Frye classify teaching—as an art or a science? In our experience, education has a relentless pressure to improve and is constantly pressed to work at identifying the human and natural world, or identifying connections between them. From Frye's perspective on art and science, we sense that teaching attends to both. That perspective encourages us to ask two questions: (1) Why should I be a teacher and not a nurse or plumber or lawyer; and, (2) What is it that a teacher does or knows that those who are not trained to teach would most likely not do or know?

Teachers Reflect on why they are teachers...

We have asked this question of thousands of experienced teachers and principals around the world. You would be surprised at the consistency of their responses. They say, "I am a teacher because I am enthusiastic, humorous, caring, organized, and able to communicate." They usually generate around 20 to 30 similar items. For example, at a recent International Conference in Assessment and Evaluation, we asked 76 educators from around the world to identify what factors defined them as teachers: "Why should we be teachers of business education and not chartered accountants, or teachers of art and not artists? " When finished, they were asked to take away the factors that groups who are not teachers would also most likely have (for example, if lawyers are organized, then cross "organized" off the list). So, what was left on the sheet should have been the key characteristics that differentiate those who teach from those who do not. What characteristics do you think remained?

In most cases the groups had no characteristics left on the sheet. They made little or no mention of pedagogy. If any characteristics did remain, at most there were one or two ideas. Those ideas were usually broad concepts such as "understanding child development" and "knowledge about how to teach." When teachers were pressed for specifics about that understanding and knowledge, the conversation was stilted. What distills from this activity is the difference between what is essential and what defines us as a profession. Teachers clearly realize that everything they crossed out (a sense of humour, care, respect, etc.) is essential—that creating a meaningful and safe learning environment is impossible without these characteristics—but that these same characteristics are insufficient in differentiating those who should and should not teach. My mother loves kids and has a sense of humour—why shouldn't she be a professional teacher?

What defines teachers is their ability to integrate all those things they crossed off their sheet *with* an extensive understanding of how students learn *and* an instructional repertoire that allows them to respond meaningfully to what is known about how and what students must learn. Interestingly, effective teachers have that repertoire and knowledge; they simply fail to mention it and connect it to what defines them as a teacher. They are also deeply aware that one's instructional approaches mean little and stand little chance of having an effect if the essence of teaching (being caring, kind, respectful, organized, etc.) is absent.

If someone were to come and observe you for the next two or three months, what instructional processes would this person see?

In Table 1 on the next page is one component of the results of a study by Bennett, Anderson & Evans (1997) related to the instructional repertoire of experienced and effective high school teachers in two school districts. The table represents three teachers' responses to the above question. In Figure 1 on page 13, you will also see a one-page summary representing one teacher's instructional repertoire after eight years of intensive work. The key point is that, like the three teachers in the study, he also owns and integrates the items in his repertoire.

TABLE 1. A LIST OF THREE SECONDARY TEACHERS' INSTRUCTIONAL REPERTOIRES

Below is an unsorted list from three experienced and identified effective secondary teachers from one school district. One of the questions they were asked was: "If someone came into your class to watch you teach over the next two to three months, what would they see you doing to make a difference in student learning?" This list was taken from their taped responses. We also asked them to explain what each meant. They could explain and provide examples of how they employed each in the classroom. Note, they did not get the questions in advance. When observed, they employed far more than what was on the list. The following compilation is just what they could recall.

Teacher One: Science
- mental set, accountability, meaningful
- modelling, checking for understanding, sharing objective
- cooperative learning, Tribes activities
- Kagan structures: think pair share, think pair square
- teams games tournament, brainstorming
- self, peer, teacher evaluation
- cooperative learning: jigsaw, Johnson's 5 elements, project work
- concept attainment, concept formation
- advance organizers: concept mapping, lecture/Socratic
- senses: auditory, visual, movement, Tribes program
- brain literature re short and long term memory, students' values, goals, beliefs

Teacher Two: French
- motivation, meaningful, interesting, need, fun, relevance,
- higher order thinking, 100% participation, student centered
- teacher as facilitator, negotiated curriculum
- anticipatory set, input, modelling
- monitor, check for understanding, reflection
- graphic organizers, Tribes, gallery tour, group carousel
- small group, whole class, individual centres, games, task analysis, portfolios
- media: computers, video productions, overheads
- cassettes, print materials,
- project driven, performance based evaluation, cooperative learning: jigsaw
- concept attainment, concept formation, mind mapping
- lesson design, role play/drama, pre-reading strategy
- multiple intelligences, at risk kids, multiple models
- senses: viewing, listening, writing, speaking, hands on/concrete

Teacher Three: English
- mental set, objectives, project work, literacy through the curriculum
- modelling, checking for understanding, practice
- cooperative learning: think pair share, gallery tour
- graffiti, 3 person interview, talking chips, pairs check, four corners
- graphic organizers: Venn diagram, flow chart, word webs
- agenda on board, oral reading, negotiation
- cooperative learning: jigsaw, Johnson's 5 elements
- academic controversy: lesson design, mind mapping
- learning styles, multiple intelligences, Tribes
- Bloom's taxonomy: knowledge, application, analysis
- senses: auditory, visual, tactile, movement

Figure 1. ONE TEACHER'S INSTRUCTIONAL REPERTOIRE

These are instructional processes one secondary science teacher uses to make a difference for students. What would yours look like?

LESSON DESIGN MODEL

MENTAL SET
- this is the anticipatory set
- get the students' attention to actively involve all of them
- link back to past experience

OUTCOME AND PURPOSE
- select an appropriate lesson type (see examples) with all required elements, hands-on (lab) activities and appropriate assessment

CHECK FOR UNDERSTANDING
- use a variety of strategies and levels of questioning to actively involve all students to assess their learning
- give students immediate feedback

PRACTICE AND APPLICATION
- provide both guided practice (one-on-one help or peer tutoring in a group) and unguided practice (working independently)

CLOSURE
- the final summary of the lesson
- should relate to the outcome and purpose
- involve all students in the summary

EXTENSION
- extend or apply the learning to new situations
- further questions for enrichment
- real world applications

TYPE OF LESSON

1. Cooperative Group
2. Socratic
3. Lecture/Drill
4. Socratic Dialogue
5. Concept Attainment
6. Concept Formation
7. Mastery
8. Academic Controversy
9. Role-Play
10. Mnemonics
11. Synectics
12. Scientific Inquiry
13. Group Investigation

COOPERATIVE GROUP INSTRUCTION

1. Five Elements
- positive interdependence
- individual accountability
- face-to-face interaction
- social skills
- processing

2. Grouping
- size and types of groups
- how are groups assigned?

3. Collaborative Skills
- taking turns
- staying on the task
- conflict resolution
- extending answers
- celebrating success
- clarifying ideas
- disagreeing in an agreeable way
- following directions carefully
- asking for clarification
- sharing
- praising
- negotiating
- elaborating
- helping others
- summarizing
- criticizing ideas, not people
- playing a role actively

MULTIPLE INTELLIGENCES
- verbal/linguistic
- logical/mathematical
- bodily/kinesthetic
- intrapersonal
- musical/rhythmic
- visual/spatial
- interpersonal

USE OF COMPUTERS
- word processing
- spreadsheet
- CD-ROM
- data bases
- graphics
- software

ASSESSMENT/EVALUATION
- anecdotal
- tally sheets
- peer evaluation
- self-evaluation
- checklist
- write up lab activity
- pencil/paper test
- portfolio
- rubrics
- project
- presentation
- performance
- PMI chart

LEVELS OF QUESTIONING

KNOWLEDGE (identification/recall of information)
- who, what, where, when, how

COMPREHENSION (organization/selection of facts/ideas)
- what is the main idea of ...?
- retell in your own words ...

APPLICATION (use of facts, rules and principles)
- how is ... an example of ...
- how is ... related to ...?
- why is ... significant?

ANALYSIS (separation of a whole into component parts)
- classify ... according to ...
- outline/diagram/web ...
- how does ... compare with ...?

SYNTHESIS (combination of ideas to form a new whole)
- what would you predict/infer from ...?
- how would you create/design a new ...?
- how would you go about solving ...?

EVALUATION (developing options/judgements/decisions)
- what do you think about ...?
- prioritize ... according to ...
- what criteria would you use to assess ...?

THINKING SKILLS
- brainstorming
- comparing/ contrasting
- hypothesizing
- visualizing
- associating ideas
- classifying
- evaluating
- analyzing
- sequencing
- prioritizing
- intrapersonal

POSSIBLE STRATEGIES
- small group, whole class, mind maps
- concept attainment, Venn diagrams
- lab work, problem solving, KNL grid
- T-chart, diagrams, posters, mind maps
- synectics, concept attainment, right angle thinking
- concept formation, using a matrix
- scientific inquiry, academic controversy
- scientific inquiry, concept formation, group investigation, jigsaw, fish bone
- open-ended problem-solving
- ranking

Is it important to be consciously skilled?

In stepping back and looking at the teaching and learning process, the public is asking why you are a teacher or principal or superintendent. Hopefully they will soon be asking why some of us are university professors—besides simply having a Ph.D. and doing research. If you are a principal, how do you convince someone that you are an instructional leader? Although an extensive answer exists, unfortunately, even when an administrator is highly effective, he or she may be unconsciously skilled. In other words, they are instructional leaders but are not articulate in describing why or how. The same is true for many teachers.

Reflect on the grade four teacher we discuss at the end of Chapter One. She had the students construct a simulation in the design and layout of a farm. As part of that simulation they had to solve problems based on their construction. They worked in cooperative small groups where the students were all involved and accountable. She employed wait time, she cross-referenced student responses, she probed, she distributed responses, and she asked a variety of questions both convergent and divergent and at different levels of Bloom's Taxonomy. Interestingly, she did not consciously know what wait time meant, did not know or understand Bloom's Taxonomy, did not think of whether a question was convergent or divergent, etc. Of course, you might ask: "Is it important to be consciously and unconsciously skilled?" We argue "yes." Both are important. Being unconsciously skilled allows you to act more automatically. It frees up "space" for you to think and respond to

Here is a quote from James Michener's book *Chesapeake:*

"But always he lacked the essential tool without which the workman can never attain true mastery: he did not know the names of any of the parts he was building, and without the name he was artistically incomplete. It was not by accident that doctors and lawyers and butchers invented specific but secret names for things they did: to possess the name was to know the secret. With the correct names one entered into a new world of proficiency, became... a performer of merit."

situations that are novel or unpredictable. Being consciously skilled allows you to reflect.

If the lesson does not work, how do you deconstruct the lesson to find out where it went amiss? How do you efficiently and effectively communicate with others about what you attempted, what worked and what did not? If you have a student teacher, how do you assist in the deconstruction of a teaching moment to talk about why it did or did not go well? Too often we hear of teachers throwing out an innovation after trying it once or twice. Yet, talking with them revealed that the problem related to another issue that they did not consider connected to the effective implementation of the innovation. They were not consciously skilled about how a variety of variables interconnect to create an effect.

For example, if you are trying to build a garage from a blueprint, but you do not have the skills of squaring the foundation or calculating roof pitch, then don't blame the blueprint. You don't have the skills to enact it. Relate that to attempting to implement the strategy of Concept Attainment when you do not have the skills of framing questions and providing enough wait time when asking questions. Designing learning environments for students is too complex and important for teachers not to be thoughtful (consciously skilled) in their decisions and actions.

So...

Perhaps one of the reasons we do not identify everything we do in the classroom is the swirling multiplicity of unassimilated knowledge in the education community. **Specialization and balkanization have created a division that works against clarity.** If you study cooperative learning with David and Roger Johnson, you are unlikely to hear much about Spencer Kagan, or Robert Slavin, or Jeanne Gibbs, or Elizabeth Cohen, and vice versa. If you study with a constructivist, you are unlikely to spend much time in the behaviourist literature, and vice versa. **We are unwittingly forced into a position of making either or choices: either you are a behaviourist or a constructivist. Why can't we be both? We like the idea of integrationist—the position we take in this book.**

From our experience over the last 25 years observing and working with teachers around the world, we have learned **that in the hands of a creative teacher, almost everything works.** Not simply because the specific idea was particularly the best idea, but because of the way the teacher integrated it with other ideas. Synergy. Similar to the observations made by Howard Gardner when referring to multiple intelligences and how they interact when the other intelligence are steeped in interpersonal intelligence, a synergistic effect results. One of the fallacies of critical thinking is the fallacy of either/or choices—of being pushed into polar opposites. Or worse, not knowing that the opposite, as well as other positions, exist.

When you consider the variety of patterns that appear with the prolific number of instructional possibilities, then you must conclude that teaching effectively must be a creative act within a complex environment. We must appreciate that teaching has historically been considered as both an art and a science (as reflected in the analysis of the behaviourist and constructivist literatures). For the authors, those literatures are functionally inseparable in the design of learning environments. **And although art and science both involve a creative process, we must also appreciate that, in most cases, they approach the world from different perspectives.**

As you observe a pianist or violinist, that musician will be playing from memory, or creating as she plays, but if you wrote down the notes that were played, those notes would represent what she played – a piece of music. The educational equivalent would be the teacher teaching——the notes, the lesson. The pay-off is that now someone else can take the notes and apply and extend that thinking—they are free to copy, adapt, extend, and integrate those ideas.

On the following three pages is a lesson by a preservice teacher who is just starting the journey. That lesson is followed by her reflection on her teaching. Feel free to copy, adapt, extend or integrate.

Lesson: Changes in the Physical World: Science Big Books

Age Group: Grade 3
Group Size: 27 Students
Subject: Cross-curricular–Language Arts and Science
Duration: 50 Minutes

LESSON SEQUENCE:

This lesson is the introductory period to a series of cooperative lessons/work periods that culminate in a presentation to the class by each expert group.

LESSON DESCRIPTION:

This is the initial lesson that begins a series of cooperative work periods that lead up to oral and visual presentations by each group. Students must work together on a shared Big Book in the area of Science, focusing on the physical world around them and identifying all changes that occur within their particular study area (e.g., Garbage and Recycling). They then teach the rest of the class through their presentation by elaborating on details and following a distributed graphic organizer. In the end, group members evaluate themselves as contributors, and each other as a group, as part of the final assessment.

OBJECTIVES:

Academic

- Students will demonstrate an understanding of change by identifying and considering all examples of change in various aspects of the physical world around them.

Topics are randomly assigned per group
  i) Matter
  ii) The Earth and Volcanoes
  iii) Garbage and Recycling
  iv) Animal Migration
  v) Animal Defenses
  vi) Bugs, Bees, and Honey
  vii) Chickens and Other Creatures that Hatch

- Students will show an understanding of change by interpreting this information, paraphrasing into their own words, and preparing a 4 minute group presentation for the class (being topic "experts" and "teaching" the rest of the class).
- Students will follow the distributed graphic organizer in preparing their presentation.
- Students will reflect on their individual contribution and group effort as an extension of the social skills content of the lesson.

Social

This lesson was preceded by a mini social skill lesson on group work using concept attainment and "yes" and "no" examples of effective group work.

- Students will work cooperatively to meet one common goal in groups of 4, sharing only one resource (Science Big Book).
- Students will identify and carry out individual designated roles in preparing and carrying out the presentation.
- Students will monitor and motivate each other in keeping participation equal in the group.
- Students will reach this goal by meeting the social skills of participating equally, sharing materials, and paraphrasing information.

MENTAL SET:
(Students are gathered at front of classroom.)

Briefly recap previous work on personal changes and changes in attitude (as studied in read-aloud, *Julius, the Baby of the World*).

- lead students to consider different types of change—ones we can see and recognize physically

- give brief "think time" for identifying 2 different physical changes in nature—lead into THINK, PAIR, SHARE

- have students share their partner's answer (raises accountability and motivates poor listeners)

- answers charted

- instructions given and groups designated after discussion

Student Language
"A few days ago we read about Lily and how she kept changing towards her new baby brother. You all did a great job explaining how her feelings kept changing and even WHY you thought she felt that way. But those were all changes INSIDE of her. What kind of changes do you think can happen AROUND Lily and around us? Look out the window. What do you see that can change again?"

Take Call Outs (2 or 3)
"Now, with a partner, think of 2 more things that change outside in nature. You have 40 seconds and then I'll be calling on some of you to give your partner's answer. So remember, you are listening, and waiting your turn. Ready, set, go!"

Wait Designated Time, Chart Answers
Acknowledge All Answers
"Now you will be working in groups and becoming experts on one thing in nature that has a lot of changes. Each group will get one book (display one Science Big Book) and you will prepare a group presentation about your topic. Remember to read carefully because you will be teaching the rest of us about your topic. Now let's think back to some of the important things to remember about working in a group."

Take call outs and acknowledge all ideas.

INPUT:
- Detailed discussion of what it means to work well in a group—equal participation, sharing one book without fighting, helping each other out, etc.
- Drawing of topics out of a hat by one group member each
- Distribution of presentation graphic organizer
- Detailed explanation of rules to follow, what to look for, and tips on presenting

MODELLING:
Another student teacher and I do a mock presentation on the changing seasons. We take turns reading out information and vocally stress all sentence beginnings that are straight from the graphic organizer. (Students follow along on their own organizers.)

Practice And Check For Understanding:

(carried out simultaneously)

- Students proceed with group work, starting with the oral reading of their book, taking turns—stronger readers helping weaker ones
- I monitor group work and the academic work as they progress
- help and guidance are offered and given as needs are identified
- I ask strategic questions about process and academic information and keep notes on checklist (on academic work and social skills central to the lesson)

Note: Check for understanding also carried out in Closure, with assessment of final product (presentation).

Closure:

Each group presents their topic—are called upon as "experts" of their given area (assessment here also applies to checking for understanding).

- Group reflects and processes questions and feedback from audience (class)
- All changes are charted, as identified by audience members (maintains everyone's accountability—must listen and pay attention)
- Charts/lists with titles and all examples of changes are left up around the classroom—reminders of changes in nature and of unit completion
- All group members reflect on their own contribution and their collaborative work as a group.

On the following three pages are the teacher's reflections on this lesson.

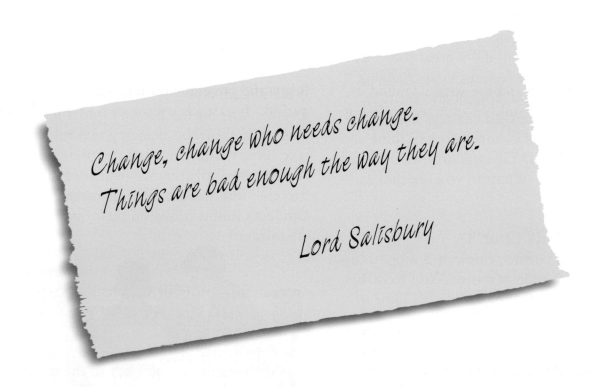

Change, change who needs change.
Things are bad enough the way they are.

Lord Salisbury

REFLECTION
REFLECTION

My placement in a grade 3 class was both a revelation and a challenge. I think I found my "nook" in teaching— high primary and junior is for me! I found this placement challenging for several reasons. The class itself was not an easy one, with a great split in the competencies of the students and a very wide range of behaviours. Furthermore, a major chunk of my placement was to focus on a cross-curricular CHANGES unit that was to prepare the students for their grade 3 standardized testing in May. The anticipated focus of these tests is the theme of change. My job was to put together this unit, touch on various areas of the curriculum, and heighten the children's awareness of any and all examples of change. I felt a bit overwhelmed at first, but I decided to think rationally and divide my lessons into themes that would make it easier for me to teach, and for the children to follow. As I grappled with physical change, I decided to focus on changes in nature and the world around us, and I thought it would be effective to link it with arts and public speaking and group work. The idea was a success and the reflection that follows relates this lesson and activity as it began, evolved, and culminated.

The basic format of the lesson is simple. The class was divided into groups, each group was randomly assigned a Science Big Book on a particular topic, the book was read, and all examples of changes were identified. The group then followed a speech/presentation graphic organizer that I supplied in preparing an oral presentation for the rest of the class. Every member was accountable for contributing to both the process and the actual presentation. As I

quickly learned, things would not be quite as smooth as initially predicted.

I put a lot of thought into my groups as I formed them before the class started. After consulting with my host teacher, I had a basic understanding of the kids' reading and comprehension levels. I applied this knowledge, making sure that each group had one very strong reader and writer, one weak, one higher-average, and one average. It was a long process with a lot of revising and erasing but I am very grateful that I persisted. For the most part, it made for very effective group dynamics, with a few exceptions. As was to be expected, the stronger readers guided their groups and helped and motivated their weaker partners. It automatically heightened everyone's individual accountability without my having to go around and remind everyone of their responsibility to contribute and participate.

I must mention that this project does not begin and conclude during one lesson or period. It extends over a week, with fair and calculated amounts of time allotted for reading, preparing, practicing, and finally, presenting. This was crucial in establishing a safe and comfortable environment for the kids where they knew they had to work effectively. I did not give excessive or unnecessary work time but at the same time, they knew that the time I gave them was fair and carefully monitored. I had to keep all the time limits I established to maintain my own accountability.

In retrospect, there are a few things I would change as I look back to the students' actual group work in progress. I did not anticipate huge gaps between the first early finishers and the rest of the class. I found myself scrambling to find meaningful and relevant activities to occupy the first group while the rest of the class kept working. Although I had predicted that some groups would finish a bit sooner, my prepared activities (self and peer evaluations) did not fill all the free time of the quickest finishers. I would now know to plan something else change-related that would maintain the theme for the students and keep them engaged in learning as their peers finished off their projects.

I preceded this whole lesson/project with a social skills lesson on group work, where vital aspects of effective and ineffective group work were identified and discussed. I used concept attainment to display "yes" and "no" examples of effective group work. This way, I was not sending the kids into a setting they were not familiar with or did not know how to act in. It also raised their accountability, because they now had rules that they knew they must follow. They also knew their behaviour was being observed. My mental set was effective because my kids not only eagerly participated but quickly caught on and followed my lead into physical changes in nature. They willingly shared many, many, many ideas and I had no doubt they were on the right track. Here, however, I did notice one of my weaknesses—I was so pleased with the enthusiasm and creativity of responses that I did not seem able to draw the line. Where I had promised to hear two or three call outs, I ended up taking seven or eight. I had a hard time ignoring eager voices and fluttering hands. I don't think this is necessarily good, because I did not follow my own initial guidelines, and spent more time than needed recording and charting obvious examples. If I were doing this again,

I would attempt to keep within my own designated limits.

The earlier lesson on group work was a success because the kids knew instantly what would be expected of them so I sent them off into their work groups. I am glad we reviewed everything in the mental set of this lesson because the kids seemed to have a sense of duty and responsibility as they found their given work areas. (This is not to say there were no complaints about whom I had placed in their groups).

Work areas were not randomly chosen, nor were the children free to pick their own spaces. I strategically placed chart paper and markers in specific areas that were far enough from each other to avoid disruption and to make for good proximity and face-to-face interaction. I feel this was a contributing factor to the success of the lesson.

Modelling was an important factor in this lesson. My associate and I followed the same graphic organizer that I gave the students in showing them an example of what I expected from their presentations. This also heightened accountability because they were not only given explicit instructions, but also a clear example of how to present.

Another thing I would probably add if I had the chance to re-teach this lesson is a brief in-group activity of charting "yes" and "no'" examples of group work that would hang in a each group's work space. This may have helped with classroom management situations that arose as individual members either strayed off task or found themselves in conflict with one another. (The problems focused mainly on some individuals not paying attention or expecting others to do all of the work.) I feel that such a list would have been an effective visual reminder, a great reference for me in classroom management situations and would have increased accountability. It is harder to break a rule that is hanging in plain sight. Overall, I am happy with the lesson. The final presentations were excellent, and I am most pleased with the individual reflections and group peer evaluation that I provided for the kids after their project was finished. They were honest and fair and all of the questions and answers applied directly to the activity.

My kids truly analyzed their own roles within their work groups and the success of their work as a group. I am confident that they learned both about physical changes in nature and about working collaboratively with others. I am including their self and group evaluations in my marking of the changes presentations. This is my way of rewarding and acknowledging their accountability and ensuring that I have many examples for a fair evaluation.

Final Thoughts

What connection can you make between a teacher's instructional repertoire, creativity, expertise, and student learning? If someone asked you to identify the factor that most clearly explains increases in student achievement, what factor would you share?

Research shows that teacher knowledge about the teaching and learning process (content knowledge and process knowledge) is the most powerful predictor of student success (Marzano, 1998; Greenwald, Hedges, Laine, 1996). That same research reports that spending money on teacher learning is the best investment in terms of student learning.

Darling-Hammond (1998) reports on a number of studies in the area of what makes a difference in student learning. She writes:

> We also know that expert teachers use knowledge about children and their learning to fashion lessons that connect ideas to students' experiences. They create a wide variety of learning opportunities that make subject matter come alive for young people who learn in different ways. They know how to support students' continuing development and motivation to achieve, while creating incremental steps that help students progress toward more complicated ideas and performances (p. 7).

She adds:

> What teachers know and can do makes the crucial difference in what children learn. And the ways school systems organize their work makes a big difference in what teachers can accomplish (p.12).

The unequivocal implication is that we will improve learning when we collectively, intelligently, and creatively focus our efforts on improving the teaching and learning process. The more we understand about the learner, the more we understand about meaningful and responsible assessment and evaluation, the more we understand about what is to be learned, the more we understand about the instructional processes, and the more we understand about collectively acting on what we understand, then the more likely we are to make a difference. Teaching is a complex and creative undertaking.

What have we learned
so far?

- Teaching is complex

- Teaching is demanding

- Teaching is important

- Teaching effectively is an art informed by a science...and personal experience

- It takes years of practice to become an expert (that applies to most activities such as gymnastics, playing the piano, or art)

- Effective teachers increase their ability to recognize and respond to patterns

- No one best way to teach exists; each teacher can teach differently and be equally effective...or ineffective

-

-

Chapter *Two*

Instructional Complexity: Creating the Patterns

Instructional skills

Instructional strategies

Instructional concepts

Instructional tactics

Instructional organizers

Chapter Two

Instructional Complexity: Creating the Patterns

In the last chapter we argued that teaching effectively is a complex, demanding and important process. Specifically, to be effective over time, teachers must become creative experts who collectively make wise decisions related to the teaching and learning process. The idea of 'collective' is not unusual in art. For example, often we see two, three or four glass artists whose knowledge of the science of glass allow them to simultaneously blow and design one piece – its complexity demands collective intelligence. Teaching complexity demands the same kind of collective intelligence.

We also shared aspects of the research literature on expert and creative thinking and actions. That literature informs us that experts have an ever-increasing base of knowledge in multiple domains with concomitant skills and strategies—they understand patterns. This chapter focuses on one area of teaching and learning complexity —'instructional patterns.'

This chapter has seven interconnected areas:

1. Providing the introduction and rationale to the chapter
2. Integrating a variety of instructional processes – a rationale
3. Experiencing an activity related to determining instructional design
4. Explaining Perkins' work on Knowledge as Design
5. Applying Knowledge as Design to understand eight instructional areas
6. Assessing this line of thinking
7. Applying what you learned - a sample lesson.

Key Questions

1. How are each of these instructional 'areas' different: Multiple Intelligences, Mind Mapping, Think/Pair Share, Wait Time, and Accountability?
2. What is the relationship between them—how do they inform or assist one another?
3. In terms of classroom complexity, why is it critical to understand the relationships between instructional options (how they help each other)?

Introduction and Rationale

How can any educator possibly integrate and apply the seemingly endless number of instructional possibilities? Some programs have described the variety (e.g., *Dimensions of Learning*, Marzano, 1992); however, we want to move beyond the description to the actual application and integration. In this chapter we explain a critical step. We begin by identifying and clarifying some of the instructional concepts, skills, tactics, strategies, and organizers that represent the science component within the art of teaching. This step assists in clarifying the instructional language of our profession. Increasing what Perkins, in his book *Outsmarting IQ*, labels symbolic intelligence.

As we play out that instructional language as a defining or necessary attribute of teaching, we must realize, that on its own, this technical or scientific perspective is insufficient. We are not after a reductionist view of teaching; rather, we are searching for a more integrative approach. Below are other areas that assist in shifting the technical aspects of instruction into the art of teaching.

If we simply embrace the technical component and develop the ability to routinely apply those possibilities in an unconnected, unthinking, checklist-like manner, then we are simply operating with a mechanistic mentality that mitigates against creativity.

Additional areas that assist educators in shifting to a more artful approach to teaching.

- the idea of 'intelligence' (making effective decisions or responses through innovative combinations of ideas based on 'knowing' the learner through multiple lenses) implies creativity
- one's personality and interpersonal intelligence; Goleman (1998) calls this self awareness and awareness of others…two key areas in Emotional Intelligence
- an ever-deepening understanding of subject matter knowledge
- a wisdom about the use of assessment data and how to act on what those data tell us

One More Step

On the previous page we mentioned four areas that are critical to shift the science of teaching into the art of teaching. Obviously, other important areas exist; for example, understanding the process of change; understanding how one learns over time; and, carrying out our professional work in an environment that supports intelligent and creative teaching.

As argued in the introduction to this book, teaching effectively is a highly creative, inquisitive, reflective, and interpersonal process. William Hare (1995) identifies these interpersonal and inquisitive components in his book, *What Makes a Good Teacher*. He lists a number of affective qualities: humility, courage, impartiality, empathy, enthusiasm, judgment, and imagination— and those certainly meaningfully connect to the cognitive. Kieran Egan (1994) argues the importance of the practical value of tools and techniques as we attend to the centrality of imagination in the teaching and learning process.

Such tools might be skills such as wait time and framing questions, and strategies such as Academic Controversy and Mind Mapping. The effective teacher has an artful mix of both the affective and technical dimensions.

Please remember the list is most likely endless; and tangentially, you only have about 35 years in which to acquire and integrate. Perhaps the sequence is like those individuals who live to play music in all its forms, they learn one instrument and then another. Soon they're an ensemble of one, a conductor putting it all together. Michael Fullan's change maxim, "start small, think big" makes sense.

This chapter simply clarifies terminology, or how we apply the terms. Most of the terms have been around for a long time, and most have multiple meanings. We believe an understanding and use of terms is critical to understanding how to integrate or weave together multiple processes. On the following page are four comments that provide a rationale for this chapter.

Although we do not focus specifically on the educational change literature... this book is fundamentally about change. We encourage you to read, understand, and act on the knowledge in Fullan's (2001) book: *The New Meaning of Educational Change.*

Rationale for Integrating and Stacking Instructional Processes.

1. **Teaching is becoming more complex** and more demanding and stands little chance of becoming less complex or less demanding. Teachers must increase their repertoire to respond to those complexities and those demands. Why 'must?'

    First, the Multiple Intelligence, Learning Styles, and the Human Brain literature communicates what effective teachers have known for years—students don't all learn in the same way or at the same rate.

    Second, Susan Rosenholtz's (1989) research reports that 20 - 30 percent of first year teachers do not return for the second year of teaching. And, another similar size group has left by the end of five years. The reasons those teachers left relate to their having no sense of efficacy about how to teach, how to manage the class (discipline), and how to deal with being isolated within the school.

2. The nature of teaching has changed. **The real world does not work in rows** nor do people interact by simply recalling facts in the absence of discussion … unless they are playing 'Trivial Pursuit.' Rather, people must be able to work in groups to inquire, to process information, to confront and resolve authentic issues, problems, and task demands. Listen to your conversation with friends and determine the nature of your thinking—is it analysis, evaluation, diverging, converging, resolving, and creating, or simple recall of facts? Listen to students. Their dialogue is no different.

Bennett and Sampson (1995) report on speech and language delayed Kindergarten students who worked on six group investigations during one academic year related to topics such as *"Why don't gorillas have tails? Why do germs make us sick in the winter? How does ice form?"* Even children this young engaged in discussion beyond the use of mere facts.

3. Instructional strategies increase the chances students are actively and meaningfully involved in complex forms of thinking and communicating. Learning improves. **The strategies place the learning in the hands and minds of the learners** – the process becomes as important as the product.

4. Integration allows the heart to meet the mind. With the large number of students coming to school being at risk students (approximately 1 in 6 in Canada) it seems that if we desire to create meaningful learning environments, we must provide safe environments and meaningful content in a variety of ways.

Determining Instructional Design: An Activity

The purpose of this chapter is to understand how to connect instructional 'ideas' such as the ones below. One way to develop an understanding of different instructional ideas is by classifying them into groups based on the role they play in designing learning environments, and then discussing the relationship between the groups. (Note: this is Hilda Taba's Inductive Thinking strategy as described in Chapter 9.)

How would you classify these instructional terms? How do they work together to assist in creating a powerful learning environment?

The authors suggest you work alone or in a small cooperative group to classify these instructional ideas based on the role they play in the design and enactment of effective learning environments.

Note: we are not suggesting that you must use or attend to these. We could do this same activity with a completely different list. The idea here is simply to begin exploring teaching complexity. If you prefer, create your own list of all the things you employ to make a difference for kids, then inductively make sense of how they interact.

1. Multiple Intelligence
2. Wait Time
3. Inside/Outside Circles
4. Bloom's Taxonomy
5. Diversity
6. Children at Risk
7. Think Pair Share
8. Ethnicity
9. Academic Controversy
10. Demonstrating
11. Reading Recovery
12. Concept Mapping
13. Suspending Judgement
14. Triple Entry Journal
15. Lecture
16. Check for Understanding
17. Role Playing
18. Enthusiasm
19. Whole Language
20. Gender
21. Group Investigation
22. Cooperative Learning
23. Portfolios
24. Concept Attainment
25. Motivation
26. Success
27. First Steps
28. Mind Mapping
29. Venn Diagram
30. Jigsaw
31. Accountability
32. Team Analysis
33. Caring
34. Learning Styles
35. Humour
36. Inductive Thinking
37. Learning Disabilities
38. PMI (positive, minus, interesting)
40. Practice
41. Inquiry
42. Challenging
43. Brain Research
44. Active Participation
45. Critical Thinking
46. Emotional Intelligence
47. Experiments

On the following page, we take the idea of knowledge as having a design from the work of David Perkins in his book *Knowledge as Design*. You will find *Knowledge as Design* a practical process that helps ensure that students more deeply understand key ideas.

We employ Perkins's process to assist us in more accurately understanding instructional ideas such as those listed above.

Knowledge as Design

David Perkins (1986) in his book *Knowledge as Design* argues that too often we are limited in our thinking and actions as a result of our lack of deep understanding of the concepts that guide our thinking and actions. He calls this having "knowledge as information" as opposed to "knowledge as design." This is certainly true related to many teachers' understanding of instructional design.

In this chapter our objective is to push your thinking around the idea of instructional design. Additionally, we are encouraging a deeper understanding of how instructional processes work together, almost like a weaving. The ideas in this chapter are an extension of our work and research over the last 15 years (Bennett, Anderson, & Evans 1997; Bennett, Rolheiser, & Stevahn, 1991; Rolheiser, 1986). As part of the discussion, we work at making the terms we use in this book meaningful by employing David Perkins's questions related to knowledge as design.

1. **What is the structure of the concept?**
2. **What are the purposes of the concept?**
3. **What are the model cases of the concept?**
4. **What are the arguments supporting or not supporting it?**

For example, if the concept were "screwdriver" we would respond with:

1. **Structure:** a handle, a shaft, and a shape on the end that fits into screws
2. **Purpose:** to assist in putting screws into objects
3. **Model Cases:** Flat Head, Robertson, and Phillips
4. **Argument:** it gives us mechanical advantage

We employ those four questions to clarify the concepts of **Pedagogy, Instructional Organizers, Instructional Strategies, Instructional Tactics, Instructional Skills, Instructional Concepts, Integration and Stacking Instructional Processes, and Instructional Power.** Obviously, Monet did not paint with one colour. Nor do master chefs limit themselves to one salad. Hair stylists, dentists, and contractors all have an extensive repertoire of responses for different situations. Obviously your students are more important than paint, lettuce, and hair. What is your repertoire, how do you integrate it, and how powerful is it in meeting the diverse needs of learners?

Note: Other categories exist such as instructional dispositions (caring, politeness, enthusiasm, humour); instructional materials (videos, puppets, storybooks, computers) and instructional philosophies (differentiated instruction, whole language, constructivism, direct instruction). Due to space limitations we did not include these other categories in this book.

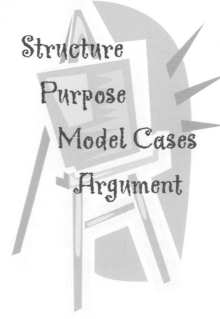

Structure
Purpose
Model Cases
Argument

Application of "Knowledge as Design" to Extending One's Instructional Repertoire

The design framework by Perkins, described on the previous page, is employed to analyze and organize the extensive instructional literature. In addition, we employ it to clarify our thinking about how a variety of instructional options can be integrated to explore the nature of teachers' instructional repertoires.

Bennett, Anderson, and Evans (1997) applied Perkins's framework in an inductive analysis of experienced and identified effective teachers' instructional repertoires. The chart below illustrates the labels for the groups. Each of those groups is explained in more depth at the end of this section.

Chart 2-1
Classification of an Instructional Repertoire

- Instructional concepts (variety, active participation)

- Instructional skills (modelling, asking a divergent question)

- Instructional tactics (Venn Diagram, 3-Step Interview)

- Instructional strategies (Concept Attainment, Inductive Thinking)

- Instructional organizers (Brain Research, Bloom's Taxonomy)

What follows for the rest of this chapter is an important analysis of instruction. **Do not attempt to read this section unless you are wide-awake, having sipped three expressos.** As mentioned previously, David Perkins argues that if a learner can respond to the four questions identified on the previous page and repeated below, then the learner is more likely to own the concept—to be able to think or problem-solve with that concept. He compares this to the idea of "knowledge as information"—where the knowledge is passive and cannot be brought into the realm of problem solving or the connecting of ideas. The concept owns the learner.

1. What is the **structure** (critical essence) of the concept?
2. What is the **purpose** of the concept?
3. What are the **model cases** of the concept?
4. What are the **arguments supporting** the concept?

We have adapted these design questions to determine the extent to which the teacher has control over a specific instructional approach that is part of their pedagogy. What follows is how we applied Perkins's questions to the concepts of pedagogy, concepts, skills, tactics, strategies, and organizers.

Something to Ponder

How many useless things have you acquired in your life? Or, we could ask, how many of the useful things in your life do you really own? Or, do they own you? One of the authors knows why boomerangs return. That knowledge allows him to not only design boomerangs, but how to design both left-and right-handed boomerangs. It is one thing to recall what a boomerang is; it is another thing to understand how to design, throw, and catch.

What about these questions?

- What is the difference between a concept and a fact? Do you really know?
- Can curved lines be parallel? Can lines be curved?
- Why does −2 times −2 = 4? Why the change in signs? Provide a real life example.
- Do you provide Wait Time when you ask questions? Why? Why not?
- What are the critical attributes of effective choices in classroom management?
- What is the difference between Learning Styles and Multiple Intelligence?
- You teach 30 brains—what do you know about the brain and learning?

Obviously, understanding the design of everything is not possible. And of course, for some knowledge we really don't need to know … at least that is what we think. What if we really knew—would we approach learning differently?

For example, let's apply the four "design" questions to Cooperative Learning (as contrasted to "group work") or we could simply say effective versus ineffective group work.

What is the structure of effective group work? What is its purpose?
What are model cases of effective group processes?
What are the arguments that support its use in education?

If we as teachers cannot act on a deep understanding of what is known about effective group work, then we may be employing one of the least effective of all instructional processes. In our experience, it is the ineffective application of group work that upsets parents and students alike. That ineffective application results in prolonged and unnecessary challenges to the teacher. Such application can also result in dissatisfaction for teachers, as they witness the less-than-desirable results of such instruction.

Conceptual Framework for Describing Instructional Repertoires

The first component of our conceptual framework, as portrayed in Chart 2-2 on pages 36 and 37, assists in clarifying the nature of teachers' instructional repertoire...their symbolic intelligence.

The second component of our framework, as mentioned previously, is derived from David Perkins's work regarding *Knowledge as Design*.

Perkins's questions provide a process to determine the extent to which teachers have control over a specific instructional approach that is part of their pedagogy. In Chart 2-2 we present the instructional components we are defining, employing Perkins's questions to structure a set of working definitions for our proposed meta-language that will help describe and compare teachers' instructional repertoires. The components are:

- **pedagogy**
- **concepts**
- **organizers**
- **strategies**
- **tactics**
- **skills**
- **power**
- **integrating pedagogy**

That said, we are mindful of the difficulty, if not the impossibility, of developing unambiguous operational definitions for the concepts that comprise our proposed meta-language. Yet, we firmly believe that the components of pedagogy we have attempted to capture in these concepts do correspond empirically to different categories of teachers' instructional actions and ideas. When given the opportunity to inductively classify random sets of instructional terms, experienced and effective teachers readily (within about 10 minutes) sort those terms into clusters that resemble the categories of pedagogy we have represented in our meta-language for instruction.

> As a comparison, why have we classified chicken, fish, grapes, apples, carrots and corn into the food groups? They each provide part of a balanced diet. Although some may be more nutritionallly powerful than others, together they provide a nutritional synergy. Understanding the role each plays assists us in making wiser nutritional decisions

Before we move to this meta-language here are two important pages to consider.

Prepare Yourself...
What is in the Box Below is Important.

Read the first paragraph and then read what's in the box.

Then ask yourself whether you have a definitive answer to the difference between Strategies, Tactics, and Skills, and how they are employed.
More importantly, ask yourself, "does this difference matter?"

Long ago, the noted sociologist Herbert Blumer argued that the "ambiguous nature of concepts is the basic deficiency in social theory" (Blumer, 1954). Rejecting the theoretical and empirical integrity of operational definitions for social concepts, Blumer proposed an alternative approach to theorizing about the social world in terms of "sensitizing concepts."

Blumer justified his proposal for sensitizing concepts in social theory on the grounds that common objects of inquiry in the social world are always manifested in distinctive ways in distinctive contexts. *"What is common (i.e., what the concept refers to) is expressed in a distinctive manner in each empirical instance and can be got at only by accepting and working through the distinctive expression."*

This quote resonates with our sense of how these pedagogical concepts relate to teachers' instructional thoughts and actions. Think of the complexity of Cooperative Learning and the different approaches employed—multiple definitions (not definitive). **So how one school staff employs Cooperative Learning may be different from another school staff's approach,** and that makes sense. The contexts are different.

A **definitive** concept refers precisely to what is common to a class of objects [say chairs as opposed to love], by the aid of a clear definition in terms of attributes or fixed bench marks. This definition, or the bench marks, serves as a means of clearly identifying the individual instance of the class and the make-up of that instance that is covered by the concept. A **sensitizing concept** lacks such specification of attributes or bench marks and consequently it does not enable the user to move directly to the instance and its relevant content.

Definitive Concept

- Wait Time
- Reading Recovery
- Mind Mapping
- Venn Diagram

    Testers: caring, time lines, motivation, Jigsaw

Sensitizing Concepts

- Cooperative Learning
- Change
- Literacy
- Conflict

Both are Important!

This Page is Critical — The Heart and Soul of This Book

We are not attempting to bring a reductionisitic simplicity or ultimate clarity to each aspect of instruction. We are also not supportive of one approach (say Cooperative Learning or Reading Recovery or Inductive Thinking) or one philosophy (say Constructivism or Behaviourism) as representing "ultimate clarity" or "the best or only way" to approach the teaching and learning process. There is no best way to teach and learn. So thinking you have ultimate clarity may lead to narrow-minded, dead-end thinking. Rather we are attempting to understand how we can continuously evolve as effective teachers, and possibly all teach differently and be equally effective. The approach we are taking is a push to have teachers become increasingly refined in their understanding of how instructional strategies, tactics, skills, concepts, and organizers can be understood, integrated, and applied. Critically, that cannot occur effectively without deep knowledge of what students are learning and how students learn.

Referring to the previous page, we do not believe that simply being sensitive is sufficient. Nor are we arguing for a clear-cut definition. Perhaps we are arguing for acting on the cusp of the two—a push for clarity, but a wariness of false clarity.

What counts as instructional organizers and strategies, tactics, skills, and concepts in the practices of a specific teacher, for example, cannot really be known and understood independent of that teacher's particular pedagogy and context. Blumer argues that **a sensitizing concept can be tested empirically against the reality it is intended to represent, and that it can be progressively refined** (albeit not definitively defined) through careful investigations and portrayals of the object of inquiry. A generalized understanding of the sense of the concept is more likely to arise from illustrations of salient examples than from increasingly explicit designation of critical attributes. Here we disagree somewhat with Blumer.

In our view, Perkins's four Knowledge as Design questions provide a helpful way of framing and presenting the set of sensitizing concepts we have selected and presented in Chart 2–1, page 31. We are advocating a sense of clarity about how we understand instruction.

This page, therefore, is a caution about how you choose to understand what we are presenting in the following chart and the more in-depth descriptions on the pages following the chart.

The following work represents the thinking of a number of educators—the work of Bennett and Rolheiser over the last 20 years and the more recent research by Bennett, Anderson, and Evans. This is our attempt at moving towards one theory for facilitating instructional integration or explaining instructional intelligence. It does not mean we are right. It means we are seeking to refine what is known.

Chart 2–2. THE DESIGN OF INSTRUCTIONAL COMPONENTS

Pedagogy

1. **Structure:** The instructional concepts, skills, tactics, strategies, and organizers that a teacher can apply to affect learning.
2. **Purpose:** To increase the chances that a teacher can more effectively respond to the needs of the learner.
3. **Examples:** Interest (concept), Wait Time (skill), Think/Pair/Share (tactic), Mind Mapping (strategy), and Multiple Intelligences (organizer).
4. **Argument:** Pedagogical ideas and practices represent one of the critical distinguishing attributes of a teacher—with pedagogy, one is more likely to construct a meaningful learning environment.

Instructional Concepts

1. **Structure:** Qualities of effective teaching and learning which teachers seek to enact through the application of a variety of instructional skills, tactics, strategies and organizers.
2. **Purpose:** To provide lenses to understand how, when, and where to apply one's instructional repertoire.
3. **Examples:** Safety, Accountability, Relevance, Authenticity, Novelty, and Meaning.
4. **Argument:** They increase the chances that a teacher more effectively selects and integrates those instructional skills, tactics, and strategies that make a difference in learning.

Instructional Organizers

1. **Structure:** Frameworks that assist teachers to organize an array of instructional ideas and practices into an interrelated yet open-ended pedagogical set.
2. **Purpose:** To act as lenses to clarify or enhance communication and thought about instruction.
3. **Examples:** Multiple Intelligence, Learning Styles, Bloom's Taxonomy, Children at Risk Research, Learning Disabilities, Gender, Ethnicity.
4. **Argument:** They increase teacher wisdom in making decisions about the teaching and learning process; to make instructional decisions through the needs and inclinations of the learner(s).

Instructional Strategies

1. **Structure:** These instructional practices involve a sequence of steps or a number of related concepts. They often have applicability across grade levels and subject areas.
2. **Purpose:** They have specific, although varying, effects on student learning. They can affect logical thinking, social action, etc.
3. **Examples:** Cooperative Learning (Johnson's 5 elements; and Thelan's Group Investigation: 6 steps)—social theory; Mind Mapping (5 factors and a process)—information processing and memory.
4. **Argument:** Usually supported by research and theory. They engage students in powerful processes and meet diverse learner needs.

Chart 2–2. CONTINUED

Instructional Tactics

1. **Structure:** Actions usually invoked by the teacher, they are less complex than those found in Strategies. Tactics cut across most subjects and grade levels, and may be linked to other instructional tactics and skills in the enactment of a broader strategy.
2. **Purpose:** To involve students in an activity that has a specific purpose.
3. **Examples:** de Bono's CoRT program (e.g., EBS-Examine Both Sides of an Argument; PMI-Plus, Minus, Interesting); Kagan's simpler cooperative learning structures (e.g., Think/Pair/Share and Round Robin).
4. **Argument:** Often employed to enrich or strengthen the application of instructional strategies.

Instructional Skills

1. **Structure:** Specific and relatively simple instructional actions of teachers that enhance learning.
2. **Purpose:** To increase the chances that the more complex instructional processes (tactics and strategies) are effectively implemented.
3. **Examples:** Framing questions at different levels of complexity; providing time to think after asking a question; linking to the learners' past experiences; checking to see if students understand; providing models or visual representation.
4. **Argument:** Without them, we would find it difficult to engage some/all learners in learning. Without the skills, the power of the tactics and strategies is drastically reduced.

Power

1. **Structure:** A statement (usually a number) that communicates the educational worthiness of something.
2. **Purpose:** To inform us of the effects we can expect from one approach to learning as compared to other approaches.
3. **Examples:** how fast (time); how much (frequency or percent); what is remembered (total score); usually refers to an effect size statistic. Effect size represents how far you can move the mean score of one group (experimental group) away from another (the control group).
4. **Argument:** The size of the effect assists us in making decisions related to what we decide to employ in the classroom, as well as what we decide to learn as teachers as part of our professional development.

Integrating Pedagogy

1. **Structure:** The interconnected use of instructional organizers, concepts, skills, tactics, and strategies.
2. **Purpose:** To engage students in a variety of approaches to learning to achieve multiple effects.
3. **Examples:** Students work with a partner through a Concept Attainment strategy to identify the essence of 'simile.' Next, students work alone to classify all the NO examples and testers into groups that represent other figures of speech (Inductive Thinking). They then form cooperative groups of four, compare their classifications, and then work alone to complete a Mind Map (Strategy) on figures of speech.
4. **Argument:** To more effectively engage learners and their diverse needs and abilities.

Additional Comments:
Pedagogy, Concepts, Organizers, Strategies, Tactics, Skills, Integrating, and Power

Pedagogy is the collective term that refers to the instructional concepts, skills, tactics, strategies, and organizers available to teachers to create learning environments that encourage students to learn. As mentioned earlier, our professional literature provides a plethora of pedagogical approaches and processes. Throughout this book we use the term instruction and instructional practice interchangeably with pedagogy. We strongly believe that pedagogical knowledge and action are key defining attributes of teachers as professionals.

Instructional Concepts refers to one level at which teachers discuss instruction. It is a label we have applied to describe non-specific instructional ideas. We often encounter these concepts when teachers describe themselves (or other teachers) and what they do in the classroom. Examples of concepts related to instruction would be authenticity, variety, relevance and accountability. Concepts related to teacher qualities would be humour, enthusiasm, caring, and respect—perhaps we could label them the instructional qualities of the teacher (one part of what Goleman argues is our Emotional Intelligence).

Instructional concepts **guide** rather than **prescribe** specific courses of action. Teachers must do something (perhaps apply a skill, or

tactic, or strategy) to enact those concepts. For example, a teacher must do something to structure accountability when students are working in groups. This might occur by employing a tactic labelled Numbered Heads (where each group member is numbered 1, 2, 3, and each group assigned a letter A, B, C, etc.). The teacher could then support or enhance that tactic with an instructional skill such as how questions are framed. That skill increases the chances that most students will be accountable which, in turn, affects participation. What might that look like specifically?

"Discuss in your groups how you might balance this equation. Then in two minutes, I will randomly call on someone from three groups to share the group's thinking."

In two minutes the teacher then selects students by Letter and Number. "Group B person two".

This, of course, brings into play a number of other instructional concepts that must be simultaneously considered: failing publicly, saving face, safe classroom, the complexity of the question, etc. Connected to those concepts are the teacher's instructional skills: providing the appropriate time to think,

responding to a no response, or a guess, or a convoluted response, or a partially correct response, or a silly response, or a correct response. What appears to be a simple idea (invoking accountability) is in fact an integratively complex and demanding process.

Instructional Organizers emerge from beliefs or philosophies about teaching. Organizers are the lenses through which teachers understand or make sense of the teaching and learning process. They guide the production of open-ended and interrelated pedagogical sets or patterns. They not only guide decisions, they assist the teacher in understanding why something did or did not work.

Examples of instructional organizers would include Howard Gardner's (1993, 1999) work on Multiple Intelligences; Rita Dunn's (1990) and Bernice McCarthy's (1985, 1996) work on learning styles; and Benjamin Bloom et al's (1956) design of the Cognitive Taxonomy. These organizers are specific and have clearly identified components. Other instructional organizers are less specific or

much more pervasive in nature, such as the literature on gender, race, culture, children at risk, learning disabilities, and the literature base that guides teachers' decisions about what and how to design learning environments to maximize student learning.

Instructional Strategies are more complex processes that are often driven by theory and that usually provide theory-specific results. The most comprehensive source of a variety of instructional strategies is Joyce and Weil's (2000) book *Models of Teaching*. They identify 21 instructional strategies, or models of teaching, that affect different ways of thinking (inductive, deductive, social, memory, creative, critical, etc.). Another source that describes strategies is Eggen, Kauchak, and Harder's (1979) book *Strategies for Teachers*. They identify four strategies. Other books and articles focus on specific strategies. Examples include Buzan's (1993) and Marguilles' (1991) work on Mind Mapping; the Johnsons' (1992) work on Creative Controversy; the Sharans' (1992) work on Group Investigation; and Novak and Gowin's (1984) work on Concept Mapping.

Other strategies have been developed in relation to specific subjects or learning areas, for example Brown and Palinscar's (1982) work on strategic learning, or Madden, Slavin, and Stevens' (1986) work on Cooperative Integrated Reading and Composition (CIRC). Although extensive, the list of theory-based instructional strategies is less than that of instructional tactics and skills. The literature on instructional strategies usually provides a research link related to the effects they have on student learning (see Johnson & Johnson,

1989; Rolheiser-Bennett, 1985; Sharan, 1990; Slavin, 1980; Pressley, Levin, & Miller, 1981). Note: those effects are consistently higher than those reported for instructional skills; tangentially, little research support is available for instructional tactics, discussed next.

Instructional Tactics are less complex than instructional strategies and may not relate directly to one particular learning theory, although they often enhance or extend a particular strategy. Like the strategies, they may involve steps; however, they are less complex than instructional strategies. We assume they are not designed to make a big difference in student learning and usually have little research support related to their effect on student learning. Our perception is that they are more powerful than instructional skills, but less powerful than strategies.

Kagan's (1994) book *Cooperative Learning* provides a variety of examples of instructional tactics labelled cooperative structures, such as Think/Pair/Share and Inside/Outside Circles (approximately 100 cooperative learning tactics are described in the book). Jeanne Gibbs (1995), in her book *Tribes*, provides an additional 175 cooperative group tactics. Focusing on learners' thinking processes, Edward de Bono (1987) identifies 60 tactics in his *CoRT* program (CoRT standing for Cognitive Research and Trust). Bellanca (1990, 1992) provides 24 graphic organizers in his books *The Cooperative Think Tank* and *Cooperative Think Tank II*. Collectively, the aforementioned programs identify over 350 instructional tactics, and that number certainly does not represent the upper limit of

instructional tactics described in the literature.

Instructional Skills refer to simpler teacher behaviours that are not driven by a predetermined process. They are not driven by a theory, and do not provide theory-specific results. In terms of student learning, instructional skills are more like sandpaper, whereas strategies are like table-saws. If you want to make a bigger difference in student learning, use strategies. From our experience and our collaborative work with other teachers, applying the strategies without the accompanying skills reduces the effectiveness of the strategies.

The most common resources for accessing this rich instructional area are works such as Madeline Hunter's (1994) *Enhancing Teaching*; Saphier and Gower's (1987) work in *The Skillful Teacher*; Good and Brophy's (1994) work in *Looking in Classrooms*; and Cooper's (1986) book *Classroom Teaching Skills*. Those four sources describe a variety of specific instructional skills and the research literature that supports their use.

Waxman and Walberg (1991) summarize current research related to some of those instructional skills. (Note: in most cases this research evaluates effects but does not evolve out of a theoretical framework of teaching and learning). A number of other texts provide a variety of skills and some strategies (see Arends' (1998) book, *Learning to Teach*, and Lange, McBeath, and Hebert's (1995) book, *Strategies and Methods for Student-Centered Instruction*). Other works focus on specific types of instructional skills, such as Morgan and Saxton's (1994) book *Asking Better Questions*. Again, this list in no way exhausts the myriad of instructional skills; rather, it provides a sampling of the contemporary literature related to instructional skills.

Power is a term employed in statistics that refers to the size of the effects we can expect for the use of a particular practice. Cooperative learning, for example, when compared to a more stand-up recitation/teacher talk form of pedagogy, produces an effect size of 1.25 standard deviations related to higher order thinking in favour of Cooperative Learning (Rolheiser-Bennett, 1986). The first deviation represents approximately 34%, the second approximately 12%. This means that for higher level thinking, the "teacher talk" group mean is at the 50th percentile, while the Cooperative Learning group mean is at the 87th percentile (50% + 34% + 3% = 87%). We can now state that one approach (in this example of Cooperative Learning) is more powerful than the other approaches (for research on effect sizes on Cooperative Learning see Rolheiser-Bennett, 1986; Johnson & Johnson, 1989). While

instructional skills are not as powerful as instructional strategies in terms of their effects on student learning, they are critical in the implementation of strategies. More specifically, from our classroom experience and observations, instructional skills increase the power of the strategies, although we know of no research that explains this "skill/strategy interdependence."

Chart 2-3: Effect size for the effect of cooperative learning on higher level thinking

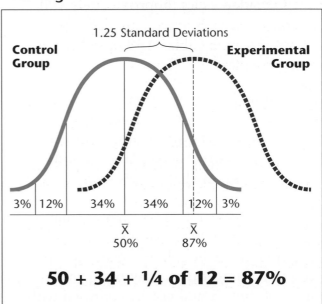

Nonetheless, instructional skills are critical to effectively implement strategies. One can imagine or wonder about the effect on student learning if the teacher integrated and stacked the instructional skills, tactics and strategies.

For example, to ignore the instructional skill of wait time (the time provided in a class for students to think prior to discussing the answer) is unwise. Not only was the concept written about in the 1800s (see Millar, 1897), it has been analyzed by Tobin (1980) in Australia, and Rowe (1974) in the United States. When given the choice to respond with first having time to think and share with a partner, almost one hundred percent of the students and teachers with whom we have worked choose time to think and share—they say they feel safer, and perceive the teacher cares. Do your own study...what would your students prefer?

We argue that ignoring the use of wait time in teaching, just like ignoring the use of the instructional tactics and strategies that form part of cooperative learning in teaching is hard to defend (unless the student would benefit from alternate approaches).

Integrating Pedagogy refers to the ways in which teachers combine instructional concepts, organizers, strategies, tactics, and skills in their instructional planning and teaching. We know that this occurs, although, as indicated in our overview of the literature, no research exists that examines the processes and effects of instructional integration in teacher planning and practice. Instructional integration may occur in the context of, but should not be confused with,

the widely discussed concepts and practices associated with curriculum integration (Fogarty, 1991).

From our own preliminary work in this area, we suggest two broad approaches: **integrating** and **stacking** pedagogy.

Integrating is like the intertwining threads of skills, tactics, and strategies shaped in part by some key Instructional Concepts or Instructional Organizers—there is a simultaneity in their application.

Stacking is sequential and is like placing blocks one-after-the-other to form a structure. In stacking one idea is applied after another while still maintaining a sense of connectedness and flow.

In summary, integrating one's instructional repertoire refers to the synergistic effect achieved by putting together multiple instructional processes: skills with tactics, skills and tactics with strategies, and strategies with strategies, etc. Integrating refers to the simultaneous use of skills, tactics and strategies. Stacking is using one model of teaching and then following up with another. Integrating is often more complex than stacking and the teacher must have an in–depth understanding of the processes they are implementing. You cannot integrate (with power or effect) what you cannot control.

The following lesson, taught as the last lesson in a science unit, is an example of instructional integration and stacking.

A Lesson

> **Just for Interest – sense how the strategies, tactics, skills, and concepts interact...**
>
> **...This is what effective teachers have always done**

Soil & the Environment Unit Final Review "Mind Mapping" Grade Three
Designed by Sherry Jones and Helen Kapsalakis

MENTAL SET:
(Concept Attainment Strategy— things you can compost)

YES EXAMPLES	NO EXAMPLES
banana peels	nails
apple cores	plastic
topsoil	rocks
leaves	chicken
grass	peanut butter
lettuce	milk

Have the students share examples, and use those as testers. Have them do a Think Pair Share around their hypotheses and their thinking.

Discuss why some food products are not put in composters, especially in a city. Be prepared to add examples and to have students provide more examples. Make the link to soil, why people compost, etc.

OBJECTIVE:
(As understood in the teacher's mind—it ties to the provincial or district curriculum). Extend students' understanding of the key ideas in the environmental unit and how they interact by having the students (in small cooperative groups) develop a Mind Map on soil and soil-related terms.

Reinforce the social skill of encouraging others by asking students what it looks like and sounds like using a T-Chart. We will let students know we will be observing all groups during the activity to find examples.

Student Stated Objective: "Today is the last day of our soil unit and each group will create a soil Mind Map and then share it with the class (Gallery Tour). We will also be practicing the social skill of encouraging others while working in groups."

INPUT/MODELLING:
- Think Pair Share – "What does it mean to encourage someone?"
- Draw T-Chart on board and have students generate examples of what this social skill looks and sounds like. Tell students we will be looking and listening for encouraging words.

INPUT/MODELLING CONTINUED:

- Review what a Mind Map looks like and why we use them.
- Hand out squares with ABCD. Assign letters and describe roles (put the roles on the board in case they forget):
  A= Materials Manager; B= Writer; C= Idea Giver, D=Supervisor.
  After each idea is written and illustrated the letters/roles will rotate.
- We will instruct the students to sign their names on the Mind Map if they participated equally and tell them in advance that anyone in the group can be selected to present the Mind Map (accountability).

CHECK FOR UNDERSTANDING:

- Make sure they all understand the instructions.
- Check to make sure they all agree who is A, B, C, D. (If you are short one person just have A, B, and C.)

PRACTICE:

- Time to brainstorm and develop Mind Maps
- Opportunity to demonstrate the social skill

- It would be a good idea at the end of Practice to do a Round Robin where each person explains the key ideas on the Mind Map. This is a rehearsal for the Gallery Tour in the Closure part of the lesson.

CLOSURE:

- Complete the Mind Map sharing using Gallery Tour. Select one person to put up the Mind Map. Then select another person, say original person B to stay with the Mind Map to do a one minute overview of the map while other groups come and listen. After two rotations, select another person to be the person who provides the overview.
- Share examples of encouraging behaviour. Ask students which group they think the comment represents (only do this with positive examples). Randomly ask groups to share examples of how they felt about how their group worked at making sure that people felt safe or encouraged in their group.

Note: this lesson was designed, taught, then written-up for us by two pre-service students at the Ontario Institute for Studies in Education of the University of Toronto.

strategies · concepts

Can you identify the Concepts, Skills, Tactics, and Strategies in their lesson?

tactics · skills

Final Thoughts

The language or symbols employed in the teaching/learning process are extensive. The *"...well worn image of classrooms where teachers talk and students listen, memorize, practice, and display knowledge has begun to fade as educators recognize that there is more to teaching and learning than words"* (Siegal, M. 1995, p. 455).

Teaching is not about "monogogy"—a term that refers to the singular and unthinking application of one approach to teaching. Teaching is about the artful and thoughtful integration of multiple approaches to teaching and learning—an integration driven by the needs and inclinations of the learner. Learning is not about recall of facts on meaningless tests. Learning is about being involved in meaningful events that increase our understanding of the world; it is about authenticity, being actively involved, and experiencing variety (Wiggins, 2000).

Interestingly, in 1945 Dale and Raths completed a study that found that the primary mode of instruction was stand-up-recitation. Goodlad's study in 1986 found little had changed since 1945. The authors' experiences inform us that teachers have extensive instructional repertoires; however, in most cases they are almost unconscious repertoires—sort of a craft knowledge, an on-the-job wisdom, something that one does rather than what one talks about.

For example, one of the authors was in a teacher's grade four class and in 70 minutes observed 27 instructional/management "moves" that the research literature identified as making a difference in student learning. For example, she had the students involved in a cooperative simulation activity related to designing a farm; questions were posed at each level of Bloom's Taxonomy to encourage more complex levels of thinking; and wait time was observed in her questions to encourage metacognition and to make the classroom a safer place.

Interestingly, but not unexpectedly, she could not identify her instructional moves. She had not heard of Bloom's Taxonomy or of wait time, etc. Unfortunately, when our university students work with teachers such as this, teachers who are "unconsciously skilled", the university students come back frustrated. Although skilled, that exemplary teacher does not communicate that she understands why she is effective; tangentially, our university students realize the gap between this teacher and themselves and see the impossibility of negotiating the gap in the short time they are together. The conversation is more aligned with activities and or broad concepts such as motivation, getting them all involved. The conversation is rarely focused on researched-based instructional skills, tactics, and strategies informed by the literature on Multiple Intelligence or Brain Research or Children at Risk or Gender or Ethnicity. Guiding the novice with comments such as: *"Well, you just have to love kids"* or *"Just do what I do"* is not good enough. We agree that loving kids is a benefit and that observation is important – but a lot of people love art, basketball, and chess, and over the years have watched Picasso, Jordan, and Kasparov. Love and observation are necessary but insufficient. Thousands of hours of practice, reflecting, and discussing goes into becoming experts.

We are arguing that to facilitate dialogue and extend learning, teachers need to consciously understand the language (the concepts, skills, tactics, strategies, organizers etc.) of their profession. They must do it in order to respond to the feedback about how students learn. Their decisions must be made by choice not by default; by intuition informed by experience combined with the experience and research of others. We encourage a collectively conscious instructional intelligence.

What do we know so far?

- a number of variables interact in the design of a powerful learning environment

- the power is NOT in the application of single innovations

- a variety of instructional processes support or play off one another; some are less complex (like concepts and skills) and others are more complex (like tactics or strategies)

- the more we understand the learner (the instructional organizers) the wiser we will be in selecting the appropriate skills, tactics, and strategies

- if students sense their teacher does not care or is unkind—then it is unlikely the ideas in this chapter will have a positive effect

Chapter *Three*

View this chapter on the internet!

www.beyondmonet.ca

Chapter Three

Internet Access

This chapter can be viewed by going to www.beyondmonet.ca. It provides a brief overview of the research related to ideas presented in the book. In addition, it lists some of the books that we have found most informative in understanding the skills, tactics, strategies, and organizers presented in this book.

Since the information contained in this chapter is time sensitive, we have posted it on the Internet to enable the text to be updated when new information becomes available. When you visit the site, you can be sure you are reading the latest version of Chapter Three.

www.beyondmonet.ca

Chapter Four

Instructional Concepts and Instructional Skills

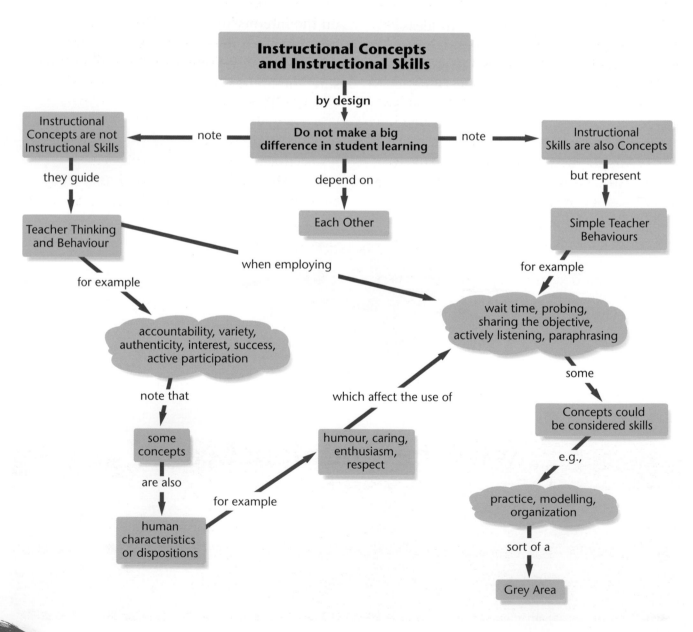

Chapter *Four*

Instructional Concepts and Instructional Skills

From what was stated in Chapters 1 and 2, you can sense the complexities and possibilities of instructional design. Given the multitude of concepts, skills, tactics, and strategies, you may realize the extensive number of ways they can be connected to meet the diverse needs of learners. Perhaps you can also more deeply appreciate why teaching is a profession and why we call ourselves teachers.

This chapter delves more deeply into two of the instructional components: instructional concepts and instructional skills. The instructional concepts usually divide themselves into those pertaining to human qualities (such as organization, sense of humour, enthusiasm, caring) and instructional necessities (such as active participation, variety, success, accountability). It would be tedious and unnecessary to cover all of the possible concepts and skills. So, we have selected a few that are relevant to all grade levels and all subject areas. We want to specifically illustrate the relationship between instructional concepts and skills. This relationship is the building block that will facilitate the application of the more complex instructional tactics and strategies explored in later chapters.

This chapter has eight interconnected areas:

1. Introduction and Rationale
2. Connecting Concepts and Skills in Art, Music and Sport to Education
3. Concepts and Skills—A Quick Review
4. The Concept of Active Participation and Related Instructional Skills
5. The Concept of Levels of Thinking and Related Instructional Skills
6. The Concept of Motivation and Related Instructional Skills
7. Summary of the Research on Instructional Concepts and Instructional Skills
8. Chapter Summary

Key Questions

1. What is a concept? What is a fact? What is their relationship? Does understanding that relationship matter?
2. What is an instructional skill? How is it different from an instructional tactic and an instructional strategy? (If you are not sure, refer to Chapter 2.)
3. If someone asked you to list the concepts and skills you act on to make a difference for students, what would you identify? Is understanding the research that supports the use of concepts and skills important?

The Concept and Skill Relationship
— a Quick Review

What would you say if someone asked you to identify the difference between a concept and a skill?

What if someone asked you to explain the interaction between instructional concepts, skills, tactics, strategies, and organizers? As an analogy, what would a skilled artist say when explaining her understanding of how to mix colours of paint to communicate an idea or emotion? Our guess is that she would be knowledgeable about how and what to mix to achieve specific effects.

Of course, you might still be wondering why understanding the difference between concepts, skills, tactics, strategies, and organizers is important. Our experience tells us that without a clear understanding of their role, we are less likely to effectively and intentionally explore the relationship among them or thoughtfully connect them to meet student needs. So, we would argue that we do need to know the difference.

One way to understand the difference and connection between Instructional Concepts and Instructional Skills is to remember that a teacher can specifically "do" the skills (like providing wait time for students to think when asking questions, or probing to encourage deeper thinking); whereas, the teacher cannot specifically "do" the concepts. For example, we do not walk into a classroom and specifically "do" Levels of Thinking or enact Motivation or Active Participation. We have to do something that make those concepts come alive. Those "do" things we label, in order of increasing complexity, as skills, tactics, and strategies. Instructional concepts act more as guides.

For example, if we know that variety is important for motivation, then that reminds us to extend our instructional repertoires so that we can use a range of instructional approaches to communicate the concept of variety.

This may sound confusing, but the difference is important. Too often our instructional thinking and resulting dialogue is vague. We often limit our talk to concepts rather than including the actions that cause those concepts to have an effect. Experienced and effective teachers often do not consciously realize the complexity that exists around something as simple as asking a question to involve all students—even though they do it effectively.

For example, we notice that when our university students are out practice-teaching, they are provided with feedback from their associate teacher to encourage them to refine and extend the effectiveness of the learning environment—to make the lesson more motivating, or to get the students more involved. When they ask the associate teacher how that should happen, the associate teacher's response may be unintentionally vague. Some have said, "Well, that is what you have to figure out, that is why you are a teacher." Others have said, "Well, just watch me and do what I do." Those options are of limited use. As we mentioned in the previous chapter, think of how many people watch Michael Jordan. How long would you have to watch him or a violinist, or a juggler, before you could passionately play or magically juggle at their level? Professionals, in order to help others learn from their wisdom, need to be able to effectively articulate their practice.

The Concept of Active Participation and Related Instructional Skills

This section focuses on one essential instructional concept called **Active Participation** as it affects the instructional skill of framing questions to encourage specific types of student responses. Note that Active Participation ties directly to the concept of **Individual Accountability** in David and Roger Johnsons' work regarding Cooperative Learning (explored in Chapter 7).

The reason for involving yourself in this section is to recall or extend your understanding of the importance of questioning skills in promoting student engagement and minimizing off task behaviour. As well, remember that the two other instructional concepts of Motivation and Levels of Thinking presented in this chapter also have dramatic effects on engaging students meaningfully in learning.

◇ MORE INFORMATION AHEAD

Section Format

This section begins by inviting you to think about the concept of active participation as it relates to framing questions through exploring a number of concepts critically connected to both framing questions and actively involving students. Next, it takes you through a lesson involving Bruner's Concept Attainment and Hunter's Lesson Design to illustrate the concept of framing questions to actively involve students. Following that lesson is the opportunity to practise the process of framing questions integrating aspects of Cooperative Learning.

PEANUTS reprinted by permission of Untied Features Syndicate, Inc.

C.A. Phase III - Application: Note that here we will select the concept of Closure and employ the tactic of Examine Both Sides of an Issue from de Bono's CoRT program.

CLOSURE:

In this phase of the lesson we want to discuss the idea that framing questions to hold students accountable is not always beneficial.

Question:

What ethical and cultural considerations should you focus on when employing the concept of active participation to the framing of questions?

Response:

In doing workshops in northern Alberta, and in our reading on First Nation cultures, we experienced a problem with framing questions. The following example, involving David, a Native student, illustrates that concern.

"Think to yourself for a few moments. Why do you believe that Canadians are not aggressive in international politics?"

(15 second wait time ... and the teacher picks David.)

Generally speaking, First Nation students do not like to look better than or worse than their peers. In discussions with their teachers, we found that if those students are first allowed to share in the group and are then invited to share the group's thinking, then they are much more comfortable responding.

The issue, then, is one of respecting the students' learning styles and lived cultural experiences.

Interestingly, regardless of culture, most students prefer the "time to think and share with others approach." In a mini-study with kindergarten teachers, we found kindergarten students also preferred time to think and share with a partner before sharing with the class. Framing questions this way is safe. The brain functions more effectively when it does not feel threatened and when it has time to "talk" with others.

In the book *Making Connections: Teaching and the Human Brain* (Caine & Caine, 1994), the authors discuss the issue of maximizing the brain's effectiveness through creating a state they call "relaxed alertness" (p. 70). This state of "relaxed alertness" is what we are attempting to achieve with framing the question to involve active participation. Of course, what is relaxed for some is panic for others—this is where the art of teaching moves away from the mechanistic or unthinking application of 3 to 5 seconds wait time for students.

Note:
On the last page of this section is a workshop activity related to PRACTISING/APPLYING the framing of questions using the concept of Active Participation. Prior to doing the activities, consider reading (or if in a group situation, Jigsaw) the ten concepts and skills presented on the next few pages.

Concepts and Skills Associated with the Framing of Questions

The following concepts and skills are part of the process of framing questions. They assist teachers and students in framing questions to more appropriately meet learning needs. Each concept or skill is presented on a separate page to make the use of the Jigsaw strategy possible. For a professional development activity, put participants in groups of three and give each person two or three of the ideas listed below to read. Participants move to expert groups, discuss what they think is important, and then return to their original groups of three to share their thinking.

A. Complexity of the Thinking   (concept)
B. Amount of Academic Engaged Time   (concept)
C. Use of Wait Time   (skill)
D. Responding to: (skill)
    1. a no response from the student
    2. a partially correct response from the student
    3. a silly response from the student
    4. a guess from the student
    5. an incorrect response
    6. a correct response.

E. Providing Knowledge of Results (feedback) (skill)
F. Covert and Overt   (concept)
G. Fear of Failure and Dependency   (concept)
H. Public vs. Private Failure   (concept)
I. Distribution of Responses   (skill)
J. Accountability and Level of Concern   (concept)

Complexity of the Thinking

This refers to the teacher's ability to apply a taxonomy of thinking such as Bloom's Taxonomy to design questions of varying degrees of difficulty. Such ability increases the chances of meeting the individual needs of students. Complexity of the thinking is discussed in more detail in the next section of this chapter that focuses on Levels of Thinking.

Bloom's Taxonomy: A Review

- **Knowledge** – recall, recite
- **Comprehension** – explain, provide examples
- **Application** – act on understanding
- **Analysis** – compare/contrast, pull apart
- **Synthesis** – reinvent, create, look at in a new way
- **Evaluation** – judge based on criteria

Consider these Questions

- Can teachers meet the individual needs of students if they do not consciously control the cognitive level of their questions to students?

- Can students meet their individual needs if they cannot consciously control the cognitive level of their answers?

- Is it possible for teachers to accurately respond to a student's response if the teacher is unaware of the cognitive level of the question they've asked?

- Does an ethical issue exist when teachers test students at a higher level of thinking than that at which the students were taught? What about testing them at a lower level than that at which they were taught?

- If teachers do not consciously think about the cognitive level at which they are teaching, is it possible that teachers are testing at higher or lower levels than at which they taught?

- Will students respond to questions more appropriately if they understand the cognitive demands of questions? That is, if they recognize the question as analysis, and what analysis means, will they respond more precisely to that question? We found that in a study of grade five and six students the answer was most definitely "Yes" (Bennett et al, 1986).

The Amount of Academic-Engaged Time

One concept reported in the research literature that positively affects student achievement is academic-engaged time. Although students often appear busy or engaged—the concern of the teacher must centre on the nature of that "busyness."

Related to framing a question… if a question is asked, should all students be encouraged to be involved in the thinking or should students be permitted to respond when, or if, they feel like responding?

If attempting to implement the concept of **"active student learning,"** which of the following teacher questions or requests encourage that concept?

Hmmmm?...

1. *"Who can tell me the difference between a fact and an opinion?"*

2. *"No hands please, think to yourself for 10 seconds and then be prepared to share an answer when asked. What is the difference between a fact and an opinion?"*

3. *"Does anyone know the major issue in the conflict between the Irish Republican Army and the government of Britain?"*

4. *"The other day we discussed photosynthesis. Discuss the process with a partner for 30 seconds and then I will select several of you to respond."*

5. *"Nicole, what is the difference between addition and multiplication?"*

6. *"Which invites a higher level of intelligence, Prose or Poetry?"* (The teacher provides 15 seconds wait time, during which time she makes eye contact with all students. She then asks Shannon to respond.)

Numbers 2, 4, & 6 provide more accountability to participate and allow less opportunity to misbehave—no guarantee, just a greater chance in encouraging participation.

Have you noticed that three or four students often answer most of your questions? Is that level of student response acceptable?

In the previous teachers' requests, which are the most commonly employed by teachers? If you said 1, 3, & 5, you are right.

So...

If we want to increase the amount of academic engaged time, then we need to be sensitive to how we structure time. One way of increasing academic engaged time is monitoring the time we give students to think during questioning. The literature refers to this as Wait Time. Wait Time is covered in the next section.

Knowledge of Results

Knowledge of results motivates students to continue. We all like to know how we are doing. We appreciate the skills of those teachers who wisely and sensitively let us know how we are doing. Additionally, feedback from other students, parents, teachers, books, films, and our own reflections, helps us to make decisions on what to do next. This is why the shift towards teaching students to self evaluate is such a powerful learning process—self evaluation give students immediate knowledge of results.

Consider This

1. If you enjoy bowling, how long would you continue to bowl if you never saw the pins you knocked down or if you simply heard a noise after the ball disappeared through a screen?

2. How long would you continue to cook gourmet meals if no one at least said, "Thank you?" Knowledge of results encourages us to do a lot of things. It becomes more effective when the information about how we are doing is:

1. provided as soon as possible;
2. specific—i.e., related to what is being learned;
3. encouraging; and,
4. perceived as "caringly meaningful."

In a study of gifted students, Marion Stelmaschuck (1986) reported that teachers who provided feedback on assignments immediately following the assignment were identified as more effective teachers. We have all had the teacher who we know skimmed and, most likely, never read the paper—and gave us our grade of 8/10 or A—with no comments or challenges. That said, one university professor we had was a master at providing feedback; the best we have ever experienced. He often gave back more feedback to students than what they wrote. He exemplified the importance of feedback—and knowing how much effort he put into our work significantly increased our thinking and effort towards the work we subsequently submitted to him. For this teacher, every word was important—it was his gift to our efforts.

> If you want the results of students' efforts to improve, the idea of letting students rehearse in their head (a covert process) before sharing (an overt process) is a useful idea that is covered in the next section.

Shifting from Covert to Overt

These two concepts provide two alternatives to student participation.
Both are useful.

Covert – means hidden from public view
Overt – means not hidden from public view

Obviously one is easier to measure than the other. Covert lessens the level of concern and overt increases it. Compare the examples of covert and overt, then contrast the examples.

Covert:
• Close your eyes and pretend you are...
• Visualize...Imagine...
• See it in your mind's eye...
• Think to yourself...
• Rehearse in your mind...

Why is covert useful?
• It increases success and
  a sense of safety
  because students can rehearse.

Overt:
• Discuss with your partner...
• Thumbs up if you agree...
• Write your answer...
• Share your answer with the class...
• Act out your feelings...

Why is overt useful?
• It holds the students accountable to think and to participate.

In terms of questioning skills, a teacher might move from covert to overt by saying...

"Take 15 seconds and think to yourself about the ways in which different animals hibernate. When I ask you to share, discuss your ideas with your partner and then I'll ask some of the partners to share with the class."

Note:
when using some of the cooperative learning structures such as Inside/Outside Circles, framing questions to include both covert and overt is important.

A philosopher once mentioned that as humans we are lucky that we can form hypotheses in our head so that the hypotheses will die in our stead. For students who must share their thinking publicly, fear of failure and, possibility a perception of being dependent on others to help them, become negative forces. These ideas are discussed in the next section.

Fear of Failure and Dependency

> The art of teaching is in providing an environment that encourages students to inquire and to risk without fearing failure or being constantly saved from involvement.

Fear of Failure and **Dependency** are two examples of extremes related to student participation. If the student perceives the classroom environment as "not safe" we increase the chances the student will not actively participate in the learning. On the other hand, if the room is so safe that the student is always "saved" from being involved, then the student will wait until someone eventually "saves" him or her.

THESE TWO CONCEPTS ARE 'EASY TO UNDERSTAND ... HARDER TO ENACT.'

Certainly an understanding of how to respond to students when they provide us with answers is one approach. Another goes back to being able to ask questions at different levels of complexity. The ability to engage the learner at appropriate levels of difficulty, while simultaneously demonstrating our ability to care and encourage, prove useful in creating an environment that prevents student misbehaviour.

If a student is reluctant to try, would you inject a low level or high level of concern into the question or activity? Why? If we never provided that student with time to think and to share his thinking with a partner before we asked him to respond, what would you predict his level of success to be and motivation to learn. You can see that what appears as a simple concept, in effect, reveals the complexity of teaching.

Remember:
The use of cooperative structures such as **Think/Pair/Share, Round Robin,** and **Place Mat** provide an opportunity for students to talk with one to three others without the stress of the whole class listening. The next section discusses the concepts of public and private failure.

Public Vs. Private Failure

We will fall off our bikes in private and get back up and try again ... but how many times will we continue to try if we fall off in public?

This concept is important from an ethical point of view. When framing questions and randomly selecting students to respond, we are in fact asking them to possibly fail in front of their peers without their having a say in whether or not they wish to respond. Although we might not consider it failure, students usually do unless we have created a safe environment.

We know of very competent teachers who are relaxed and enjoy the conversations within their classrooms. Yet, when asked to work with a group of adults (even with teachers in their own school) they are extremely reluctant to stand up and talk in front of these peers. Some will not

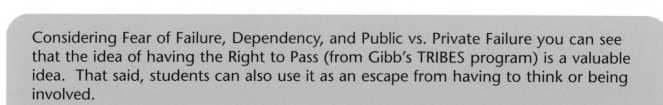

attend workshops for fear of being asked to talk publicly.

That is why developing a repertoire of skills to understand and respond to students' efforts is important in creating safe classroom environments.

Certainly, having students rehearse answers within a group or with a partner increases the chances students will experience success. As noted before, First Nations children do not want to be singled out to respond if it means making them look better than or worse than their peers. They will, however, be more willing to respond by sharing a response developed by the group. Structuring lessons in a cooperative small group format increases the chances that students who are afraid to fail will more actively involve themselves in the lesson.

Considering Fear of Failure, Dependency, and Public vs. Private Failure you can see that the idea of having the Right to Pass (from Gibb's TRIBES program) is a valuable idea. That said, students can also use it as an escape from having to think or being involved.

Distribution of Responses

This is not a complex concept. Nonetheless, given the research literature reports that when students are invited to respond in a way that encourages them to volunteer, three or four students in a class willingly answer 80% of the questions.

If you provide workshops for adults, try asking questions in such a way as to encourage voluntary participation and see what percentage of the participants respond. Adults are simply students who are just a little bit older—three or four in a group of 25 will respond to 80% of your questions.

In a recent university class, it was observed that of 70 students who were being asked questions, three answered most of the questions that involved volunteering a response. Does that mean the others had nothing to say? Of course not. They simply were more comfortable sitting back and passively listening. One has to remember it was the start of the year and they didn't know each other that well. Additionally, one also has to ask whether or not the topic was of interest or relevant—other reasons also exist as to why students do not volunteer a response.

Please do not think that we are suggesting that voluntary participation is "bad" … quite the opposite. It can be a low stress way of starting to get students involved, or it can give students who like to volunteer the opportunity to volunteer. **The art of teaching, however, is to use it by choice rather than default.**

CLOSE TO HOME   JOHN McPHERSON

Mrs. Mortleman made sure that everyone participated in class.

A Thought

As a parent, you certainly expect your son or daughter to be actively involved in their classwork. If they are not, you would hope the teacher has skills in his or her repertoire to increase the chances your son or daughter would be involved. For parents, if you get a chance to watch a teacher teach, observe the lesson for how the teacher involves students through the framing of questions.

Accountability and Level of Concern

Accountability and the level of concern of students can best be illustrated using an x and y axis. Let's say you are reviewing ideas that were covered in the previous class. Quadrants 1, 2, 3, & 4 represent different levels of concern and accountability—an example is provided for each.

The art of teaching is deciding what level of student concern to envoke(**from little to high anxiety**) and what level of accountably to envoke (**no involvement to full involvement**) to maximize learning.

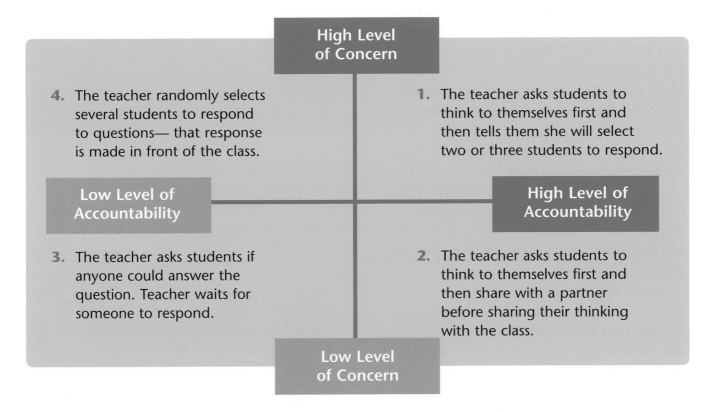

High Level of Concern

4. The teacher randomly selects several students to respond to questions— that response is made in front of the class.

Low Level of Accountability

3. The teacher asks students if anyone could answer the question. Teacher waits for someone to respond.

1. The teacher asks students to think to themselves first and then tells them she will select two or three students to respond.

High Level of Accountability

2. The teacher asks students to think to themselves first and then share with a partner before sharing their thinking with the class.

Low Level of Concern

Obviously the teacher can operate in any or all of the quadrants. The art of teaching is deciding what to invoke to appropriately meet the needs of students in any specific instance.

Of course, the difficulty level of the material and whether or not the classroom is a safe place to take a risk also determine the level of concern (sometimes considered the level of student stress or anxiety).

With a partner, develop classroom tasks that would fit into each of the quadrants. Where would students be most creative?

The Concept of "Levels of Thinking" and Related Instructional Skills

Reasons for reading this next section:

- This section is about levels of thinking. For some of you, this section provides an introduction to how thinking can be categorized (the essence of a taxonomy); for others, it is simply a review; and, for others, it might be a waste of your time in that you already effectively apply taxonomies.

- Most teachers have heard of taxonomies and when they hear of Bloom's Taxonomy some say, "Oh yeah, we did that at university." For most of us the taxonomy represented memorizing a list of verbs that fit into a pie chart representing the levels of the taxonomy—much like how kids categorize food into four food groups. In reality, almost every verb could fit into any category. To get through our practice-teaching assignments, we designed objectives using those verbs, and when we got our first classroom, we promptly dispatched the process and dived into the everyday swirl of the classroom. So we will revisit the past and hopefully illustrate how to apply the design of taxonomies as a powerful support system for thinking.

- Most teachers cannot recall the six levels of Bloom's Taxonomy. Yet when asked to explain what each component means, they have little difficulty. As well, most teachers do not consciously play with the elements of taxonomies, yet when you watch them teach you see those elements being played out.

A number of other taxonomies exist, for example, Aschner's, Krathwol's, and Guilford's. The question is not whether or not someone is an effective teacher based on whether they use a taxonomy. The question is how much better might they be if they consciously attended to levels of thinking as they designed activities and asked questions?

So, in summary, the purpose of this section and the related activities is to clarify and extend your instructional practice related to thinking — by using a taxonomy as a springboard.

Note:
Educators in the area of critical thinking (such as Richard Paul at the Centre for Critical Thinking and Moral Critique at Sonoma State University) argue that taxonomies for thinking are basic requirements for critical thinking. We would also argue that strategies such as Cooperative Learning, Biological Inquiry, Jurisprudence, Concept Attainment, Synectics, Inductive Thinking, Group Investigation, etc., would be more difficult to meaningfully integrate and apply without the use of a taxonomy. Taxonomies are one piece of the vast puzzle of teaching—a piece that makes sense once you understand how it integrates into the teaching and learning process.

Taxonomies for Thinking

The previous section on Active Participation presented two concepts: (1) actively involving students; and (2) holding students accountable. We argue that attending to those two concepts is important but insufficient. As teachers we must also consider different levels of thinking.

Levels of Thinking is certainly one lens a teacher can use to respond to a variety of student needs. (Other lenses might be Multiple Intelligence, Learning Styles, Children at Risk, Brain Research, Gender, Culture, and Learning Disabilities.)

Again, the ability to integrate a variety of concepts, skills, tactics, and strategies is what defines us as teachers. Such ability is one key reason we are teachers.

One way to refine your thinking is to complete the following activity. The activity involves categorizing thinking by employing Hilda Taba's Inductive Thinking strategy (described in Chapter 9).

Academic Task

Classify the questions and activities found on the next page into categories based on the type of thinking they would encourage of learners.

Collaborative Skill

Each person shares his or her thinking before an item is placed into a category.

GROUP SIZE: Put yourselves into groups of 2 and letter off A & B. If you prefer, you can work on your own.

When finished, please respond to the questions on page 75. Please do not look at the questions until you have finished the classifying task.

Note:
Groups will be randomly invited to share and defend their categories.

Levels of Thinking Data Set

1. List the parts of a microscope.

2. What are the similarities and differences between the Conservatives and the Liberals?

3. Explain, in your own words, how endorphins work in the human body.

4. Show how you would calculate how much carpet you would have to buy to cover the living room and two bedrooms and what the total cost would be if the carpet were $24.95 a square metre.

5. In your opinion, if Louis Reil were the son of a rich, white family, would he still have been hanged?

6. What are two present-day examples of the Industrial Revolution?

7. Role-play your interpretation of disagreeing in an agreeable way.

8. Using your understanding of international politics, devise an innovative series of steps to resolve one of the issues you consider of critical importance in Yugoslavia.

9. Which is a more powerful force in Macbeth: love or hate? Why?

10. Discuss with your partner. What is your interpretation of Canada's current position regarding free trade with the United States and Mexico?

11. Predict the long-term effect of free trade on the automobile industry in Ontario.

12. Who was the greatest artist of all time? Base your answer on the impact of that art on the people of the world.

13. Design a new way to incorporate plastic into the restructuring of this car fender.

14. Use your knowledge of graphs, to depict the effects of smoking on the different types of illnesses reported in the research article provided.

15. What is the formula for calculating the speed of a free-falling object?

16. If you were given $100 000, devise the best conservative 5-year investment plan for you as a 65 year-old retired person whose income is $18 000 per year.

17. Compare and contrast Baroque and Classical forms of music.

18. What form or style of art most affects your thinking?

19. Match the capital city to the country.

20. By the end of next week, your group has to have taken a small engine apart and be able to explain how each part affects the working of the other parts.

21. Try to balance this equation with the information you used to balance the other equations.

22. Taking the flaws of the protagonist and the strengths of the antagonist, create a new ending for the script.

23. List as many hydrocarbons as you can in three minutes.

24. Contrast the major tensions concerning people's attitude toward the First World War and the Vietnam War.

Related **?'s** are on the following page

Questions Related to the Classifying Activity

For the questions below, first read the question, then share your answer with a colleague. If on your own, simply compare your thinking with the ideas presented on the next page.

1. Looking through your analysis, which category of questions is most common in today's classrooms and on most exams or quizzes?

2. Again reflecting on your categorization, what types of questions do you think students enjoy responding to in the classroom? Why? How would your students rank the types of questions in terms of encouraging them to think?

3. In your opinion, what is the minimum level to which students must think, given they live in a democracy?

4. Explain how opinion connects to evaluation.

5. Define what is meant by "application." What is another way of connecting "application" with the other levels of thinking in Bloom's Taxonomy?

6. What do you think is one of the traps teachers fall into when they have students apply what they can recall?

7. Is it possible to meet the individual needs of students if teachers do not consciously control the level of their questions?

8. Are teachers legally or ethically liable if they test at a higher level of thinking than that at which they taught or otherwise engaged the students?

9. Do you think a relationship exists between what is known about how the brain neurons evolve, Piaget's stages of development (see below), and the higher levels of thinking that students are encouraged to pursue?

Piaget's developmental stages are:

- Sensorimotor: (birth to two years) – physical interaction with environment
- Pre-Operational: (ages 2 to 7 years) – needs concrete physical conditions
- Concrete Operational: (ages 7-11) – still learns best by doing, but can do some abstract problem solving
- Formal Operations: (ages 11-15) – thought processes like adults

Just For Interest
When finished, connect your thinking with the responses on the following page.

Answers related to the classifying Activity:

The responses of others...

1. Recall is the most common level of thinking encouraged in most classrooms. Ironically, the effect on learning is minimal.

2. In mini-inquiries completed with students, we have found the most popular questions were synthesis and evaluation. Analysis and application were next, followed by comprehension. Recall was identified as the least popular.

3. Analysis and evaluation combined. For example, in making decisions re political positions, as in the Quebec Referendum, people needed to analyze the options and make a judgement. If they did not understand the issues, it was difficult for them to decide. A lot of people were confused.

4. When opinion is judging an issue, it becomes evaluation. The extent to which you can back up your opinion with supporting evidence determines the worth of your opinion. This is where critical thinking becomes a component of the dialogue and the listener attempts to determine the flaws in your argument (e.g., through your use of inductive fallacies such as sweeping generalizations, false analogies, unknowable statistics, and either/or choices, etc).

5. Application shows you understand how to do something. A new teacher informed us that she saw application at each level of the taxonomy. She sensed that we apply our ability to recall, to comprehend, to apply, to analyze, to create, and to evaluate.

6. The trap is having students apply what they do not understand (e.g., students who can subtract with borrowing, and get the correct answer, yet do not understand what was meant by crossing out the 4, putting a 3 and moving the 1 next to the 0). We think they understand because they answered correctly; in fact, they have just memorized the process and understand very little.

7. We argue yes. Encouraging students to think at an appropriate level of understanding is more difficult if we as teachers have no conscious control over the cognitive demand of our questions. If you asked an analysis level question and got no response, what would you do?

8. We believe yes. Think back to when you were a student—would you think it fair if the teacher tested you with questions that were at a more complex level than was discussed or presented in class? How would you feel about the quality of learning if all the questions were at the recall and comprehension levels of thinking?

9. Regarding Piaget's stages of development, the answer appears to be yes. One of two theories about brain development shows that myelin release and brain growth coincide with those stages. Myelin is a fatty insulation that allows messages to travel more quickly without a corresponding loss of transmission. We discuss more about the brain in Chapter 12. Healy (1994) reports that the largest release of myelin occurs in adolescence.

Bloom's Taxonomy

A taxonomy of thinking assists the teacher in determining the type of thinking in which the students are to be involved. A taxonomy also guides the teacher in more clearly understanding what is to be learned and how the students will demonstrate that learning. In a simpler way, the previous classification activity with the thinking data set parallels what others who construct taxonomies have done. They searched for ways to organize types of thinking.

Further, and perhaps most importantly, a taxonomy guides the teacher in the design of questions and activities at different levels of complexity; questions not only to challenge the students' thinking, but to meet individual learning needs.

If you do not enjoy, or if you feel constrained by Bloom's Taxonomy, then try Aschner's or Guilford's, or create your own. As you consider whether or not to use a taxonomy, consider what research is saying about how the brain evolves (developmentally) and students' ability to operate at more complex levels of thinking. See Chapter 12.

Interestingly, the literature reports that effective teachers teach at more complex levels of thinking — yet are often unaware of it.

Bloom's Taxonomy has Six Levels

1. **Knowledge (recall)**
2. **Understanding**
3. **Application**
4. **Analysis**
5. **Synthesis**
6. **Evaluation**

Please note that these categories are not discrete; they only act as guides. More often than not, the thinking fits into more than one category. For categorization of levels 4, 5, & 6, the literature reports that disagreement is more often the rule than agreement. One reason is because of the amount of background information the student brings to the learning. For example, you might ask an evaluative question and you think the student's response was at the evaluative level; however, unless you probe, you will never know whether or not the student simply parroted someone else's thinking.

MORE INFORMATION AHEAD

The next three pages provide more ideas, related to the six levels of Bloom's Taxonomy.

Sentence starters for developing activities based on Bloom's Taxonomy

Note that some of these starters fit into more than one category; these are just suggestions.

LEVEL I – KNOWLEDGE (RECALL):
1. What is the definition for ...?

2. Trace the pattern....

3. Recall the facts....

4. Name the characteristics of ....

5. List the steps for....

LEVEL II – COMPREHENSION:
1. Tell why these ideas are similar.

2. In your own words retell the story of....

3. Classify these concepts. (could also be analysis)

4. Provide some examples.

5. Construct a model of....

6. Draw a picture to...or role-play what happened.

LEVEL III – APPLICATION:
Note: (applying without understanding is not effective application)
1. Graph the data.

2. Demonstrate the way to....

3. Practise....

4. Act out the way a person would....

5. Calculate the....

LEVEL IV – ANALYSIS:
1. What are the components of...?

2. Which steps are important in the process of...?

3. If ... then....

4. What other conclusions can you reach about ... that have not been mentioned?

5. The difference between the fact and the hypothesis is...?

6. The solution would be to....

7. What is the relationship between ... and...?

8. What is the pattern of...?

9. How would you make a...?

LEVEL V – SYNTHESIS:
1. Create a model that shows you new ideas.

2. Devise an original plan or experiment for....

3. Finish the incomplete story so that....

4. Make a hypothesis about....

5. Change ... so that it will....

6. Prescribe a new way to....

LEVEL VI – EVALUATION:
1. In your opinion....

2. Appraise the chances for....

3. Grade or rank the....

4. What solution do you favour and why?

5. Which systems are best? worst?

6. Rate the relative value of these ideas to....

THE FOLLOWING ARE SAMPLE QUESTIONS OR REQUESTS FROM STORIES BASED ON BLOOM'S TAXONOMY

(If these stories are not part of your or your students' cultures, think of other stories and identify similar questions.)

Goldilocks and the Three Bears

LEVEL I – KNOWLEDGE:
- List the characters in the story.
- Whose bed was Goldilocks in when the bears found her?

LEVEL II – COMPREHENSION:
- Retell the events of the story in your own words.
- Why were the bears upset with Goldilocks?

LEVEL III – APPLICATION:
- Tell what might have happened if Goldilocks had also made a mess.
- Retell the story from the point of view of breaking and entering.
- Using the information from the story, draw a sketch of the bears' house.

LEVEL IV – ANALYSIS:
- How was Goldilocks's experience different from that of Little Red Riding Hood?
- Identify parts of the story that could have happened to you.
- Make a list of all the events in the story that indicate it is not true.

LEVEL V – SYNTHESIS:
- Suppose that Goldilocks had found the home of the Three Skunks. What might have happened?
- What if Goldilocks had come home and three bears were sleeping in her bed? What would she do?

LEVEL VI – EVALUATION:
- Judge whether or not Goldilocks made a good decision by running away from the bears. Explain.
- Evaluate Goldilocks's behaviour as a guest in the bears' home.
- Pretend that Goldilocks was on trial for "breaking and entering". Decide whether or not you would find her guilty. Justify your decision.

The True Story of The Three Little Pigs

By: Jon Scieszka

LEVEL I – KNOWLEDGE:
- What arguments was the Wolf using to claim his innocence?
- Have you ever had to defend yourself for something someone said you did?

LEVEL II – COMPREHENSION:
- Explain your thinking about the wolf's argument that eating the pig was the same as not wasting a hamburger if it was just lying there.
- Do you believe the wolf's explanation of why he was visiting the first pig's house? Why?

LEVEL III – APPLICATION:
- How is this adaptation of the story more like what happens in courtrooms today?
- How have you argued your innocence when someone blamed you for something you did?

LEVEL IV – ANALYSIS:
- How is this approach to The Three Little Pigs different from the original story?
- Why is the wolf always seen as the villain in so many stories? Is this perspective justified?

LEVEL V – SYNTHESIS:
- What do you think the pigs would do if the wolf was found to be innocent?
- When the wolf gets out of prison after his sentence, do you think he will have learned from his mistake or will he seek revenge?

LEVEL VI – EVALUATION:
- Is this version of the wolf's innocence more interesting than the original? Why?
- If you were the judge, what sentence would you have given the wolf?

For those of you who have not read this book—it's fun! We encourage you to do so. The wolf is on trial for eating the pigs. He provides an interesting and engaging defence!

Two Continuums

SIMPLE to COMPLEX
EASY to DIFFICULT

Madeline Hunter illustrated that we could increase flexibility in our questioning at different levels of difficulty by controlling the level of difficulty of the question. We have found that she is right (for us and our students). Thinking of these as slide rulers reminds teachers that they can ask questions that range from *"complex and easy"* to *"complex and hard."*

Asking a range of questions allows teachers to engage all learners' minds in thinking at all levels of complexity. Certainly, applying the taxonomy in this manner facilitates meeting the individual learner's needs. Questions in all quadrants serve a purpose.

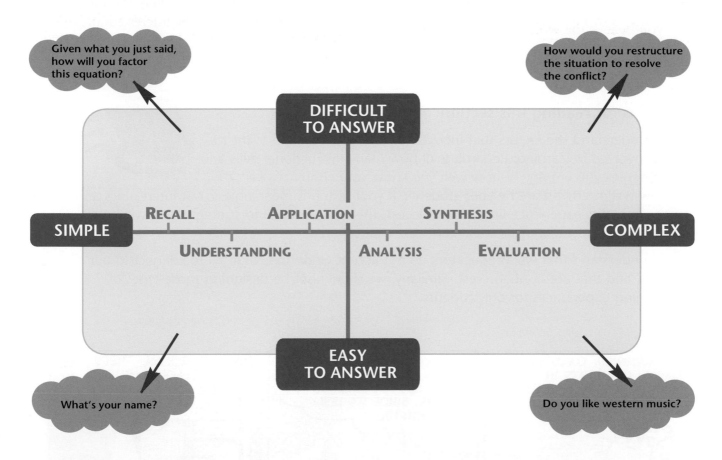

This also relates to what Millar stated in 1897. *"When teachers select students to respond...they should select the student who is in most need of the question."* How can teachers do this if they are not in control of the cognitive demand of the question?

The Concept of "Motivation" and Related Instructional Skills

The previous two sections responded to the issue of having students actively involved and accountable, while simultaneously attending to the levels of thinking. Those three areas are important; however, it is another thing to sustain students' interest over time—to keep them motivated—or even better, to have the students keep themselves motivated.

Motivation is another concept a teacher can attend to in responding to individual needs of students. A wise person would agree that the idea of one person attempting to create a learning environment for thirty others for approximately 200 days a year is a complex and creative task. Once again, the ability to integrate a variety of concepts, skills, tactics, and strategies is essential in accomplishing this task. Robert Sylwester reminds us that when we say that students are not interested, it is not that they are not interested—rather, they are simply not interested in what we want them to be interested in. (ASCD, *The Brain and Learning* video, Part I, 1998)

Reasons for reading this section:

- To understand the factors that increase the chances students want to be involved in learning. Regardless of how many instructional skills and strategies you employ or how well you know your content areas or how well liked you are by your students, if your lesson is meaningless, not interesting, and if the students experience little or no success, then those skills and strategies etc. will be of little value in your classroom.

- To understand that we as educators do not accept workshops that fail to connect to our lives, and that are of no interest. Similarly, we should not be designing those types of learning experiences for our students.

Motivation Motivation Motivation

DEFINITION OF MOTIVATION:

Who really knows? It is different for each one of us. In terms of our students, perhaps it could be as simple as "Anything that encourages the student to learn."

RATIONALE FOR INTEGRATING MOTIVATION INTO THE LESSON:

When students are motivated to learn they learn more and learn it faster. They are also less likely to misbehave.

Just for interest, ask yourself what would happen if we told all grade 8 students that, when they completed the stated curriculum with a 75 percent or higher average, they would be on summer vacation?

Educators often talk of increasing the school year to increase student achievement. Our response is that one bowl of gruel kept Oliver Twist alive—two bowls may have killed him. More isn't always wiser.

CONSIDERATIONS:

1. Attribution Theory argues that unless students attribute their successes and failures to their own efforts, little or no long-term transfer of the motivation to

learn will occur. (Note: the assumption is that the students understand the causal link between his or her effort, or lack of effort, and the resulting success or failure.)

2. If students receive reinforcement (praise, encouragement, etc.,) for a task that was easy or related to luck, ability, an effective teacher, or other factors over which they have little control, the reinforcement will not sustain their motivation to learn.

3. Through whose eyes should the use of motivation be situated: the student's or the teacher's?

Two Basic Types of Motivation

In most classrooms, students do not run through the doors breathlessly and excitedly yelling "Ah, math class ... great great; let's get started!" If they do, you most likely do not need to review the literature on motivation.

We know that one student in six in Canada is at risk. They walk through our classroom doors being victims of physical abuse, sexual abuse, mental abuse, multiple divorces, alcoholic parent(s), etc. When their basic needs are not being met, then how can they care about understanding finite math, reading a poem, or working with a partner? Yet somehow some do.

To understand more about what motivates students, it's helpful to examine the two basic categories for classifying motivation explained on the following page.

- **Intrinsic Motivation**

  In this type, the force comes from within the learner; however, the teacher can design environments and employ skills and personality traits that encourage the move towards intrinsic motivation. *Millar (1897) labelled this "natural" motivation.*

- **Extrinsic Motivation**

  With extrinsic motivation, the force comes from outside the learner. The teacher consciously does things to cause motivation to occur—hopefully moving the student to become intrinsically motivated. *Millar (1897) labelled this "artificial" motivation.*

  Unfortunately, not all of our students are intrinsically inclined—at least not at the first of the year. Although effective teachers have learned to design learning environments that invite students to be intrinsically motivated, they have also had to weave other

extrinsically motivating forces to sustain or initiate motivation.

If Adler and Glasser are right about the human needs that influence our behaviour:
- the need to belong;
- the need to have power (influence) over occurrences in our lives;
- the need to experience freedom; and
- the need for fun;

...then what **FORCES** would we see and hear in a learning environment that would increase the chances students will sustain their involvement in learning?

Below you will find a set of directions that invite you to explore what motivates you.
Following that is a list (not exhaustive) of what the literature reports.

Things that Motivate — Workshop Idea

Task: List the things that motivate you...

DIRECTIONS:

1. Take two minutes and identify variables that you use to get yourself motivated to do something.

2. Connect that information to the teachers or other individuals (parents, friends) you've interacted with that created an environment that motivated you to learn.

3. Get into groups of three and identify the motivational factors that all of you have in common.

4. Find one other group of three and identify the variables the six of you have in common.

Debrief:

Are you all motivated by the same factors? What are the implications for the teaching/learning process? Predict what would happen if you had a limited repertoire of approaches to teaching.

5. How does Multiple Intelligence Theory (Howard Gardner's work) and Learning Style Theory (the work of Bernice McCarthy, Rita Dunn, & Anthony Gregoric, etc.) connect to motivation?

When finished, compare your thinking with the information on the following two pages.

Six Characteristics of Motivation

These six concepts are some of the concepts we can control in the classroom; they increase the chances that students will be motivated. Nonetheless, if we do not assist students in learning and believing that their success and failure depend on their effort, then these six skills will have illusory effects. Also, if students who work hard do not achieve success, alternative strategies to engage their thinking must be employed. Additionally, alternative ways to structure classroom interaction must also be considered. We note that these six characteristics have been present in the literature from 1897 to present. One of the best chapters we've read was by Millar in 1897. Madeline Hunter also had these as key factors in her work.

SUCCESS – Nothing succeeds like success. If students regularly experience success and have a healthy self-concept they need to have successful experiences approximately 75% of the time. Students who are not successful and do not have a healthy self-concept require success at a minimum of 90% to 95% of the time.

One inference for teachers is that if students are to experience success, teachers need to teach at the correct level of difficulty and in a manner that actively involves the learner in meaningful learning. Also, when required, teachers must monitor the student learning and make appropriate adjustments in their instruction and in the set up of their room. In most cases teachers should sequence the learning from the easiest to most difficult—especially for students who are easily frustrated. That sounds obvious; however, it is not always that easy to do when kids are at different levels of competency.

CONCERN – If zero concern exists there will probably be zero learning. On the other hand, too much concern and some students become frustrated; too little and some students become bored. Teachers can control concern by appropriately applying one or more of the following five concepts:

1. **Increasing accountability**—Framing the question, wait time, checking homework, and having standards for learning all increase or decrease a student's level of concern. When invoking accountability remember to be sensitive to norms of other cultures.

2. **Visibility**—Moving around the room increases the chances students will be involved in the lesson. This is similar to the increase in your level of concern when you see a police car in the rear-view mirror.

3. **Consequences**—When students know they can enjoy the fruits of their effort if they complete a task or have to miss a task they enjoy if something is not completed, they are more inclined to complete the task.

Note that reward and punishment often occur as consequences; the side effects of reward and punishment decrease the chances of intrinsic motivation occurring. However, most people we've met enjoy a bit of extrinsic motivation; it is the excess that can be counterproductive.

Characteristics of Motivation

4. **Time**—If students know how much time they have to complete a task they are more concerned about the intensity of their effort. Have you noticed how people are affected by time on examinations? The more time, the lower the level of concern (for most people). Interestingly, time restrictions negatively affect creative thinking for some and positively affect it for others. For sure, it negatively affects the breadth and depth of a conversation.

5. **Help**—If students know that avenues of help exist, their level of concern is reduced. Guided practice is incorporated into the lesson because it provides the opportunity for assistance while students are practising a new skill. Nonetheless, teachers must be careful because too much help can make students overly dependent. Perhaps that is why small group Cooperative Learning has proven so useful—students depend on one another.

MEANING – The more the learning relates to the students' past, present, or future knowledge and experience, the greater the chances the students will be involved in the learning. This implies connecting to learning that is already stored in the brain. Mental Set is one place in the lesson the teacher can create meaning or help the student realize the meaning. Also, sharing/discussing/negotiating the purpose of the lesson with the student increases the chances the student will be motivated to participate. Other ways are through drama, role plays, field trips, discussion, films and videos, etc.

POSITIVE FEELING TONE – If we make what is being learned a pleasant experience, we increase the chances students will want to continue learning. Although unpleasant feeling tone is just as powerful, if employed excessively, it might cause the student to withdraw. Learning style (discussed in Chapter 12) fits in here, as does being polite and respectful. Appropriately responding to students' incorrect or partially correct responses, silly responses, guesses, etc., also fit as examples of teacher behaviours that provide a positive feeling tone.

INTEREST – People are motivated to do those things that they find interesting. We attend to things we find novel, varied, and vivid. Humour and enthusiasm are two teacher behaviours that create interest. Curiosity about something also peaks our interest. By showing interest in students we impact the feeling tone in the classroom.

KNOWLEDGE OF RESULTS – When we know that what we are doing is being done well, or needs to be improved and we know what to do to improve (and feel and believe we can do it) we are motivated to continue. How teachers respond to students' responses provides guidance for the students to either stop or continue with a line of thinking. Certainly, monitoring the students' learning and adjusting teaching (checking for understanding) is one way to provide accurate knowledge of results. Student self assessment (e.g., through the use of rubrics) is another excellent approach for providing feedback.

Motivation and the Enthusiastic Teacher

The research literature reports that when teachers are enthusiastic, students are more likely to be focused on the information being presented. Mary Collins' (1978) research reported that teacher enthusiasm increased student academic engaged time. In talking to teachers over the years, when we ask them to think back on a great teacher and what characteristics that teacher had, humour and enthusiasm rank first 80% to 90% of the time. Enthusiasm was also identified as a characteristic of effective teachers when Ken Macrorie interviewed effective teachers in his book *Twenty Teachers* (1986). Likewise, William Hare (1995) argues the importance of enthusiasm in his book, *What Makes a Good Teacher.*

The following teacher characteristics communicate enthusiasm to students:

- Vocal Delivery
- Word Choice
- Humour
- Eye Movement
- Facial Expressions
- Gestures
- Movement
- Energy Level
- Acceptance
- Variety and Novelty

Summary of the Motivation Variables

 Success
not boring, not too difficult

 Knowledge of Results
feedback

 Accountability
visibility, framing the question

 Meaningful to the Student
linking to their experience

 Positive Feeling Tone
winning over, politeness

 Interest
novelty, vividness, variety

Summary—Research on Concepts and Skills

If someone asked you which of the three following tools would be more effective for taking wood off a plank—(sandpaper, plane, or table saw)—you would most likely say table saw, if you were looking for the biggest effects. That does not mean the use of the plane or sandpaper is inappropriate. Each plays a role in getting the job done.

We see the relationships between skills, tactics, and strategies in a similar light. Each has a purpose, but strategies make the biggest difference in student learning — to the extent the teacher can effectively attend to the concepts and organizers in making wise decisions about what skills and tactics to integrate into the strategies to allow them to fully function.

The research related to a number of the instructional concepts and skills has been around for a long time. For example, if you were to do a computer search on ERIC on the research related to the concepts of humour and enthusiasm, you would find a plethora of studies (both qualitative and quantitative) related to the effects those two concepts have on student learning.

Research on Instructional Skills shows that skills make small differences in student learning. Some researchers have implied that certain programs (for example Madeline Hunter's Instructional Theory Into Practice—ITIP) were not effective because the concepts and skills in those programs did not make a noticeable difference in student learning. Our response is that those comments by researchers is akin to carpenters saying that sandpaper is not worthy in that it does not take much wood off a plank. Sandpaper is designed not to take too much wood off. Instructional Skills serve a similar purpose and enhance the learning process. When we reduce research on teaching to determining the effects of single variables on student learning, and then make decisions about that variable's worth, then we run the risk of operating in a narrow and naive manner. It is the fruitfulness of the interplay of variables that must guide our efforts.

If you calculate the effects of instructional skills on student learning, you find that the effects are small—they move the mean score from somewhere between the 50th to the 55th percentile. Some are more, some are less, but the overall effect is small. Of course there is the synergistic effect one might expect when they are artfully integrated, and more importantly, integrated with other instructional tactics and strategies.

Instructional concepts are also connected to the learning environment. Phelan, Davidson and Cao (1992), in their study of high school classrooms, report the critical importance of caring. The brain research overwhelming tells us that classrooms need to be safe places. The brain shuts down when threatened. The hippocampus, which is important in memory, atrophies under prolonged stress. Soar and Soar's (1979) research illustrated the effect of uncaring environments on student learning. However, they did not report the effects of a more supportive environment. Stelmaschuk's (1986) research on gifted children reports that students want teachers who care about them outside the classroom walls.

Additionally, David and Roger Johnson's research on Cooperative Learning indicates that the instructional concept of Individual Accountability is critical if group work is to function effectively. So, we can conclude that a number of instructional concepts and skills are clearly part of the teaching and learning tapestry.

Chapter Summary

Integrating Instructional Skills and Instructional Concepts

This chapter explored three concepts and the related skills that emerge or that encourage those concepts. The three concepts are: Active Participation, Levels of Thinking, and Motivation. Sub-concepts also emerged: Covert, Overt, Public Failure, Fear of Failure, Academic Engaged Time, Knowledge, Comprehension, Application, Analysis, Synthesis and Evaluation, Level of Concern, Success, Positive Feeling Tone, Knowledge of Results, Interest and Meaningfulness.

The skills that were discussed in this chapter related to wait time, framing questions to move from covert to overt, and asking questions at different levels of complexity.

The chapter also presented the teacher's instructional skills related to questions; that is, how teachers respond to students who provide responses that are silly, guesses, correct, partially correct, incorrect, and no response.

Some concepts such as caring, enthusiasm, and humour can also be argued as being skills we can invoke: being caring, being enthusiastic, and being humorous. That said, they are somewhat more amorphous in terms of how one goes about invoking them. As a result, we tend to see them as instructional concepts. Whether or not they are skills or concepts is not important—what is important is having a deep understanding of what they are and how they play out in creating powerful learning environments.

CALVIN AND HOBBES© Watterson. Reprinted with permission of UNIVERSAL PRESS SYNDICATE. All rights reserved

Chapter Five

Instructional Tactics

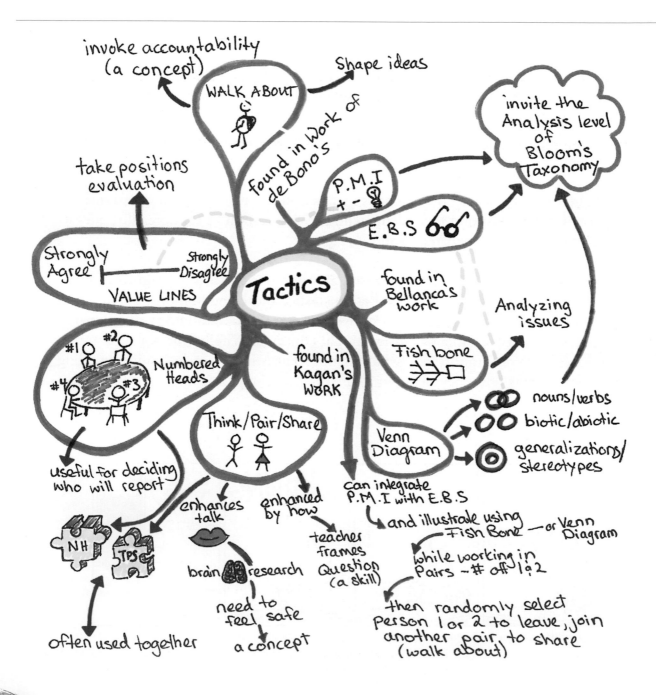

invoke accountability
(a concept)

Shape ideas

WALK ABOUT

found in Work of de Bono's

invite the Analysis level of Bloom's Taxonomy

take positions evaluation

P.M.I + -

E.B.S 6ð

Strongly Agree — Strongly Disagree

VALUE LINES

Tactics

found in Bellanca's work

Analyzing issues

#1 #2 #4 #3 Numbered Heads

found in Kagan's WORK

Fish bone

nouns/verbs
biotic/abiotic
generalizations/ stereotypes

Think/Pair/Share

Venn Diagram

useful for deciding who will report

enhances talk

enhanced by how

Can integrate P.M.I with E.B.S

NH   TPS

brain research

teacher frames Question (a skill)

and illustrate using Fish Bone — or Venn Diagram

while working in Pairs ~ # off 1 & 2

need to feel safe

a concept

then randomly select person 1 or 2 to leave, join another pair to share (walk about)

often used together

Chapter Five

Instructional Tactics

Below are two columns set up as a **Concept Attainment** data set. The items in column 1 are examples of tactics. The items in column 2 are examples of skills. What do the tactics have in common and what is the relationship between tactics and skills? (For information on Concept Attainment see Chapter 8.)

Predict what would happen if you tried to implement the processes in Column 1 (the tactics) without applying the skills in Column 2?

Column 1	Column 2
Think Pair Share	Providing Wait Time (questioning)
Numbered Heads	Checking for Understanding
3 Step Interview	Responding to a Silly Answer
Four Corners	Clarifying a Student's Response
Place Mat	Doing a Demonstration (Modelling)
Round Robin	Disagreeing in an Agreeable way
Double Entry Journal	Sharing the Lesson Objective
Inside Outside Circles	Actively Listening
Brainstorming	Paraphrasing

Below are ten testers. In which column would you place each one?

1. Positive, Minus, Interesting (PMI)
2. Examine Both Sides (EBS)
3. Fish Bone
4. Venn Diagram
5. Summarizing
6. Word Web
7. Value Lines
8. Two on a Crayon
9. Walk About
10. Suspending Judgement

Note: Testers 1 to 9 are tactics. Number 10 (Suspending Judgement during a discussion) is an example of a critical thinking skill. Suspending Judgement is a useful skill to employ when using tactics such as Think Pair Share and Round Robin.

Chapter Five

Instructional Tactics

This chapter describes eight tactics. Did you know that at least several hundred additional instructional tactics exist? Spencer Kagan illustrates about 100 tactics in his book *Cooperative Learning*. Edward de Bono identifies 60 in his *CoRT* program and Jeanne Gibbs has another 50 or so listed in her *Tribes* program. Imagine the possibilities when we integrate one tactic with another and when they are enhanced by a variety of instructional skills. For example, framing questions (a skill) and active participation (a concept) are instrumental in increasing the effectiveness of most tactics such as Think Pair Share. Now, combine that with your knowledge of Multiple Intelligence and Child Development, and with your understanding of math, or art, or French, etc., and you sense the power of an instructional tapestry.

Imagine the possibilities when the tactics are employed to enhance the more complex strategies such as Lesson Design, Concept Attainment, Mind Mapping, and Academic Controversy presented in later chapters.

This chapter has six interconnected areas:

1. Introduction and rationale for this chapter
2. Description of eight instructional tactics
3. Analysis of three lessons to illustrate how tactics are applied
4. Connection between instructional skills, tactics, and strategies
5. Understand how some tactics can be integrated with Mind Mapping
6. Summary—connection to student learning

Key Questions

1. What is an instructional tactic, and how is it different from an instructional Skill and an instructional strategy?
2. What is the research on instructional tactics? Do tactics make a difference in student learning?
3. What is the relationship between instructional skills, instructional concepts, and instructional tactics (e.g., Framing Questions, Accountability, and Inside/Outside Circles respectively?)
4. How do tactics affect/support the implementation of instructional strategies? For example, does Three Step Interview (a tactic) enhance the effectiveness of Concept Mapping (a strategy)?

Introduction and Rationale

This chapter introduces a variety of instructional tactics. The use of tactics is a shift to the next level of instructional complexity. This complexity is enhanced when there is a corresponding appreciation of the interdependence between skills and tactics and their combined role in implementing instructional strategies.

Although an extensive variety of instructional tactics is available in the educational literature, little research exists related to the effect that tactics have on student learning. Our hypothesis is that they are not as powerful as instructional strategies, yet are likely more powerful than instructional skills. Regarding student learning, the value of tactics is in how they strengthen the effect of the more complex instructional strategies. That said, tactics can operate independently to accomplish a variety of tasks in the classroom, such as organizing information, encouraging dialogue, and shifting thinking to more complex levels.

Most of the tactics presented in this book are found in the following resources.
- Spencer Kagan's book, *Cooperative Learning*
- Edward de Bono's work in his *CoRT* program
- Jim Bellanca's ideas in *Cooperative Think Tank I* and *II*.
- Jeanne Gibb's work in *TRIBES*

Note that most of the cooperative structures collected and presented in Kagan's book on cooperative learning are tactics. Some of those small group structures are more complex (e.g., Jigsaw, STAD, and Teams Games Tournaments). The authors of this book classify those three as instructional strategies, as they are more complex.

The fact that a range of tactics exist implies a continuum of complexity within the extensive variety of cooperative group structures—the simplest being Numbered Heads and Think Pair Share and the more complex (from our perspective) being Three Step Interview and Four Corners.

The most in-depth book on Group Investigation is *Expanding Cooperative Learning Through Group Investigation* by Yael and Shlomo Sharan. For a concise explanation of the six steps of Group Investigation and the corresponding planning sheets and sample evaluation forms, see *Cooperative Learning: Where Heart Meets Mind* by Bennett, Rolheiser, and Stevahn. In that book you will also see a concise explanation of Aronson's instructional strategy called Jigsaw. For the most in-depth explanation of Jigsaw, see the book *The Jigsaw Classroom* by Elliot Aronson.

Think/Pair/Share: A Simple Tactic. Do You Understand Its Complexity?

We have stated that instructional tactics are more complex than instructional skills. What does this mean?

Take a moment and think of everything you must consider if you want to effectively apply **one of the simplest** of all instructional tactics—**Think/Pair/Share**. If you are sitting with someone, take a moment and share your ideas, then compare them with what other experienced and effective teachers have told us about what they consider.

- Do students have the skills to effectively complete a Think/Pair/Share? For example, can they actively listen to one another, can they paraphrase what the other person said, can they suspend judgment when necessary, not put each other down?

- What level of thinking will be invited: recall, comprehension, application, analysis, evaluation, or synthesis? If you do not know, then how will you decide how much wait time to provide? What does the research say about how much wait time to provide and what effect wait time has on student thinking?

- How accountable will you make the students? Will they only share with a partner or will you then ask them to share with the class? If you will ask one or more to share publicly, is your classroom a safe place for students to share? Will they have the right to pass?

- What does the literature on the human brain inform you about the importance of emotional safety and talk in terms of the development of intelligent behaviour?

What does Howard Gardner's work indicate about the importance of interpersonal intelligence?

- What if you select a student to respond and she gives you a correct, incorrect, partially correct response, a silly response, a guess, a convoluted response, or a "no" response? How will you respond? More importantly, how will you respond to make sure the student saves face?

- Who will sit with the English as a second language student or with the student who is the isolate and has no friends? Will the boys sit beside the girls or vice versa? What if the classroom has an odd number of students? How will you decide who will talk with whom?

- Did you frame the question to indicate the level of thinking, how much wait time students will get and how you will ask them to share their thinking? Will you start with an open-ended or closed-ended question and will you ask them to think covertly and then overtly to make it safer?

Remember, THINK/PAIR/SHARE is one of the simplest of all the tactics. On the following pages are descriptions of seven more complex tactics.

"This structure is adapted with permission from Kagan Publishing and Professional Development. Books and resources on Kagan Structures can be obtained from Kagan Publishing, 1 (800) 933-2667, www.KaganOnline.com"

Description of Eight Instructional Tactics

On the following pages, you will see brief explanations of eight instructional tactics with a sample lesson following several of the tactics to illustrate how they are woven into the lesson. Note, as you move through the chapter, the lessons get more complex. In the chart below you see the name of the author and the title of the book in which each tactic is described. We encourage you to peruse the works of these authors. They collectively describe a rich variety of instructional tactics. Our initial purpose in this chapter is to have you understand the characteristics and potential power of instructional tactics. As the chapter progresses we hope you will sense the interplay or relationship between instructional tactics, instructional skills, and instructional strategies.

Tactic	Book Author	Source of Additional Tactics
1. P.M.I	deBono	CoRT
2. E.B.S.	deBono	CoRT
3. Fish Bone	Bellanca	Think Tank I
4. Venn Diagram	Bellanca	Think Tank II
5. Think Pair Share	Kagan	Cooperative Learning
6. Numbered Heads	Kagan	Cooperative Learning
7. Value Lines	Kagan	Cooperative Learning
8. Walk About	author unknown	source unknown

The first two tactics (**Plus, Minus, Interesting** and **Examine Both Sides**) are two of 60 tactics from de Bono's CoRT program. They push students to be more analytical in their decision making. They also weave easily into aspects of critical thinking.

The next two (**Venn Diagrams** and **Fish Bone**) also push for analytical thinking, but employ a graphic organizer to assist in the organization of information.

Think Pair Share and **Numbered Heads** encourage accountability in group work — with Think Pair Share encouraging student dialogue and Numbered Heads affecting accountability and assisting with controlling who will talk first.

Note: In Chapter 7 on Peer Mediated Learning (a chapter that provides a more practical and integrative focus on Cooperative Learning) five more tactics for effectively structuring small group learning are described:

1. **Inside Outside Circles**
2. **Place Mat**
3. **Four Corners**
4. **Three Step Interview**
5. **Graffiti**

"This structure is adapted with permission from Kagan Publishing and Professional Development. Books and resources on Kagan Structures can be obtained from Kagan Publishing, 1 (800) 933-2667, www.KaganOnline.com"

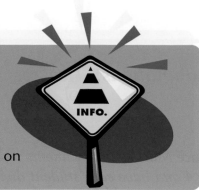

2 EBS (Examine Both Sides)
A Thinking Organizer

Remember the story about the two people on opposite sides of the river—one called over and asked how to get to the other side. The other person responded, "You are on the other side."

EBS is connected to the process of critical thinking—searching for truth. This tactic encourages students to look at the world from another's perspective. Unlike a debate, where students select and defend one position, this encourages a wider understanding. Note: students can often do a PMI on each side of the issue to determine where they want to position themselves. Once an issue is identified, side A argues in favour of the idea, Side B argues against the idea. Note that this connects to the strategy of Academic Controversy explained in Chapter 11.

If you want your students to take advantage of the power of Academic Controversy (also known as Creative Controversy) you would be wise to have them first develop the skill of **examining both sides of an issue**. Note: if your students struggle with a simple tactic like Think Pair Share, they will not benefit as much from EBS. You can see how two tactics can be snapped together for a more integrative effect.

For example, perhaps someone is trying to convince you to become a vegetarian. The examination of this issue would focus on factors related to be or not to be a vegetarian. Having explored both sides of this issue, you can make a more informed decision.

Situation: A school rule may be in question (e.g., wearing hats in class). The students explore both sides of the issue (wearing and not wearing hats.) Once again, EBS can weave naturally into PMI. In this case, do a PMI on each side of the issue.

Situation: Children's literature books are excellent resources to encourage students to explore both sides of the issue. Below are two books that can be adapted K to Adult.

 Story: *Maxine's Tree* by Diane Legér-Haskell. This is a story about a girl who comes up with an idea to save trees. Interestingly, this book was challenged in the Canadian courts. The question to ask the students is: *"Why was this book challenged?"* The answer: the book portrays those in the lumber industry as "bad people." The book does not explore both sides of the issue. This book is excellent for introducing students to the importance of exploring both sides of an issue.

 Story: *The Littlest Mole Who Knew It Was None of His Business* by Werner Holzwarth & Wolf Erlbruch. This story is about a little mole emerging from his burrow to see the sun. In the process, another animal (a dog) drops something nasty on his head. The mole did not see who did it as his eyesight is not that good. Nonetheless, he is upset, so he seeks out who did it and enacts revenge. The question the students attempt to answer is "What was the flaw in the mole's actions?" The answer is that he does not consider the dog's perspective. This is a great book for Academic Controversy.

Situations

Situation: Think of a fallacy of inductive thinking known as the "sweeping generalization." It refers to the failure to explore both sides of an issue. Below is a data set presented in Chapter Eight, page 198. On the following two pages you see how it is woven into a lesson.

EXAMPLES of the FLAW	NOT EXAMPLES of this FLAW
The pesticides are causing the birds, eggs to be too fragile. We need to stop using pesticides.	One possibility is that the earth is warming up because of pollution. But I think we need to explore other reasons.
Trees are important; people who cut down trees are destroying our planet. We need to ban tree cutting.	I like your idea, but I'm not sure what you meant by the last part. Would you please explain that?
Solar energy is free. We should pass a law that would provide money so that everyone could switch to solar energy.	I agree, but could we consider this from another perspective. What do you think, Ali?
Making people pay more taxes on gasoline is smart. Then we will have enough money to cover the cost of helping feed the poor.	I agree that car exhaust is hurting the environment, but we need to consider what would happen if we forced people to use another form of transportation.
That raccoon got at the chickens last night. I'm going to trap and destroy all the raccoons that step onto my farm.	No thanks, I don't eat fish. I got sick on it once and developed an allergy.

Situation: On the following page is a lesson containing Bruner's Concept Attainment process. You can employ it to introduce students to the concept of examining both sides of an argument.

A Lesson

Objective: **Develop an understanding of what is meant by Examining Both Sides of an issue**

MENTAL SET: Each team has their **Place Mat** set to go. In your individual section, please jot down reasons why you think people get into arguments that often go unresolved. In 90 seconds, I will ask you to rotate your group's sheet so that you can see what others in your group thought. If you are not sure what to put down, leaving it blank is fine.

INPUT: I have an idea related to how to increase the chances of disagreeing with someone and not getting mad. We are going to use **Concept Attainment** to explore this idea. Below are five examples of that idea and five examples that do not represent the idea. Compare the YES examples and contrast them with the NO examples. When you each have an idea, go to the testers on the top of the next page.

YES EXAMPLES
- I agree that pesticides control insects, but have you considered the effect pesticides have when they seep into streams?
- Well, we all understand why cutting down those trees is a problem in terms of soil erosion. We also have to consider what will happen if the mill shuts down and there is no work.
- Yes, I realize he is always late for school. I was wondering if we should look at what is happening at home to see if that can help us understand why.
- Okay, you can decrease the cost of producing each computer and we will make more money in the short term. Do you think you need to consider the long-term increase in cost for repairs?
- I understand your argument for more amateur sports, but does that mean that professional sports have no place in our community?

NO EXAMPLES
- Those raccoons are destroying all my chickens — I say get rid of the raccoons.
- Teachers are paid too much as it is. They get two months holidays and only work from 9 a.m. to 3:30 p.m.
- All students should wear school uniforms. Then we would all be the same and no one would get picked on because of the way they are dressed.
- The fastest solution is to push for electric cars. That will reduce the pollution caused by car exhaust.
- Competition simply causes too many problems. We need to get rid of it; people need to learn to cooperate, to work together.

Below are four testers. In your group, take turns using a Round Robin to determine which testers are YES examples and why.

TESTERS:

a. The gun laws in Australia are a great idea. Without guns, this world would be a safer place.

b. The big malls save a lot of money for the developer, but what about the effect on the small corner store?

c. The advertisements that show people as skinny and attractive are useful because they encourage all people to stay fit.

d. Building cheaper cars is important in that not all people can afford expensive cars. My concern is that the poor may then be more at risk in road accidents.

CHECKING FOR UNDERSTANDING:

We are going to share our thinking about what the YES examples have in common by doing a **Walk About.** Take one more minute to make sure your team has a consensus around what the YES examples have in common. Place your idea in the centre of your **Place Mat.** When I say move, one person in each group will put up their hand (person A, B, C, or D.) Another person will get up with their group's Place Mat and go to a new group and explain your group's position. The other group will then share theirs with you. When I say return, that person will return to their home group. Okay, take two minutes to share. (After two minutes ask person A to put a hand up, and ask C to move. A's hand goes down when a new C joins their group.)

Once they return, randomly call on individuals using **Numbered** or **Lettered Heads** (e.g., Group 2 person B, what does your group think?)

PRACTICE:

Provide an issue from the above data set. The two As take the pro side, the two Bs take the con side. They get several minutes to plan their comments and then take one minute (for each side) to share. When finished, they discuss their comments.

The social skill is active listening—you may have to pre-teach this skill if your students are not skilled at active listening. If your students put each other down and are not able to listen in a fair-minded way, then they are not ready for this type of experience.

CLOSURE/EXTENSION:

Have students discuss the relationship between teasing, prejudice, apartheid, and their original comments on their **Place Mats.** How do these ideas relate to the willingness and ability of people to explore both sides of an issue? Clips from movies are also excellent for illustration (e.g., Gandhi, near the beginning of the movie, where he is defying the law regarding travel passes).

Note: If your students do not have the skills and disposition to involve themselves in this lesson, then what are the chances they could effectively participate in the more complex process of Academic Controversy explained in Chapter 11?

3 *Fish Bone*
A Graphic Organizer

Fish Bone (like **Venn Diagrams**, described next) is used to organize information. It is often used in problem solving or to identify and organize factors. It ties to de Bono's tactic of **Consider All Factors** (CAF). Although CAF is not discussed in this book it is self-explanatory.

The diagram below illustrates the structure of the Fishbone Organizer. It illustrates one teacher's initial thoughts related to factors to consider when developing a successful lesson. Fishbone can have as many extensions as is appropriate or necessary.

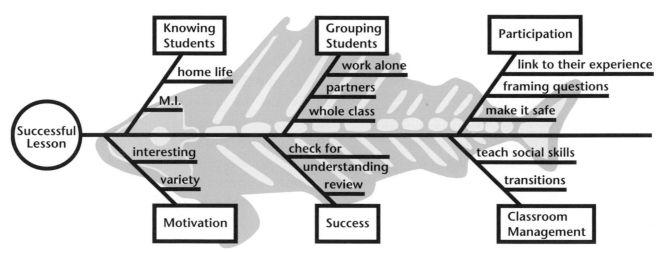

Notice how the head of the Fish Bone provides the issue or idea that acts as the focus for the thinking. In a way, Fish Bone is a more sophisticated form of **Brainstorming** or **Considering All Factors**. Now the students do more than simply identify or recall ideas; they also organize them according to some type of classification of the main ideas and the sub ideas (this is the analysis and evaluation level of Bloom's Taxonomy).

Situation: The students may be exploring how to pass an exam. They put "Passing the Exam" in the head, and then explore the factors that will affect their passing. They can then explore the ones over which they have control.

Situation: The students may have read the book *The Giving Tree* by Shel Silverstein. They first brainstorm the ways that the boy can be a better friend to the tree. They then do a Fish Bone on the things to do and not to do if they want to make friends.

Situation: The students may be discussing why people bully. They could do a Fish Bone to explore the issue of why some people become bullies.

Adaptation: Have the students complete a PMI using the Fish Bone so that the POSITIVE is on the top part of the Fish Bone and the MINUS is on the bottom. When finished, they then do a 3 Step Interview around their thinking, which includes what they thought was most interesting, important, or intriguing.

4 Venn Diagram
A Graphic Organizer

A Venn Diagram is a graphic organizer. Although it looks simple, it is not. Using a Venn diagram invites the learner to operate at the analysis level of Bloom's Taxonomy. How are things the same and how are they different? If someone asked you to do a Venn diagram on nouns and verbs, the first thing you would realize is how many nouns can be verbs (e.g., rock, chair, book). On the right is a Venn diagram on nouns and verbs. You could employ it to graphically represent both those concepts.

Think About Integrating Venn Diagrams with Other Tactics:

If you are having students construct a Venn Diagram in small groups, you might ask yourself questions such as: "How could **Numbered Heads** increase accountability and focus their talk? How could **Walk About** assist in both increasing accountability and the spreading of ideas? Could the students work alone and then do a **Three Step Interview** on their diagram? Could students create their own Venn diagram using **Place Mat** and then rotate the Place Mat to check others' ideas, and then in the centre create a Venn diagram, which they can all agree on and explain?

Note that Venn diagrams do not have to overlap and can occur as one circle within another or two circles not touching. For example, with the two concepts of stereotyping and generalizations, see the Concept Attainment data set on the following page – then decide whether or not the circles should be one inside the other, should overlap, or should not touch at all.

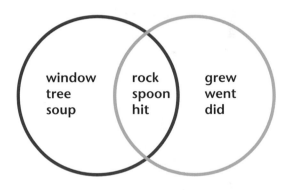

Situation: When you are encouraging students to differentiate (e.g. between addition and Multiplication story problems), ask them how they know the problem is one of multiplication and not addition.

Situation: When you are asking students to look at figures of speech such as simile and personification, ask them what they would call the phrase, *"crests like cruel smiles."* Is it a simile, personification, or something in between?

Situation: You are asking kindergarten students to sort items into two groups: Ingredients (chocolate chips, sugar, flour) and the Whole Object (cookies, cake, pizza). Where would they put pineapple, rice, and chocolate bar?

When you get to the chapter on Concept Attainment, you will understand that by putting two hula hoops on the floor, you can create the location for the YES and NO examples. Then for the examples that seem to fit into both categories, you bring the hoops together so that they overlap, and place those items in the middle (as illustrated previously with nouns and verbs).

Stereotyping is a specific type of Generalization. Below are six examples of stereotyping followed by six examples that are not stereotyping. On your own, try to decide what the stereotyping examples have in common and how they differ from generalizations. Then look at the testers and decide whether or not they would be examples of stereotyping.

Stereotyping:
1. Boys are stronger than girls.

2. A woman's role is in the kitchen.

3. Movie stars live glamorous lives.

4. Wolves are evil.

5. Kids today don't show respect.

6. Old people are dangerous drivers.

Generalizations that are not stereotyping:
1. People who exercise tend to live longer.

2. If you don't eat properly, you are more likely to get sick.

3. Italians appear to enjoy pasta.

4. Drivers who are tired are more likely to have accidents.

5. People who study tend to do better in school.

6. When you say nice things to people, they tend to treat you better.

TESTERS:
a. Politicians and lawyers are like snake oil hucksters.

b. Life can be dangerous.

c. People who cry are sissies.

d. Video games are a waste of time.

e. Football players are dumb jocks.

Now, on your own or with a partner, decide which Venn diagram best illustrates the relationship between stereotyping and generalizations.

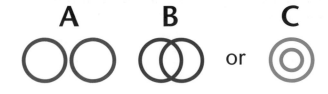

5 Think/Pair/Share
A Group Organizer

The teacher puts students into groups of two, three, or four. Students are asked to think to themselves, then share with a partner. Sounds simple, but it is a bit trickier than it looks. Think Pair Share is often not applied effectively. The problem is that too often, one student does all the talking. How do you know the students listened to each other? Another alternative is Think Pair Square. In this tactic, one person talks, the next person has to paraphrase what the person said, then that person shares, and the next person has to share what that person said, etc.

That said, Think Pair Share still works. We simply have to weave a bit more accountability into it and integrate it with other tactics. One option is to first have students letter off A and B (**Lettered Heads**). Then ask your question, give them time to think, and then ask A to start. When A is finished have B share what A said. Now reverse the process. Or, have A start, then say PASS when finished. Now B shares. Then tell students they have 30 seconds to discuss what they think is the best answer and that you will randomly call on them to share their group's thoughts with the class.

CONSIDERATION (read Chapter 4 on Instructional Skills) How you frame your question (an instructional skill) is critical in effectively weaving Think Pair Share into the learning process. You need to move from covert to overt (e.g., "Think to yourself, now share with a partner."). You also need to consider the amount of wait time. As the questions become more complex, the wait time must increase. Effective use of wait time also implies you can easily play with different levels of thinking as described in Bloom's Taxonomy (knowledge, comprehension, application, analysis, synthesis, and evaluation). If you are not aware of the cognitive demand of the question, then how do you know how to respond to an incorrect or partially correct response, a convoluted response, a no response, a silly response, or a guess? If students do not feel you are skilled in framing questions and do not feel safe when responding in your class, then Think Pair Share will not be effective.

Situation: Another way to increase accountability is to connect Think Pair Share to another small group instructional tactic called **Walk About**. First students think, then they share, and then you ask all the As to put their hand up. Bs are then asked to leave and sit beside another A and to exchange ideas. (See the explanation of Walk About later in this section.)

After they discuss what they think is the best response you can randomly call on them to respond: "This pair here please, person A."

Utilize Wait Time!

Situation: The students have individually worked on their **Mind Maps**. You now have them pair up. You frame questions and they share their thoughts. For example, you might say, "Think to yourself for 20 seconds. What component on your Mind Map would have the biggest impact on other components if it were removed?" (Note that this question is at the analysis and evaluation levels of thinking in **Bloom's Taxonomy**.)

Situation: Students have just taken the time to compare and contrast the YES and NO examples in a **Concept Attainment** data set. With a partner they now discuss how all the YES examples are the same. They then share their thinking of their mind's journey as it selected and rejected or selected and confirmed hypotheses. (Note that this represents Phase II: *Sharing the Thinking* of the Concept Attainment strategy.)

6 *Numbered Heads*
A Group Organizer

This is one of the simplest and most useful of the group tactics. It simply means to have groups number off (1, 2, 3) or letter off (A, B, C). Numbered Heads is one of the most effective ways of **increasing the concept of accountability**. It also assists in initiating a transition, or in handing out and collecting materials, etc. Most teachers also number or letter the groups as well. If you number the students, provide the group with a letter (or vice versa). Employing Numbered Heads alongside a mini-lecture is also effective. For example, before you start a mini-lecture on factoring equations, inform students they will have two minutes to discuss in their groups before you randomly call on someone from several groups to share their group's answer.

In terms of **framing questions**, even our university students prefer weaving in the use of Numbered Heads with small group work.

They say that although students are more accountable, they are under less stress because they have someone with whom they can talk before having to share publicly. When **making a transition** or handing out materials etc., the last thing you want to do in a grade seven or eight class is to ask for someone in each group to get up and get an atlas for each person in the group. They will either all get up, or no one will get up, and when they do get up, you know that the closer they get to the atlases, the faster they will move. You also know that someone will get tripped … which will push you to the fringe of frustration. Therefore, asking person 2 from each group to come and collect an atlas increases the chances of this being a successful request.

CONSIDERATION: Remember that even in Think/Pair/Share, one person can take over and do all the talking. If you add Numbered Heads to Think/Pair/Share, you can ask the question, give students time to think, and then ask person A or B to start. When that person finishes they say PASS, and then the other person shares. Some teachers invoke **Flip It** — that simply means that one person in the pair talks until you say "Flip It," and then the other person starts talking. You can tell them to share their idea or to extend that person's idea, or to paraphrase what that person said.

Situations: When doing **Inside/Outside/ Circles,** you can increase accountability by lettering off each group, having each pair number off, asking your question, giving wait time, then selecting a person: Group D,

Pair 4, Inside. Now that person shares with the class. If you want to make it safer, then say Group D, Pair 4, share with your group. Now two students share with a smaller group. At the start of the year the second approach is safer. Students don't have to share in front of the whole class.

Situations: In a **Three-Step Interview,** numbered heads is used as a management or organization process. It informs the students who will be the Interviewer, the Recorder, or the Interviewee for each of the three rounds. This way they do not fight over who gets what role. Note that for your peace of mind it's wise to assign the letter first, and then assign the role. That way, you increase the chances students do not argue over the role. If the roles rotate, then they are not as concerned about who gets what role.

7 Value Lines
A Thinking/Emotions Organizer

Value Lines pushes the analysis and evaluation levels of Bloom's Taxonomy — it has a subtle complexity. Remember that the quality of the students' decisions increases as they become more informed and feel safer to present their ideas without fear of being ridiculed. Value Lines work more effectively in classrooms where students are skilled at working collaboratively.

From one perspective, Value Lines is a simpler version of Four Corners (see page 162 in Chapter 7 on Peer Mediated Learning for a description of Four Corners)—rather

than four or five choices, you have only two. Nonetheless, even though you have only two choices, you have a much wider range of values between those two extremes. This continuum allows the students much more flexibility as to where they stand on an issue.

One of its strengths is that Value Lines connects to the work on the Emotional Brain (LeDoux, 1996; Goleman, 1995). The students weave their feelings and explore their thinking around those feelings—often making complete reversals in their positioning.

Situation: Students are exploring the complexities and issues in Russian society. Based on their reading, they have to position themselves on a value line. The line represents a more Democratic form of government or a more Communistic form of government.

Situation: Students are studying two paintings. They have to position themselves on a value line (e.g., a painting that creates the most tension, or specific emotion, etc.).

Situation: Students are listening to and exploring Baroque music. A piece of music is played and they have to position themselves according to whether or not it clearly represents Baroque music.

Complex Situation: A grade four class was studying the issue of quarantine. This was extended into a discussion related to whether or not students with AIDS should be allowed to attend their school. If they were strongly in support of a student with AIDS attending they went to one wall, strongly against to the opposite wall. As well, they were also allowed to position themselves anywhere in between. They then did a **Think/Pair/Share** to discuss why they made the decision to stand where they did. Students were randomly selected to respond. They then moved into an **Academic Controversy** where they debated both sides of this issue. Following the debate, they returned to the Value Line to assess how much they had shifted their thinking. Interestingly, students from both extremes switched sides to the other extreme. Only a couple of students did not shift their thinking.

Adaptation: Put a piece of tape on the floor, then have the students stand on the value line and sign their name to represent where they stand on an issue. (Note, if you have read the Chapter on Lesson Design, this adaptation of Value Lines would make an interesting Mental Set or Introduction prior to starting an inquiry.) The rationale for using the tape is that at the end of the inquiry students can return to a new tape and sign their name. You could bring out the first tape and have them note any shift in thinking. This makes an interesting Closure for Lesson Design or Processing the Academic Task. (See Chapter 7 on Peer Mediated Learning for a discussion on processing.)

8 *Walk About*
Building Relationships

Walk About is a process that links other more complex processes. It builds individual accountability, physical movement, and variety into the learning process. It involves one member from one group joining another group. Basically it is akin to cross-pollination—ideas being taken from one group to the next. Note that it is best to have the students letter off or number off while in these groups prior to moving (for example, use **Numbered** or **Lettered Heads**). Walk About can be used in any subject area and all grade levels, including kindergarten.

Scenario: The grade one students have just listened to you tell a story (e.g., *Franklin in the Dark*). They then get into groups of two or three and they talk to each other about the things that make them feel afraid. Perhaps provide several focused questions such as, "What things frighten you?", or "Why were you scared?", or "How did you solve the problem?" Then ask one person from each group to go to another group to share some of their group's ideas.

Note that if you have a person whose sharing skills are weak, then have that person go with a buddy to share.

Scenario: Your students were working in groups of three using **Place Mat** or creating a **Fishbone** on a particular issue or problem. You would now use **Numbered Heads** to identify which person in the group will go on the **Walk About**. One person is asked to put up their hand (say person C), then another person is selected to get up (say person A) and take any relevant materials with them to join a new group. When a new A arrives at the group, person C puts their hand down. The new person now shares their group's thinking while the group members actively listen. Upon completion, the group can then share their comments, add ideas, etc. Person A then takes that information back to their original group.

Ideally, the students should know in advance that one person will be selected. That increases accountability to make sure they all understand what they are to do.

Remember: Integrating these instructional tactics is complex. If the students do not feel safe, or if they are not skilled at actively listening and paraphrasing, then they are not going to benefit from this process. This is why creating a safe and inclusive school and classroom environment is critical. (This is also why a number of schools are employing programs such as TRIBES to build learning communities.) Of course a number of teachers will say, *"I can't do that with my*

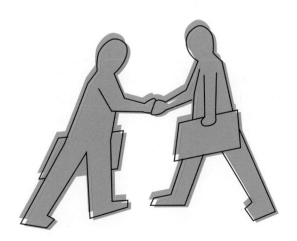

students." Our response is *"We have seen it used in classrooms all over the world—where teachers have collectively taken the time to create a safe, collaborative learning environment."* You have to take the time to develop students' listening and sharing skills if you want these tactics to have a pay-off in your classroom.

Adaptation: Have the group generate questions around the topic or problem they were discussing (say the topic of "tragic flaw" or "endangered animals" or "interpreting a graph"). These might be questions that they would like to ask the new person from another group who is joining their group. The students get time (say 3-5 minutes) to generate questions, the new person arrives, and is interviewed by that group. Once the interview is over, the teacher randomly selects students from the group to share what they learned from their interview. Again, this builds in accountability, gives them the opportunity to orally respond to interview questions, and to present the results of their interview. Note that the students can also do the Walk About in pairs or in groups of 4 or 5. This makes it safer for the person being interviewed.

A Lesson

A Grade 6 Science class is studying systems and system components with a focus on leaf structure (Pinnate, Palmate, and Parallel vein patterns). Leaf functions are then compared to systems or system components in the human body.

The lesson involves all of or parts of the instructional ideas listed below. Can you identify where the instructional ideas are used in the lesson and why?

Mind Mapping, Venn Diagrams, Numbered Heads, Think Pair Share; Concept Attainment; Place Mat, Round Robin, Walk About, Jigsaw, 5 Basic Elements, Brainstorming, Inductive Thinking, Lesson Design Components, Framing Questions, Wait Time, Covert to Overt, Accountability, Active Participation, Variety, Meaning, Safe Classroom, Bloom's Taxonomy, Brain Research, Multiple Intelligences, Learning Styles

As you read the lesson, think about how the skills, tactics, and strategies intersect or support each other.

Also consider that the lesson content does not have to be 'leaves' but could be different geometric shapes, types of poetry, different figures of speech, types of physics problems, styles of painting, algebraic equations, types of graphs, etc.

Teacher: I have just numbered you off from 1 to 9 (30 students in class). When I say move, would the ones sit here, the two's here, etc. You can see I have a number on a folded card at each table. Please move to those tables. (They moved; it took about 45 seconds.)

Teacher: Could you please letter off A, B, C. One group has four, you will have a D as well (wait 10 seconds). Okay A's, who are you ... hands up. B's, C's, okay and Erica, you are a D. Thank you.

I have 9 manila envelopes and sheets of chart paper at the table. When I call out a letter, would that person please come up and get the envelope and one sheet. Please don't open it—just wait for the next instruction— thanks. Person C please. (This took about 30 seconds.)

Teacher: Would person A please come up and get a different coloured felt pen for each person in the group. Just a minute A, my fault, don't move until I ask you to move. (This took about 30 seconds.)

Teacher: Okay, in the envelope are a number of leaves from a variety of plants. Before we analyze them, I want you to write down everything you know about leaves on the sheet of paper. I will give you 30 seconds to think, and when I say "start," write. When I say "stop," get up and move to the table that is the next highest in number (this clarifies how they will move). You will get 60 seconds to repeat your information on another sheet. You will not move to every sheet, only four in total. I will be the time keeper. Don't worry about reading what is there—just write your ideas. Having the same informa- tion written twice is not a problem. Take 30 seconds to think. No talking please. (This took about 30 seconds.) Please write. They

then completed the four rotations. Teacher moved around the groups as they wrote.

Teacher: Thanks. What you have is a list of what about 15 people in the class understand or know about leaves. Take one minute and read that information and start to see if you have anything that can be grouped together. (One minute passes). Now, do a Round Robin starting with D if you have a group of four, or A, if you are a group of three. See if you can find any patterns. If you are not sure, just say "Pass." When you have all passed, then you are finished.

Teacher: Now Person B, open the envelope and gently dump the leaves on the Chart Paper. You have approximately 20 different leaves. Each of you take about one minute and see if you can see any patterns that you did not discuss when you looked at the ideas on your chart paper. (One minute passes.) Person C, would you please start. If not sure, say "pass", then go clockwise. If it is not your turn, please just actively listen. See what you can find. You have 3 minutes. Go.

(3 minutes pass)

Now, would you work together, making sure that everyone is involved. Be sensitive to avoid one person taking over and doing all the work—we worked on that the other day. The one thing we will talk about at the end of this lesson is the extent to which you are working thoughtfully at involving everyone in grouping the leaves into categories based on their design. Don't focus on the colour of the leaves or size, rather, focus on design. You have four minutes. Go. (4 minutes passed). Stop please. Thank you.

Now at the two sides of the room, I have set up two centres. Groups 1 to 4 will go to one side, 5 to 9 to this other side. Without talking, and on your own, look to see what all the leaves on the left side of the table have in common—then compare them to the leaves on the right side. How are the left-side leaves the same? As you are quietly analyzing, think to yourself whether or not you had a similar group at your table. (This took about 5 minutes—they had to mill around a bit.)

Thanks. Now return to your table, and see if you have any new ideas (two minutes).

Teacher: Thanks, now I want you to think to yourself for about 30 seconds—what do you know so far about the leaves and their design? Also think about why they are designed the way they are. Now share in your group. You have one minute. I will then randomly call on students from each group to share. Go. (They discuss.)

Teacher: Okay, group 4, person C, what is one thing that your group mentioned? The teacher then asked one person from each group to share the group's thinking. (Note, instead of evaluating the students' answers, the teacher just said, *"Thank you for sharing,"* and then selected another group.)

Teacher: Up front, I have three sheets of paper. When I say move, person D (if group of 4) or A (if group of 3) come up and get one of each sheet. A will get the blue sheet, B the green sheet, and C (D) the yellow sheet. Everyone has a sheet? Good. Take 5 minutes and read your sheet. Identify what you think are the 3 or 4 key ideas. When I say move, the A's will move to this corner, B's to this corner, and C's and D's to this corner. When you arrive, find one or two others and discuss what you believe is the most important idea. Okay, please read it (about 6 minutes to read.) Okay, please move (it took about 3 minutes to move and share). Thank you. When I say move, you will return to your group, flip over your chart paper and construct a Place Mat, like we did the other day. Person B, you will draw the Place Mat. Okay move.

Teacher: When I say start, you will list in your section the key ideas from the discussion you had with your partner. You will have 2 minutes. Stop please. The recess bell is going to ring in about 60 seconds. Before you go out, think to yourself about what you have seen or done to encourage everyone to participate—to make sure one or two people did not do all the work. Don't share just think. When the bell goes, you can leave quietly for recess.

Recess Break

Teacher: (Gets students settled.) I will now do a 10 minute talk on vein structure. I will also refer to the three patterns of pinnate, palmate, and parallel. As I talk you can add ideas to your area. Also start to think about what systems in the human body perform what leaves do for plants. When I am finished, I will ask you to share ideas from your section with the other two or three members in your group. Then you will summarize what you believe is the most important information in the centre of the Place Mat. I will then call on one person to get up and go and share with another group. (Teacher did about an 8 minute mini-lecture on each of the three types of leaf patterns and the role of veins in plant growth, etc.)

Teacher: Person A, would you please raise your hand and put it down when a new person joins your group. Person D (if group of 4) and person C (if group of 3) will you please join a new group, taking the chart paper with you. (Students then shared their group's thinking. When they finished, the other group shared their thinking for a total of 4 minutes. Person D/C then added that to their chart and when told to move back to their home group, did so and shared any new information with their group).

Teacher: Thank you. Okay, I have handed out pieces of paper (8 1/2 X 14). On your own, I would like you to now Mind Map everything you know about leaves. I have the directions up here on the board. Go back to what you initially wrote. Select what you want from that information; also select the ideas that others wrote, from the discussion in the corners, and from the lecture. On one part of the map, identify using a Venn Diagram (we have used them a lot this year) how veins in plants compare to systems in the human body.

Also, on one part of the map, indicate which vein pattern you find the most interesting or that you think is the most efficient, and briefly explain why. Tomorrow, we will take time to finish these and then share them using a Gallery Tour.

Stop please. We only have about 2 minutes before we need to finish. I want you to think for 20 seconds about what you saw or what you did to make sure that everyone in the group was encouraged to be involved. When I say share, please identify one specific thing that happened that would tell someone in the group that everyone's voice was valued and encouraged.

Note: Gallery Tour is when the student tapes or pins up the work, and then stands by it and explains it to a small group of other students who visit. So about 2/3 of the class are touring (in this case, predetermined tour groups) and 1/3 are sharing. They then rotate until each person has had a chance to share.

A Lesson Coming Together:
...Can You Find the Tactics?

Chapter Summary

Connection to Student Learning

Interestingly, we found scant research to directly support the use of these tactics or any of the instructional tactics we frequently use and see applied in elementary and secondary classrooms. That should not deter you from using them; our experience tells us they are useful. If you are involved in action research, perhaps you can consider inquiring into the effects of these tactics on student learning.

That said, studies at the university level illustrate that in classes where the lecturer stops every 8 to 10 minutes and asks students to discuss what was just presented, students' test marks almost double those of students in classes where they just listen for the entire lecture. These findings suggest that tactics such as Think Pair Share have a positive effect on short-term memory.

Additionally, we know from the brain research that talk is critical to intellectual growth. Many of the tactics focus on the use of talk. Additionally, Howard Gardner argues from his research related to multiple intelligences that Interpersonal Intelligence is one of the strongest predictors of whether or not a person will be successful. This was true in all cultures they studied. Piaget and Vygotsky's work also support the importance of social interaction in learning.

We have found from our classroom experience that the tactics described in this chapter often enhance the level of thinking, the accountability, the participation, and the motivation to learn. More importantly, they enhance the effectiveness of the more complex strategies such as Mind Mapping, Concept Mapping, Concept Attainment, Inductive Thinking, Academic Controversy, and Team Analysis.

The effect that various instructional tactics have on student learning is virtually unknown. Yet, we would argue that limiting research to determining the effects of single innovations is not a wise idea; the teaching and learning process is not that simple. Rather, we would suggest that inquiry is needed that explores the effects of integrating tactics, the effect of integrating instructional skills with tactics, or of integrating tactics with other more complex strategies. Such inquiry may reveal a more interactive and authentic effect.

Chapter *Six*

Lesson Design...An Activity

Let's say your students are involved in an investigation of the abuse of human rights and the concept of Apartheid came up. They did not understand the concept of Apartheid and how it relates to teaching and prejudice so you decide to create a lesson for your students that would take 5, 15, 50 or more minutes. What building blocks or components would you employ to assist in the design and flow of the learning? Jot them down beside the puzzle pieces provided below, and then compare your ideas with some of those identified by Madeline Hunter in the Fish Bone on page 122.

Chapter Six

Lesson Design Chapter Overview and Discussion

This chapter has seven interconnected areas:

1. Introduction and Rationale for Lesson Design
2. Exploring the Instructional Concepts and Instructional Skills Connection
3. Discussion and Description of Lesson Design
4. An Activity: Becoming Consciously Skilled with Lesson Design
5. Inductive Lessons on each of the Lesson Design Components (on Web site only)
6. Sample Lessons Employing Lesson Design that integrate Active Participation, Motivation, and Different Levels of Thinking (See Web site for more sample lessons in different grade levels and subject areas.)
7. Summary—Connection to Student Learning

Key Questions

- Is checking to see if students understand an issue or concept etc., important?
- Is discussing the "what" and "why" of learning with students important?
- Should the learning be meaningful, interesting, and authentic?
- Are demonstrations important? What about using models?
- Can teachers weave a variety of instructional skills, tactics, or strategies into the introduction of the lesson or use them to generate information or to check for understanding?
- Should students' have time to discuss the link between what they are learning to their life experiences?
- Should students be actively involved?
- Is the chance to practise (rehearse) and discuss with peers—as well as alone—important?
- Why might a lesson crash or succeed? If it crashed, do you throw out the complete lesson or do you add/refine/delete one, two, or more components?
- What may happen if you choose to ignore one or more of the above questions?

Introduction and Rationale

This chapter presents a strategy (Lesson Design) employed throughout the rest of this book. **Lesson Design is one strategy that facilitates the creative process of *designing lessons*.** By designing lessons we are referring to selecting and integrating instructional processes through the needs and inclinations of the learner. The selection of those options is based on an ever-increasing understanding of the learner (see Chapter 12) and the content to be investigated.

Note: we are not suggesting that this Lesson Design strategy is the only way to organize a learning opportunity. Nonetheless, given the difficulty of communicating creativity in a book format, we decided to employ Lesson Design as one way to more clearly illustrate how a variety of instructional concepts, skills, tactics, and strategies may be integrated.

More specifically, this chapter illustrates how a group of eight instructional components can be organized in a variety of configurations to assist in making wise decisions in the design of a learning experience. One way to configure them has been labelled "Lesson Design." Two useful perspectives on Lesson Design and related ideas are found in Hunter, 1994, and Gentile, 1993.

You might ask, *"Why should I pay attention to this idea called Lesson Design?"* We might respond, *"Madeline Hunter, a Canadian who worked at UCLA, spent her professional life observing and working with teachers, trying to understand why they were or were not instructionally effective."* That work involved the identification of a sense of instructional necessity and flow in more effective learning environments. She put labels on what most teachers do day in and day out. One way of appreciating or understanding that "flow" is through her process of Lesson Design—as she says, *"It is not a rigid formula but a launching pad for creativity."*

Unfortunately, some educators employed her work, especially the idea of Lesson Design, in a restrictive and unthinking manner. That is not what Hunter intended. Like her, we see the Lesson Design process as one containing optional building blocks (as in a LEGO set) or threads on a weaver's loom, or colours on an artist's palette. Once you understand the different ways that lessons can flow (Lesson Design being one of them) you begin the shift towards the more powerful process of designing lessons or opportunities for learning.

This "artful" metaphor has three implications. **First,** the components of Lesson Design can occur in any sequence. **Second,** they do not have to be included or they may be used as many times as is appropriate. And **third,** they can be stacked (used one after another) and integrated (employed simultaneously) as you move in more creative directions. If you paint, you pick and mix the colours that best meet the needs of the painting. If you teach, you and the students select and integrate the design processes that most effectively meet the needs of the learners.

The Connection between Instructional Concepts and Instructional Skills

Lesson Design is a framework based on eight components. Five of those components we classify as instructional concepts and the other three instructional skills (see Chapter 2). Mental Set, Input, Practice, Closure, and Extension are concepts; you cannot directly **do** them, you must **employ** a skill, tactic, or strategy to make them come to life. Sharing the objective and purpose for the lesson, checking for understanding, and demonstrating or employing a model are things you can **do** directly; therefore, we see them as instructional skills. That said, we could select and apply any number of instructional tactics and strategies to increase the effectiveness of the instructional concepts and instructional skills. For example, to make Mental Set come alive, we could apply Place Mat or Mind Mapping, or invite a guest speaker.

Of course, other instructional concepts, such as those presented earlier in Chapter 4 (e.g., active participation, motivation, and levels of thinking) can also be connected to each of the components of Lesson Design. For example, you most likely want the students to be "actively participating" in the "checking for understanding." You also want them to be "accountable" and "successful." A check for understanding that does not actively involve the students, that does not hold them accountable, and that does not increase the chances they are going to be successful is not likely to be effective. We would also want to be sensitive to the cognitive demand of the "check for understanding." If it is too easy, students may get bored; too hard, they may get

frustrated. Both those situations can lead to classroom management problems.

Additionally, you need to consider how you are going to engage students based on their strengths in a variety of domains. Here are a few considerations: (1) the different senses (auditory, tactile, visual, kinesthetic, smell, taste); (2) their learning styles (how they approach learning); (3) their strengths in the different intelligences; and (4) their ability to work with a partner, etc. Furthermore, how will you make learning meaningful and interesting? What level of thinking should be encouraged? Will the learning link to the students' experiences? When should demonstration or modelling occur? This makes the idea of Lesson Design and designing lessons an interesting option.

In addition to the concepts identified in Chapter 4, hundreds of other concepts exist. Some are personal characteristics such as caring, respect, and enthusiasm, and others are more instructionally focused such as being organized and attending to variety, and authenticity. All of these can and should be integrated into the process of Lesson Design. **Lesson Design is a process that acts on its own or as an advance organizer representing one of many ways to connect the limitless possibilities of pedagogy.**

The possibilities are endless.

Discussion and Description of Lesson Design

In this book, Lesson Design acts as one way to integrate or organize what we understand about instruction. As stated earlier, it was initially conceptualized by Madeline Hunter in the 1970s and was employed widely in some parts of Canada and the United States. Unfortunately, its use was too often stilted by the rigid and unthinking application of the instructional concepts that form its structure. (For an interesting discussion of the pros and cons of Lesson Design, see the February 1987 issue of *Educational Leadership*).

Regardless of your philosophy, the concepts that form its structure can work with any philosophy of teaching and learning. (The skeleton components of Lesson Design are listed on page 122.) Note: Arends (1991) in his book *Learning to Teach*; Good and Brophy's (1994) work in *Looking in Classrooms*; Sahpier and Gower's (1987) work in *The Skillful Teacher*; and Cooper's (1986) work in *Classroom Teaching Skills* provide other components that enrich teaching and learning and contribute to the design process.

Lesson Design assists teachers in developing a sense of instructional confidence around the design and flow of a lesson. It can increase one's sense of instructional efficacy. Lesson Design is often employed in a more teacher-directed manner when a teacher is preparing students to work more independently and interdependently, or when information must be presented effectively and meaningfully when time is short.

Lesson Design is a totally different concept from Designing Lessons. The agenda in the rest of the chapters in this text is to shift away from Lesson Design towards *Designing Lessons*—a much more creative, powerful, and integrative process than Lesson Design.

The strength of Lesson Design is in the number of instructional concepts that produce the process. Perhaps the most interesting point of this strategy is the ease with which the components within the strategy can be employed in other approaches to teaching. Think of how strategies such as **Academic Controversy**, **Concept Attainment**, **Inductive Thinking** and **Mind Mapping** etc., (see Joyce, Weil, 2000, for a list of approximately 20 strategies or models of teaching) can be woven into Lesson Design. Although Lesson Design appears simple, do not be fooled. That simplicity is its basic structure. When used thoughtfully by instructionally creative teachers it can be a complex, interesting, and demanding approach to teaching.

No one way of designing a learning environment represents a panacea in the teaching/learning process. So we can confidently state that Lesson Design is not a panacea. Rather, it is simply one possibility, one option in a teacher's repertoire. For the authors, we appreciate its strength in assisting us to integrate ideas—to act as an advance organizer for instructional integration (see Ausubel, 1960 re Advance Organizers.)

Fish Bone Organizer of Lesson Design

Caveat

This book is about the creative process of designing lessons—of integrating instructional processes. Easy to say; not easy to do. This chapter illustrates an instructional strategy that facilitates one way of integrating a variety of instructional concepts, skills, tactics, strategies, and organizers. If you are an effective teacher (regardless of whether you see yourself as a constructivist, modernist, behaviourist, post-modernist, etc.) you will already be employing most or all of the instructional concepts and skills that constitute Lesson Design. The piece that may be new is the idea of integrating more powerful instructional tactics and strategies to take the place of each of the Lesson Design Components. We are naming the shift to intentionally weaving multiple processes an "Integrationist's" approach.

So, let's start. To more effectively integrate instructional approaches to meet the diverse needs of students, teachers can employ design structures. The components (concepts and skills) of Lesson Design represent one such structure. Those components allow teachers to enter into a more powerful process of designing lessons through the thoughtful integration of multiple instructional processes.

The reason: In previous chapters we discussed instructional concepts and skills. This chapter takes those two instructional areas and illustrates how they can be stacked to create a strategy known in the literature as Lesson Design.

A caution: If teachers organize Lesson Design in a simplistic and unthinking manner, they limit their ability to powerfully respond to the ever-increasing classroom complexity and diversity.

Lesson Design is made up of a series of Instructional Concepts and Instructional Skills—none of which are very powerful alone. Consequently, teachers must integrate more powerful approaches to the teaching and learning process into the strategy of Lesson Design. This integration occurs in the following chapters and illustrates how Lesson Design provides a backdrop to construct a conceptual flow that is sensitive to student needs.

> So although Lesson Design provides a sense of flow, it does not necessarily provide "learning power." The idea of learning power was discussed in Chapters 2 and 3, and refers to how much of an effect the design of learning environments have on student learning.

Fish Bone Organizer of Lesson Design

At the start of the chapter you were invited to think about the components that would be part of most lessons. The Fish Bone Organizer below illustrates the components of the strategy of Lesson Design.

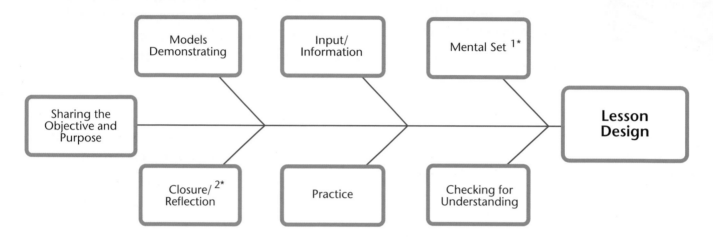

Ask yourself whether or not you agree with those instructional ideas. We did. We asked ourselves:

- Is linking to the past experiences of students important? (Mental Set)
- Is actively and meaningfully involving students important? (Mental Set)
- Should students have a say or opportunity to discuss or debate the learning objectives? (Sharing the Objective and Purpose)
- Should we be sensitive to the variety of ways in which students can obtain information? (Think about Multiple Intelligence and Learning Styles.) (Input)
- Is modelling or demonstrating or role playing a useful process?
- Should teachers and students check to see they understand?
- Should students practise or simply be able to explain? Is a tutor or a mentor sometimes useful? (Guided and Independent Practice)

- Is a summary of the key learning and integration with previous learning a worthwhile idea (Closure and Extension)

If you read Madeline Hunter's 1994 book: *Enhancing Teaching* and the in-depth discussion of Lesson Design and related components, you will note the absence of more powerful instructional processes. This failure of educators to integrate or move beyond the simple elegance of the concepts and skills was their tragic flaw.

Later in this chapter are four sample lessons.

1. *The Body's Defences against Disease (high school)*

2. *Friendship through Understanding Reconciliation (elementary)*

3. *Introductory Lesson to Death of a Salesman (high school)*

4. *Equal Participation (elementary)*

1* Madeline Hunter labelled this Anticipatory Set
2* Madeline Hunter did not include Closure

LESSON 1:
High School Biology

Title of lesson:
The Body's Defences against Disease

Grade level:
Biology, grade 11 advanced

Type of activity:
Lesson Design with Jigsaw and the Johnson's 5 Basic Elements

Length of period:
80 minutes. (All times below are approximate.)

OBJECTIVE:
To understand the mechanism by which the body fights disease caused by foreign bodies (particles or micro-organisms) by completing a Jigsaw process.

MENTAL SET (8 MIN.)
Our body is under constant threat of attack by foreign particles, such as smoke, bacteria, and viruses, which can cause discomfort or disease. Throughout time, the body has evolved ingenious methods to combat foreign intrusion. Use Place-Mat (see page 172) to bring out students' ideas on the subject. (I then share the objective in students' language with the students.)

INPUT & MODELLING (8 MIN.)
Explanation of Jigsaw activity:
- Form home groups of three, letter off A, B, and C (if extra student have two C's).
- Expert groups are A's, B's, and C's from each home group.

- Equal participation needed (check to make sure they understand – T-Chart)
- Note-taking and summarizing skills required.

PRACTICE (40 MIN.)
- (10 min.) Each home group gets 3 instructional input sheets (1 per student): A (pink) = Antibodies, B (green) = White Blood Cells, C (blue) = Histamines. Give time to read sheets. Ask class if ready for quiz. Answer is resoundingly negative, so students understand logic of proceeding to discuss in expert groups.

- (15 min.) Move to expert groups and discuss sheet. Each sheet has about 60% text, 20% illustration and 20% questions to guide the discussion in the expert groups. Students summarize the main ideas in writing to explain later to their home group.

- (15 min.) Return to home groups. Each member explains the main ideas from the expert group to other two members.

CHECKING FOR UNDERSTANDING (20 MIN.)
Group quiz among members of each home group (in preparation for individual test).

CLOSURE/REFLECTION (3 MIN.)
After students hand in their quiz, give each student the other two original sheets. Note: I found that interest in reading the other two sheets was high after the quiz.

Nora Rivaud designed this lesson.

LESSON 2:
Elementary Literature

Note, this lesson includes two additional strategies: Concept Attainment and Cooperative Learning (the Johnsons' 5 Basic Elements and Kagan's Structure Think/Pair/Share)

Title of lesson:
Friendship through Understanding Reconciliation

Grade level:
Grade four - Literature Study
Theme - friendship

Type of activity:
Lesson Design with Concept Attainment and Cooperative Learning

Length of period:
60 minutes

OBJECTIVE:

Students will understand and apply how reconciliation is part of friendship by analyzing the data in a Concept Attainment strategy in the SET portion of this lesson.

Students will evaluate how these characteristics are exercised by studying the characters in the book *The Orphan Boy*. This is an African story of a boy who befriends a poor village and, as a result, the villagers become self-sufficient. He informs them that this can only occur on the condition that they never follow him at night. Some time later, one person is tempted to follow, the boy realizes it and disappears into the sky. The villagers are left to poverty. The question is how to

reconcile the error. The Concept Attainment lesson is designed to assist students in clarifying the concept of reconciliation.

Students will devise ways in which the characteristics of friendship will be practised in class.

TASK ANALYSIS:

1. What does reconciliation mean? How does it connect to friendship?

2. What does a friend act like; and, just as importantly, not act like?

OBJECTIVE SHARED WITH STUDENT/SET:

"In our last class we discussed the word reconciliation. Think to yourself. What does reconciliation mean and why do we need it in our lives? Share your thinking with a partner and discuss why reconciliation is important." I will randomly ask some partners to share their ideas with the class.

"Reconciliation, then, is a time to come together, to build upon friendships. It is also a time to re-evaluate what kind of friends we have been to our peers. In order for us to become and continue to be good friends, it is important that we understand what friendship means and be able to reflect on how friends behave with one another. Today we will be looking at extending what being a friend means."

INPUT/MODELLING/CHECKING FOR UNDERSTANDING:

Concept Attainment is used to check Student's understanding of the characteristics of reconciliation. Students will think silently until example four. Then they will Think/Pair/Share and be prepared to discuss how the YES examples are the same.

Concept Attainment Data Set

YES	NO
1. Julie is sitting by herself, head down, staring at her hands. "Hey Julie, you look down. What's going on?"	1. "Hey Julie, you are always so depressed! Give your head a shake—you are definitely no fun!"
2. "George, do you remember yesterday when you wouldn't let me play ball? I felt bad. What happened? Why wouldn't you let me play?"	2. "George you were such a jerk yesterday. You act like no one else in the world is important except for you."
3. "Whoa, Jordan, I know we ignored you yesterday, but Lisa wasn't finished what she was saying. Can you hold on until she's finished, then we (the group) will hear your idea better."	3. "Jordan stop interrupting! What's your problem? That's why no one ever wants you in their group."
4. "Sorry about yesterday. I know you think I was ignoring you. I wasn't feeling that great and just wanted to be left alone. I didn't mean to be mean."	4. "You are such a bump on a log. Ever thought that maybe you could put in some effort? I'm sick and tired of doing all the work."

TESTERS

A. "I really want to thank you for bringing my homework every day while I was at home sick. I heard you missed your basketball game after school. I know the walk isn't easy. Thanks."	C. "Here are your books! I am getting real tired of this slave labour. You are always inconsiderate. No one is important except for you. Why should I have to wait for five minutes?"
B. "Tom, I'm sorry about not asking you to play ball. Sometimes I'm acting like a jerk so that I can play with the cool guys." Tom's reply: "It's hard when I'm left out of the game. It's good to know that I'm still your friend."	D. Tom responds to Fred, who ignored Tom yesterday when he wanted to play with the guys. Tom says: "You're just trying to be cool so that they'll like you. Some friend you are!"

MODELING:

The Modeling portion of this lesson was completed in the Input phase. This also occurred when the teacher and the partners reviewed their ideas related to the YES and NO examples.

CHECKING FOR UNDERSTANDING:

This was completed in the Input phase; specifically, in the portion of the Concept Attainment strategy where the testers were displayed. The idea being that a problem or concern existed and something happened to re-establish a relationship.

Checking for Understanding will also be completed as the teacher observes the groups in the process of their working together. The Check for Understanding will be completed by the students at the end of the lesson when they present their answers to the questions related to the book.

PRACTICE:

A) "You have explored the characteristics of friendships within your pairings. Let's take a look at a friendship in this book by Paul Morin, *The Orphan Boy*."

Ask the students to pay attention to the illustrations, as they are not only award-winning works of art, but clues to the boy's identity. Read the book.

Ask the students to think silently and in their minds answer the questions: Who is the boy and why do you think he is who he is? Share your answer with a partner. Teacher then randomly asks for several hypotheses.

B) Roles: recorder, social goal reminder, materials manager, and timer.

Social Goal – active listening (students are well aware of this term and what it means—we did a T-Chart with them the previous day).

Academic Task – Answer the following questions on a sheet of paper. Be prepared to hand this in at the end of the lesson.

1. How were the boy, old man, and the shadow good friends? How were they not good friends?

2. Give examples of how trust is broken in this story. How is that relationship mended?

Record your answers on a sheet of paper.

You have 20 minutes for this task. The class will reconvene when all groups are ready.

Each group will be asked to answer one of the questions. The teacher will choose the presenter.

CLOSURE:

"I'd like each of you to consider how you did with the active listening. Did you show that you were listening with your body? Did you refrain from interrupting? Without sharing any names let's hear from each group. I will randomly pick the presenter from each group." (I will also have been evaluating the individuals in the groups as I visited each and made anecdotal notes.)

"We have spent a great deal of time examining the idea of friendship today. Let's see how the word friendship applies to us in this class. I'd like you to think to yourself for 30 seconds. No hands please, I will choose a few of you to explain your thinking."

"I'd like to know what you think we as a class could do to be better friends to one another. Think of two simple things that we could practise in this class. Sometime during the day come and put your ideas on this large brainstorm sheet on the wall."

Maria Giampa designed this lesson.

Building Block Nature of Instructional Concepts and Skills

The following section provides a brief overview of each of the Lesson Design components. The building block metaphor for Lesson Design simply reminds us that we can choose to play with these instructional concepts and skills in any order. Remember, though, that some might not be required and some will be employed a number of times. As professionals, we need to make informed decisions about their application.

Of course hundreds of additional blocks exist.

Mental Set - Brief Description

Mental Set is an instructional concept a teacher invokes to get students focused and actively involved in learning. Another label could be "lesson introduction" or the "hook." This instructional concept is often initiated in a lesson through the teacher playing with three critical attributes (the essential characteristics of something). Of course, if students run through your classroom doors with palpitating hearts, passionately demanding to begin your class work immediately, then you can most likely dispense with Mental Set.

CRITICAL ATTRIBUTES:
(See Examples on Web site)

1. Linking to the past experiences of the students through questions or activities.

2. Having all Students (or as many as possible) actively involved.

3. Connecting Students' involvement to the learning objective.

WHEN USED:

Usually at the beginning of a lesson or to re-focus the students after an interruption in the lesson (e.g., someone at the door). Remember though, that the learning may be so intrinsically interesting that you do not need a Mental Set. This is no different from art. If you don't need a colour, you don't use it.

WHY USED:

To increase the chances all students are meaningfully connected and involved in the learning. We often think students are not interested in learning; not true. They are interested in learning—they are just not interested in what and how it is being presented. Remember that students have an intense and demanding life outside of the classroom. Other things are often on their mind (e.g., birthdays, competitions, divorces, new puppies, deaths, falling into or out of love). Mental Set must attend to those competing demands.

CONSIDERATIONS:

Mental Set can occur in a matter of seconds or, if students don't have the experiences, it may take as long as a film, a story, or a field trip—the time needed to create the experiences. At times the Mental Set can have a complete lesson embedded inside it. Simply said, Mental Set is about getting the mind ready to learn. Mental Set is also a place to invoke the power of the skills that enhance motivation.

The fascinating aspect of MENTAL SET is that like a puzzle piece, it has receptor sites. Those receptor sites allow other tactics such as Mind Maps and Word Webs, as well as other strategies such as Inquiry, Concept Attainment, Role-Playing, and Inductive Thinking to become the Mental Set. The Set can be pointedly precise or mythically magic. Regardless of what you do, it will set the tone for the students' involvement in the lesson.

Sharing the Objective and Purpose

This is the place in the lesson where the teacher decides whether or not to share and/or discuss with the students what they will be learning in terms of the cognitive, affective, or psychomotor domains. In addition, a discussion often occurs as to why it is important for them to inquire into this particular area and how it connects to their lives. Shared Objectives and Shared Purposes represent the statements that assist students in understanding how to meet learning outcomes or bench marks. As Madeline Hunter (1994) states: "It is not the pedantic: At the end of today's lesson you will be able to ...". Although that objective is in the teacher's mind as a guide, the objective is shared in student language. "Today we are going to extend our thinking about the types of energy you have explored. I thought we might employ a Mind Map to assist us to pull the ideas together and then we can see how you respond to some questions that will come out of your thinking from your Mind Map."

CRITICAL ATTRIBUTES:
(See Examples on Web site)
1. The objective is stated in student language and states what will be learned and how the students will demonstrate that learning. It can also include the level of performance re the assessment of the learning (say 90% accuracy) and the conditions (given 30 minutes). (For example: Given 30 minutes and the opportunity to work with a partner, the students will construct at least three arguments that communicate their understanding of both sides of the issue re the conflict of clear cutting.)

2. The objective is clear, and if required, measurable.

3. The objective is specific i.e., the level of thinking is considered.

4. The objective is meaningful or relevant.

WHEN USED:
Usually the objective is shared near the beginning of the lesson—unless the objective is to be discovered through student involvement in an Inquiry-oriented lesson. In this case, you might want the student to identify the objective and purpose for the lesson as part of the summary or Closure to the lesson.

WHY USED:
If students know where they are going it increases the chances they will get there—especially if the purpose for the objective has meaning and interest.

CONSIDERATION:
As teachers, we often have a passion for our subject ... a passion that is not always shared by the students. Although that passion is useful to us, we must remember that our students seldom walk through the door with that same level of appreciation. It's not that they are not interested, they are simply not interested in what we want them to be interested in. **If we as teachers are not sensitive to the learner's disposition to the content being learned, then we increase the chances students will not be sensitive to ours.**

Note that an objective might be relevant, but we need to ask if it is also meaningful and relevant. Is working on worksheets in math an example of brain-friendly learning? If a learning objective is lacking authenticity and relevance the human brain is more likely to reject it. The brain is designed for survival, not boredom.

Input or Information:
A Brief Description

Input or information refers to what the students receive to facilitate the learning. That information can emerge from a number of sources:

- from other students (for example, in a Cooperative Learning lesson)
- the teacher
- computer searches
- a video, film, slides, pictures
- guest speakers
- field trips
- a trip to the library
- books
- the student's own experiences and thinking
- activities such as drama or role playing
- other instructional strategies such as Mind Mapping, Concept Attainment, Inductive Thinking, Inquiry, Group Investigation, etc.

Although stated previously, as many of the senses (auditory, visual, tactile, kinesthetic, taste, and smell) should be stimulated as *appropriate* to accommodate the sensory strengths and weaknesses of the students.

CRITICAL ATTRIBUTES:
(See Examples on Web site)

1. The Input relates to the learning to be achieved.
2. The Input supports/encourages an appropriate level or area of thinking.
3. The Input should facilitate a meaningful and interesting inquiry.

Of course, the other decision the teacher must make about the use of information relates to the percentage of time students will work individually, in small cooperative groups, or in large group discussions. The authors believe that no single approach is best; variety and balance is the key.

Obviously Input is not as simple as Input. All of the above can be situated on a continuum of teacher-influenced to student-influenced or postivist to constructivist. The options are richly complex.

CONSIDERATION

Stepping back to other literatures that inform or guide Input we must also consider the literature/research on:

- gender
- culture and ethnicity
- learning disabilities
- the human brain
- children at risk
- multiple intelligence
- emotional intelligence

Modelling/Demonstration: A Brief Description

Modelling usually refers to the visual representations of what is being learned (like a model of the human heart). It can also refer to "hearing" or "feeling" representations such as a poem or piece of music or the idea of rough or cold respectively. Demonstrations usually refer to an action or simulation or a process (as in an experiment or solving a math problem).

CRITICAL ATTRIBUTES:

(See Examples on Web site)

1. The Model/Demonstration contains the critical elements or steps to be learned.

2. The Model/Demonstration is not confusing or ambiguous.

3. The students can see and, if necessary, hear or touch the attributes.

4. The students can talk about what they see, hear, or touch related to the critical elements.

Note: a student cannot 'see' all the attributes (characteristics) of a mammal by analyzing a picture (life, birth, hair on body, warm blooded); so we must be sensitive to what is 'discernable.'

WHEN USED:

In most cases, Modelling comes after or along with the information being presented. At times it can occur at the beginning of the lesson as part of the Mental Set to generate input or information. As well, it can also be applied in the process of Checking for Understanding, Practice, and Closure.

WHY USED:

Modelling helps students remember what was learned by acting as a visual check on what was presented orally. As well, it provides variety and interest and, if possible, hands-on experience.

Note that if you integrate the Concept Attainment or Inductive Strategies into the lesson, the Modelling occurs in the presentation of the data sets. Also, when using Mind Maps, the drawings completed by the students are one of the factors that make Mind Maps effective in assisting students to retain information.

CAUTION:

When teachers are encouraging divergent thinking or creativity, they must be thoughtful about whether or not to employ Modelling—it can control or encourage students to replicate the model and work against divergent/creative thinking.

Checking for Understanding: A Brief Description

This is a process that assists teachers in monitoring the learning and determining if students have attained an appropriate level of competence related to the targeted learning. Based on that finding, a check for understanding helps teachers make adjustments in their teaching. Adjustments can include actions such as re-teaching the same way; break into simpler steps and re-teach; to trying a different approach; leaving it until later; or, if successful, to go on to the next step.

The use of rubrics or benchmarks is one way for students to check their own understanding. Rubrics can also involve student self-assessment, which is another process that allows students to take more responsibility for checking their understanding.

CRITICAL ATTRIBUTES:
(See Examples on Web site)

1. It involves all the students (the concept of active participation).

2. The teacher asks for an overt response.

3. Students get specific feedback.

4. It relates to the objective and the desired type or level of thinking.

5. The teacher responds appropriately to the students' efforts. (e.g., if a student is asked a question and gives an incorrect, partially correct or correct response).

WHEN USED:

Usually the Check for Understanding is used before the students are asked to Practise. It can also occur in the Mental Set to check what students know before starting the lesson or in the Closure to summarize the key ideas in the lesson.

WHY USED:

A Check for Understanding increases the chances the students will experience success rather than frustration or confusion during the Practice. Successful students are more likely to be motivated to continue learning—discouraged children are not so apt to become a management problem because their concerns are being picked up and resolved.

"I lift, you grab . . . was that concept just a little too complex, Carl?"

Practice: Guided & Independent: A Brief Description

Practice is the time given in the lesson or outside the classroom (e.g., homework) to allow the student to try out or experience what was learned. It is an opportunity to apply their understanding. Two types of practice that exist on either end of a continuum are working completely alone (Independent Practice) or having intense help (Guided Practice). Practice can also be massed (intense period, then finished) or distributed (shorter periods that occur over time).

Guided Practice – the student receives or can ask for assistance from the teacher, parents, other students, etc. The idea of peer tutors, coaching, and mentoring also relate to this type of practice, as would aspects of Cooperative Learning. In Guided Practice you are intending to make sure the student is comfortable with the ideas before allowing her to work more independently.

Independent Practice – the student completes a task with no help from another source. Homework usually falls into this category.

Note that some students will need more Guided Practice than others. As well, some students will prefer to be totally independent.

CRITICAL ATTRIBUTES:
(See Examples on Web site)

1. Amount. How much should be practised? (suggestion: a small, meaningful amount)

2. Duration. How long should they practise? (suggestion: a short, intense period)

3. Frequency. How often should they practise? (suggestion: a variety, from massed to distributed)

4. Feedback. How will they find out how well they did? (feedback or knowledge of results)

5. Timing. Is the practice to be massed for immediate use (a lot of practice with no or little other learning between practices) or distributed for long term retention?

6. Appropriateness. Does the practice relate to the objective (the intended learning) and the appropriate level of thinking?

WHEN USED:

Practice usually occurs after what has been learned has been Modelled or Demonstrated and the students understand what they are to apply during the Practice.

WHY USED:

Practice is used to increase the chances that students not only remember what they have learned, but also that they transfer that learning to new situations. "To know something is to act on it—to act on it is to remember it."

Closure: A Brief Description

Closure is often a final summary of the lesson that occurs in the minds of the learners, not the mind of the teacher. It can be similar to a Check for Understanding although it usually focuses on the major learning of the lesson. It can be simple. It can be complex. It can also encourage the students to extend their thinking, to make connections to what they have already learned, or will be learning next...like a transition phase.

WHEN USED:

Usually at the end of the lesson or a phase of the lesson.

WHY USED:

Closure brings the major ideas in the lesson into a sharper focus. It provides time for the student to gel the learning. It might be as simple as explaining the major ideas in a lesson, or as complex as having students argue the value of what was learned. At times it invites the students to be creative with what was learned or to apply it in a different situation. Somehow, during the lesson the students must obtain what David Perkins (1986) discusses as Knowledge as Design. That is, have they...

1. understood the structure of what was learned?

2. discussed the purpose of that learning?

3. experienced model cases of that learning?

4. inquired into the arguments or value of that learning?

If not...then of what value was the learning?

CRITICAL ATTRIBUTES:
(See Examples on Web site)

1. Closure actively involves all the students.

2. The Closure relates to the objective (often by extending the objective).

An Example of Closure:

We have finished discussing the effects of the Industrial Revolution on men and women in the late and early nineteenth century. I am going to ask you a question. Think to yourself and be prepared to defend your answers in about 30 seconds. No hands, I'll randomly invite responses.

"Given what you know about the Industrial Revolution, can we assume it is over? If yes, what proof do you have? If no, what proof do you have?"

Caution: Often the teacher does the summary or checks with one or two students and asks "Now does everyone understand?" and assumes that because no student responds, that all students do. When in fact the hidden response is: "Yes-I-do-but-really-I-don't-because-I-don't-want-others-to-know-I-don't."

Two more Complex Lessons: Integrating Aspects of Cooperative Learning and Mind Mapping with Lesson Design

 ## LESSON 3:
Introductory Lesson to Death of a Salesman
Grade 11 Advanced

MENTAL SET:
"We are about to begin reading a book called *Death of a Salesman.* Before we begin, I would like you to collect your thoughts about the concept of a salesperson. Take 20 seconds to think. Okay, we are going to do a Three-Step-Interview. Please organize yourselves into your base groups of three and letter yourself off A, B, and C." (Note: my class does a lot of cooperative learning.)

    A= Interviewee
    B= Interviewer
    C= Recorder

"Okay C, use this recording sheet to collect person A's ideas. Each interview will only be 60 seconds. I will tell you when to rotate the roles." (Time 10 min.)

OBJECTIVE:
"Your objective will be to find all of the aspects common to the salesman—what we are doing is collecting the class's initial thoughts and emotions about the concept of a salesperson. We are going to do that by constructing a Mind Map. You have done these last year. If some of you are new, the students will explain it to you. We will then put these away and have you revisit them at the end of the book to see if your ideas have changed."

DIRECTIONS:
"This is how we will proceed.

Person A =   Drawer (captures the concept in image)

Person B =   Manager (responsible for passing the ideas from 3-Step Interview to the drawer)

Person C =   Scout/Map Checker (responsible for having a look around at other groups for ideas re Mind Mapping as well as making sure all the component parts of a Mind Map are on your Map).

    When I say 'Switch,' the roles in the group change (A moves to B, B to C, C to A)."

    "We are going to shift this topic re gender. Write "salesperson" in the centre of your page. I want you to think of salespeople that you have met. Think of the things that you feel are associated with the salesperson. Draw all of these things around the word salesperson and connect the ideas with a line—remember key words, pictures, and colour are important in communicating your thoughts and emotions."
(Total time = 15 min.)

3. Using the Concept Attainment process, provide a data set that gives YES examples of how to include everyone equally.

On the other side (right), give some NO examples (what to avoid). Ask students to think about what the YES examples have in common (encouraging equal participation). Have students brainstorm other possible YES examples or ways to include everyone equally.

MODELLING: Occurs Primarily in the Presentation of the YES Examples

YES	NO
"Okay, let's go around and each take a turn sharing our ideas."	"Okay Monica, these were all your ideas, so you should share them."
"You draw first and then we will rotate every five minutes."	"I'm too nervous to talk in front of the class. You do it."
When the teacher went around the room she noticed that the students were listening to one another as each person shared their ideas.	When the teacher observed the group she noticed that one or two students were doing all the work.
"Okay, we still have not heard what Alison's thoughts are."	"You draw the pictures I can't draw. You are better than I am."

TESTERS

Look at A and B below. Decide with your partner, if each is a YES or a NO.

A. When the students were working , the teacher noticed that one student did all the talking, one did all the drawing, and one did the reporting at the end.
B. As the group worked, they stopped every so often to check to see if everyone felt that their ideas were being listened to.

CHECK FOR UNDERSTANDING:

Is carried out in the Input phase when students generate YES and NO examples of equal participation and have to discuss the Testers (A is a NO, and B is a YES). Also during the Mental Set (Circle) when students discuss personal experiences or thoughts about not being included.

PRACTICE: (GUIDED)

Students are divided into Legend writing groups of three or four. Rather than give them assigned roles (to ensure individual accountability) i.e., person A is the participation monitor, B is the timer, the students were asked to problem-solve together to ensure equal participation.

CLOSURE:

After working in their Legend groups (on-going) students process how effectively they were able to include everyone equally by rating themselves from one to five. The groups reflect and, in their individual journals, record how they can improve for next time.

Summary: A Few Questions

DISCUSSION QUESTIONS: Mental Set
1. Predict what would happen to the classroom if no introduction or mental set occurred—keeping in mind that kids (especially students at risk) often come to class with everything on their minds but the subject at hand.
2. How could a field trip, or a guest speaker, or creating a Mind Map, or a role-play, etc., be like a larger mental set? Could a Mental Set last all day?
3. Do you always need a Mental Set? If the activity is intrinsically meaningful and interesting, is Mental Set a waste of time?

DISCUSSION QUESTIONS: Practice
1. Is there something that you do well that did not involve practice?
2. Should all students have the same amount of practice?
3. What is the relationship between feedback and practice? What about homework?

DISCUSSION QUESTIONS: Checking for Understanding
1. Predict what would happen if the teacher didn't Check for Understanding before having students Practice.
2. Could Check for Understanding happen in Mental Set?
3. Identify how Check for Understanding could be used throughout the other components of the lesson (e.g., during the Mental Set.)

DISCUSSION QUESTIONS: Providing a Model/Doing a Demonstration
1. Could Modelling occur in the Mental Set or Check for Understanding, etc.?
2. Do you see a difference between a Model and Demonstrating?
3. How does modelling affect the retention of information?

DISCUSSION QUESTIONS: Objectives and Sharing the Objective(s)
1. What might happen if no opportunity was provided to share or discuss the direction and purpose of the learning with the students?
2. Who determines the objective? What are the pros and cons of involving students in the design of learning outcomes?

DISCUSSION QUESTIONS: Closure
1. How are Closure and Checking for Understanding the same and different?
2. What is the key mistake made in most attempts to bring Closure to a lesson?
3. Could students identify the objective of the lesson in Closure rather than having the teacher share or discuss it with the students at the beginning of the lesson?

Chapter Seven

Cooperative Learning: A Concept Map

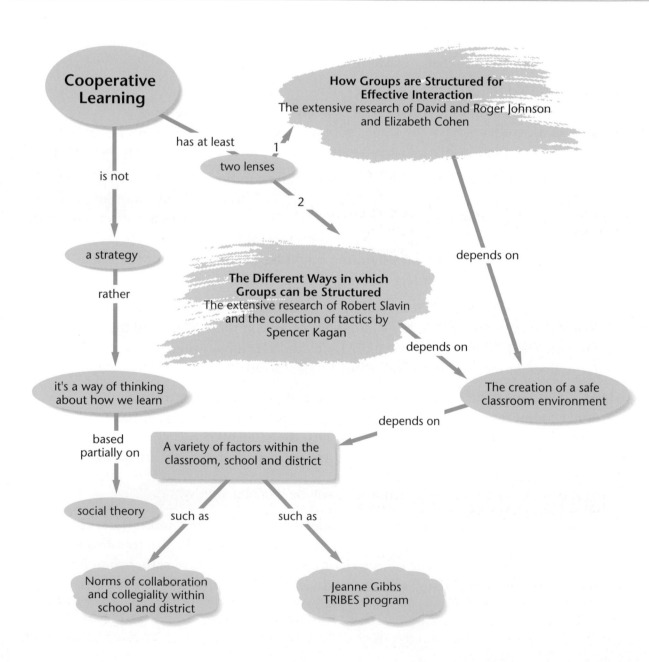

Cooperative Learning

has at least → two lenses

1 → **How Groups are Structured for Effective Interaction**
The extensive research of David and Roger Johnson and Elizabeth Cohen

2 → **The Different Ways in which Groups can be Structured**
The extensive research of Robert Slavin and the collection of tactics by Spencer Kagan

is not → a strategy → rather → it's a way of thinking about how we learn → based partially on → social theory

depends on → The creation of a safe classroom environment

depends on → A variety of factors within the classroom, school and district

such as → Norms of collaboration and collegiality within school and district

such as → Jeanne Gibbs TRIBES program

Chapter Seven

Cooperative Learning

What is the difference between effective and ineffective small-group learning? Would expert teachers know? The educators, researchers and literatures listed below provide part of the answer for teachers who push to be experts, and who want to grapple with the intricacies of small-group learning.

- The Johnsons' research on the five basic elements
- The Schmucks' book *Group Process in the Classroom*
- DeVrie's research on Teams-Games-Tournaments
- Sharan's research on Group Investigation

- Cohen's book *Complex Instruction*
- Johnsons' book *Creative Controversy*
- Gardner's work on Interpersonal Intelligence
- Kagan's collection of group structures
- Goleman's writing on Emotional Intelligence

- Slavin's summaries of the research
- Aronson's research on Jigsaw
- Jeanne Gibb's book *TRIBES*
- Children at Risk research
- Brain research
- Vygotsky & Piaget's work

Pieces of wisdom emerging from this collective work:

- learning is socially constructed; we seldom learn isolated from others
- the need for everyone in the group to be accountable for the learning
- the importance of actively teaching social skills, communication, and critical thinking skills
- the importance of having the group process how it functions as a group
- the necessity of worthy tasks or objectives, appropriate for group work and face-to-face interaction
- groups of 2, 3, & 4 encourage interaction
- larger groups decrease the amount of individual talk time
- taking the time to be thoughtful about who will be working with whom will have long term benefits

Pieces of wisdom from the authors' experiences:

- Cooperative Learning is not a panacea; it's one of many instructional processes
- you can be an effective teacher and not consciously employ aspects of Cooperative Learning
- the power of Cooperative Learning occurs when integrated with other strategies
- group work that is not structured thoughtfully is one of the least effective approaches in the teaching and learning process

Chapter Seven

Cooperative Learning

This chapter introduces the literature and the corresponding instructional processes labelled as Cooperative Learning. This chapter is about how aspects of Cooperative Learning weaves into teaching—how they integrate with other processes to create a synergistic effect on learning. Although this chapter will extend your understanding of Cooperative Learning, it is not intended to develop an in-depth understanding of any one approach (see the work of the Johnsons, Cohen, Slavin, Gibbs, etc., for a more in-depth understanding). We find integrating multiple voices more powerful than focusing on only one educator's or researcher's approach.

Currently, Cooperative Learning is a catch-all label for a lot of small-group instructional processes that happen in the name of group work. Some of those processes are simple (such as Think-Pair-Share) and others more complex (such as Academic Controversy).

The simpler ones we consider "tactics," the more complex ones "strategies."

The tactic/strategy dichotomy is often confusing. The Johnson's Learning Together Model is based on five basic elements, and the more complex Cooperative Learning structures such as Jigsaw, Group Investigation, Team Analysis, and Academic Controversy would be examples of Cooperative Learning strategies. They are designed around a theory of learning, have a series of steps, or components, and have a research base. If we are talking about the less complex Cooperative Learning structures such as Think-Pair-Share, Inside Outside Circles, and the Three-Step Interview, then we are talking about Cooperative Learning tactics (simpler, structures that are highly useful but are often lacking a research base). For example, most of Spencer Kagan's work fits into the tactics category. Refer to Chapter Two for a detailed discussion on skills, tactics, strategies, etc.

This chapter has six interconnected areas:

1. Introduction and rationale for the chapter followed by an organizer for understanding the different perspectives on Cooperative Learning
2. A one-page set of questions to consider when applying Cooperative Learning
3. Understanding how Cooperative Learning weaves into lessons through the examination of two lesson plans
4. Reviewing the Five Basic Elements that comprise the Johnsons' Learning Together model
5. Explaining six additional small group structures. (Note that well over 200 small group structures exist, with most of them being tactics and most not researched.)
6. Presenting a brief summary on Cooperative Learning.

Introduction and Rationale

Cooperative Learning is one of the most amorphous and researched of all the instructional processes. Interestingly, a variety of Cooperative Learning approaches exist with no single approach representing the best approach—each approach has its strengths and weaknesses. The wise teacher recognizes that a variety of approaches exist, most of these can be integrated simultaneously or stacked. Stacking refers to using one process to enhance the next.

When a teacher first starts employing Cooperative Learning with students who are not skilled at group work, it is akin to throwing a rock to a drowning person. Effective group work is complex. It takes thoughtful work over time in order to achieve results. Attempting to implement Cooperative Learning without the support of others is an act of courage (and perhaps unwise). A first year teacher we know enthusiastically raced back to his classroom to attempt an Academic Controversy with his grade seven students. He told us the next day that it was a disaster. He had attempted to implement one of the most complex of all group processes when his students were not even ready to do a Think-Pair-Share.

Consider this: the research on how the brain thinks and the emergence of knowledge regarding intelligence, creativity, and learning styles all argue that social interaction is critical in the development of intelligent behaviour. Perhaps look at Csikszentmihalyi's (1996) work in *Creativity* and Gardner's (1997) work in *Extraordinary Minds* to explore this idea further.

Howard Gardner identifies Interpersonal Intelligence as the most powerful predictor of whether or not an individual will be successful in life. Gardner's statement is also supported in Daniel Goleman's 1995 work on *Emotional Intelligence*. Gardner states that a synergistic effect results when the other intelligences (Spatial, Musical, Bodily Kinesthetic, Logical-Mathematical, Intra-personal, Linguistic, and Naturalistic) are integrated with the Interpersonal Intelligence.

Cooperative Learning is an example of an instructional approach that values Interpersonal Intelligence in classroom and school environments. It also facilitates the use of other instructional strategies that attend to the different ways in which students think (such as Mind Mapping and Concept Mapping).

Cooperative Learning is complex. It has many advocates who approach it from different perspectives. On the next page is an organizer; it represents one way of making sense of those different perspectives.

As you read through this chapter, remember that Cooperative Learning enhances the effectiveness of many other instructional strategies. Without Cooperative Learning being integrated into those strategies the strategies "wither on the vine." As well, remember that ill-conceived group work is one of the least effective approaches in the teaching and learning process.

Three Dimensions of Cooperative Learning

In our experience with Cooperative Learning, we have found it useful to understand cooperative learning through three lenses— we are calling them dimensions. The diagram below illustrates those dimensions.

- **Structural Approach**—the literature in this dimension provides a variety of ways groups carry out tasks to achieve different effects. For example, read or experience the work of
  - Robert Slavin
  - Spencer Kagan

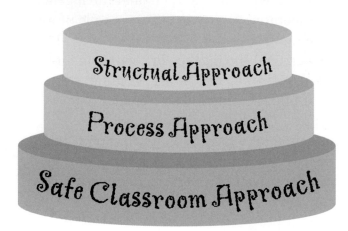

- **Process Approach**—The literature in this dimension focuses on the social theory of how groups function in relation to both academic and social learning. For example, read or experience the work of
  - David and Roger Johnson: Learning Together model (five basic elements)
  - Elizabeth Cohen: Complex Instruction
  - Richard Schmuck: Group Processes in the Classroom

- **Safe Classroom Approach**—this dimension connects to the brain research which informs us of the brain's need to avoid threat. Students who live in a state of fear or who feel at risk do not learn as effectively as students who feel valued and respected. Cooperative Learning helps create this dimension and at the same time depends on it in order to achieve the benefits of working with others. Without a safe classroom, you play at a superficial level of Cooperative Learning and you will at best achieve minimal levels of success. For example, read or experience the work of
  - Jeanne Gibbs: *Tribes,* which encourages attention to the following

1. *Attentive Listening*

2. *Appreciation Statements*

3. *The Right to Pass*

4. *Mutual Respect*

Questions to consider are on the following page.

Cooperative Learning: Key Questions

What other approach to teaching has as much research support as Cooperative Learning? In a way, this question is asking, *"How do we as educators justify not having Cooperative Learning as one of the options we employ to create an effective learning environment?"*

If the brain research reports that one of the three things that every brain needs is a safe environment, do we as educators have a responsibility to develop an extensive repertoire of processes that encourage students to work respectfully and thoughtfully with others?

If the research on intelligence (see Calvin's 1996 work in *How Brains Think* and Perkins' 1995 work in *Outsmarting IQ*) argues that intelligence is greatly affected by social interaction, then are we responsible for creating learning environments that encourage students to talk in meaningful and engaging ways?

If interpersonal intelligence in Howard Gardner's 1983 work on Multiple Intelligence is one of the most powerful predictors of success in life, does this suggest that developing interpersonal intelligence in school is essential?

Paulo Freire in his 1984 book *Pedagogy of the Oppressed* informs us that dialogue is a powerful way to resolve the revolution-like behaviour in society. He adds that dialogue cannot exist in the absence of trust, hope, love, humility, critical thinking, and faith. In accepting that argument, should we encourage our students to develop skills to dialogue effectively?

Should we, as educators, reflect this ability in our interactions with students and our peers?

The research by Karen Seashore Louis and Matthew Miles written up in their 1990 work, *Improving the Urban High School: What Works and Why*, reports that resolving conflict is the number one predictor of whether or not a school staff will become and/or stay effective. How will we do this if we cannot dialogue—if we cannot collectively work effectively within groups?

Where will students pick up the appropriate social skills, communication and critical thinking skills needed to live and work in harmony? What might the effect be of cumulatively acquiring and practising these social, communication, and critical thinking skills throughout their school years?

The Learning Styles research reports that some students learn best while working in groups. Do we (from a moral stance) have to attend to that research?

And last, when was the last time you read a job ad in the paper that asked for employees to be skilled at sitting in rows while listening to the boss talk, and in addition, when confused, sit and do nothing until the boss comes around to help?

On the following few pages are two sample lessons that weave Cooperative Learning into the learning process.

Lesson One:
Cooperative Learning
Kindergarten Science:
Parts of a Tree

Note:

The students were doing a unit on living things and what makes them grow. This lesson was part of their inquiry related to trees. Feel free to shift or delete parts. This lesson simply represents how this teacher used Cooperative Learning in designing a lesson.

OBJECTIVE:

To extend the students' understanding of trees by having them experience trees and then to work in pairs to discuss the parts of a tree. The social skill they were to work on was sharing—mainly ideas and materials with a partner.

MENTAL SET:

a. Group the students in pairs (one is called Buddy A and the other Buddy B).

b. Think-Pair-Share: *"Think to yourself for five seconds about a time when you were in a park or maybe a forest or even your own backyard—someplace with trees. Were the trees all the same or were they different?"* Now ask Buddy A to tell Buddy B ... now Buddy B tell Buddy A. *"Now discuss with your partner—How were the trees different?"* Let them have about 15 seconds and randomly ask students to share. Write the words on chart paper. Go over the words.

c. Introduce and discuss with the students in their language, the **academic objective** of identifying the various parts of a tree and understanding that not all trees are the same.

Outdoors

a. Students will walk around the schoolyard with their partners observing a variety of trees.

b. Hug and rub the trunk of different trees. Talk about the *bark*.

c. Pick up and distinguish between sticks on the ground (dead) and branches on the trees (live)—*branches, buds*.

d. Touch and feel pine and spruce needles— *needles*.

e. Touch and feel maple and pussy willow buds—*buds*.

f. Discuss the fact that some trees have leaves and some trees have needles.

g. Discuss what we can't see—*roots*.

Indoors

a. Introduce the **social objective:** sharing materials nicely.

b. **Model** the objective by demonstrating ways of not sharing nicely; rudely saying *"It's MINE!"* and taking materials away from others.

c. Discuss what the teacher would see and hear when students are sharing nicely. You might use a T-Chart, using words and simple pictures (like a happy face).

d. Instruct students that at the end of the activity the teacher will be calling upon some of them to tell the class how they shared the materials nicely.

INPUT:

a. Student pairs are given a plastic bag containing four tree twigs:

- willow (yellow/green twig, long, pointy, alternate buds)
- maple (dark green twig, short, round, opposite buds)
- white pine (five, long, soft needles in a bundle)
- spruce (one, short, prickly needle)

b. Students are asked to hold up a twig having needles and then instructed to pass the twigs back and forth with their partner and discuss how they are different.

c. The teacher leads a class discussion on the differences between the pine and spruce twigs.

d. Students are asked to hold up a twig that does not have needles and then instructed to pass the twigs back and forth with their partner and discuss how they are different.

e. The teacher leads a class discussion on the differences between the willow and maple twigs.

CHECK FOR UNDERSTANDING:

a. Teacher circulates and observes/notes how the partners are sharing their twigs and discussing their observations.

b. The teacher calls upon individual students to tell how they worked at sharing the twigs with their partner.

COMBINATION OF GUIDED AND INDEPENDENT PRACTICE:

a. Students are assigned individual envelopes of 'tree part puzzles'—pictures and words of various parts of a tree (needles, buds, branches, bark, roots, needles and leaves)—that have been cut into interlocking puzzle pieces. The words and pictures are to be matched and glued to a worksheet.

b. Students are directed to hand their completed worksheet to the teacher. The teacher engages each child in a brief discussion to determine if further instruction is required.

CLOSURE/EXTENSION:

a. As part of Friday afternoon "week-in-review," the parts of a tree can be discussed while sitting in the reading corner. Discussion can focus on how we treat trees and the idea of being friends with trees. The book, *The Giving Tree* by Shel Silverstein, was used to talk about who was the better friend, the boy or the tree. Discuss how the boy could be a better friend and what trees need to grow.

b. Note that the ideas learned in this lesson will connect to what makes living things grow—it will weave into the next unit on rain.

Lesson Two:
Cooperative Learning Grade Nine French

Lesson prepared by Sonia Ricci

ACADEMIC OBJECTIVE:
Through group work, students will demonstrate the ability to identify and categorize images of *le bien-être* (**well-being**) taken from recent magazine issues.

SOCIAL OBJECTIVE:
Students will have the opportunity to state their own opinion, listen to their colleagues' opinions, and reach agreement through discussion.

TASK ANALYSIS:
1. Do the students understand what *bien-être* means?

2. Do the students know what is meant by Think-Pair-Share?

MENTAL SET:
Teacher writes *le bien-être* on the board and asks students to look at this new word and try to figure out its meaning from what they already know. They know *bien* and *être*; however, together the compound means much more. Students are asked to privately think about this and then discuss their idea with their partner before being called upon to share with the class (i.e., students participate in a Think-Pair-Share).

Input:
1. Using flashcards, the teacher provides sentences of various examples (both physical and mental/emotional) of **well-being**. The teacher also makes sure that students understand the vocabulary being used before taping these flashcards to the board and proceeding.

2. Once all the flashcards have been presented, the teacher makes use of magazine cutouts that illustrate these examples of **well-being** to spark interest and focus their attention. Learners are asked to look at the images and determine whether or not the image portrayed is a good example of *le bien-être*, and if so, which one(s)?

3. The teacher asks one student to share his/her opinion. The teacher demonstrates that she is listening by nodding, looking directly at the student speaking, using expressions such as *"Oui, je comprends,"* waiting until the student has finished speaking to state her own opinion. The teacher then asks two other students to share their opinions. She then initiates a discussion and encourages the three students to help her reach some sort of agreement.

4. Teacher shares the objective with the class and uses the heterogeneous co-operative groups of four already in place in the class (desks are arranged in clusters of four.) Each group receives four magazine cutouts

Person A: collects materials for group (pictures, paper, marker)

Person B: records agreed-upon answer

Person C: makes sure everyone's ideas are heard

Person D: acts as timekeeper

5. When the groups complete their work, the teacher randomly chooses one person from each group to report the group's findings to the class. Students are made aware of this before they begin group work to increase individual accountability.

OBJECTIVE:
Teacher makes students aware of the academic goal and explains to students the social goal of the lesson. She establishes with them the importance of taking turns when working with others. Together they establish what taking turns (i.e., voicing your opinion, actively listening to another's opinion) looks like and how one could express it in French. Students decide to use the following phrases: *"Et toi, qu'est-ce que tu penses de ça?,"* *"Qu'en penses-tu?,"* and *"A toi la parole!"*

MODELLING:
This will occur during Step 3 of Input.

PRACTICE (GUIDED):
This will occur during Input.

CHECK FOR UNDERSTANDING:
During Input: occurs during Step 3 of Input.

During Practice: teacher circulates and observes the groups in action to see if their answers are correct, if students are taking turns, and to see how agreement is being reached.

During Closure: see below.

CLOSURE/PROCESSING:
When the groups have decided on and written their answers, a Reporter is chosen. This Reporter presents the pictures to the class and tells the class how his/her particular group categorized each picture.

At this time, the teacher or the other students may ask the reporter why the group has chosen to categorize the image in this manner. The reporter will relate how the group reached its decision and why they eliminated certain possibilities.

Last, the group does a Round Robin to quickly discuss how they thought they did regarding taking turns – making sure everyone's voice was heard and respected.

Lesson Analysis:
What happened in the previous two lessons to increase the chances the students functioned effectively while working in groups?

On your own or with a partner, take the time to identify what happened in the previous two lessons that pushed students to more effectively involve themselves in group work.

A **Fish Bone** graphic organizer is provided below. Fishbone is discussed on page 102 in Chapter 5 on Tactics. The excercise below is a chance to provide practice in using this particular graphic organizer. Fill in your ideas.

When finished, compare your thinking about effective group work with what the Johnsons argue from their research and experience concerning the five basic elements (presented on the next two pages) and what you know about the different Cooperative Learning structures such as Think-Pair-Share.

Note:

It would be unfair to the teachers designing these two lessons to hold them accountable to teach a perfect lesson. They were courageous enough to share what they tried. The lessons demonstrate how concepts, skills, tactics, and strategies weave together. The lessons were planned and taught with the intention of weaving in aspects of the research on how Cooperative Learning can increase the effectiveness of group work.

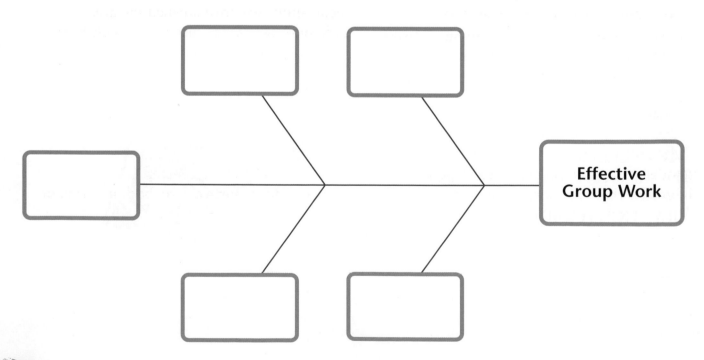

The Johnsons' 5 Basic Elements of Effective Group Work

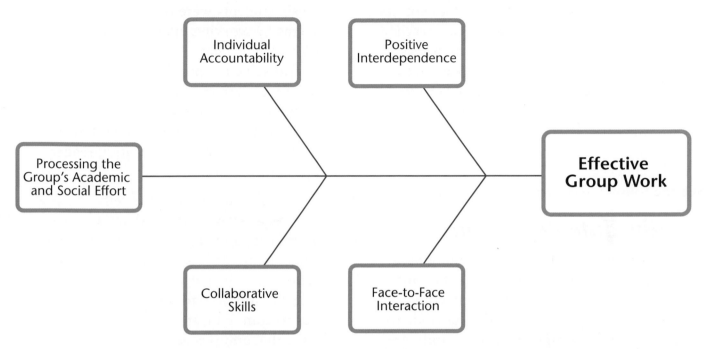

Individual Accountability refers to making sure each student in the group is responsible for their own learning and willing to encourage and support the learning of others in the group. This is one of the most important concepts. If a student can hide, or hitchhike off the efforts of others, or take over and do all the work, then the group will not function effectively.

Face-to-Face Interaction refers to setting up the group environment so that it encourages students to interact and dialogue with one another. That means they need to be sitting in groups that are approximately two to four in size, are close enough to one another to easily hear each other's voices, and see each other's faces. Obviously a circle or square shape facilitates face-to-face interaction. The larger the group the easier it is for students to hide on the edge of the group. They can escape being responsible or being involved.

Collaborative Skills refer to the social, communication, and critical thinking skills the students need to work effectively in groups. The Johnsons refer to this area as social skills; we have labelled the area Collaborative Skills, with social skills being one of the components. We see this as a hierarchical sequence. Communication is hard if one does not have the requisite social skills; and likewise, thinking critically is hard if one has neither the social skills nor communication skills.

Processing refers to reflection, and assessing the group's efforts both in terms of their academic and collaborative interaction. This metacognitive function is very important. Without it, groups do not develop as effectively over time which negatively impacts social and academic learning. Perkins, in his book *Outsmarting IQ* explains why reflection is an essential component in developing intelligent behaviour.

Positive Interdependence refers to students working together in supportive (positive) ways and being accountable and caring for one another. Positive Interdependence does not always occur naturally. Accordingly, a teacher can select from a number of ways to increase the chances students will be interdependent in a positive way. Romains, a French dramatist and novelist refers to this concept in his work back in the early 1950s. The Johnsons identified nine ways to invoke positive interdependence.

See the following descriptions of each.

Positive Interdependence

- **Goal:** Providing a clear and meaningful task or goal is one of the most important attributes or characteristics of effective group work. Why would you put students into groups to complete a boring and meaningless task? That is akin to putting a lit match to a stick of dynamite. We strongly encourage you to put the task on the board or overhead or chart paper so that those students who struggle with auditory memory can review it if necessary. As well, record the directions.

Note that this relates directly to the instructional skill of Sharing the Objective and Purpose of the Lesson. Refer to the research that clarity around objectives has on student learning and disposition towards learning (Marzano, 1999.)

- **Role:** This refers to each student having a job to do in the group—e.g., reader, recorder, checker, etc. Roles need to be selected and utilized carefully. Roles can get in the way at times. For example, if grade six students were reviewing math problems by working in groups to classify word problems related to the operation needed to solve the problem (whether they would add, subtract, multiply, divide or some combination of those four operations) then they may find employing and rotating the roles of the cutter, reader, and paster more useful.

- **Resource:** Sharing resources is self-explanatory. Here students share a resource, e.g., a microscope or paints. For example, in an art lesson you might have students share the pastels as they complete a Place Mat on how to use lines and shapes to communicate feelings such as lonely, calm, and puzzled.

- **Incentive:** This one is often the most controversial. Incentives refer to students getting perks for working together, e.g., free time or a story. This means that everyone in the group works to get the incentive and that every group can achieve it if they accomplish the goal—they do not compete for one prize or incentive. Competition for an incentive or reward that only one group can receive fits under Outside Force.

- **Outside Force:** This 'force' sets up a competitive situation where students compete against other standards or for a single prize, e.g., time, a standard, no homework.

- **Environmental:** When teachers attend to the structure or structures within the environment (e.g., students sit or work around a defined area, or around a table or hula-hoop or Bunsen burner) they are more likely to work collaboratively.

- **Identity:** Identity is often selected when students are going to work together over time to complete a project or task. They often develop a group name or design a group logo. The impact of identity building becomes apparent over time.

- **Sequence:** When each student in the group has a task that each must complete and put together to finish, then the teacher is invoking Sequence Positive Interdependence. In real life, building a

house would be an example.

- **Simulation:** This is similar to role-playing and can often involve the skills needed in drama. When employed in a more complex way, simulation becomes a strategy unto itself—one that is extensively researched. Again, this often implies the use of roles to act out a situation or resolve a conflict, etc.

Note: With the exception of Goal Positive Interdependence, the rest are optional in any given collaborative task. Employ them with care.

Five Basic Elements: Practice

Analyze the Lesson Below. Identify where and how the teacher applied the Johnsons' five basic elements.

Note: The following lesson was designed by a student teacher for a grade nine class in a large suburban, multicultural secondary school. Previous to this lesson, the students began a work-profile project that would span a three-week period and would eventually be used in an integrated math assignment. The objective of the assignment was to help students familiarize themselves with the complications of creating a résumé, finding a job, pursuing a career, and balancing a budget. For this lesson the class were at the stage of inventing a fictional, prospective job-hunter who would become the subject of the entire task. The students, at this point, were vaguely aware of why they were to list certain characteristics pertaining to the fictional person. It was time to do a lesson on the résumé. They sat in groups of three or four and the group members were labelled A, B, C, etc., and the groups were numbered off. (Numbered Heads.)

MENTAL SET:

"Did anyone have trouble doing yesterday's assignment?" (The assignment was a personal data worksheet to get them prepared to complete a résumé.) *"Did you find it difficult to organize your information? Take about 15 seconds to think about the difficulties you had while doing the worksheet. Share your ideas in your group. Make sure you are sensitive to each person's voice being heard. I will randomly call on people to share the group's comments, so be prepared, it could be you."*

After 60 seconds ask for some ideas.

OBJECTIVE AND PURPOSE:

"Today, we will apply our understanding of what is meant by a résumé. We will organize the meaningful, personal data you collected into a document called a résumé. Since most of you will have to look for a job, knowing how to sell yourselves to a prospective employer is important. The résumé is a short and easy way to quickly tell someone about you.

You will get a chance to write résumés about your fictional characters by the end of the week."

INPUT:

Students were regrouped into working partners so they would learn to work with everyone in the class. *"Okay, with your partner, label yourselves A and B. Take about five minutes to write down all of the possible types of things that you would consider including in a résumé. Remember to make sure you are aware of equal*

participation—one person should not be taking over and doing all the work." (We discussed this social skill in a previous lesson.) *"Write your ideas down in point form first."* Once students have completed this, ask them to organize the information into categories (a simple Inductive Thinking strategy). Let them know that once all groups finish, one person from each group will be asked to shift and share with one other group. (This small group structure is known as Walk About or One Stay Some Stray; it increases accountability.)

MODELLING/INPUT:

After about five minutes hand out a sample résumé and tell them not to turn it over until everyone gets one.

When everyone has one, they turn it over and take a look at the headings on the résumé. With the same partner, they take 10 minutes to examine Gloria's résumé closely and then think about the following questions. (Write these on the board.)

- What do you like or dislike about this résumé?
- What kind of job do you think Gloria is applying for?
- If you were an employer, would you hire Gloria? Be prepared to first explain why and then to take a vote.

CHECK FOR UNDERSTANDING:

> **Note:** The teacher of this lesson wanted to focus on equal participation but wanted it to emerge from the lesson. She did not want to teach it or introduce it up front. This approach makes the communication skill more realistic and meaningful.

"Before we start, I just want to share that as I walked around, I noticed that everyone was involved, no one was taking over and doing all the work. That's important. Thanks."

The following questions are asked and the students share their ideas with the class. When the questions are asked the teacher makes sure the students are all involved and accountable to think.

The students are asked to think individually. They are then randomly selected to respond to these two questions:

* What is the purpose of learning to do a résumé?
* Why do you think that a résumé is so important?

GUIDED PRACTICE:

"I have booked some lab time in the computer room over the next couple of days so that you can create résumés for your fictional characters. I will give you some other sample résumés to help you decide on other categories that you might want to include. Today, we will stay here for the remainder of the class so that you can get started on planning the résumé." (I hand out the other résumés.) *"Okay, let's get started, you still have 20 minutes to plan."*

IDEAS FOR EXTENSION:

After they have completed their résumés, they will get into groups of four and work together to decide on what jobs they could apply for based on the information in the résumés.

On the next page we present the teacher's reflection on this lesson. The reflection is followed by examples of six Cooperative Learning Structures.

Teacher's Reflection...

The classes were generally small (20-25) and the rooms were ideal for working in pairs and small groups. The various strategies that I used worked well in such a flexible atmosphere. I was especially pleased with the "unofficial" grade 9 curriculum that emphasizes real life and skill development specifically designed for these students. The concept of résumé is both relevant and interesting to students of their age. They were able to understand the purpose of the résumé from the point of view of a boss, which is the only point of view that matters with this sort of writing. Most of the students got involved during the discussions and all of them participated in the 'like/don't like' exercise and in the final vote.

During the mental set and the objective/purpose activities, there was an incredible show of concern and interest. The first question addressed to the students, as I had predicted, was answered by a unanimous show of hands. They were confused about the difficulty of grouping together information. Some of the students evidently had some knowledge of the résumé, and shared their thoughts with the class, referring to brothers, sisters, and friends who were in the job market.

They were thrilled to see a real résumé and immediately attacked, praised, or questioned the document. Most agreed that it was well organized, others suggested that the candidate was too sporadic with part-time jobs and experience. There seemed to be a split in the class after a while as the students drew their conclusions as to whether or not she would land the job. They all voted and gave reasons for their decision. I think this part of the lesson was very successful because they had a sense of decision-making, an important skill for people of their age. There was only one management problem during the entire lesson. One student thought that another student's justification was "stupid". I intervened to say that it was okay not to agree on things, but that it was not acceptable to use words like "stupid" in reference to another student. Then I said, "Continue to tell us why you disagree," and the lesson continued. I am not sure if I reacted appropriately, but in that instant, I didn't want to tamper with the positive energy of the class.

During their partner work, I walked around the room helping with difficult words and ideas. They asked many questions. They were all very excited about lab time to create résumés. Some started their outlines, while others graphically expressed their ideas about their résumés. I stopped once in awhile to make sure they were sensitive to participating equally. I talked briefly about how the job ads in newspapers wanted people who could work as part of a team and that team work included the idea that people participate equally whenever possible.

I believe that when we teach students about real life or connect what we teach to real life, they will be motivated. The nature of such an assignment calls for group or partner work as well as individual expression and large group discussions. I felt good about the lesson, the dynamics of the class, and the motivation with which the students approached the task.

Cooperative Learning Structures

Cooperative small group structures are, for the most part, examples of what we call tactics; a few of the more complex structures we consider strategies (see Chapter Two for an explanation of tactics and strategies). As mentioned earlier in this chapter, structures range in complexity from simple to complex and serve a variety of purposes. The simple structures would be Think Pair Share and Round Robin. Three-Step Interview and Place Mat would be of average complexity. Teams Games Tournaments, Jigsaw and Group Investigation are more complex.

What makes these structures useful is that they invoke three of the Five Basic Elements in the Johnsons' work: individual accountability, face-to-face interaction, and at least two of the nine types of positive interdependence (goal and environmental).

Spencer Kagan's work includes the most extensive collection of cooperative small group structures. Jeanne Gibbs' work, encapsulated in TRIBES, is a practical and clearly articulated philosophy around creating a community of learners. It likewise contains numerous small group structures. Robert Slavin's work also provides a range of structures; we consider his structures instructional strategies. Two of the more complex cooperative group structures presented in Chapter 11 of this book are Team Analysis, (Richard Elson's); and Academic Controversy, (David and Roger Johnson's).

We recommend the chapter on Group Investigation in Joyce, Weil, and Showers (1992) book *Models of Teaching* and Sharan and Sharan's (1992) book on *Group Investigation* as the most in-depth resources

for this powerful group structure.

Don't forget that the structures can be integrated one within the other or stacked (one used after another). For example, in applying Inside/Outside Circles, you can also employ Numbered Heads to keep all the students accountable to think. At the end of a Three-Step Interview you can connect a Round Robin where each person shares what was learned. With Jigsaw, in the last phase, you can weave in Three-Step-Interview to hold the learners accountable and to check or extend understanding.

Of course, structures can also be employed to drive the more complex strategies such as Bruner's Concept Attainment explained in Chapter Eight. For example, Place Mat can be applied as the process to have students gather their thinking re the development of their hypothesis during the sharing of the YES and NO examples.

> Following is a sample lesson that integrates the Jigsaw process with the five basic elements.

Following the lesson on fractions is an explanation of six cooperative group structures. Each structure is briefly described and is followed by a number of situations that illustrate how or where it might be used.

- **Inside/Outside Circles**
- **Place Mat**
- **Four Corners**
- **Graffiti**
- **Three Step Interview**
- **Teams Games Tournament**

Fractions Lesson: Grade Six

This is the end of a unit on fractions. This lesson is a pre-test review.

OBJECTIVE:

The students will review for an upcoming test and reinforce their understanding of fractions, specifically: equivalent fractions, expressing fractions in simplest form, addition/subtraction of fractions with like/unlike denominators, expressing improper fractions as mixed numbers, and vice versa. A Jigsaw strategy will be used, whereby students become "experts" in one or two areas and then teach their area of expertise to the other students in their Home Group. Jigsaw is explained below.

MENTAL SET:

The students are put in Home Groups of six (teacher-determined based on level of performance in math) and have lettered themselves off AA, BB, and CC. Put them into pairs to have stronger and weaker students working together—like peer tutoring. *"In your groups of six, brainstorm on the piece of paper at your table all the areas you have studied related to fractions. In 90 seconds I will randomly ask some of you to share."* After they've finished, collect their ideas. Assign the following task.

"I am going to assign each pair two areas in which you will become the expert. You will have three minutes to discuss these with your partner in your Home Group before I ask you to move and work with two other A's, B's, or C's where you will take turns sharing your ideas in your Expert Group."

- **A's:** equivalent fractions and expressing fractions in lowest terms
- **B's:** changing mixed numbers into improper fractions and changing improper fractions into mixed numbers
- **C's:** adding/subtracting fractions with like denominators and adding/subtracting fractions with unlike denominators

OBJECTIVE AND PURPOSE:

The students are reminded of the upcoming test and told that today is an opportunity to extend their understanding of fractions by involving themselves in a review session using Jigsaw. They will be responsible for teaching the other members in their group their two areas. Following that, they do a short quiz at the end of the Jigsaw involving these six areas. Last, they do a **Three-Step Interview**.

"Okay, please start." (They are given three minutes.)

JIGSAW

Step 1: Students work with their partner in their Home Group to review these two areas. They do a check for understanding with each other. The three minutes are a warmup for when they move to their expert groups. Students then pick up a sheet that provides information and questions concerning their area. Prior to moving, students are reminded of what they discussed earlier in the unit about checking for understanding and involving everyone's voice. They know they will reflect on this at the end of the Jigsaw.

Step 2: Students now pair up with other group of A's, B's, or C's to form their expert group. This is predetermined.

Step 3: Students thanked their Expert Group and returned to the Home Group. A's shared first (checked for understanding) then B's and C's. They were then asked to discuss how effectively they checked to see if everyone understood and the extent to which they encouraged everyone to share their thinking. Several students were randomly selected by the teacher to share.

PRACTICE (GUIDED):

Practice occurred in Step Three. As part of the expert's responsibility, the members of the group complete the same sheet as the one completed in the expert groups. The expert guides them through completion of the sheet. This means each person completes all three sheets, but is the expert for one.

PRACTICE (INDEPENDENT):

Students now push their chairs away and work on their own to complete a short quiz that mirrors the questions that will be on the test. They then go back to their Home Group and mark each other's work and explain how to correct mistakes.

CLOSURE:

Students now get into groups of three and complete a Three-Step Interview around the questions posed. After each question, they rotate. Each person had to be interviewed for three questions—so each person is the interviewer, the interviewee, and the recorder three times (this takes about 15 minutes).

Note:

Part way through, the teacher stopped the students and asked them to think about how they were doing re checking for understanding and making sure everyone's voice was being heard. The teacher also reminded the students that they were going to have to come back to their Home Group and take their group through the same sheet to explain their areas and illustrate how to solve the questions. They were reminded to think about how they were going to teach the others in their group and to check for their understanding.

EXTENSION:

To make the connection between what students had just done and how it applied to problems they might experience outside of school, the teacher put real life problems on the board and asked them to discuss in their triad the connection between the problem and what they just learned. The teacher then randomly called on students.

Inside/Outside Circles

Inside/Outside Circles involves placing students in two circles—one circle within the other. It can be employed with groups of six or more students (with half of the group forming the inside circle and half the outside—with each student in one circle facing a student in the other). This structure facilitates dialogue between students. It encourages community building at the first of the year, while providing for movement and interaction at any time throughout the year.

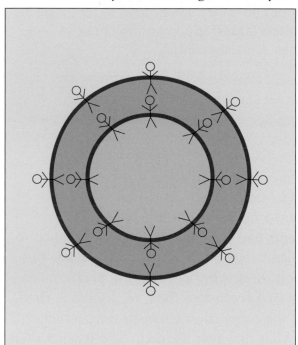

Application of this Tactic:

Situation: You put a question on the board. You then tell the students to think about how they might respond to the question. Give them wait time (say 15 to 30 seconds). Now say *"Person on the inside, tell the person on the outside how you would attempt to solve it. When you are finished sharing, say 'pass,' and then the outside person will share or extend the thinking of the inside person."*

When finished, have the outside people rotate one to the left or right. They are now ready for the next question and interaction with a new person.

Situation: It is Friday afternoon and the students are a bit listless. You need to get them moving a bit. So you put them into Inside/Outside circles and have them respond to questions related to the content they have been studying. Don't forget to give them time to think (wait time) before you ask them to share—this makes the process safer and they are more likely to be successful. Rotate after each question.

Situation: You are studying poetry, so you read a short poem. The students then get 30 seconds to think about its meaning. You then pick either the outside or inside person to start sharing their opinions. When finished, they say *"pass"* and the other person then shares their thinking.

Situation: As part of your French or Spanish class, you are doing a unit involving language related to the legal system. You put the class into a large Inside/Outside Circle with a table separating each pair of students. On each table is a role-play situation. One person is the police person, the other the person who just got the ticket (parking, speeding etc.). They have to engage in a dialogue as to why they should or should not get the ticket. Give them 90 seconds. They then rotate one desk in the opposite direction. This time the roles reverse (the situation and roles are stated on the card on the table).

Situation: You are editing a paragraph or piece of art or identifying figures of speech in a piece of writing. Put the item on the overhead or on the wall and ask students to analyze the piece of writing and then have them share (inside with outside and vice versa). Showing the work visually is important—just reading it to the students is too hard for those students whose auditory memory is not strong.

Inside/Outside Circles... Considerations

- We suggest you letter the Inside/Outside groups as A, B, C, etc. (i.e., if you are using more than one Inside/Outside Circle). Then number each pair within the circle (one, two, etc.). Now you can ask your question and give them time to share. Now say, *"Group B, pair two, outside, what is your response?"* This means you are integrating the group structure of **Numbered Heads** into this process. This holds the students more accountable.

- When using Numbered Heads and the outside persons rotate, this mixes the pairs number. We solve that by telling students that the inside person carries the "dominant gene" (in this case, a number). The inside person's number does not change. The new outside person adopts the inside person's number.

- Provide wait time for thinking prior to asking inside or outside to share. Be sensitive to the complexity of the question and how long you give the students to think.

- When employing Numbered Heads in order to select a student to respond publicly, be prepared for students not to respond or to respond incorrectly. One way to assist them to save face is to tell them they have the right to pass if they are not sure. Or, when discussing, to turn to another group who appears to know and get the answer from them. See Chapter 4 for more information on asking questions.

- If you have an odd number of students, simply have two people on the outside circle act as one person. This works well if you have special needs students. They can be paired up with a stronger student. This also applies to students who have been away. They can be paired up with another student when you use this process as a review.

Inside/Outside Circle... Adaptations

1. Have the outside circles from each group shift and stand around a different inside circle. This brings in new information and also helps if someone is fooling around. We also move pairs—for the same reasons—avoiding pairing two students who will not talk or will argue. Simply make sure you know the number of the existing pairs and say, *"Okay, pairs, one and three move to the group to your right."* Given each group has someone who moves, the intervention does not single anyone out.

2. To decide who begins, you can vary how you select who starts. For example: the person whose birthday is closest to April Fool's Day; the person born the furthest distance away from the school; the person whose first name would appear first in a dictionary, the person dressed the warmest, or the person who has the most brothers and sisters, etc. If it's a tie, then tell them that the person on the inside (or outside) starts.

Four Corners – K to Adult

With Four Corners you begin with a statement, an issue, or a question. Next, the students choose a corner that best captures their perspective, view, or response. They move to that corner, pair up (if there is another person with whom to pair up) and share why they made that decision. They should be prepared to share their response or their partner's if asked.

Four Corners is an ideal structure for getting students to operate at more creative and evaluative levels of thinking, and is especially useful if you are interested in getting the students into debating. Of course, you can have three, five, or six corners or places students move based on their thinking or attitudes towards an issue.

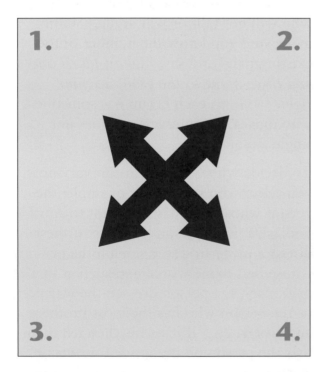

Application of this Tactic

Situation: You are discussing an issue, such as "Students with AIDS should be allowed in our school.' You label the four corners: "STRONGLY AGREE," 'AGREE," "STRONGLY DISAGREE" and "DISAGREE." The students get time to make a decision (say 30 seconds) then without any discussion, they move to the corner that best represents their stance (when they get to the corner, they form groups of two or three) and share why they chose that corner. The teacher then randomly calls on pairs of students from each corner to identify why they made that decision.

Situation: Your grade two students have just done an investigation on organs of the body: brain, heart, stomach, lungs. They have to decide which organ they think is the most important and why. They get time to think, then they move to the corner that represents that organ (wise to have a picture or word up in the corner for younger students—they get confused remembering which corner is which). Now they pair up, share, and defend their ideas.

Situation: You are reading a novel or children's story. The students have to decide who was most responsible for what happened or what is the best solution to an emerging problem. Each corner represents one of the responses. For example, if you have the children's book *John Brown, Rose and the Midnight Cat*, the class could identify conditions under which the cat could join the family. The students could then move to the corner they believe represents the best solution—and share/defend their answer.

Situation: You are studying World War II. You put up each of the causes in different areas of the room. The students have to make a decision as to which one they believe was the major cause and why. You could start your unit this way and then redo it at the end of the unit; students could compare their thinking.

Situation: You are studying energy systems or pollution. The students have to decide which source of energy is most efficient, or most costly. Or, they have to decide who is most affected by oil spills (plumbers, gill netters, cooks, bankers).

Four Corners... Considerations

- Encourage students to make up their own minds regarding what corner they select. Give them time to think. Then tell them not to be influenced by others—to follow their own thinking, and not to be controlled by others. If you do not encourage independent thinking, students will go to the corner that their friend(s) selects—or that the most popular or smartest person selects.

- Make sure the students do not get into larger groups once they are in their corner; encourage groups of two or three. Students need to know they are accountable and responsible for thinking. In pairs they are more accountable, and have more time to talk. For the first few times, be sticky on this one—don't let them start until they all have a partner. Then let them discuss. Once this norm is set, they will follow it unless you suggest modifications.

"This structure is adapted with permission from Kagan Publishing and Professional Development. Books and resources on Kagan Structures can be obtained from Kagan Publishing, 1 (800) 933-2667, www.KaganOnline.com"

Four Corners... Adaptations

1. If only two positions are to be taken, then the Four Corner process becomes known as a Value Line (in Jeanne Gibbs TRIBES program they call it "Putting Yourself on the Line"). Here the students position themselves along the continuum—a line from STRONGLY AGREE to STRONGLY DISAGREE.

Some teachers will put a piece of masking tape on the floor between the two extremes, the students then take a stance (on the tape) prior to the discussion/debate or unit of study. They sign their name on that spot. Then after the discussion, debate etc., they return to the tape, stand and sign their name. They then measure the distance they shifted. You can integrate this measurement into a math activity (graphing, averages).

2. You can use a variety of themes for metaphorical thinking related to each of the corners. For example, we have used Song Titles, Movie Titles, and Types of Food or Animals. We sometimes use the theme of roads to have people identify how they have experienced a situation (with teachers, how they have experienced change in their district: 1. Yellow Brick Road, 2. The Road Less Travelled, 3. the Trans Canada, or the 4. Ho Chi Min Trail).

3. Remember: Four Corners can be integrated or supported by other tactics and for problem solving. For example, say you are having a problem with teasing in your classroom/school. You identify why students tease one another. Then you put each reason in a different location in the room. The students think, then move to the area they believe is the major reason why students tease one another. Their views then become a catalyst for change.

APPLYING FOUR CORNERS:

On the following three pages is a complex Cooperative Learning lesson that involves the Johnsons' five basic elements, as well as several small group structures including Four Corners.

Four Corners Woven Into a Science Lesson: *Grade 6 Static Electricity Lesson – Part of a Unit on Electricity*

Lesson designed by Renee Lyon

OBJECTIVE:

Academic Task

1. The students will gain an understanding of the characteristics of static electricity (especially that opposite charges attract and like charges repel) and demonstrate this understanding by completing a written report of in-class investigations and observations.

2. The students will use appropriate vocabulary, including correct science and technology terminology in describing their investigations and observations.

SOCIAL SKILL FOCUS:

To have students work congenially in groups. This will be demonstrated by individual group members encouraging each other's efforts (verbally and through body language) during their static electricity investigations.

TASK ANALYSIS:

1. Can the students identify the characteristics of static electricity?

2. Can the students conduct proper scientific investigations and write up their findings using scientific vocabulary?

3. Can the students demonstrate their understanding of the social skill addressed by refraining from using put-downs and instead using encouragement in the group activities?

MENTAL SET:

Teacher Demo #1: Blow up balloon (students to do). Ask if they think the balloon will stick to the wall. Have them **Think/Pair/Share** regarding what would make the balloon stick to the wall. Why? Try it and see what happens.

DISCUSSION:

When I rubbed the balloon onto my hair, the balloon picked up electrons from my hair. We know electrons have a negative charge, so now the balloon also has a negative charge. The wall, on the other hand, is positively charged. Concept: charges that are not alike (unlike) attract each other—draw on board. Electrons from hair negatively charge the balloon and the board is positive.

Teacher Demo #2: Blow up second balloon that is attached to string. Rub against hair. Rub first balloon (attached to string now) against hair again. Ask students to predict what will happen when both balloons are held together by their strings.

Using the **Four Corners** tactic, students demonstrate their predictions. Depending on their predictions, independently arrived at, students will move to the following centres:

Centre #1: Balloons will push away from each other
Centre #2: Balloons will stick together
Centre #3: Balloons will do nothing
Centre #4: I don't know

Concept: charges that are like, or the same, repel each other—draw on board—electrons from hair negatively charge both balloons.

Note:

I now have students standing in four groups around the classroom. From this point I rearrange students into four groups of four students each (pre-selected by me so that they are mixed according to level of performance, sex, and ability to work in groups). Direct students to now move desks into four groups of four.

OBJECTIVE (SHARED):

Well done. You all did a pretty good job of predicting how static electricity affected the balloons in both demonstrations. Now you're going to have a chance to evaluate what we think just happened (electrons moving from atom to atom creating electric charge on the surface of the object) by conducting your own investigations.

We are working on two main things today:
1. *Static electricity—you will hand in one report per group (titled: My Investigation Results) showing what you learned in your investigations. (Students are familiar with this form.)*

2. *Group work—you will work at understanding that your group will work more effectively when you encourage and praise each other in all your efforts rather than spending precious energy criticizing and putting each other down.*

"We've discussed this before but let's review what we will see and hear while we're working in groups that shows that we are encouraging each other." (Note that the T-Chart previously done involved the social skill of no put-downs.) Remind students of previous T-Chart. Have students **Brainstorm** a new list or recall from the old **T-Chart**. Record items (what they would see and hear) on the chalkboard. Then put up their previous T-Chart to compare their thinking.

Have students read over the list and choose two items they will personally work on today in the science activities. Have students jot them down on index cards handed out. Collect cards and remind students to pay attention to the See/Hear items they selected to work on.

"At each of your four centres you will find the following materials (detail for students). These are now laid out neatly on this front table. We'll get to them in a minute but first I'll give you directions on how to proceed with your group investigations." Explain rotations, which materials stay at centres and which they take with them, and the time allotted. Go over the Static Attraction sheet, which details how to proceed with investigations—elaborate especially on how to write-up their findings using proper vocabulary and scientific fair-test procedures. Remind them that their group is responsible for handing in one completed "My Investigation Results" sheet. Have students create chart on back of this sheet so they can easily record results shown on the board.

MATERIALS TESTED	RESULTS
Pin	attracted to charged straw

Teacher randomly assigns Group Roles: (each student is an Encourager)

1 person – manages material
1 person – records results
1 person – tidies table after finished at centre
1 person – double checks/edits completed report and hands in to me

Remind students that they will be completing an evaluation to assess how they did individually and as a group.

Begin by having the Materials Manager (from each group) retrieve the materials from the front table. Be there to ensure proper materials are retrieved.

Circulate during student group activities.

MODELLING:
Academic task was modelled during Mental Set and Input. Social skills were modelled during shared objective and throughout lesson by teacher's use of encouraging words and positive body language.

CHECK FOR UNDERSTANDING:
• Observe students working in groups
• Students to hand in completed report

PRACTICE:
(INDEPENDENT AND GUIDED):
see Mental Set, Input, Shared Objective

CLOSURE/EXTENSION:
"We've seen that static electricity is the building up of an electric charge on the surface of an object. Did your group discover something surprising or unexpected?" Allow each group to share two findings with the whole class.

"Think to yourself, can you think of any other everyday occurances when we see static electricity?" Let them think for about 10 seconds and ask for hands if they have an idea (clothes in dryer, flyaway hair, TV screen, lightning, etc.) *"Do you think it happens more often on a dry day or on a damp day?"* Get them to share and explain their response.

SOCIAL SKILL:
Open discussion on group performances. Ask them how well they encouraged each other. Share positive observations of their work.

Return the students' individual index cards on which they recorded what two items in particular they were going to work on (e.g., saying *"You did that well," "I really understand it now,"* or seeing nodding heads in encouragement).

Hand out Evaluation Sheet for each student to complete and hand in. Remind them to comment on how they did with respect to the two items they selected from the T-Chart to work on. Were they successful in practising what they wanted to do?

Three-Step Interview...K to Adult

Three-Step Interview is a focused way to encourage students to share their thinking, ask questions, and take notes. It works best with three per group, but it can be modified for groups of four.

Each student is assigned a letter, then each letter is assigned a role: A= Interviewer, B= Interviewee, C= Reporter. The roles rotate after each interview. You need to decide the length of time for each interview based on the age of your students, and their experience with this Cooperative Learning structure. When finished, they do a Round Robin and share the key information they recorded when they were person C.

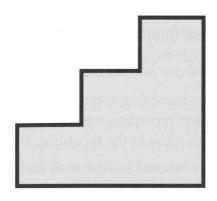

Application of this tactic:

Situation: The students have just completed a report on endangered animals or a biography on an important person. They now do a Three-Step Interview to share the key ideas in their report.

Situation: The students have just finished a Mind Map or Concept Map on the most important ideas in the geometry unit or the application of different formulae in the physics units. They now interview each other about the construction and conceptual flow or connections in the Map.

Situation: The students have just completed a Concept Attainment process on heat transfer equations or figures of speech or effective graphs. They now interview each other about their thinking as they attempted to identify what all the YES examples had in common. Here, the Three-Step Interview is used to invoke Phase Two of Concept Attainment.

Situation: The school year is just starting. The students interview each other on why math makes people nervous or what they think are the most important classroom rules. Perhaps employ Place Mat first to gather their thoughts.

Situation: The students are interviewed around their thoughts and feelings concerning a book they recently read (or a chapter, article, experiment etc.).

Situation: Problem solving (these could be real life problems such as when they were teased or issues of prejudice) or they could be specific content (e.g., science) problems. Students interview each other about how they solved (or could solve) the problem.

Data Set: *Questions/Requests*

The students just finished individual reports on endangered animals. The following data set was designed to act as a model of types of questions for students who may need help developing questions.

1. What animal did you study?

2. Explain why the idea of animal rights is important to you.

3. In what countries is this animal found?

4. How do you take the laws involving animal rights and use them to solve this problem?

5. What does it normally eat?

6. What do you see as the relationship between animal rights and extinction?

7. Would an endangered animal make a good pet?

8. What kind of zoo would you create to respond to all these pressures on animals?

9. What is its life expectancy in the wild?

10. What is the biggest threat to this animal, development or pollution, and why?

TESTERS:

A. Do you believe that putting these animals in zoos is a solution?

B. Explain why zoos are bad if the animals are protected and assisted to reproduce.

C. Is this animal found in zoos? Why?

D. You mentioned that elephants' feet were being used as ashtrays. To what extent does demand for this animal's body parts affect its chances for survival?

As an extension: Do numbers 1, 2, 4, 6, 8, & 10 have a pattern? Think of Bloom's Taxonomy. When students have control over a taxonomy of thinking, they think more precisely.

Three Step Interview Form

Interview One: _____ (name)

_____
_____
_____
_____
_____

Interview Two: _____ (name)

_____
_____
_____
_____
_____

Interview Three: _____ (name)

_____
_____
_____
_____
_____

Round Robin: Key Idea(s) from Interviews

_____
_____
_____
_____
_____

Place Mat...K to Adult

Place Mat involves groups of students working both alone and together around a single piece of paper to simultaneously involve all members. The paper is divided up into pieces based on the number of members in the group with a central square or circle. Ideally, groups of two to four work best. It can be used with groups of five, six, and seven, but if you do, the students should be skilled at group work.

Materials: piece of chart paper, pen or pencil for each person and a place to set the paper. Place Mat also works with regular 8-1/2 x 11 inch paper; however, the chart paper is more enjoyable as it provides the students with a bit more room and it's easier to read what others have written.

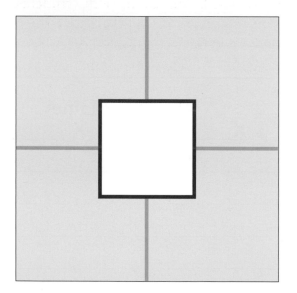

Application of this tactic:

Situation 1: You have read a story or a poem and you want the students to take the time to reflect, write, and share their ideas related to a key question or issue. Then do Place Mat.

Situation 2: You are starting a unit on energy or spring or government and you want to know what the students already know. You put them into groups of two or three and do Place Mat.

Situation 3: You have illustrated how to balance an equation or factor an equation or solve an addition story problem. You then put one question on the board and each student works out the solution in their space. They then share their thinking with others in the group. As an extension, you can put different questions on the board (one for each student in the group) and now students work on their own question. When finished, they share their solution with the rest of the group.

Situation 4: You are attempting to come to consensus around an issue. Each person writes (in their space) what he or she thinks are the most important issues. They then circle two or three ideas and star the most important idea to consider. They then take turns reading their list to the group and identifying the most important issue. The next person writes that key idea in the box in the middle. Repeat for each person. When finished, the group has the key ideas of the group, with each person knowing their voice was heard and respected.

Situation 5: You are watching a video and you want the students' minds engaged and accountable for key information (you can even assign them different questions to answer about the video). They jot down ideas during the video and share the ideas with their group.

Place Mat... Considerations

- Get a piece of chart paper and have the students divide it into the number of students in the group. You can decide whether to have the square in the middle or not. See Situation #4 on the previous page concerning how to use the centre square or circle.

- Students are provided with time to work alone. The social skill is respecting silence and privacy.

- Students then share their thinking with the group. Here you can decide whether you want the communication skill of *active listening* or *probing for clarification* etc., to be introduced to support the Place Mat process. We recommend you weave a social, communication, or critical thinking skill into the process.

- Students use the Round Robin tactic and rotate clockwise or counter-clockwise around the group, sharing their thinking. One option in the sharing, especially when it is their first time or they do not know each other well, is to allow them to have the right to pass—and either not share, or share later.

Place Mat... Adaptations

1. Weave in **Walk About**. Have one student take the sheet and go to another group to share the key ideas in the centre square.

2. If the students are in groups of three, you can have them do a **Three-Step Interview** focusing on what they constructed in the centre square.

3. With kindergarten students, they draw pictures—e.g., of what spring means to them.

4. Place mat works well when doing **Concept Attainment**. When the data set is being presented, the students can write their hypotheses in their space and later share their thinking using the ideas they wrote. Then, in the middle, they put their group's consensus.

5. When doing **Mind Maps** or **Concept Maps**, students can use this process to prepare for doing the Map by identifying the key ideas for the Map. They can put the most important ideas that should be placed on the Map first in the square.

6. In **Brainstorming**, some students will take over and others will try to do nothing. Place Mat encourages all the students in the group to brainstorm—it increases the chances of holding them accountable and getting them actively involved.

7. Once finished, you can have the students cut out their section, and then have them recombine with two or three others from another group. They then share.

Other Formats

large table – 2 groups

Graffiti... Grade One to Adult

Graffiti is a creative brainstorming process that involves collecting the wisdom of all or most of the students in the class. It starts by placing students in groups of three or four and providing a large piece of paper for each group. Each piece of paper has a topic (same or different) in the middle. The students get 30 seconds to think and then 60 - 90 seconds to individually but simultaneously record their ideas on the paper. They then stop, stand up, and go, as a group, to a different piece of paper. They then once more write their ideas. They continue until each group has visited each of the other groups. When they return to their original group they now have the collective wisdom of everyone in the class.

Note, instead of using words, students can draw an image (good for younger students.)

Application of this tactic:

Situation: You are in a music class. You play a piece of music and the students have to identify all the things that come into their minds when they hear this type of music (such as feelings and memories etc.). When finished, you will have a variety of thoughts and emotions related to the different types of music (e.g., country western, classical, jazz, blues). Now ask them to make a statement related to music that emerges from their analysis of the data on the sheet.

Situation: You are studying a novel or play such as Romeo and Juliet. The next lesson

involves having the students write a character sketch. You realize the most difficult part is collecting the information about each character. You put each of the main characters in the centre of five pieces of paper. The students then write everything they know or examples of situations that communicate this person's personality. They write for 90 seconds and then rotate (every 90 seconds) until they return to their original sheet. They now have the class's thinking. Next, they prioritize the data and write the sketch.

Situation: You want to classify the students' understanding of all the different machines that involve levers. They write down all their ideas, then repeat that on each group's sheet. The students then group the examples into classes of levers based on characteristics they have in common. Note: this is using Graffiti as Phase One of Hilda Taba's Inductive Thinking model, as discussed in Chapter 9.

Situation: The students are to identify examples of parts of speech. Each paper has a different part of speech (improper nouns, proper nouns, adverbs, etc.). They move from paper to paper (every 60 seconds.) writing down as many examples of each as they can. The students return to their sheet and look for incorrect or confusing examples.

Situation: Before starting the unit on Egypt, you want to know everything students currently understand about Egypt. Each sheet has Egypt in the centre. They then get 90 seconds to identify everything they know about Egypt. When they get back to their original sheet, the group makes up five questions to which they would like answers based on the information on the sheet.

Graffiti... Considerations

- Use coloured markers. This makes it more interesting. It also holds students more accountable to stay focused and not write something inappropriate (which will happen ... expect it and be prepared for how you will respond). If the inappropriate comment is green, and only three students have green markers, it makes it easier to be the detective.

- Remind students not to take time to read the other responses. Whether or not they write the same thing is irrelevant; from one perspective it communicates that perhaps the idea is important.

- Introduce graffiti as a concept and what it means. Discuss where they typically find it. You might want to talk about the history of graffiti. This makes the process more meaningful.

Graffiti... Adaptations

- You are a teacher of second languages. This time the Graffiti has no word in the centre—the students take five French or Spanish or German words. They get 30 seconds to record their words. Then they repeat those words on each group's sheet. When they return to their original sheet, they compete to see who can list the English equivalent or French equivalent for each word.

- Have the students pass the paper instead of the groups moving. This is simpler if you think you might have classroom management problems when students move about the class.

- Graffiti is an excellent way to initiate Phase One of Hilda Taba's Inductive Thinking strategy discussed in Chapter 9.

- With kindergarten students, we have seen Graffiti used to have students respond to something they know about a letter, e.g., 'A.' They move around from sheet to sheet (each with a different letter) and they print the letter or draw something that starts with 'A' or a word that has an 'A' in it.

On the next page is a sample of math Graffiti by elementary students.

- When working on spelling, have students take 6 of the words and have them spell 3 correctly and 3 incorrectly. The incorrect words are misspelled in terms of the most common mistake the student thinks others would make when spelling those three words. Students then put the six words on the other group's sheets. When time is up they return to their group, decide which words are spelled correctly, and correct those that are not.

Chapter Eight

Concept Attainment

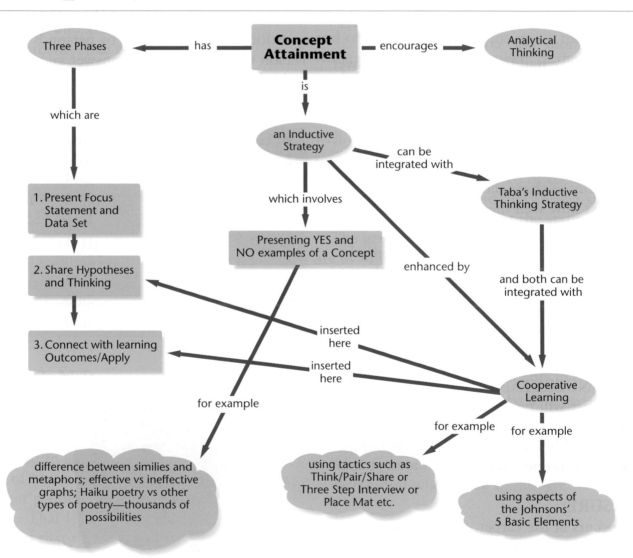

Three Phases ← has — **Concept Attainment** — encourages → **Analytical Thinking**

Three Phases — which are ↓

1. Present Focus Statement and Data Set
2. Share Hypotheses and Thinking
3. Connect with learning Outcomes/Apply

Concept Attainment — is ↓ — **an Inductive Strategy**

an Inductive Strategy — can be integrated with → Taba's Inductive Thinking Strategy

an Inductive Strategy — which involves ↓ — Presenting YES and NO examples of a Concept

enhanced by

and both can be integrated with ↓

Cooperative Learning

inserted here

inserted here

for example → difference between similies and metaphors; effective vs ineffective graphs; Haiku poetry vs other types of poetry—thousands of possibilities

for example → using tactics such as Think/Pair/Share or Three Step Interview or Place Mat etc.

for example → using aspects of the Johnsons' 5 Basic Elements

Note: see *Models of Teaching* by Joyce and Weil for more information on this model of teaching

Chapter Eight

Concept Attainment Chapter Overview

This chapter contains the following interconnected areas:

- Introduction and Rationale
- Sample Data Sets and Lessons
- Clarifying Inductive Thinking
- Explaining Concept Attainment
- How Concept Attainment attends to David Perkin's Work on Knowledge As Design
- Increasing the Complexity: Sample Integrated Lessons
- Activity: You Play the Game
- Concept Attainment: The 3 Phases
- Concepts—Three Types
- Concept Attainment Strategy
- The Integration of Strategies
- Summary—Final Thoughts

Key Questions

1. What are concepts? How did you attain them when you were two years of age?
2. What is meant by "Knowledge as Design" as compared to "Knowledge as Information"?
3. How does Cooperative Learning integrate with Concept Attainment?
4. Is framing questions a critical skill to integrate with the process of Concept Attainment?

Introduction to Chapter

Everything you can touch, see, feel, and taste is a concept. Look around the room you are in – everything in that room and their characteristics are examples of concepts: wall, window, smooth, cold, small, girl, friendly.

Could we argue that concepts are the essence of life? Well, maybe not, but concepts are the building blocks for communication regardless of whether that communication is visual, verbal, or acting out—and communication is certainly important in all our lives. Once we are clear about a concept we can begin to make generalizations and discriminations, which are critical to effective communication. The greater the clarity we have around an ever–increasing number of concepts, then the more likely we are to understand and communicate that understanding with others. Concept Attainment is one approach that brings clarity to concepts—and clarity often enriches life.

This chapter introduces the instructional strategy or model of teaching known as Concept Attainment. Concept Attainment is an inductive strategy developed by Jerome Bruner and explained in the book *A Study of Thinking* (Bruner, Goodnow, & Austin, 1986). Bruner is a research professor at New York University and in 1987 was awarded the international Balzan Prize for his lifelong contribution to human psychology. His work has increased our understanding of how people construct meaning and how instruction affects learning.

We apply Concept Attainment because we find it a useful "colour" or "thread"—another way to respond to the diverse ways in which students learn. Concept Attainment pushes the analysis level of thinking. It invites the

brain to find patterns. Students remember information longer and understand the design of concepts more quickly and more deeply when asked to think at more complex levels and to discuss their ideas with one another.

Brain research informs us that the brain is a pattern seeker and that talk is important for intellectual growth. Concept Attainment helps to uncover those patterns and to facilitate opportunities to talk.

As you will discover as you start your journey, the difficult part of the Concept Attainment process is the time it takes to put together quality data sets. You will also discover how much you don't know about the things you thought you knew something about (e.g., Can parallel lines curve if they remain the same distance apart and never cross?).

To begin responding to the "start up" difficulty, we have created a Concept Attainment data bank for all grades and all subject areas. It is accessible on the Internet. See Chapter Three.

Caution: Concept Attainment does not, by itself, encourage students to play with the purpose of the concept, nor to push how the concept plays itself out in our world; nor does it invite the student to judge the value, the power, or the effect of the concept. The teacher must weave other processes such as Academic Controversy into the learning experience in order to facilitate such opportunities.

Rationale for Reading this Chapter

- Teachers can choose to think for students or create opportunities for students to think for themselves. Concept Attainment invites students to think for themselves.

- As mentioned previously, this strategy encourages students to operate at the level of analysis—an essential skill in the process of critical thinking. More importantly, most (if not all) people have played with the process of Concept Attainment most of their lives...they just didn't know it was called Concept Attainment.

- This approach to encouraging students to develop or clarify or extend their understanding of a concept is much like how we learned concepts as young children. Consider the following scenario:

You are a parent or someone who is taking a young child for a walk. Without giving it a label, you will be naturally forced to apply the Concept Attainment process. Let's take a closer look at what happens when you take Deborah for a walk.

Deborah points at something and you say, *"Oh, that's a dog Deborah. Here, puppy. Yeh, that's a dog. He goes woof woof. Feel his cold nose. Yeh, see he wags his tail when he likes you"* ...etc. Now, from that interaction with the dog, the child is starting to figure out the concept of "dogness". Of course, within two minutes, Deborah sees a cat and says, *"Dog."* You then start the process all over again and say, *"No, that's a cat. Cats go meow, meow and they purr..."* etc. Now from that last interaction, the child is starting to figure out what dogs are not and what cats might be—that the idea of tail—although important to the dog and cat—does not easily differentiate a dog from a cat. Of course if you are a parent, you have also experienced the problem of explaining that a Great Dane is not a horse. Fortunately, over time the child will also realize that a skunk is not a dog and that a gopher is not a cat. All of that will have occurred because someone took the time to point out the YES and NO attributes of the concepts "dog" and "cat".

- Novelty and variety are components of motivation that encourage students to learn. Concept Attainment is an enjoyable instructional strategy, one that can create a game-like environment in the classroom. It adds variety and novelty to your instructional repertoire.

- This approach encourages students to identify the critical essence of concepts. As well, it provides examples or model cases of the concept they are learning.

- When we look at the literature on learning styles and multiple intelligence, we see that Concept Attainment can encourage students to learn in different ways.

On the following pages is a teacher's first attempt at trying concept attainment with a reflection on how it went.

THE CONCEPT

I introduced the concept of a "portrait" to the class. I explained that the yes examples were all portraits and that the no examples were not, because they did not fit the definition of a portrait. I restated the attributes that the class had already discovered:

- it is a descriptive piece of art of a person or animal (the still life was a no example)
- the person or animal is the true focus of the artwork, not what's going on around them or in the background
- it can be a painting or sculpture
- it can depict the whole person, or just their upper body or head
- it can be a side view or some other angle (some of the cards depict side views of the subject, also called "profile")

I explained that the tester card that had a painting of a man and woman on it may at first look like a portrait. However, the focus is not on them, but more on the Coca-Cola advertisement in the painting. This was in fact an ad, not a portrait. They seemed to understand this quite well.

I asked them if they felt they would feel comfortable creating portraits of someone in the class and they were very excited about it. I went on to tell them that they, like the artists in the examples, could use any style they wanted to create a descriptive portrait of someone they knew.

FURTHER REFLECTION

We moved on to the art lesson quite nicely after using this data set. I felt very comfortable presenting it because I have a strong art background. It was my first time using a data set, so I was happy I chose a familiar topic to try first. I would definitely use this concept attainment method of teaching again. It worked very well for this group, because they constantly need to be involved in something challenging, or they get very unfocused and unsettled. They love anything to do with art, so they were drawn to this lesson. Having done this, I think they would be open to trying it again in any other subject area. It is a very effective way to introduce a concept and addresses a variety of learning styles and multiple intelligences.

7 More!!

On the following four pages are seven sample data sets. Following those data sets are three more complex lessons (labelled A, B, and C) where Concept Attainment is carried out by teachers. See if you can figure out the process of Concept Attainment before we explain it near the end of the chapter.

Data Set: Example One - Cartoon Characters

This is a sample data set used to provide students with practice hunting for attributes—they find it fun. Easy for non-readers and readers alike. Such examples can be provided at different levels of complexity. Remember that colour is not important.

MUFFS

Look at these MUFFS:

Stacy Wagstaff

These are not MUFFS:

Are any of these:

Can you and your partner create a MUFF?

Data Set: Example Two - Art

Below is an example of a data set related to art...the concept of line. Other possible data sets include: shape, form, space, texture, etc.

LINE

The following are examples of *LINE* :

The following are not examples of *LINE* :

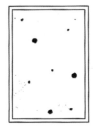     

Which of the following are examples of *LINE?*

 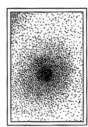    

Definition: A path traced by a moving point or a mark, streak, scratch or stroke.

A line may be horizontal, vertical, diagonal, thick, thin, curved, straight, fuzzy, clean or implied.

> Note: When you give this to students do not provide the definition until after they have created theirs.

Data Set: Example Three - Geometry

Rather than providing students with information regarding 3 Dimensional Shapes, create a data set to let the students' brains look for the pattern and to discuss with one another what they think. You can do this with Kindergarten students and use triangles on one side and other shapes on the other. Perhaps place the examples and non examples in two Hoola Hoops and for testers, give the students a shape and have them discuss where they would put it and why. "In the data set below, what do the shapes on the left have in common? How are they different from the shapes on the right? Think to yourself, then share with a partner. When you think you both have an idea, take turns discussing where you would put the Testers."

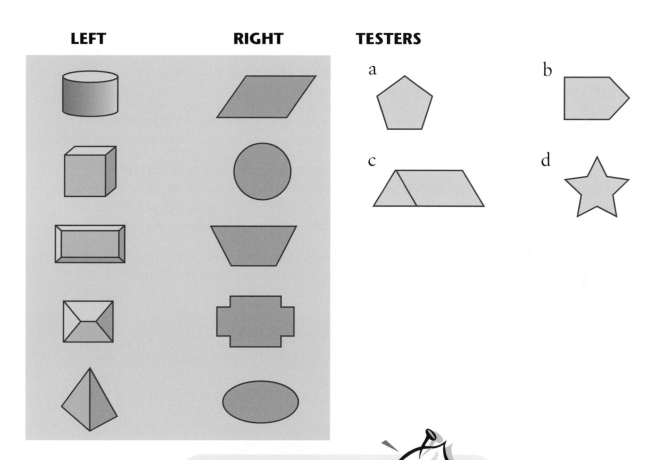

Note that you can use chart paper, overhead Transparencies, or the actual shapes as a means of presenting the exemplars. Or you can modify the data set to use shapes in the room. For example, the concept of parallel works well using objects in the room: Show students yes and no examples of edges that are parallel and not parallel.

Data Set: Example Four – A Critical Thinking Flaw

This data set would be useful as Input to assist students in understanding the design of a specific flaw in a critical thinking skill.

"Read the items on the left and compare them with those on the right; the left ones all represent one fallacy in critical thinking. Work on your own. Then when you have read them all and have an idea, share it with your partner. Then decide where you would put the two testers."

EXAMPLES of the FLAW	NOT EXAMPLES of this FLAW
The pesticides are causing the birds' eggs to be too fragile. We need to stop using pesticides.	One possibility is that the earth is warming up because of pollution. But I think we need to explore other reasons.
Trees are important; people who cut down trees are destroying our planet. We need to ban tree cutting.	I like your idea, but I'm not sure what you meant by the last part. Would you please explain that?
Solar energy is free. We should pass a law that would provide money so that everyone could switch to solar energy.	I agree, but could we consider this from another perspective. What do you think, Ali?
Making people pay more taxes on gasoline is smart. Then we will have enough money to cover the cost of helping feed the poor.	I agree that car exhaust is hurting the environment, but we need to consider what would happen if we forced people to use another form of transportation.
That raccoon got at the chickens last night. I'm going to trap and destroy all the raccoons that step onto my farm.	No thanks, I don't eat fish. I got sick on it once, and now I have an allergy.

Below are two testers. Which one is an example of the 'Flaw'?

A. We don't have that much money so I think we should buy the cheaper computer; then we could have two in every class.

B. We have heard from everyone in the group except Carl. Did you understand how to solve that problem, Carl?

The FLAW examples represent a failure to Examine Both or multiple Sides of an issue (EBS). This is one of the tactics in de Bono's CoRT program. You could design a Concept Attainment data set for most of the 60 tactics in the CoRT program.

Note: the students may need many more examples—do not expect all the students to get the attributes after seeing only 5 or 6 examples. We have often presented over 20 pairs of YES and NO examples before the students grasped the concept.

Data Set: Example Five – Microscope Magnification

In a grade seven class the students were struggling with drawing what they saw in the microscope with the correct perspective relative to the magnification shown on the stage. Telling them did not work. So the teacher created this data set and the students got it within a few minutes and after that drew with the correct perspective.

CONCEPT Estimating the Size of an Object through a Microscope

attributes: the object approximates its size in relation to the view size (beware of changes in magnification)

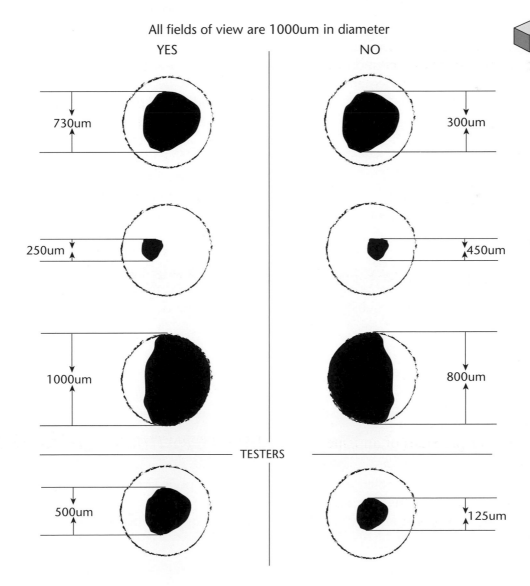

All fields of view are 1000um in diameter

YES	NO
730um	300um
250um	450um
1000um	800um

TESTERS

| 500um | 125um |

Data Set: Example Six – Romanticism

Romanticism means that the principle or the belief comes above all else, regardless of the cost or whether it is good or bad for society.

POSITIVE EXAMPLES

1. A boy challenges a bigger neighbourhood bully who has offended his friend.

2. An employee reports his own company to environmental authorities for pollution and safety violations after top management refuses to correct the problem.

3. A woman persists in resisting the authorities, despite the threat to her career.

4. With his family sick and hungry, a man robs a bank to get money for food.

5. A boxer faces a vastly superior opponent and, with no chance of winning, avoids a knockout on his record.

NEGATIVE EXAMPLES

1. A coach follows the team owner's wishes to play an athlete whom he does not consider good enough for pro hockey.

2. An employee applauds his boss's decision at all meetings... even if he disagrees.

3. A man works for a political party whose policies he detests, but which has a good chance of winning the election.

4. A teenager remains silent in a large group of "in" people who are ridiculing an absent friend of the teenager.

5. An inventor sells his rights to produce his product to a large multinational company which threatens to crush him and his small company if he doesn't.

TESTERS

a. A man drives a car bomb into the midst of his enemies, killing them and himself in the process.
b. A tiny nation bordering Russia abstains in a UN vote on the Soviet Union's invasion of Afghanistan.
c. A wealthy but grouchy uncle is tolerated during his visits to a poor family where no one contradicts his bigoted opinions.
d. A student sticks up for a new student who is being teased by a group of bigger and popular kids.

Data Set: Example Seven – High School Physics (complex)

The objective in this lesson was for the students to construct a relationship and formula to illustrate the gas law relationship between pressure (P) and volume (V) and to solve problems based on this relationship. Temperature and mass are constant. Note: You may have to show them a large number of YES and NO examples. That aside, you can see that it would be easy to add an infinite number of YES and NO examples on the spot.

The students are asked to focus on the final volume (V2) relationship to the initial volume based on the pressure initially (P1) and finally (P2).

V1(L)	P1(kPa)	P2(kPa)	YES V2(L)	NO V2(L)	How Pressure was Changed
10.0	100	200	5.00	20.0	
10.0	100	300	3.33	30.0	
10.0	100	400	2.50	40.0	
10.0	100	50	20.0	5.00	
10.0	100	1000	1.00	10.0	
10.0	100	1	1000.0	.0001	

"Discuss in your groups of four what you believe is the relationship between pressure and volume. (Give them one minute.)

Based on your group's discussion, decide on your own, no talking, whether the answer of **100.00** in bold below is a YES or a NO." (Give them 30 seconds.)

V1	P1	P2	V2
10.0	100	10	**100.00 (YES or NO?)**

"If you said YES you are right. Make sure everyone in your group can explain why."

"Take turns in your group discussing the process and the answer for the following:

V1	P1	P2	V2
20.0	100	200	____
20.0	100	50	____
20.0	100	250	____
20.0	100	75	____
35.5	22	45.2	____

When done, construct a formula that represents the process. Be prepared in your group to share your formula with students in another group. You do not know who will be selected to share."

Lesson A: *Apartheid and Prejudice*

APARTHEID

Rule: Apartheid is legislation or policy that promotes segregation

Critical Attributes:
1. legislated
2. causing segregation

PREJUDICE

Rule: Prejudice is an unfavourable and irrational judgement or opinion made before the facts are known; often against a particular group. A more severe form of bias.

Critical Attributes:
1. unfavourable and unsupported judgement against a particular group
2. results in some form of damage

Objective for the lesson: Students will have a clearer understanding of the concepts of apartheid and prejudice as they relate to issues in equity education. Associated concepts will be "bias" and "teasing."

This lesson integrates the strategies of Concept Attainment and Cooperative Learning and deals with two important concepts that will extend our thinking into other related concepts later in the lesson.

Academic Task: Compare all the ODD numbered examples and determine how they are the same. Contrast them with the EVEN numbered examples.

Collaborative Task: Suspend your judgement until you have heard the ideas of each person in your group. Then, as you complete the testers, deal with them in a way that does not make you go against your values, yet still allows you to communicate to others that you want them to be right about their thinking.

Directions:

1. Get into groups of 2 or 3.

2. Have only one data set between you.

3. On your own, read the 10 examples. Read one ODD then one EVEN until you have read all 10. Compare the ODDs and contrast them with the EVENs.

4. On your own, form an hypothesis as to how the ODDs are the same and how they are different from the EVENs.

5. Share your hypothesis with your partner(s). When you have all shared your ideas, please re-trace and share your "mental map" of how you arrived at your hypothesis as you compared and contrasted the data set—starting at 1 and moving to 10.

6. Now look at the testers and decide which ones would fit under the ODD and which ones under the EVEN. Are there any that do not fit as ODDs or EVENs? Remember the collaborative task of suspending judgement.

Apartheid/Prejudice: Data Set:

1. In South Africa, policy prohibited blacks from living in homes in areas designated as "white only" neighbourhoods.
2. In Canada, the First Nation People were denied access to most classy cafes.
3. In Germany, during World War II, Jews were required by law to have travel passes in order to move about their community.
4. In North America, it is not unusual to have all white juries hear the case of a non-white person.
5. In Canada, during World War II, legislation was passed that sent Japanese Canadians to special camps. They had to leave behind virtually all their possessions. German Canadians and Italian Canadians did not have to move to these camps.
6. In some states in the United States, if a black person killed a white person, that person was almost always found guilty. If a white killed a black, that person was almost always found innocent.
7. In the United States, blacks were obliged by law to sit at the back of the bus.
8. In Israel, a Jew was walking down the street and was shot by a terrorist.
9. In some Middle Eastern countries women are forbidden to drive.
10. In England, three people were killed by a bomb planted by the Irish Republican Army.

Testers:

a. In Malaysia, if your hair is longer than a certain length (as shown by pictures in the banks) you will not be served until everyone else in the bank has been served.
b. In Canada, women did not have the right to vote by law, but men and most women accepted this law.
c. In North America, immigrant children are teased on the playground.
d. In North American schools, men hold over 90 percent of all administrative positions, although there are more women teachers than men.
e. As set out in legislation in some states and countries, women are not allowed to terminate a pregnancy without permission.
f. In Canada, we have created laws that support men and women being paid the same wage if they do the same job.

Now have the students connect their thinking to the concepts of apartheid and prejudice. They could now go back to a novel they are reading and discuss whether or not a specific incident is an example of apartheid. Or, they could identify examples in today's society. An interesting discussion would be to have them determine the relationship between teasing, prejudice, and apartheid. Is teasing what kids do, prejudice what adults do? Is apartheid normed prejudice?

Lesson B:
Economics
Concept Attainment
Integrated with
Cooperative Learning,
Inductive Thinking, Mind
Mapping, and Concept Mapping

SUBJECT AREA: Economics—Primary, Secondary and Tertiary Industries

GRADE: Seven

OBJECTIVE: Students will apply their understanding of Primary, Secondary, and Tertiary Industry by responding to questions asked in Phase III that arise from their initial Mind Map on industry.

Note: To start the lesson (the Mental Set or Activating Prior Knowledge) I constructed a Mind Map on a large piece of chart paper that illustrated their Brainstorming of all the things they could think of that connected to the idea of "industry." The purpose of this activity was to check to see what they understood or had lurking in the corners of their minds related to industry. (For more information on Mind Mapping, see Chapter 10.)

The following data set was then used, using "green" for the exemplars and "red" for the non-exemplars. The phases are explained following the data set.

Data Set for Concept Attainment Lesson on Industry	
Green	**Red**
Fish Farming	Banking
Fur Trapping	Restaurant
Ranching	Meat Packing Plant
Apple Orchards	Lumber Mill
Coal Mining	Furniture Factory
Oil Wells	Computer Assembly
Wheat Farm	Photocopying Store
Rubber Tree	High School
Plantation	Plumber
Rock Quarry	Carpentry
Diamond Mine	Veterinarian
	Hospital
	General Motors
	Radio Station
	Stock Broker

Testers:
Dairy Farming
Making Computer Chips
Teaching
Movie Theatre
Sport Fishing
Professional Baseball Team
Welfare Department

Explanation of the Phases

PHASE I: Provide a Focus Statement and present the data set

"Remembering the Mind Map, I would like you to continue focusing on industry. Try to identify what the items in the Green column have in common. Compare the Greens and contrast them with the items on the Red side. It doesn't matter if the item communicates the work is done indoors or outdoors.

PHASE II: Students share their thinking and their hypotheses

Once most students think they have the concept, have them share their thinking with their partner. This is where Cooperative Learning integrates effectively with Concept Attainment (C.A.). While working in Phase I, the "task" was individual; in Phase II, the "task" is small group. Now the students can start to dialogue around the essential characteristics (attributes) of the concept, and then begin to share the road map of their thinking from the first example to the last example (metacognition—thinking about one's thinking; intrapersonal intelligence).

PHASE III: Application and Extension of the concept

Note, at this point the students did not shift into Phase III of C.A.; rather, the students were put into small cooperative groups of three and flipped into Phase I and II of Taba's Inductive Thinking (see Chapter 9). The students grouped the Red Examples and again reflected on their thinking in order to pull out the concepts of secondary and tertiary industry. They then did Phase III of

Inductive Thinking and Phase III of Concept Attainment at the same time because Phase III is identical. Phase III involves the application and/or extension of the concepts attained or formed.

PHASE III: Application of the concept of Primary Industry

Now go back to the Mind Map and ask questions from their original thoughts about industry as they related to Primary, Secondary, and Tertiary industry.

For example:
- Where would you make the most money, Primary, Secondary, or Tertiary? (They couldn't come to an agreement—great arguments.)
- What is Canada? (They said, "Primary.")
- What is Japan? (They said, "Secondary.")
- Whose currency is worth more, Japan's or Canada's? (They said, "Japan.")
- Who is the most fragile, Japan or Canada? (They said, "Japan.")
- If Japan is most fragile, then what should Japan do? (They said, "Buy Canada.")
- What then should Canada do? (They said, "Nationalize." Teacher could respond with, *"Who would invest in Canada if it nationalized?"*).

When Phase III was finished, students constructed a Concept Map for homework (see Chapter 10 for information on Concept Maps). The next day they were put in groups of four and they presented their Concept Maps in their group using the cooperative group structure of Round Robin.

Lesson C: An Example of Concept Attainment used within a Lesson based on the Short Story "The Revolt of Mother"

Objective for the Concept Attainment process is to have students recognize the difference between colloquial and standard speech. This is important so that they are not confused with the irregular speech patterns illustrated in the story they are about to read. (Note that these students are low English ability students.) The Concept Attainment component was only a small piece in the overall lesson and fits into the Input Component described on the following page. Below is the Concept Attainment data set.

Concept Attainment Process—"The Revolt of Mother"

"Below you will see a set of sentences. The even numbered sentences (2, 4, 6, and 8) have something about them that the odd numbered sentences do not have. I am not going to tell you what that something might be.

With your partner, please read one odd numbered sentence and then one even numbered sentence. Please compare the odd numbers to see why they are the same and how they are different from the even numbered sentences. Please focus on how they are communicating information; do not focus on the length of the sentence or whether there is a man or women talking—that is not important."

1. "I wish you'd go into the house, Mother, and 'tend to your own affairs."
2. They were in the barn, standing before the wide open doors.
3. "You ain't going to build another barn. Why, we was going to have a house over there, Father."
4. "What are they digging for, Mother?"
5. "Didn't think it would do no good."
6. "I've got a letter from Hiram."
7. "Why don't do so, Father?"
8. " I had no idea this meant so much to you."

"Now, when you and your partner think you know the pattern, try the following testers."

TESTERS

"Which of the following sentences would follow the same pattern? Please explain why."
(Note that 1, 2, & 3 are all examples, number 4 is not.)

(1) "I ain't gonna go to school no more."
(2) " What on earth you all down here for?"
(3) "What'cha goin to school for?"
(4) "I don't want to go to school anymore"

Objective for the major part of the Lesson

To have students understand the idea of not compromising their standards or values and not giving up ... persevering to solve a problem. To understand how compromise often occurs by default. That is, when we are so close to someone we do not really know them as well as we thought we did; or, we took them for granted and never looked at the world through their eyes; or, we were never encouraged to persevere to solve a problem.

Note that you could also create a Concept Attainment data set on "Persevering to Solve a Problem." This data set could also be used below. Then tell the story and/or show the video and have the students make the connections and relate it to their life experiences.

SET:

Tell the students a story of a time when you wanted to say something or do something but you didn't, so you ended up going in a different direction. Now, ask the students to think of a time that they didn't want to do something but for whatever reason, they did not speak up and they ended up doing something they did not want to do. Have them share. (This is where the Round Robin cooperative learning structure can be woven into the lesson—groups of three or four.)

• Show the beginning of the Ghandi video, so students will recognize that Ghandi was put in a position to either compromise or act on his values and standards of what was right and what was wrong.

• Put students into groups of two and have them discuss. Did Ghandi speak up? Did he compromise or did he act? Then have them combine with one other group and have them share among the group of four. (The video clip refers to burning the travel passes.)

SHARE THE OBJECTIVE AND PURPOSE:

"Today we want to explore what it means not to compromise what you believe is important, by analyzing a story about a mother who decided things had to change."

INPUT:

1. Do a Concept Attainment lesson to clarify the language and irregular syntax in the story. Discuss why it is used. Check to make sure they understand.

2. Clarify any confusing terminology.

3. Read story. Have them discuss in groups how what the mother did was similar to what Ghandi did. Have them discuss the pros and cons of not compromising your values, etc.

4. Have them extend their learning in the closure by looking at the civil rights movement.

MODELLING:

This is found in the video clip, as well as, in the students' personal experiences and in the story of the mother's revolt.

Lesson continues on the next page

CHECK FOR UNDERSTANDING:

Have the students discuss in their groups the essence of the story "The Revolt of Mother" and what it means by not compromising one's beliefs or standards. (Note you could also show the clip from the movie *Stand and Deliver*, about a high school math teacher.)

CONCEPT ATTAINMENT: NOT COMPROMISING ONE'S VALUES

Focus Statement – Determine what human stance is illustrated by the statements on the left.

1. Ivan knew that he had to study to pass the exam so he did not go to the show with his friends.
2. "No thanks, I'm not drinking. I am the designated driver."
3. "I don't care if you don't talk to me again. Teasing him is wrong."
4. Even though Dolci wanted to go with her friends, she didn't. Instead she visited her grandmother who was lonely.

1. "Well, I shouldn't be late for supper, but I guess we could play one more game of pool."
2. "I know smoking is bad for my health, but I'm nervous, so maybe I'll have one."
3. Even though she believed gossip was wrong, she did it because her friends did it.
4. "I know it's cheating but I need to copy your answer. I went to the hockey game last night and didn't do mine."

TESTERS

a) Although she would be late for school, Jan made sure her little dog Ana was fed before she left for school.

b) Adam knew he should not have stolen the radio, but then his friends would have thought he was a chicken.

CLOSURE:

"We have just discussed the idea of not compromising what you believe, what you want to say, what you want to do. Go back to the beginning of the lesson when I asked you to think of one thing you are currently doing that you would prefer not to do. How would you have acted if you had not compromised your standards or values? Think for 15 seconds. Would any of you like to share?" (Note that active participation was not invoked because this is a personal response.)

What is Inductive Thinking?

Thinking can be classified into a variety of types: creative thinking, critical thinking, divergent thinking, convergent thinking, etc. The classification that Concept Attainment fits most logically into is Critical Thinking. In most critical thinking texts, critical thinking is divided into Deductive and Inductive thinking. With deductive, we often think of science or of detective work (e.g., trying to find a cure for a disease or the person who stole the jewelry). With inductive, we can also think of science and detective work (e.g., trying to classify insects into groups based on common characteristics or looking for a pattern in a series of robberies to predict where they might hit next).

Concept Attainment is an inductive strategy that encourages students to look for patterns, to hunt for characteristics. The brain research tells us the brain enjoys searching for patterns. In the next chapter we introduce another inductive strategy called "Inductive Thinking." The difference between the two is that in Concept Attainment the teacher provides the group of ideas already classified—the students simply have to study what the group of ideas have in common and tease out the characteristics.

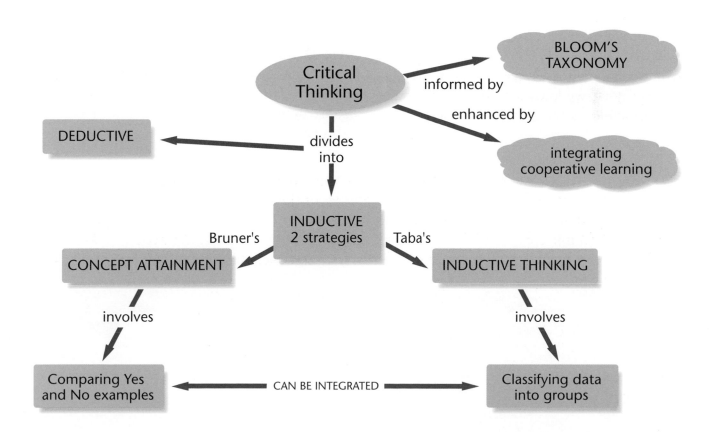

An Explanation of Concept Attainment

What is it? Concept Attainment is an inductive process that helps bring meaning to concepts or helps construct concepts through the searching for common characteristics (called attributes). In Concept Attainment, the student compares like examples and contrasts them with unlike examples.

Those characteristics can be applied to distinguish examples of a concept from non-examples of that concept. For example, to distinguish "metaphor" from other literary techniques such as simile, hyperbole, oxymoron, etc.

Why use it: One role the teacher plays is to engage students in thinking related to concepts; to help them meaningfully grasp the design of a concept; to own it; to think and be creative with it. The reason for this is that our understanding of concepts is how we represent what we know; it brings meaning to facts, principles, systems, theorems, etc.

You could argue that for every concept the students do not understand, the less likely they are to understand the meaning of the fact, or principle, or whatever. Obviously some concepts are more important or more complex than others. The teacher's role is to decide what concepts need to be understood in order to bring clarity to thinking. So, the **science** of teaching is, in part, represented by the instructional strategy of Concept Attainment; the **art** is represented, in part, by the decisions of when to employ it given the nature of the learner.

David Perkins's (1986) work on **Knowledge as Design** vs. **Knowledge as Information** connects to the thinking process involved in Concept Attainment. He states that when students are learning concepts, they should be able to respond to four questions related to the design of that concept. This pushes the idea of actively constructing knowledge rather than passively absorbing it.

Take something as simple as this widely accepted *fact,* "Christopher Columbus sailed the ocean blue in 1492."

Embedded in that fact are the concepts of:
- explorer
- sailed
- colour – blue
- ocean
- A.D. – year

David Perkins's ideas regarding "Knowledge as Design" are discussed on the following page.

David Perkins' work on Knowledge as Design

4 Questions

1. What are the critical attributes of the concept?
2. What are the purposes of the concept?
3. What are model cases of the concept?
4. What are the arguments for learning the concept?

For example, we can explore the design of the concept **"Screwdriver"** using Perkins' 4 questions:

1. Attributes — it has a handle, a shaft and an end that fits into a screw
2. Purpose — it is designed to put in screws
3. Model cases — flat head, Robertson, Phillips
4. Argument — it gives us mechanical advantage

MORE INFORMATION AHEAD

Now it gets tougher....

Another example, the concept of **"Disagreeing in an Agreeable Way"**

1. Attributes	Letting a person know that they might not be right in such a way as to encourage dialogue and resolution or search for clarity as opposed to resentment and polarized arguments.
2. Purpose	It focuses on an issue without ruining a relationship.
3. Model cases	"I see your point; can I share one thing that I think you might not have considered?" "I understand why you are upset, but you have not asked me why I did what I did." "I am sorry you feel that way; nonetheless, I believe you have made a mistake. Would you like to know, or should we just forget it?"
4. Argument	It promotes discussion as opposed to shutting it down. It works to depolarize a situation. It promotes inquiry into issues rather than narrow-minded exploration of one side of an issue.

Increasing the Complexity: Integrated Lessons

Now it begins to get more complex—and the lessons more powerful. On the following page is a lesson that involved part of a one-month unit on a novel study that incorporated having the students become more conscious of the cognitive demand of questions. Students began to generate questions and to classify them based on the type of thinking. This data set was designed to have them begin to pull their thinking together and make a connection to Bloom's Taxonomy after they had constructed and applied their own taxonomy.

The strategies involved are	Tactics	Skills	Concepts
Concept Attainment Lesson Design Inductive Thinking Mind Mapping Cooperative Learning (5 basic elements)	Think Pair Share	Framing Questions - covert to overt Wait Time	Accountability Active Participation Safe Classroom

Note: More instructional expertise occured in this lesson than those ideas listed above, but these were the ideas that were consciously integrated and adapted as the lesson evolved. This is what a teacher does who is consciously skilled.

Simple example of the Concept Attainment Process —Grades 5 to 8 then moves to Inductive Thinking and ends with a Mind Mapping activity which is done in Cooperative Groups

Concept Attainment: Levels of Thinking

Explanation: This data set was designed as an introduction to getting students to think at different levels of complexity. The teacher has 2 initial objectives: (1) to extend the students' clarity of the idea of recall level questions (a simple activity and one where they would experience success); and (2) to extend their understanding of other types of questions by having them classify the 10 NO examples and testers that are not Recall examples into other levels of thinking (the Inductive Thinking strategy). In this case the students are building their own taxonomy for classifying. When finished, they will complete a Mind Map on their Taxonomy. Later (about 2 or 3 weeks) the students will do a simple Jigsaw on Bloom's Taxonomy and compare their taxonomy to Bloom's. During this next two weeks, each time a student is asked a question, the student must first identify the cognitive demand of the question before giving the answer (e.g., "That is an evaluation level question, here is my answer ....").

Remember Bloom's Taxonomy?

- Knowledge/Recall
- Comprehensim/Understanding
- Application
- Analysis
- Synthesis
- Evaluation

Directions: On the following page are two sets of questions/requests. The first ten represent a specific type of thinking. The next ten do not. With a partner, decide what the first ten have in common. Then take turns discussing the testers. Make sure you are both prepared to share your hypothesis as to what the first ten have in common re their cognitive demand. You will be randomly called upon to share your thinking.

Note: you could do the same lesson for a grade 9 to 12 class by changing the questions.

WHAT DO THESE HAVE IN COMMON?

1. Name 2 monsters that are destroyed by mythical heroes.
2. List examples of pollution we might find in our community.
3. How many legs does a spider have?
4. Share with your partner the different types of triangles we have studied.
5. What are the parts of a flower?
6. What are the provinces of Canada and each of their capital cities?
7. Identify the primary colours.
8. Can someone repeat the definition of an island that Sari gave yesterday?
9. Brainstorm as many types of transportation as you can in three minutes. Go.
10. Think to yourself and then share with a partner. What are three social skills that we have been practising?

OTHER TYPES of THINKING

1. As a citizen of this school, write a letter to a friend describing what you are doing in your school to work against bullying.
2. Explain in your own words the role of the sun in the life cycle of all living things.
3. Given what you know about war, where do you think it starts and why?
4. Which has a greater affect on our emotions-music or sports?
5. Share with your partner examples of things in this room that are symmetrical.
6. Graph the number of times you have had junk food during this week. At the end we will explain the implications this has for your health.
7. With your partner, discuss the difference between teasing and prejudice.
8. Identify a food that you do not like. Now, you are an inventor, think of one other food that you blend with this food to make it more likeable.
9. People in cities should not be allowed to have pet dogs and cats. In your pairs, person A will argue YES; person B will argue NO.
10. Provide your own examples of where light gets refracted into rainbows.

TESTERS

a. Name three study skills you could use to help you pass the test.
b. Assess the quality of food served at McDonalds based on the four food groups. Based on that assessment, you are going to compete with McDonalds with your franchise—what would you put on your menu and why?
d. In what ways are the nomads in Afghanistan and street people the same?
e. Take what you understand about multiplication, and find a quicker way to find out the cost of washing the windows on that eight-storey building.
f. Identify the five most recent prime ministers, and decide which one has had the biggest impact on shaping Canada's identity.

CHECK FOR UNDERSTANDING
Randomly call on pairs to have them explain their thinking.

EXTENSION/SHARE NEW OBJECTIVE AND PURPOSE:
(Inductive Thinking)

Hand out scissors. Have person A cut the NO examples and the Testers that are NO examples into strips. "We are now going to take you a bit deeper into understanding the complexity of questions. If you understand what questions are asking you to do, then you are more likely to respond more precisely."

PHASE 1.

"With your partner, group the strips into categories based on other types of thinking. There is no right or wrong number of groups; be prepared to justify why you put them into the groups you did. Please do not group them by subject matter—that is not important—rather focus on the type of thinking. Remember that the YES examples were simply asking you to recall memorized information. The NO examples push thinking into more complex areas."

PHASE 2.

Students paste their strips onto a larger board, identify the characteristics that each group has in common, and then provide a label that represents this type of thinking. When finished, they meet with one other group and exchange ideas. They then tape them to the wall and do a Gallery Tour. This allows them to compare their thinking with other groups.

PHASE 3.

Students now go back to their novels and read. As they are reading, they have to design questions that relate to their novel and that fit each of their categories. Although they work alone, they check with their partner each time they design a question.

CLOSURE:

Students will construct a **Mind Map** working with their partner to communicate their Taxonomy of Thinking. These will go on the wall for other students to check. These will be used as the reference point to compare their thinking with Bloom's Taxonomy later in the unit.

The students focus on Equal Participation in the Mind Mapping process and at the end of the lesson they process how well they did in involving each other in the Mind Map. (Note: this ties into David and Roger Johnsons' work on Cooperative Learning covered in Chapter 7.)

On the next page is a more complex grade 12 English example of Instructional Integration.

A Complex Example of Integrating Concept Attainment with a Variety of Instructional Processes
Purpose: to Extend Students' Understanding of the Use of Figures of Speech

The Strategies are: Concept Attainment, Cooperative Learning, Inductive Thinking, Mind Maps, Lesson Design

The Organizers are: Multiple Intelligence, Learning Styles, Motivation, Levels of Thinking

The Tactics are: Think/Pair/Share

The Skills are: Sharing the objective and purpose of the lesson, framing questions, wait time, checking for understanding, modelling, practice

---

The Lesson:

MENTAL SET/OBJECTIVE:

"We have been exploring the writing process. You asked if we could spend some time trying to establish more clarity about what figures of speech mean and from that to create a more organized understanding of the techniques writers employ to create images in the reader's mind."

"To do this you will be working alone, in small groups, and as a class. Could you please sit with your partner? If yours is not here, join another person whose partner is not here or form a group of three. I will hand out a sheet that has the directions."

DIRECTIONS AND DATA SET:

"On the next page is a data set that consists of YES and NO examples. Both sets contain examples of techniques that writers, for a variety of reasons, employ to create images in the readers' minds (e.g., to paint with words so as to make meanings clear or exciting)."

"All the YES examples represent one specific technique. First, by yourself, read the YES and NO examples. Then, with your partner, read aloud one YES and then one NO. Go back and forth until you have read the first five examples. See if you can find what all the YES examples have in common that allow us to classify them as one specific writing technique."

"Once you have done the first five examples on your own, discuss with your partner if you have an idea. Once you and your partner have completed the YES and NO examples and have a hypothesis, try the testers."

1. She stared intently into his eyes *like an optometrist seeking a flaw.*

2. ...I woke up early in our family's large, quiet, shabby Ottawa house and looked straight up at the ceiling where there was a long circular crack shaped *like the hunch in an old crone's back, high and rounded at the top, then tapering down.*

3. Now that I have circled around sorrow, time and again, and can read my life *as a map drawn with wrong turnings*, now that I haven't a trace of self pity and can review my life without emotion because I have found a little peace, all I regret is the loss of innocence.

4. This nameless wind scraping the Rock *with an edge like steel.*

5. Petal Bear was crosshatched with longings, but not, after they were married, for Quolye. Desire reversed to detestation *like a rubber glove turned inside out.*

6. They shudder with the heat of their own dramas, awestruck by the doubleness of memory, the hold it has on them, *as mysterious as telephone wires or the halo around the head of the baby Jesus.*

7. For fate had long ago taken a shine to Tert Card, filled him *like a cream horn with itch and irritation.* His middle initial was X. Face *like cottage cheese clawed with a fork.*

8. He and Alice and Joan are joined together *like the little dolls Alice cuts out of newspaper*, that's how he thinks of himself and his sisters. He's located there in the middle, always in the middle, the one who was born in the early days of the war....

9. Memory could be poked with a stick, savored in the mouth *like a Popsicle*, you could never get enough of it.

10. Today the fog was *as dense as cotton waste*, carried a coldness that ate into the bones.

11. Diddy Shovel's skin was *like asphalt, fissured and cracked, thickened by a lifetime of weather, the scurf of age.* Stubble worked through the craquelured surface. His eyelids collapsed in protective folds at the outer corners.

12. "Seventy years young and they're forcing me out. Intend to learn how to play the banjo. If I can keep from bursting the strings. Sometimes I don't know me own strength. What about you?" Flexed his fingers, making the joints pop like knotwood in a fire. Showed a little finger *like a parsnip.*

NO Examples:

1. "Suppose we might 'ave a cup of tea," he murmured Yark, first wiping his nose on the back of his hand, then leaning over the *shavings to snort out sawdust and snot.* Sang his bit of song, "Oh it ain't no use, 'cause every nut and bolt is loose."

2. The looming wall tipped at Sunshine who scrambled up and ran, *deliciously frightened.*

3. *The sky a net*, its mesh clogged with glowing stars.

4. *A crack, a whistle as a cable snapped.* Glass burst. The house slewed on grating sills. *The cables shrilled.*

5. Henry, rigid in his blankets, experienced immensity, *became a solitary ant* in a vast ball.

6. Or is love something less, something slippery and odorless, a transparent gas riding through the world on the back of a breeze, or else—and this is what he more and more believes—*just a word trying to remember another word.*

7. Her present *sinking of spirit, the manic misrule* of her heart and head, the ounering of her reason, the decline of her physical health—all these stem from some mysterious suffering core which those around her can only register and weigh and speculate about.

8. I'd only been home a few days when I realized she was relishing all this, the pure and beautiful force of her hatred for Pinky Fulham, the ecstasy of being wronged. There's a certain majesty in it. Nothing in her life has delivered her to such a pitch of intensity—why wouldn't she love it, *this exquisite wounding*, the salt of *perfect pain.*

9. What has it been? I make it twenty years. Lordy, it does go by, *time that is, the filthy robber.* And Alice off to college next fall! And all this so soon after your dad dying.

10. And a damned good chance of drowning all alone in the *freezing boil.*

11. I liked him as soon as I heard the calmness of his *mind's metaphorical memories.*

12. The tuckamore all black tangle, *the cliff a funeral stele.*

13. "Poor thing," said the aunt, inspecting Sunshine's red knees. The waitress came across the worn carpet, *one of her shoes sighing as she walked.*

14. I came because of Hemingway, in search of *my manhood, the myth of the macho*, the definition of masculinity, pride in the muscles and endurance I acquired during training, wanting to prove my valor, because at heart I always suspected I am a coward....

15. A curtain moved in the window of the house behind *the rioting wooden zoo.*

1. At sixteen he was buried under a casement of flesh. Head shaped like a crenshaw, no neck, reddish hair ruched back. *Features as bunched as kissed fingertips.* Eyes the color of plastic. The monstrous chin, a freakish shelf jutting from the lower face.

2. *As if it had been waiting for the seasons to be pronounced the snow started*, flicking a few grains against the windows.

3. *These trousers carry an odor of sanctity*, as well as a pattern of symmetrical whisker-like creases across the front.

4. ...the age gap became her hobby and profession, being a young wife to an older husband - it kept her girlish, *made her a kind of tenant in the tower of girlhood.* There she remained, safe, looked after.

5. During the night *a warm fluke, a tongue of balmy air, licked out* from the mainland and tempered the crawling ice margins.

6. Do you remember that day last October when I experienced my first terrible headache? I found you in the kitchen wearing one of those new and dreadful plastic aprons. You put your arms around me at once and reached up to smooth my temples. I loved you terribly at that moment. *The crackling of your apron against my body seemed like an operatic response to the longings, which even then I felt. It was like something whispering at us to hurry*, to stop wasting time, and I would like to have danced with you through the back door, out into the garden, down the street, over the line of the horizon. Oh, my dear. I thought we would have more time.

7. *People like to think of memory as a low-lying estuary*, but *my memories of myself are more like a ruffed-up lake*, battering against the person I became. A nice person.

8. He had never had his boat in such rough water. The swells came at him broadside from the mouth of the bay, *crests like cruel smiles.* The boat rolled, rose up, dropped with sickening speed into the troughs.

9. These waters, thought Quoyle, haunted by lost ships, fishermen, explorers gurgled down into *sea holes as black as a dog's throat.*

10. *Was love like a bag of assorted sweets passed around from which one might choose more than once?* Some might sting the tongue, some invoke night perfume. *Some had centers as bitter as gall*, some blended honey and poison, some were quickly swallowed.

11. Imagined wind in his inner eye, saw its directions in the asymmetrical shapes of windstars on old maps, roses of wind whose elongated *points pictured prevailing* airs.

INPUT AND MODELLING CONTINUED:

"Now with your partner, take the TESTERS that were not similes, along with the NO examples and group them into categories based on other figures of speech or techniques that writers employ, you may want to cut them into strips with the scissors provided." (Note: this is the Inductive Thinking strategy - Concept Formation—see Chapter 9).

CLOSURE:

When finished classifying that data, the students create a Mind Map of all the figures of speech—Mind Mapping assists them to remember. They can do this alone or in small cooperative groups. They will then take a sample reading from Anne Proulx's book *Shipping News* and Carol Shield's book *Stone Diaries* and identify examples of each of the figures of speech and the effect they had on them as readers. They will be asked to share that effect using the Cooperative Learning structure of Inside Outside Circles. (You could also use a number of other cooperative structures such as Round Robin or Community Circles.) In addition, you could ask them to identify what they think is the most powerful example and be prepared to debate why.

EXTENSION:

(This is designed to illustrate how figures of speech can be integrated—used simultaneously—much like how this lesson integrates a variety of strategies. The first YES example employs: simile, personifica-tion, alliteration and oxymoron.)

The teacher now finishes with another Concept Attainment lesson employing the following data set. *"Focus on what the YES examples have in common. Both YES and NO examples are examples of figures of speech, but the YES examples are special. Compare the YES examples and contrast them with the NO examples. Take 3 minutes working alone. Then I will give you a minute to share with your partner, before randomly calling on some of you to share."*

Yes:	No:
Crests like cruel smiles glanced above the bow.	Dancing across the keys *his fingers sighed disdain* towards complexity.
Shriekingly silent the ship slipped beneath the surface	The pencil, *guided by a mind of its own,* turned me into an instant genious.
One of her *shoes sighing as she walked*	his *mind's metaphorical memories*
A curtain moved in the window of the house behind *the rioting wooden zoo.*	Drowning all alone *in the freezing boil*

TESTERS:

- People like to think of memory *as a low-lying estuary*
- Sea holes *as dark as a dying dog's throat*
- His mind raced *like freshly frozen ooze*
- He was a *simpleton seduced by the sinister side of knowing.*

Activity: You Play the Game

Given you have been involved in the Concept Attainment process since birth and if you are a parent, you have no doubt done several hundred of these mini-Concept Attainment processes. Let's see what you remember.

First, as we mentioned earlier, everything you can see, touch, feel, smell, and do is a concept. Look around you, there are hundreds of concepts: rough, red, round, parallel, chair, patterned, soft, flexible, ring, container, floor, light fixture, tall, old, straight, yuppie, warm, aloof, things you write on, and things with which you communicate. Identify one concept and then find four examples in the room that you could go and touch. For example, take the concept of, "communication": mouth, hands, pen, pictures. Now find four NO examples (socks, purse, coffee mug, and floor). Now find three testers: eyes, print, and wallet. You are now ready for the game.

ACADEMIC TASK: To apply your current understanding of the process of Concept Attainment by teaching a concept using the Concept Attainment process. (Note: this lesson is designed for people who are working in small cooperative groups. If you are alone, follow the steps and then find someone who will allow you to practise with them.)

COLLABORATIVE TASK: *To reflect on the action as it is occurring.* That means attempting to determine what the steps of the process should be, **OR**, if you are familiar with Concept Attainment, to decide where and how critical thinking tactics and/or other models of teaching such as Concept Formation and Cooperative Learning can be integrated with Concept Attainment.

DIRECTIONS:

1. Find a partner (or do this alone if you have no partner) and look around the room...there are hundreds of concepts. Pick a concept (make sure you can provide the label and the attributes of that concept) and design four YES and four NO examples of that concept. Then find three testers; they can all be NO or YES examples or a mix. Take 15 minutes to construct the data set and decide how you will present your data set to two other groups.

2. When instructed to move, get together with two other pairs (this will give you a group of six) and take the other four people through what you believe is the process of Concept Attainment. Share your YES and NO examples, and when they think they have an idea, have them share it and then try the testers.

3. When finished, discuss with your group of six what happened. Do any additional components need to be added to make Concept Attainment work? If you are familiar with other models of teaching such as Cooperative Learning or Inductive Thinking, discuss how they could be integrated. As you discuss, make sure everyone's voice is heard.

4. Compare your analysis with the steps on the following page.

pair's hypotheses, the pairs shared their hypotheses with the small group where they were seated. Then each group presented one or two of their hypotheses to the class. A final tester was presented to the class and the same method of discussion was used as the first tester. In the small groups each group came up with one hypothesis and labelled the common attribute found in all the YES examples.

PHASE 3: THE APPLICATION AND EXTENDING OF THEIR THINKING ABOUT THE CONCEPT

Since this was the first time my students had ever done Concept Attainment, I collected their thoughts about how they felt their thinking had progressed during the analysis of the data. Many of my students were confused at the beginning with trying to figure out the common attribute. They attributed this to focusing on the whole sentence rather than breaking the sentences up. They sometimes found that the content was distracting because they would switch their train of thought from the focus statement of "looking how the sentences were formed and connected to one another" to looking for similarities in the sentences content. Many students broke the sentences up into parts and looked at how each sentence began. They enjoyed discussing how individuals came up with their hypotheses because they were able to see how different people look at and solve similar situations.

Satisfied with the hypotheses presented by the students, we went on to an application of the concept since the students now had a basic understanding of transitional words and phrases. Students then worked on creating a paragraph, linking sentences together with transitional words and phrases.

The sentences and transition words were all glued onto individual popsicle sticks so that the students could manipulate them and try out different combinations without having to write them down every time. When students were happy with their final paragraph they wrote down every other line on a piece of paper and then had a fellow student edit it.

Another follow-up activity to the Concept Attainment was given to the students as homework. It was to take one of the NO examples and turn it into a YES example.

PERSONAL REFLECTIONS

My Concept Attainment lesson went very well. I attribute a lot of the success of the lesson to the data set. I created my examples around the grade eight subculture, using popular television/movie stars and musical groups. I found by using peoples' names the students knew and liked captivated and maintained their attention more effectively than having content that they were unfamiliar with.

Several positive outcomes resulted from my lesson. First, students were very enthusiastic about the lesson and enjoyed the challenge of trying to determine the concept being presented. They viewed the lesson as a game and, consequently, I saw more participation. Second, all my students were thinking. I could see all of them thinking when I allowed for silent reflection. They were very eager to share their thoughts and hypotheses when it came to sharing with a partner or group. As well, because time was given to think in between exemplars, I found that I received more responses from all my students, including my special education students. The lesson flowed very smoothly. I found myself more comfortable with the lesson since I could see all my students engaged in the lesson. The progression through the three phases of a Concept Attainment lesson seemed so natural.

After completing the lesson I asked my students what they thought about the lesson, specifically what I should continue, stop or start. The students were very positive towards the lesson. They said that they enjoyed being taught this way as opposed to being lectured to or reading about concepts in a textbook. They felt that the concept was easier to learn and understand as they were able to create and change hypotheses depending on the examples that they saw. They weren't presented with one example of the concept and then told how to use transitional words and phrases. Rather, they liked the fact that they were presented with more than one example and that they were given non-examples of the concept. By giving both positive and negative examples not only did they find it easier to identify the concept being taught, but they also found it easier to understand the concept since they could actually see when transition words were used and not used.

There were only a couple of difficulties students had with the lesson. One was that sometimes I used vocabulary that they were unfamiliar with, for example "attribute." Although I later defined "attribute", I should have explained what an attribute was when I was introducing the lesson. Another problem students had was they had difficulty remembering to stick to the focus statement. Some students tended to drift away from the focus statement and focus on some other aspect of the sentences. I tried to correct this by repeating the focus statement each time I had them thinking or sharing their hypotheses. I think that with time and continued practice with Concept Attainment this problem would be solved.

Many of my high achieving students showed signs of understanding early in the activity. A couple of them began to fidget throughout the remainder of the lesson. Next time if I see this happening (or I could set it up before the lesson) I may have them sit next to a special needs student. That way if they see the special needs student struggling they can help, not by giving the answer but by asking appropriate questions to help guide the special needs student in figuring out the common attribute.

Another thing I would do differently next time if teaching this to a class who has never done Concept Attainment before, is give a simple data set first and work through the three phrases of concept attainment with the class. That way students would have more of an understanding of the process and what to do, and how to go about finding the commonality among the YES examples.

Remember: It will likely take 15-20 practices before you and your students own Concept Attainment and it doesn't own you!

A description of each of the 3 phases of Bruner's Concept Attainment Strategy

PHASE 1 - PRESENTATION OF THE DATA AND THE IDENTIFICATION OF THE CONCEPT (WITH FOCUS STATEMENT) ...
note this is similar to phase one of Hilda Taba's Inductive Thinking Strategy.

The teacher provides a focus statement prior to presenting the data set to guide the students' thinking. It can contain both *what* and *what not* to focus on.

For example, if the concept attainment lesson was to be on 'sonnets', or Haiku poetry, then the teacher might say, "I am going to present you with examples of a specific type of poetry. All the examples under the YES side have a certain quality. The NO side, although also forms of poetry, do not have the same characteristics. Please compare the YES examples and contrast them with the NO examples. Do not focus on the subject matter or the type of print, only focus on the structure or design of the poems."

Next, the teacher presents the examples and the students compare the attributes of the YES examples and contrast them with the NO examples.

Here the teacher has several options, each of which invites the students to think differently. One option is to show one YES or one NO example, and slowly build the data set; another option is to

simultaneously provide all the examples in two columns. You can also provide the examples in a mixed list with a explanation of which ones are YES and NO examples.

In the last part of this first phase, the students generate and test their hypothesis as the data set is presented or as they scan the data set (at first covertly and by themselves, and then overtly with partners).

The students are usually provided with individual quiet time for the first analysis of the data set. If the data is built slowly in pairs, the students are presented with approximately four pairs before they are asked if they have an hypothesis—this provides some safe time to think without students calling out "I got it" or "That's easy." When most of the students seem to have an idea, the teacher can then have them share their hypothesis either with a partner and then with the class, or with the class directly. We encourage the students to share with a partner first. If the data set is provided all at once, allow the students to work individually until they have an idea or hypothesis to share. Note: when they share they should just listen to their partners' ideas and not pass judgement. Just listen and say, "Thank you."

Phase 2 is described on the following page

PHASE 2 - TESTING THE ATTAINMENT OF THE CONCEPT

(This is like phase 2 of Taba's Inductive Thinking Strategy. This is where the students can apply some of the critical thinking skills—see the appendix for a list of critical thinking skills.)

Once about half of the students have developed hypotheses, you can have students identify a few **unlabelled** examples to determine whether they are YES or NO examples. (Note: at first the students can think privately, and then they can begin to share their ideas.)

Note: if members of the class are undecided as to whether the example is a YES or a NO, we suggest you place it in the middle and come back and discuss it later after the students have brought some clarity to the concept. This is similar to what happens when we use the VENN DIAGRAM option where the circles overlap.

For example, once most of the students think they have an idea or an hypothesis, the teacher provides testers to allow students to confirm, refine, or refute their hypotheses. At this point, how you frame your questions is critical to the success and participation of all students. To illustrate that point, notice the difference in student accountability when you ask these three questions:

(1) "Gilda, tell me whether this is a YES or a NO"
(2) "Who can tell me whether this is a YES or a NO?"
(3) "Think to yourself please, and be prepared to share your decision with a partner; remember, don't evaluate the other person's thinking, just listen, say thank you, and then share your idea. Is this a YES or a NO? (5 second wait time). Okay, person A tell person B and then person B tell person A."

The first and second questions do not hold the students accountable. The third question does by integrating into the process the Cooperative-Learning structure of Think/Pair/Share and one element of the Johnsons' approach to Cooperative Learning—the element of a social skill. In this case, the communication skill of non-evaluative feedback was employed.

Now they are ready for Phase 3 - Applying the Concept.

When most students have shared their hypotheses, the teacher then sets up a situation that confirms or eliminates hypotheses through asking questions about the students' hypotheses and providing additional examples. At this time, the label can be provided if students do not have the label, and the students can state their definitions according to the attributes identified.

PHASE 3 - ANALYSIS OF THINKING STRATEGIES AND EXTENDING OF THE THINKING RELATED TO THE CONCEPT

Students now describe their thoughts about how their thinking progressed during their analysis of the data.

Note: the students' thinking will depend on how the data were presented. If the data were presented in ordered pairs, they will either select one or two hypotheses and constantly review the data. Or, they may generate multiple hypotheses, and then slowly eliminate hypotheses. If the students are provided with the complete data set (including positive and negative exemplars) they are more likely to scan the data and select a few hypotheses with which to operate.

Next, Students discuss the relationship between their hypothesis and the attributes of the concept.

Here the students look at the connection between the concept and the attributes, and discuss how important the essential and non-essential attributes are in defining the concept.

Students extend their thinking related to the concept.

At this point the students have an understanding of the concept. Now you can choose to have them apply the concept and/or to extend their thinking with the concept.

Note: Older students will be able to recall the development of their hypotheses, changes they made, and the reasons they made the changes. This provides an interesting map of how they were thinking. Students often enjoy hearing the different ways students come up with ideas as well as the different ideas. Younger students are less able to do this. For the first few times, have the students use a Thinking Sheet such as the one below to record their thinking processs as they go along.

Thinking Sheet

Each time you see an example and a non-example, quickly write down what you think makes the YES examples special—what they have in common—how they are the same. If you are not sure, just put an 'O' in the space. When another idea comes along, quickly write that idea down in the next space. At the end, you can see how your thinking changed.

1. _____

2. _____

3. _____

4. _____

5. _____

6. _____

7. _____

8. _____

9. _____

10. _____

See a variation of how a recording sheet was employed in the following lesson.

Chemistry Lesson: Investigating Chemical Change

By: Carolynn Scholtz
Designed for a Grade 9 Academic Class

PHASE I: PRESENT THE FOCUS STATEMENT AND THE DATA SET

By the end of this lesson it is expected that students should be able to describe, through observations, the evidence for chemical changes (e.g., changes in colour, production of a gas, formation of a precipitate, production or absorption of heat, production of light).

I wanted the students to think about what they observed during the reaction and to record their observations using descriptive words. In order to focus the students' thinking I had the students set up a data table in their notebooks with the following headings:

YES examples			NO examples		
Description of components *before* reaction	Description of components *after* reaction	Description of components *during* reaction	Description of components *before* reaction	Description of components *after* reaction	Description of components *during* reaction

I used demonstrations to present the data set to the students. I presented one pair of examples at a time. The following data set was used:

YES examples	NO examples
Lighting a match	Boiling water
A rusty tin can	Shredding a newspaper
Adding magnesium metal to hydrochloric acid (followed by a gas test)	Cutting a carrot
Mixing copper sulfate and sodium hydroxide	Stretching an elastic band
Burning toast	Dissolving salt in water

After presenting the data set I had the students review the observations they had made in their tables. From their observations I asked them to write down a list of characteristics to describe the YES examples. This was done silently and independently. When all students had completed the list I then presented the testers to them. I instructed the students to record their observations and, based on the observations, decide whether it was a YES example or a NO example. They did this independently and silently. The following are the testers I used:

TESTER #1 Burning of magnesium metal
TESTER #2 Oranges to orange juice

Phase II: Sharing their hypotheses and their thinking

For this phase of the lesson the students did a Think Pair Share activity. I instructed the students to decide by themselves where they thought the two testers belonged. Next they turned to their lab partner and discussed where they placed the two testers and why. As a pair they were to come to an agreement as to which group Tester #1 and Tester #2 belonged. After the students were done I randomly selected groups to discuss their conclusions. After the discussion the students regrouped with their partners and together came up with a definition to describe all of the reactions in the YES group. Through their own investigation they were able to define chemical change.

Phase III: Application or extension of the concept

As a class we reviewed the formal definition of a chemical change and the clues or evidence that indicated that a chemical change had occurred. As an extension of the concept the students carried out a lab in the next class which investigated physical and chemical changes. I set the lab up as a 10 station lab in which the students got the opportunity to conduct mini experiments and develop their inquiry skills such as recording observations in a proper data table and analyzing observations. In preparation for the lab, I sent students home with worksheets to practise identifying chemical changes. This gave me an opportunity to check for understanding before they performed the lab.

My First Attempt at a Concept Attainment Lesson

I was very happy with my first attempt at a concept attainment lesson. The students were very receptive and thoroughly enjoyed the lesson. One of the students said, "I like the way you taught us. We learned something but it didn't feel like learning." Another student remarked "The demos were cool. I liked how we figured out what we were supposed to be learning without you lecturing us." From a previous survey I already knew the students found the classes where I did notes BORING! By having the students involved in the teaching process, they were more attentive and genuinely interested in completing the data table. I knew my lesson was successful when the students picked out the clues that indicated a chemical change. Although they did not know what they were defining until after the fact, their definitions were pretty close to what I would have given them. When I told them that they all had a definition in their notebooks for a chemical change, it was as if I had given them a puzzle to figure out and they got the right answer. We did review the definition and a complete list of clues to a chemical change to make sure their notes were complete.

On the following page are **3** types of concepts

1. conjunctive
2. dysjunctive
3. relational

Three types of concepts from Bruner's perspective

The idea of "Concept" can be categorized into three additional concepts. Understanding the three types will help you design and critique your concept attainment lessons.

Rather than tell you what they are, let's do an inductive analysis—given this chapter is about inductive thinking. Examples of the three concepts are provided below. Read each of the columns. Pick any one column and contrast it with the other two. When you have an idea of what the attributes are of that column go to the testers below and determine what examples fit under that column. Do the same with the other two columns. Note that some examples can fit into more than one column.

> **Note:** in the three columns below, the concepts in column **b** will be an easier place for you and the students to start developing data sets for the Concept Attainment process—concepts in columns **a** and **c** are usually more difficult

A	B	C
1. love	1. car	1. deep
2. justice	2. leaf	2. strong
3. symbolism	3. cup	3. rough
4. equality	4. hug	4. easy

Testers: computer, huge, opposite, hypothesis, insect, soft, prejudice, controversial, radio, democracy, gravity, normal

We would put controversial under column a; computer, hypothesis, radio, democracy, insect, and gravity under column b; and huge, opposite, and soft under column c. Normal could most likely fit under all three, as could prejudice.

What are other examples of these three types of concepts from your curricular area(s)?

See the next page for an explanation of the three types of concepts.

Dysjunctive, Conjunctive, and Relational Concepts

(Remember some concepts can fit into more than one category.)

Note: For a productive teacher activity, divide into groups of three and Jigsaw these 3 terms.

A. DYSJUNCTIVE

(with no common juncture):
Concepts in this category have exemplars that have nothing in common and are therefore more difficult for students to analyze for common characteristics.

For example, take symbolism: what does a wedding ring, a Hell's Angels Jacket, a Mercedes car decal, and a flag have in common? (very little) Concepts of this type are perhaps a bit more abstract and the teacher will have to have longer data sets and be more patient. When you are first starting to apply Concept Attainment, start with the next category—conjunctive.

B. CONJUNCTIVE (having a common juncture):
Concepts in this category have common characteristics that are more easily observable—personification, right-angled polyhedrons, a sonnet, and symmetry. Almost everything you can see and touch is conjunctive. There are some interesting exceptions. Take the concept of the strike (a "swing-and-a-miss" in baseball)

For example, imagine taking someone who has never seen a baseball game and who knows none of the rules of baseball to a baseball game. The first pitch is thrown, the batter swings and misses, and the umpire shouts, "Strike one." You now explain that if the batter swings and misses it is called a strike. Of course, on the next pitch the batter hits the ball, but it goes foul. The umpire, calls "Strike two." Your friend looks at you quizzically and you now explain if the batter swings and hits the ball and it goes outside those lines, it is also a strike. Of course, on the third pitch, the batter does nothing, the ball blows right by him and the umpire yells, "Strike three." Appreciate your friend trying to see the common link for the concept "strike" given none of the examples had anything in common. As you can see, the "strike" in baseball is somewhat dysjunctive.

C. RELATIONAL (relying on the context or past experience for clarity):
Concepts of this type do have common characteristics, but they depend on the context of the experiences a student brings to the situation. These concepts can be easy to develop data sets for (rough, smooth, soft, cold) or more difficult (fair, opposite, greater than, less than). Again, if you pick a concept for a Concept Attainment lesson, look to see if it is relational. Once you realize it is relational, you will more easily develop an appropriate way to communicate the data set.

For example, one teacher struggled over how to develop the data set for the concept "opposite" until she realized it was relational and that she would have to use diagrams as well as place objects around another object.

Putting the Concept Attainment Process Together

PHASE 1:
Present the focus statement and the data set
a. What is your focus statement?
- this tells students what to look for and sometimes what not to look for

e.g., If you wanted to assist the students to think more clearly about the essence of effective paragraphs, you might say "Focus on what makes the paragraphs effective, do not focus on the number of words." Then present your data set of effective and ineffective paragraphs.

b. How will you present the data set?
- all the examples at once
- one pair of examples at a time

c. What medium will you use to present the data set?
- pictures • overhead • role play
- objects • words • chart paper/chalkboard
- typed sheet, etc.

d. When will you decide to present the testers?

e. When will you decide to stop presenting the data and move into Phase 2?

PHASE 2:
Sharing their hypotheses and their thinking
a. How will you have the students share their hypotheses and thinking?
- individuals volunteer
- randomly select students to share with whole class
- pairs share then volunteer or teacher selected
- small groups of 3 or 4 (round-table sharing) then with whole class

b. How will you deal with incorrect or partially correct hypotheses? Remember that students may see things you didn't realize were in the data set or simply err in their analysis. If they provide an hypothesis that is in the data set that you did not see or that the NO examples did not eliminate, then agree with them and tell them you are looking for something else. Another option is to provide another example that would eliminate their hypothesis. If they err in their analysis, take them back to the data set and show them an example that eliminates their hypothesis.

c. When students have determined the essence or the critical attributes of the concept, how will you start to move to Phase 3, the application of the concept? This is a key part of the process. This is where you move back into the lesson. For example, think back to the start of the chapter with the lesson on "The Revolt of Mother" The teacher created a data set to clarify colloquialisms before shifting into the lesson.

PHASE 3:
Application or extension of the concept
a. How will you make this concept come alive so that students understand the purpose of this concept and its value to them?

b. What questions could you ask? What level of Bloom's Taxonomy are your questions? Could you insert any other strategies or critical thinking skills at this point to extend their thinking about this concept?

Teaching a Concept Attainment Lesson

ACADEMIC TASK: to apply your current understanding of Concept Attainment by teaching a concept using this process.

COLLABORATIVE TASK: to reflect on the process as it is occurring and to determine what the steps of the process should be **OR,** if you are familiar with Concept Attainment, to decide where and how critical thinking tactics and other models of teaching such as Concept Formation and Cooperative Learning can be integrated with Concept Attainment.

DIRECTIONS:

1. Get in groups of two. Take a newspaper—it contains hundreds of concepts. Pick a conjunctive or relational concept (make sure you know which one it is and why) and design five YES and five NO examples of that concept. Take 25 minutes to construct the data set and decide on your process.

2. When instructed to move, get together with two other pairs (groups of six), and take the other four people through what you believe is the process of Concept Attainment related to your concept.

3. When finished, discuss with your group of six what happened. What were the phases of the strategy that you observed? Follow that by discussing what other instructional strategies (models of teaching), or critical thinking skills could be integrated into the process.

4. Compare your analysis about integration with the information on the following page.

5. Now, take a concept that you will teach soon in your own class (start with a less complex concept—preferably a conjunctive concept) and prepare a data set.

The Start of the Art: How Concept Attainment Integrates with Other Models of Teaching

First, in order to integrate Concept Attainment with other strategies you must be "comfortably skilled" at applying Concept Attainment. You must be able to control Concept Attainment ... it should not control you. Few people learn to play five musical instruments simultaneously. Yet this is what is meant to integrate—you are becoming the conductor, the weaver, the painter, the artist—through the judicious selection of instructional approaches. You begin to construct lessons that assist others to construct their own understanding of concepts. Bruce Joyce and Beverly Showers (the authors of *Models of Teaching*) told us we would need to practise 15 to 20 times before we would use it effectively. They were right—and we are still learning fifteen years later.

Second, you must understand the purpose each model serves, i.e., the theory that drives that strategy. For example, Cooperative Learning is a social model driven by social theory. Concept Attainment is an information-processing model driven by learning theory. By integrating these two strategies, you weave social theory and learning theory into the learning environment. What is important in integrating these two processes is recognizing where the potential exists to integrate aspects of Cooperative Learning within and after the Concept Attainment process.

The selection and integration has to happen based on the learners' needs, not yours. This is the same idea as when an artist mixes colours within the context of shadows and light. The artist understands each of those concepts in isolation in order to understand the potential they have when integrated. The difference is that you have 30 canvases in any one classroom, and the artist has only one. And your canvases move. Additionally, they will have different learning styles, different strengths in the different intelligences, they might not have had breakfast, they will be male or female, from different cultures, and so forth. This is what we mean by "Beyond Monet."

Third, just as the artist must have skills related to brush techniques, and the ability to mix and match colours, to sketch, and create perspective, the teacher must have control over the instructional concepts, skills, and tactics that drive or give energy to the use of strategies. For example:

- knowing when to provide a demonstration
- mindfully framing questions to encourage active student involvement
- being skilled at framing questions at different levels to challenge thinking
- understanding how to include concepts such as interest and meaning in the lesson
- sensing when a tactic, such as Three-Step-Interview may be useful to share thinking.

Note: The above concepts, skills, and tactics are presented in previous chapters.

Final Thoughts

Concept Attainment

It is at heart a game ... a detective game. The clues are presented and the observers have to hunt down the pattern. The process is enhanced when the detectives can discuss their thinking.

In a grade one class that had played with this strategy during kindergarten and now into grade one, they would not give up and after the 23 pairs of examples, produced the key characteristics for "biotic" and "abiotic." The data set began with five flowers and five things that were not biotic (rocks, windows, etc.). This then shifted to trees, which caught them a bit off guard for a few seconds. Finally after about 10 plants, the shift was made to animals and then humans. After about the thirteenth example, they all knew where the testers fit, but they could not say why. By the twenty-third pair of examples, they had it. Interestingly, the teacher had put basketball and car on the abiotic side, and one girl reminded him that basketballs are made of rubber and that rubber comes from trees and that the teacher needed to change it. A boy told the teacher that he should put car in the middle (the students used Venn diagrams to conceptualize how to group data). The reason is that the tires are rubber and the seats might be leather.

You have to remember that the students must be able to see all the characteristics of the concept in each example. That is why concepts such as "warm blooded animals" and "mammals" are difficult; the students cannot sense the attributes. For example, if you were doing "cold and warm blooded animals" and you had the animals in your classroom, you could pass them around the room ... telling them that the snake and alligator represent the concept; the elephant and horse do not. The same thing applies with the concept of flightless birds. You would have to have them on the roof of the school and toss them up in the air. Of course the penguins and ostriches may not enjoy the process (and you may end up in jail).

With younger students we have seen Concept Attainment Centres set up in the classroom. An example is the GUESS MY RULE centre. The centre has a lot of junk and a table with a piece of tape down the middle. The students create data sets and then invite other students to come and guess their rule. It could be "shiny" or "rough" or "colour red" or "triangles" or words or things that start with 'T' or pictures of winter and not winter, etc. They enjoy it.

In all of this, though, it is important to have the students discuss their hypotheses and to share their thinking about how they got to where they are regarding their thinking. Thinking about thinking and sensing how we all think differently is not just interesting; more importantly, it is part of being a fair minded and reasonable critical thinker.

Key Things to Remember about
Concept Attainment

- it is an inductive strategy—rather than telling students it encourages students to find out what things have in common for themselves; the pay off is that students remember

- identify what you think are the key concepts in a unit of study and decide whether or not Concept Attainment would be the best process for the students to gain understanding

- it involves presenting examples and non-examples of a concept—and when the students appear to be getting the idea—then you present them with testers to check their understanding

- start with a few fun/easy data sets first so that students get the idea of the process

- everything that you can see, touch, feel, taste, smell, hear, describe, or label is an example of a concept (except when there is only ONE of something (e.g., Toronto is not a concept—it is however an example of the concept "city")

- remember, you can always do a mini-lecture to clarify or extend their thinking if they get stuck

- when showing examples, you should be prepared to share at least ten YES and NO examples—plus three or more testers; the more complex the concept for the learner, the more examples you should be prepared to share

- the focus statement is important in assisting students to more clearly analyze the data set—the more you tell them, the easier it is for them to form hypotheses, but the less likely it is that their "brains" work at finding the pattern—the art is learning to provide the most appropriate focus statement—this only comes with practice

- given talk is critical for intellectual growth, then using cooperative group structures like Think/Pair/Share in Phase Two is wise

Introduction

This chapter introduces another inductive instructional strategy or model of teaching known as Concept Formation (the previous chapter dealt with Concept Attainment). Like Concept Attainment, this strategy is also an information processing strategy. It encourages the learner to process (classify/sort) information in order to make sense of that information. Given everything around you has been classified through analysis, one could safely say that Concept Formation is a useful process.

In the early sixties, Hilda Taba took the inductive process and created a structure that takes the classification process much deeper than what typically occurs in classrooms. At first it was employed in social studies curricula. Today we see it integrated into the learning process in every subject for all ages of students.

Think of biologists or botanists that have classified the animal and plant kingdoms. What about periodic tables, or the classification of types of furniture, music, and art? How could you have students inquire into the Impressionist, Cubist, Realist, Expressionist, Abstract, and Surrealist artists? Perhaps you could tape up four or five of each and have students classify them based on the style of art. Then have them Jigsaw information about one artist in each area. From there, have them generate questions and do a mini-group investigation on questions/interests that evolve from that initial inquiry.

The initial organization of information through Concept Formation allows us to communicate ideas more precisely. It provides a point for pushing more deeply into thinking.

This chapter is not designed to provide in-depth knowledge on Inductive Thinking. Rather, it is designed to illustrate how this strategy can be integrated with other instructional processes. For example, if students are skilled at Inductive Thinking then they will more easily and thoughtfully employ Mind Maps and Concept Maps (see Chapter 10).

We strongly encourage you to refer to books such as *Inductive Thinking* (2000) by Joyce and Calhoun, and the chapter on Inductive Thinking in the book *Models of Teaching* (2000) by Joyce and Weil, which provide a more focused and precise insight into the Inductive strategy.

As you start to play with Concept Formation, consider that the authors of this book took ten days of training on this strategy with Joyce and Showers and have applied it extensively over the last fifteen years. It is a complex strategy. Do not expect to be comfortable with it until you have "played" with it 15 to 20 times. The more you work with it, the easier it gets and the more powerful it becomes.

Rationale

Inductive Thinking is about the process of classifying. Look around you ... everything that you can see or touch or hear has been classified. Look in your closet ... do you have things classified based on common characteristics, say by colour, or by seasons, or by pants, shirts, dresses, socks? Some of you might use the random pile approach, but most of us have some semblance of order.

Like Concept Attainment, Concept Formation is also an inductive thinking process that encourages students to think analytically. The big difference is that with Concept Attainment, the teacher controls the data set. With Concept Formation, the students control the classification (and often the generation) of the data to be classified. For example, they collect the leaves, then sort them.

This process can be used in any subject area and at any grade level.

- The inductive process helps students make sense of large amounts of information—to break it into more meaningful bits and to see relationships between those bits.

- It helps students understand the essence of a concept; or to extend, or refine their understanding of the concept.

- It provides novelty for teachers as an instructional method – it allows teachers to attend to different learning styles and different intellectual strengths (i.e., Gardner's work on Multiple Intelligence).

- It provides an opportunity for the integration of social theory through a variety of Cooperative Learning tactics such as Three-Step-Interview, Round Robin, and Place Mat.

- It integrates and allows the integration of other instructional strategies such as Concept Attainment, Mind Mapping, and Concept Mapping.

- It can be used at all grade levels and in all subject areas.

- It can be employed to teach concepts and skills related to critical thinking, communication, and socialization.

On the following two pages are eight examples of data sets you can create to have students familiarize themselves with the process of Concept Formation (warm-up data sets). These are followed by two sample data sets. Following that are five additional data sets and three lessons that weave in the process of Concept Formation.

How does Inductive Thinking connect to the Naturalistic Intelligence? (Gardner, 1999)

Sample Data Set— Understanding Emotions

Below are faces representing different emotions. Look over the emotions and see if you can find a way to group them into themes of emotions.

Sad

Tired

Suspicious

Excited

Angry

Content

Afraid

Frustrated

Hurt

Shocked

Confused

Lonely

Happy

Aloof

Surprised

Grouchy

Irritated

Sleepy

Calm

Interesting

Sample Data Set—Cartoon Characters

Below are a number of cartoon characters. Look at them carefully. What do some of them have in common? Put them into groups based on common characteristics. Remember … colour is not relevant.

Sample Data Set—Elementary Math—Story Problems

Below is a set of math problems that need to be classified based on the operation you would employ to solve the problem. In your group of three, one person will be the cutter, one the reader, one the paster. Rotate roles after each question. First cut out the problem. Next read it. Next discuss how you know whether to add, subtract, multiply, or divide or some combination of these. Last, glue the problem into one of the four or five groups.

1. If it took you 15 minutes to have a shower, 10 minutes to get dressed, and 25 minutes to have breakfast, and you must leave for school no later than 8:00 P.M., what time should you get out of bed?

2. I gained an average of 2 kilograms a year for seven years. What was my total weight gain?

3. You ordered four pizzas (a total of 32 slices – 8 slices per pizza). Sixteen friends are coming for lunch. Will anyone get three slices?

4. I lent $150 dollars to my brother to purchase a bicycle. I had $250 dollars in my account. Do I have enough left to purchase skates worth $110 dollars?

5. I purchased a pizza for $6.99, a coke for $.99, and chips for $1.25. What should my bill read?

6. My bill for the three pair of socks totaled $6.75. How much for each pair of socks?

7. I have been in elementary school for six years, middle school for three, and high school for four. If my total number of years in education is twenty years, then how long was I in university?

8. Over the period of one year, my car travels on average 60 kilometres per day. How far does it travel in January?

9. If you lost the $10 dollars your mom gave you to buy lunch, and the lunch in the cafeteria was going to cost you $5.25, how much would you have to borrow?

10. If your CD holder is full and contains 50 CDs and the CD holder in the car is also full and holds another 25. How many CD's do you have in those two locations?

11. Each person will most likely eat about 8 ounces of steak. If I have twelve people coming over for a barbecue, and each steak is 6 ounces, how many steaks should I purchase?

12. If you, your sister, and your brother want skate boards for your birthday, and each board is worth $69.99, then how much money will be needed to purchase the three skate boards?

13. You agreed to wash the windows in a building at a cost of $1.25 per window. The building has 8 windows on each floor and it is a 24-story building. What will you bill the person who owns the building?

14. Your allowance for the year is $624 dollars. How much would you get each week?

15. The soccer game is tomorrow. You have three vehicles. One holds 4 passengers (plus the driver), another holds 12 (plus the driver) and another holds two (plus the driver). You have 15 players on the team. Do you need all three vehicles for the team?

Sample Data Set—Secondary English—Figures of Speech

Below are examples of figures of speech—the more complex techniques that writers employ to create images in people's minds. Read through the techniques and see if you can see techniques that have something in common. There is no right or wrong number of groups. Just be prepared to defend why you grouped them the way you did. Use the numbers to group them. For example, you may put 1, 7, 10, and 11 in the same group. Work on your own for five minutes and then share your thinking with a partner. Then the two of you finish classifying the data making sure you both participate equally.

1. I should have listened to my feet. They told me I was not ready to walk so far.
2. Laughing and dancing, the water trickled amongst the rocks.
3. His hands grasped my arm like a vice.
4. The buzz of the saw rang in my head.
5. Screaming like a crazed ghost, he slipped into the night.
6. As I leaned out the window, I heard the silent swoosh of the grass.
7. She can calculate numbers in her head faster than the best computer.
8. I'm sure the walls laughed at my naïve attempts to escape.
9. Her heart was like a vault with no combination.
10. As she chewed the food, the clacking of her teeth made me sad.
11. If I've told you once I've told you a million times.
12. My memory returned like the water flowing over Niagara Falls.
13. Tornadoes of wind escaped from the horse's nostrils.
14. Walking down the street the slosh of the water echoed between my toes.
15. I think the principal has a nose bigger than a pumpkin.
16. I turned and felt the fire licking my heels, trying to prevent my escape.

Are there any of the above that could fit into more than one category?

Where would you put this one:

The clock's tomb-like tick was predicting my test-taking doom.

In your group, create an example of each of the techniques.

When you think you understand the different figures of speech, read the poem "The Highwayman's Daughter" and see if you can find any examples of these techniques.

Sample Data Set—Secondary Science

This lesson was designed by Connie Tindall. It relates to science experiments and the five steps one might employ during an experiment (the scientific method):

• State the Problem
• Predict a Reason for the Problem (Hypothesis)
• Collect Information
• Test Your Hypothesis
• Present an Explanation
• Accept or Reject your Hypothesis

Present the students with a data set from a few problems. They have to classify them according to the steps in the Scientific Method. Below is a data set for three problems. (Note to teacher: Please feel free to change the steps and the examples.)

A Data Set for Three Problems

1. My car won't start.
2. Maybe I could turn it off and then on again.
3. Maybe it came from her house.
4. Look at the dashboard and under the hood.
5. The computer screen suddenly freezes.
6. His guess was correct; the radiation came from her home.
7. The detector says her house is full of radon.
8. Maybe I am running too many programs.
9. I added gas and it started right up.
10. It must be out of gas.
11. The computer worked fine after it was restarted.
12. He discovers she is radioactive in the morning.
13. It's running fine so it must have been out of gas.
14. I had too many programs running at once.
15. The radiation must have come from someplace other than work.
16. It will start if I put some gas in it.
17. The engineer is radioactive every day after work.
18. He shuts down his computer and starts it up again to see what happens.

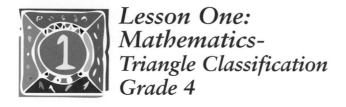

Lesson One: Mathematics- Triangle Classification Grade 4

OBJECTIVES:

1. Students will classify triangles by angle measure and the length of their sides by identifying, stating, and applying the properties of triangles. They will do this by involving themselves in an Inductive Process.

2. Students will apply their understanding of the social skill of equal participation during the classification process and during the sharing of their thinking.

MENTAL SET:

Yesterday we discussed types of angles and the labels we give to those angles. In your groups, do a Round Robin starting with the person whose birthday is closest to January 1st. See if you can come up with all the labels and what each label means. I will randomly call on someone from each group for at least one answer.

OBJECTIVE SHARED:

Today we are going to classify an envelope of triangle shapes. I want you to focus on angles and size of the sides. Be prepared to defend your classification with another group. I will ask one of you to stay at the desk to explain to one other group who will visit to check your analysis. The rest of your group will visit another group. We are attempting to sharpen our understanding related to triangles.

INPUT:

Could you letter off in your groups please (wait 5 seconds)? Could person A put up their hand? Please come up and get one envelope.

MODELLING:

I quickly showed them what was in the envelope by dumping one envelope on the overhead.

Each group was given an envelope with 3 or 4 examples of each type of triangle. They were on coloured transparency paper so that I could have a group come up and put their classification on the overhead and explain why they classified them the way they did. Once finished, they were to check their analysis with the description in a handout on the different types of triangles.

CHECKING FOR UNDERSTANDING:

Person B, please share with your group what you are going to do.

PRACTICE:

The students then classified the data into groups. They had about 10 minutes. I then asked them to do a check for understanding to make sure everyone in their group could explain each group and the label for each group. We had previously talked about what an effective check for understanding would look like and sound like. I reminded them of that discussion. I then selected one person from the group who would stay and explain (person C).

CLOSURE:

Following the group sharing, I selected several students to come up to the overhead and share/explain one of their classifications to the rest of the class.

Lesson Two:
Language Arts - Communication - Grade 6

Teacher's Name: Rhonda Safont
Theme: Communication/Messages

OBJECTIVE: Students will identify different means of sending messages, compare and contrast those means, as well as determine their appropriateness to a variety of situations involving communication.

Note: The teacher read the poem - *"Messages"* from a Networks (Nelson) anthology to provide the students with a Mental Set for the Concept Formation process.

Messages by John McInnes

Messages
Enclosed in envelopes, carrying your name
Scribbled on the backs of pretty postcards
Stuck magnetically onto refrigerator doors
Addressed to you in shouts or whispers
Given warmly in a hug or handshake
Extended silently with a wink or smile
Sent to you mysteriously, in the night
      dream-wrapped
Messages
    written and read
    spoken and heard
    unwritten, unread
    unspoken, unheard
Messages

PHASE I: Collect Data

Have the students watch a segment from the movie *Star Trek: The Voyage Home* (Part IV.) Scenes deal with the issue that whales are becoming extinct and show a probe contacting Earth and trying to communicate with a humpback whale who has been sending out signals. Have the students complete this task: View the film segments and record examples of how messages are conveyed or communication is carried out (types of communication).

Data Set generated by the students from the Star Trek video clip.

- alien to earth radio signals
- computers with people—voice and typed
- interplanetary distress signals
- federation to Kirk—radio and screen
- transmission to Earth—distress signal
- signals by words and music
- eye contact between Spock and McCoy
- whales communicating with whales
- orders to subordinates
- underwater messages through microphone
- whaling ship captain gives orders
- spouting of whales communicates presence
- Spock Vulcan mind meld
- questions being asked   • Spock guessing
- McCoy doesn't agree, uses sarcasm
- Kirk sends message he is trying to help
- McCoy prays to God
- Dr. of Cetology (whale study) gives information—lecture
- concern by tone of voice and words
- expresses fear for their survival
- talking   • radio   • TV
- looking (eye contact)
- body movement   • touching   • sounds
- gestures   • mind reading

PHASE II: Group The Data

Ask the students to group the data into categories based on the ways that messages get communicated. Let the students know there is no right or wrong number of groups. Also, make sure they know they must be prepared to explain why they placed items within a group. Anyone from the group can be asked to share (invoke the concept of individual accountability from the Johnsons' work).

Remind them to beware of the trap of labelling too early. If students predetermine the categories, they are not implementing the inductive process the way Taba intended. The best way is to pick one type of communication and try to find another that has something in common with it. When you cannot find any more for that group, then select another one for a second category and go through the same process. Once you have finished, go back and find appropriate labels for each group.

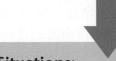

> The groupings the students created were: body language, electronic communication, words or language, voice, feelings, and instructions.

As part of Phase II, the students can now create a Mind Map or Concept Map to organize the data and begin to determine relationships between categories. This push to find relationships can overlap into Phase III.

PHASE III:

Application of the Concepts from Phase II

Start to get the students to make predictions and inferences from the different ways we communicate. Have them look for connections and the situations that lend themselves to specific forms of communication.

For example, ask the students to imagine what verbal communication would be like without body language or actions. Is it possible to say one thing and then through body language say the opposite? Which of our senses is the most powerful in terms of interpreting and being sensitive to messages—taste or smell? (Scientists say smell.) You could get into a delightful discussion of point of view and perception.

Provide situations involving communication and ask which of the groups or categories would be most important to that situation.

> **Sample Situations:**
> - Teacher with students
> - Mother or father with child
> - Two people arguing
> - TV newscaster as compared to radio announcer

An Explanation of Inductive Thinking

The following information is a result of the work of Hilda Taba (1967) in her book, *Teacher's Handbook for Elementary Social Studies*.

What is the strategy? At the simplest level, Inductive Thinking invites students to put things into groups to develop expediency, or clarity related to the communication of ideas. They identify the characteristics or critical attributes of a concept, and this allows them to move on to making generalizations and discriminations, to compare and contrast, and to evaluate, to create because they own the design of the concept.

Inductive Thinking is a process that encourages students to organize information by having them group items, words, pictures, formulas, processes into categories based on common characteristics (or attributes). Those characteristics can be applied to distinguish examples of a concept from examples that do not represent that concept. Everyone has played with the process, and has been affected by aspects of it most of their life. Virtually everything (if not everything) you see around you has been organized or categorized inductively—you cannot escape it.

For example, you have no doubt had a closet that was out of control. To put it into control, you most likely put the pants with the pants, or dresses with the dresses, the shirts with the shirts, the sweaters with the sweaters, etc. You no doubt did it based on the concepts of "pants," "dresses," "shirts," etc. On the other hand you might group them based on the concept of colour coordinates—with an almost endless number of possible groupings;. Once you understand the concept of "blue" or "skirt" then any new object that appears can be sorted based on your being able to discriminate and generalize.

Hilda Taba has taken the process from its historic application to what might occur in today's classroom. She operates from a set of beliefs about thinking. Two are mentioned below:

1. Thinking is a transaction between the individual and data.

2. Processes of thought evolve by a sequence that is lawful.

What Taba argues is that mental operations cannot be taught or given directly from the teacher to the student as in spoon-feeding a young child. Rather, the teacher can create an environment or process that encourages students to mentally involve themselves in complex mental operations in a sequence of events that invites the students to move from less complex to more complex thinking.

She identifies three strategies in that sequence:

1. Concept Formation
2. Interpretation of Data
3. Application of Principles

> **These 3 phases or strategies of Inductive Thinking are described on the following page.**

THREE PHASES WITHIN TABA'S INDUCTIVE STRATEGY

Taba's Inductive Strategy has 3 phases. The teacher can invoke one, two, or all three. The further you go, the more you push into critical thinking.

1. Concept Formation
   - Enumerate or list the data
   - Group the data
   - Label the groups
2. Interpretation of the Data
   - Identify the critical relationships between groups
   - Explore those relationships
   - Make inferences from those explorations
3. Application of Principles
   - Predict consequences, explain unfamiliar phenomena, hypothesize
   - Explain or support the predictions, etc.
   - Verify predications

Note: Concept Formation is like Concept Attainment except the students assume greater control over the process and the concepts being formed. Also, remember that Phases 2 & 3 are where the students can apply critical thinking strategies to make the concepts come alive—see Chapter 11.

AND, you will see that a Mind Map and Concept Map—when done in a sophisticated way—are in fact powerful Inductive Strategies...see Chapter 10 on Mind Mapping and Concept Mapping.

A description of the 3 Phases

1. Concept Formation

The students enumerate or list the data. In the initial part of the process, the students are either presented with or generate a list of data.

For example, the list could be generated from a question such as: What are all the different sources of energy? or What are the different ways in which we are polluting our environment? In a math class dealing with measurement, the teacher might have placed actual items around the room that have been measured by gradations of grams, litres, metres (items such as jam, chocolate bars, milk, chain, etc.,). Or, in an English class, the students could be presented with a variety of poems. In a grade one class, the students were given numerous items found in a large food store. The students had to organize the food based on how the food should be located in a food store. The students then went on a field trip to compare their thinking with how the store manager thought. Interestingly, the students put bread, butter, meat, jam, peanut butter, and milk together in the 'sandwich group' and were most surprised that that was not the case in the store.

Group the data. Now that the students have the data (either presented by someone or generated by them), the students group the data into categories by identifying common properties and deciding what belongs together and what criteria allows them to be together. In this phase be careful not to come up with predetermined labels for categories that might limit the creative and divergent nature of this activity.

Phase 1: continued

For example, if you have young children who have had some experience with food groups, they will immediately place items into groups based on what they have memorized, not based on a set of criteria. When you ask them, "Why can't you put sausage in the fruit group?", they will say, "Because sausage is meat." When you ask them, "What is meat?", they are confused. When you ask adults, "Why can't you place carrots in the fruit group?", they get caught. Adults will say, "Because it's a vegetable." When asked what a vegetable is, they are confused. There are fruits, tubers, nuts, seeds, stems, and leaves...no vegetables.

Now the students label the groups. Through questions and discussion, the students are encouraged to identify labels for the groups. Be careful of predetermined labels like "These are all examples of prejudice." The teacher should ask, "What do you mean by prejudice?" Often students will have the label, but will not understand the design of the concept (remember Perkins's four questions about design discussed in Chapter 8). See page 260 for a quick review.

Note: This is where the students can begin to apply some of the critical thinking tactics and strategies identified in Chapter 11.

2. Interpretation of the Data

Identifying critical relationships. At this point Taba is inviting the student to engage in the mental operations of interpreting. Here the teacher (or other students) asks students what they noticed about the data within groups (e.g., How they are the same? Why do certain things belong in one group and not the other?) The teacher can set up the environment so that the students are challenged to justify their groups and what they placed within those groups.

> For example, if the students have placed the Pyramids in the group of items that involved "construction using the inclined plane" (after being asked to group items into groups based on the simple machines employed) the students might be asked, "How does the shape of a pyramid prove the use of an inclined plane?"

Exploring those relationships. Here the students are invited to explore relationships between groups in a cause and effect process.

> For example, if the students had one group labelled "pollution" and another group labelled "primary industry," the students might be asked the following questions: What effect does pollution have on primary industry? Is pollution more of a concern for primary, secondary, or tertiary industry?

Making inferences from those explorations. Students are now invited to go beyond the immediate issues within and between the data. They are moving more into the area of vertical or high-road transfer.

> For example, if we take the pollution issue, students could be asked questions such as: "Given the polluting effects of the automobile, and the effect that issue has

on health and the quality of life in cities such as London, San Francisco and Toronto, does the federal government have the right to step into a state or province issue if the people in that area do not want the changes because it will increase their taxes?" And, "What about the issue of the acid rain caused by industries in the United States that is currently destroying Canada's forests. Does or should Canada have the right to stop the United States from polluting?"

3. Application of Principles

This phase takes the issues discussed in the previous phase or strategy and applies the principles. Note, this is a powerful place to integrate or initiate the use of other models of teaching such as Group Investigation and Jurisprudential Inquiry. (See *Models of Teaching* by Joyce and Weil.)

> **Note:** This is another point where the students can apply the critical thinking skills identified in Chapter 11.

Predicting consequences, explaining unfamiliar phenomena, hypothesizing. Students would now probe more deeply into the issues or concerns discussed in the previous two phases or strategies. They might get into groups and explore issues of importance and make some hypotheses or predictions that would attempt to bring more clarity and understanding.

For example, you might ask a question such as. "Predict what would happen if Canadians told the Americans that they would not trade with the United States until the United States made moves to resolve the acid rain issue."

Explaining or supporting the predictions. Here students attempt to support or validate their hypotheses. This can be initiated by questions such as "Why do you think this will happen?"

For example, they might access other pieces of information, do reports, have debates, bring in guest speakers, films, etc., to attempt to validate, reject, refine and/or extend their hypotheses.

Verifying those predictions. As a result of the discussions the students assess the value of the information, its practicality, its strengths or weaknesses, or its logic. They may critique the worth of the arguments, and the worth of the effort.

For example, the students may have grouped data around aids to transportation. One category the students constructed may have been "man-made canals." When asked to verify the hypotheses that the Panama Canal "was worth the effort," the group, after reading a brief history of the Panama Canal, would have to justify their hypotheses. Was the Canal worth the effort based on juxtaposing the excessive loss of life with the economic growth for Panama and dollars saved by other countries who use the canal?

> On the next page are a few reasons for employing this strategy.

Why Employ Taba's Inductive Thinking Strategy?

Why use it: One role the teacher plays is to engage students in thinking related to concepts. Without an understanding of basic concepts—the building blocks of knowledge—it is more difficult to learn facts, develop principles, comprehend theorems, etc.

Take something as simple as this statement:
When teaching, if the teacher can integrate taxonomies of thinking into their framing of questions, then the use of wait time becomes more powerful.

Embedded in that statement are a number of concepts. For example:
- teaching - teacher
- integrate
- taxonomies - thinking
- framing questions - wait time
- power

The more concepts stated above that you do not understand, the less likely you are to understand the meaning of the statement. Obviously some concepts are more important or more complex; the teacher's role is to decide what concepts need to be understood in order to bring clarity to thinking.

So, the **science** of teaching is represented by the instructional strategy of Inductive Thinking; the **art of teaching** is represented by the decisions you make concerning when to employ it and how to employ it given the nature of the learner and time you have available to teach. Initially you can learn to apply the strategy from a more teacher controlled stance, but that is not where the power is in terms of student learning. When approached from a constructivist perspective it facilitates a more thoughtful application of the strategy.

Reflecting back to Chapter 8, this is where David Perkins's work on **Knowledge as Design** vs **Knowledge as Information** brings clarity to the process. If you recall, he states that when students are learning concepts, they should be able to respond to four questions related to the design of the concept:

1. What are the critical attributes of that concept?

2. What are the purposes of that concept?

3. What are model cases of the concept?

4. What are the arguments for learning that concept?

When you engage the three phases of Concept Formation they attend to those four questions.

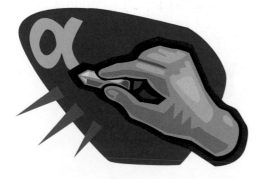

On the next few pages are three more complex inductive lessons.

Three Complex Inductive Lessons

Lesson One: Grade One – Preparation for a field trip to a grocery store.

OVERVIEW: The students had been discussing food groups and classifying foods into the food groups. This lesson is an extension of that inquiry and prepared them for a field trip to a large grocery store in their community. Students came to a large table at the back of the room in groups of four and worked with the teacher. The other students worked on another activity related to the field trip. The perishables (such as vegetables, meat) were placed in sealed plastic bags.

ACADEMIC TASK: Group food into categories based on where you think you would put this food if you were the manager of the food store.

COLLABORATIVE TASK: Make sure that everyone gets a chance to talk.

DIRECTIONS:

PHASE I:
Food was placed on the table at the back of the room (items like bread, butter, jam, meat, fruit, vegetables, cereal, candy, canned foods, etc.) Students were asked to look at all of the items and then to decide how to group them in terms of which ones should be together when you visit a food store.

PHASE II:
Students had to explain why they would put items together in particular groups. They knew they would have to explain their reasons to the manager of the food store when they went on the field trip.

They grouped things like bread, butter, jam and meat together because they thought you might want to make sandwiches.

The students then drew pictures of the foods that belonged in a group on a piece of paper. When they were all done, they all sat in a circle and they discussed the groups on their piece of paper.

PHASE III:
The students went to the food store and shared their ideas with a store employee. They compared their classroom thinking with what they found when they walked around the store. They then discussed why they thought the food was sometimes grouped differently than they thought it should be. For example, how refrigeration determines where some things will be found, and why soap and cleaners are not too close to perishable food.

Lesson Two: Elementary Science Lesson

Designed by Brooke O'Brian

Structures Unit: Learning about Buildings

Note: the teacher begins with Bruner's inductive strategy Concept Attainment – she then shifts to Taba's Inductive Strategy

OBJECTIVE:

Students will extend their understanding of specific building structures (i.e., their function, materials, size, shape, tools, geographic location) through Concept Attainment and Conept Formation while working in cooperative groups. While in their cooperative groups, students will work on the social skill of equal participation.

MENTAL SET/SHARING THE PURPOSE:

Bring students to the carpet and quickly review last day's work on observations of structures. Then, tell the students "Today in science we will be learning more about structures in terms of buildings. We will begin our investigation of buildings by playing a YES/NO game (Concept Attainment) together at the white board, and then we will split into groups and work cooperatively to sort buildings into categories (e.g., the material they are made of, size, shape). Then we will have a Walk About so you can see how other groups have categorized their buildings. Once that is completed I will pick someone randomly from each group to present their ideas."

INPUT/MODELLING:

(Step One) Begin by playing the YES/NO game. Have 16 cards of different buildings drawn, coloured, and labelled (8 YES and 8 NO examples). Place cards face down on white board with sticky tack in a vertical line down the board, with the YES examples on the left side and the NO examples on the right side. Explain game to students. Make sure they understand that they are trying to figure out what the YES side has in comparison to what the NO side doesn't have. Tell students they are to keep their guesses in their heads until the game is over so they don't spoil the fun and learning for others in the class (**5 min**). Begin by revealing one example at a time from each side, each time emphasizing that the YES side has something that the NO side does not have. (The YES side contains examples of buildings that we live in, the NO side contain examples of buildings in which we work or visit, but in which we do not live.) After all the examples have been revealed, bring out testers (three for each side, much harder than the ones just presented) to check and see if students understand the rule. Have students come up to the white board and put the tester under the category that they think it goes (**10 minutes**). Do thumbs up/thumbs down/thumbs sideways to see if most students know the rule. Have students Think/Pair/Share their guesses, and then randomly select a few students to justify the rule (**5 min**).

(Step Two) Inductive Thinking Strategy: Put students heterogeneoulsy into groups of 4 or 5 (seated at desk clusters) according to their ability in science (this provides an opportunity for positive peer-mentoring between the weaker and stronger students). Each group receives an envelope filled with 22 pictures of buildings that were used in the

Concept Attainment segment of the lesson (This is Phase One). Groups are to sort those buildings into categories that make sense to them; however, they are not allowed to sort them as experienced in the Concept Attainment lesson (Phase Two). That means they can sort them according to topics already covered in previous lessons (e.g., the materials from which they are made, uses, size, etc.). Remind students they are working on the social skill of equal participation in the lesson. Talk about what it sounds like, looks like, and feels like when done properly. Each person is expected to contribute equal ideas to the sorting exercise (1) decide on categories to sort by; (2) take turns putting buildings under proper categories; (3) encourage group members to participate; (4) check to see all categories fit (**10 min**). After the groups have finished their sorting exercise, they do a **Walk-About** to see the different ways other groups have sorted their categories (**2 min**). Then randomly choose one student from each group to present their categories (Phase 2 continued—sharing their thinking). (**10 min**)

CHECK FOR UNDERSTANDING:

In the Concept Attainment part of the lesson check students' understanding of the YES concept (buildings we live in) with testers provided, and randomly pick students to justify their answers. In the sorting part of the lesson, the students' understanding can be checked by having the students go over the information in their groups before they start, and later by doing the Walk-About to see how other groups had categorized their buildings.

As well, when the groups present their categorizations of buildings to the class they all can be expected to know and agree on the categorization of their buildings because the teacher will randomly call upon one person from each group to present.

PRACTICE:

Doing the Concept Attainment with the class provides a warm up practice to the work that comes later in the sorting task (Inductive Thinking). In the sorting task students practise their categorization skills with group members as well as practise their development of the social skill of equal participation.

CLOSURE:

After the Walk-About is completed, the students return to their groups and the teacher chooses one person to present their categorization of the buildings. Students share the categories they used to sort their structures and justify their choices. After the presentations are finished discuss as a class their ability to work in a group with equal participation using thumbs up/thumbs down/thumbs sideways (**3 min**). Then in their own groups thank each other and tell one good thing about their group participation and one thing they could work on. (**5 min**)

Lesson Three:
Fallacies of Inductive Thinking

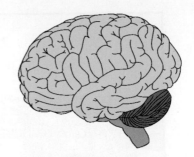

Secondary Lesson: Secondary Critical Thinking Unit

ACADEMIC TASK: to experience the process of inductive thinking by organizing concepts. In addition, to extend your understanding of fallacies of critical thinking as they relate to inductive thinking.

COLLABORATIVE TASK: to disagree in an agreeable way or to accept and extend the thinking of others

MENTAL SET: "We have already discussed the two major divisions of thinking: Inductive and Deductive. You sense that one often leads to the other. That said, people often try to argue from an inductive stance to prove a point—the result may be that their thinking is "wrong-headed." For example, consider the following statement: If someone said to you: '80 percent of men in Canada disagree with the government's gun policy.' Think to yourselves, what type of "wrong-headed" thinking does that statement represent?" Randomly ask students and then discuss the fallacy of the unknowable statistic. (See p. 267).

DIRECTIONS: On the next page is a list of fallacies of inductive thinking.

1. Please get into groups of two (or if you prefer, do this by yourself).

2. Read over the data set twice.

3. Pick any one example to start and identify why you think that form of thinking is fallacious or open to criticism.

4. Now read through the data set and identify any other examples that contain that same fallacy. Remember to disagree agreeably or to extend each other's thinking.

5. When you have placed as many as possible into that group, pick another example that does not fit in that group and continue the process until you have categorized all the examples in the data set into groups.

6. When you have finished, compare your classifications with that of at least one other group.

Data Sheet on the Fallacies of Inductive Reasoning

1. I waited half an hour for him to get dressed. All men are more vain than women.

2. When you see a person from another country coming toward you on the street, do you rush forward and thank them for coming to our country or do you cross to the other side?

3. Only 106 of an estimated 895 cases of rape that occurred in Toronto last year were reported.

4. Everyone that I talked to in my neighbourhood said that they had guns. This whole town is armed.

5. Of course I cannot approve of hecklers disrupting my opponent's speeches. However, I would also say that in a democracy, they also have the same right to be heard as the speaker.

6. Are you in favour of a prime minister who stuck up his middle finger and told people where to go?

7. The universe is like a clock; both are systems of moving parts. Clocks have makers; so it is likely that the universe had a maker.

8. The corruption of North American youth has been caused by role models provided by its singers who have encouraged experimentation with drugs and promiscuity.

9. If you offer people unemployment insurance, they will become lazy and expect the government to support them for life.

10. It is a known fact that people only use 10 percent of their potential.

11. Do you act with passion or are you always this cadaverous?

12. Most poor people who live in cities are anti-rich. That's because their landlords are too well off.

13. I love mankind; its just that I can't stand people.

14. Are you saying you could love somebody knowing he or she killed someone?

15. There is no convincing evidence to show that cigarette smoking is harmful. Too much of anything is harmful. Too much apple sauce is harmful. (Cigarette Manufacturer)

16. Canadians buy Japanese cars, cameras, and stereos because they are unpatriotic. An ad campaign appealing to their patriotism could reverse this trend.

17. Sex education in the schools leads to promiscuity, unwanted pregnancies, and cheating in marriages.

18. Students in classrooms where the teacher uses whole language have scored lower on the standardized tests. We should ban whole language.

19. In the politics of confrontation the rules of poker apply. Once you begin to run a bluff, never show the slightest hesitation.

20. All the literature I've read said activity-based learning is the best way for kids to learn. Teachers had better use activity centres all the time.

21. If you teach critical thinking in an Indian university, the young people would go home and question, then disobey their parents. Their families would quarrel and break up. Then they would question their bosses and everyone else. The next thing you know the whole country would fall apart.

22. Do you ever search for friends or do you just stay at home alone?

23. Yes the children in the inner city are behind and we must provide more funds for inner-city schools. But please remember, we try to treat every school equally.

24. You either use Cooperative Learning techniques and have effective groups or don't use it and have groups of kids who will never function effectively together.

25. Do you mean after the child told me my lesson was boring, and that my class was run like a prison, and that I was a dead head, you will not suspend the student?

26. Teaching humanistically doesn't teach students to respond to authority. They will become undisciplined, disrespect their friends, their teachers, their parents, and eventually their country by ending up on welfare.

27. If the Roe vs. Wade decision remains in force until the beginning of the twenty-first century, our nation will be missing more than 40 million citizens, of whom approximately 8 million would have been men of military age.

28. Yes, I believe teachers should be empowered to make choices about how and what they teach. Nonetheless, we live in a democracy so they must teach what we know students need to survive in a democracy.

29. Given you have 3 beautiful children, are you seriously going to support women's rights for abortion?

30. Mothers of young children can either have careers or stay at home. But they can't expect to have both.

31. In life as in basketball you cheat if you can get away with it—that way you have a better chance of winning.

32. Teachers who are proactive only spend between .95 to 3.5 percent of their time dealing with behaviour problems.

33. Since the Boeing jumbo jet flying over Korea was full of space age technology, it could not have failed unless there was some sinister design on the part of the West to make it fail. (Soviet interpretation of the Korean jet incident in 1983.)

CHECKING FOR UNDERSTANDING/PRACTICE: Have the students do a **Walk-About** to see how other groups classified the data. Then randomly select group members to share their thinking about why they put certain examples together—why they thought they represented a specific type of "wrong-headed" thinking.

Next, put students into groups of three and complete a **Jigsaw** on the different fallacies of inductive thinking (sweeping generalizations, unknowable statistics, false analogy, etc.; see the list to the right). Then have them go back to their data and see if they would classify them any differently, trying to find examples of each of the different types of inductive fallacies. Maybe there are no examples for some fallacies—students might have to constuct their own.

EXTENSION: Provide students with newspapers, and give them fifteen minutes (working on their own) to find examples of inductive fallacies. If they get stuck they can work with someone else. Have examples already selected so if they get stuck you can give them an example and ask them to find the inductive fallacy. As an easier option, you can provide examples in an envelope and have students do a Round Robin, with each person getting two or three examples. They then read and discuss the fallacy in their examples.

Eight Common Fallacies in Inductive Reasoning

- **The Hasty or Sweeping Generalization** – this refers to a person making a judgement or broad statement based on limited information.

- **The Either-Or Fallacy** – this refers to polarizing an issue when in fact other positions or both positions are possible.

- **The Unknowable Statistic** – this refers to making a statement based on a statistic that is impossible or unrealistic to calculate.

- **Inconsistencies and Contradictions** – this refers to arguing a point while going against or acting in a way that negates your argument.

- **The Loaded Question** – this question does not allow for any answer but the one the person who asked it wants. (A dead end question)

- **False Causations** – this involves invoking a cause/effect relationship when it is at best a correlation or a coincidence.

- **The False Analogy** – this occurs when a comparison is made which is not accurate.

- **The Slippery Slope (or domino effect)** – this implies that if one thing happens then all these other things will happen as a consequence.

On the following page are some directions for planning an Inductive Thinking lesson.

Planning a Lesson that Incorporates Concept Formation

ACADEMIC TASK: To develop and plan the process for an Inductive Lesson; a process that includes all three strategies or phases within Taba's Concept Formation model of teaching.

COLLABORATIVE TASK: Maintain integrity to the model and to the instructional skills and tactics needing to be woven into the lesson to make the Inductive strategy come alive or have more "learning power."

DIRECTIONS:

1. With a partner (or alone) develop a data set from a set of concepts you teach or identify the objects that would be part of the data set.

   For example, if I were in business education, I might develop a database of four or five examples of different types of business letters that students would have to categorize. If I were in a wood-working class, I would have the students classify pieces of wood based on the grain of wood and make predictions about how to work with and use different types of wood. If I were in English, I might pull different examples of the parts of the novel for students to categorize. In physics, at the start of the year, examples of different types of physics problems students might have to solve would be put into an envelope—once they develop the categories, they match formulas to the category.

2. Predict the types of categories the students would construct and then design the questions that would take you through Phase II and Phase III. Check to see if you were true to Taba's process.

> **Note:** In your own classroom, if the students do not give you the groups you need to continue through the lesson, how could you use Bruner's Concept Attainment strategy to get the groups you want? Hint: pull out two or three examples and tell the students that these three have something in common ask them if they can find one or two more. Once they have done that, then ask them to work to find one more group.

3. When finished, share your data set and process you would employ to engage the students through the three phases with one other group.

> *Now turn to the next page and read through a lesson that focuses on how we deal with the fear in our lives. Notice how Inductive Thinking (Concept Formation) could be part of this lesson.*

How Could You Integrate Concept Formation into a Lesson

Note: Mark was a pre-service student and his task was to create a lesson that attended to the work of David and Roger Johnson (see Chapter 7). The intention was not to weave in Concept Formation. Mark designed this Cooperative Learning lesson as a result of students in his class being afraid to share ideas because they might be teased. So, although he was not trying to play with Hilda Taba's Inductive Thinking strategy, you can see how the lesson could lend itself to the inductive process by having students group types of fears. They could then do a Jigsaw to teach each other about the types of fears and discuss how people deal with or overcome them.

The purpose of this lesson is to illustrate that most of us already have lessons that can be re-designed to integrate Concept Formation.

Cooperative Learning Lesson: Children's Literature (Grade Six)

The art of teaching is the art of assisting discovery. —MARK VAN DORAN

INTRODUCTION

During my final student teaching placement I guided a lesson in Social Studies on facing one's fears. I selected this particular subject for my lesson because I had observed several students in the class (grade 6) who seemed to give up on things for fear of failing at them. It was my intention, in the presentation of this topic, to get the idea across to the class that to try something, in itself, is an achievement one can be proud of.

I attempted, as best I could, to get across the importance of the process of doing something, rather than concentrating solely on the final outcome (be it a score or a mark). One of the examples I gave to illustrate the importance of process over outcome was a personal story I told the class. When I was in Grade 9 I had an art project to do for class. I took a good deal of time to work on this assignment, and had enjoyed the process of putting together this piece of work. I did my drawing for myself and I was pleased with what I had done.

Unfortunately, my art teacher was not so appreciative of my artistic genius (all modesty aside) and I received a C for my grade. Well, as I told the class, at first I was rather bothered by the mark I had received. I did not feel it was a fair representation of the work that had gone into my piece. But then I thought: Hey! it's my drawing and I like it and that's all that is really important. From that perspective I saw my drawing as a success not as a failure, because I had enjoyed the process of creating my picture. Interestingly enough, I stopped taking art in high school after a few years because I enjoyed drawing and painting so much that having my work graded took a good deal of the pleasure away from the activity.

THE LESSON

I began my lesson by reading the class the tale of "Brave Molly" from Terry Jones *Fairy Tales* (1981). To summarize the story: A little girl, whose name is Molly, is caught in a thunderstorm. She spots a hut on a hill, and finding the door open, runs inside to escape from the rain. Once inside Molly senses something inside the hut with her. When lightning strikes she glimpses the terrible shape of a huge monster. The monster asks Molly if she is frightened, to which she replies that she is. The monster then tells Molly that he eats little girls for supper. Molly, who is terrified at this point, thinks to herself: Well, if he's going to eat me, he's going to eat me. Being frightened won't help anything. So Molly stopped being frightened, picked up her satchel, and hit the monster right on the nose. At this development the most remarkable transformation began to take place. First the monster turned green, then black, and then bright pink. Then a bunch of flowers grew out of the top of his head and a ribbon appeared around the monster's waist. Molly took hold of the ribbon and pulled, releasing the monster from its shell. Out of the monster's belly sprung a little rabbit who was frightened and said: "Oh, please! Don't put me in a pie!" To which Molly replied: "I won't put you in a pie this time, but don't go around trying to frighten little children in the future." The rabbit promises he won't and quickly hops away. At this point in the tale the storm has passed and Molly makes her way on home.

As you read this next section, can you sense that this is where Phase I (classify data set) might emerge?

After reading this story to the class, I began to explore (orally) the themes in the story. I elicited the themes from the class: fear, bravery, deceptive appearances. I then began to explore the idea of fear with the class. I asked them questions such as: **What are some of the things you are afraid of, or people you know are afraid of? Did you ever find something initially frightening, but after you gave it a try the fear subsided? I then took the answers the class provided and wrote them on chart paper that I had taped to the blackboard.** After a few minutes I had some 20-30 fears listed on the board. Then, on another sheet of chart paper I listed one fear and asked the class for some ways one might go about alleviating or possibly eliminating the fear (I chose the fear of dogs as an example). Then, as a class, we came up with several ways that this fear might be reduced. At this point I told the class that I was going to group them into categories in which there were some similar fears expressed. I then set up 6 categories that had related fears (eg., fear of animals) and placed people in those groups if they had an interest in exploring those themes. I then had everyone move to their assigned space depending on what they wished to study. **How would Phase II be employed to make sense of all the different types of fear? You could also bring in the language of phobias in a mini-lecture or a Jigsaw.**

THE ASSIGNMENT

(As you read the next section, can you sense how Phase III (application) would be employed in this section?)

At this point I outlined for the class what they were to do in their group. I provided each group with a sheet of chart paper and coloured markers. I numbered the members of each group 1-4 and assigned duties to 1 (writing) and 3 (choosing the colours of markers used).

I let the class know that every 5 minutes I would alternate people's responsibilities in the group so that everyone had a chance to write and choose colours. I then let the class know their assignment: they were to brainstorm ideas to go about alleviating or eradicating the fears their group had been given. Each group was to come up with as many ideas as they could in regards to helping someone get over the fear they were looking at. Each individual in the group would receive a participation mark, and also the group as a whole would be evaluated on how well they functioned as a group. They had 20 minutes to work on this, and then they would be presenting their results to the class. Thus, every member of the group had to understand and participate in the process for they would be presenting it at the conclusion of the period.

MARK'S REFLECTION

This cooperative lesson went very well. In fact, I was a little surprised by how well it went. During the time when I was reading the tale of "Brave Molly" the class was attentive. And when I began discussing the themes of the story the class participated and got into it. As I said earlier, when we began listing fears on the board the students were quite willing to let others know some of the things they were afraid of. It turned out that one person's fear often turned out to be five people's fear, or more. After the excellent discussion the class had regarding fears, and then taking an example and brainstorming ways to conquer that fear the class easily moved into their respective groups and worked on their assignment. During the 20 minutes that the class had to brainstorm ideas, the groups worked cooperatively and respectfully. This

lesson took place midway through my placement, so the kids were familiar with me and were responding to me in a positive manner. I think the fact that I had an excellent rapport with the class had a lot to do with the success of this lesson. A lot of the ideas that were being expressed in regards to how one might go about conquering certain fears would have made Freud proud. There were some really great ideas. At the end of the 20 minutes each group had 2-3 minutes to present their information to the rest of the class. The presentations were well done, and the class was quiet when the other groups were presenting. I really experienced no difficulties in getting this lesson off the ground, nor did I have to deal with any problems during the group work. Everything ran smoothly. After the presentations were done it was recess. After recess I had students evaluate themselves individually and as a group. I then collected these evaluations, put them together with my evaluation and came up with an individual mark for everyone, as well as, a group mark. Everyone did quite well.

I followed up on this cooperative lesson the next day when we began to discuss peer pressure and the fear of not fitting in. The fact that I'd done a cooperative lesson on fear with them the previous day, really helped to move our discussion along in regard to peer pressure. I also noticed a carry-over through actions during the last week-and-a-half of my placement. The class seemed less concerned about failing in front of their friends and more interested in participating in what was going on. A nice carry-over from my lesson, if that was what it was.

Children's Literature Cited
Jones, Terry. *Fairy Tales*.
England: Puffin Books, 1981.

Teachers' Comments Regarding how Aspects of Cooperative Learning Weave into Inductive Thinking

These comments are from kindergarten to grade twelve teachers who have been working at implementing this strategy in their classrooms. The reason we included their comments is that talk is essential for intellectual growth – learning is socially constructed.

- Aspects of Cooperative Learning are critical to this process. Do not assume that students have the skills to work in small groups or to share information with one another. Students need to develop the skills to work together to arrive at consensus and to make sure everyone's voice is heard and valued in the process.

- You have to take the time to 'teach' the social aspect – such as how to deal with different opinions (disagreeing agreeably, taking time to make sure everyone gets a chance to talk, and learning to suspend judgement).

- Provide time for the students to look at how other groups classified the data. Here you could use the cooperative structures of Walk About or Gallery Tour. Also, make sure you provide time to have the students share their thinking in their small groups.

- Take time to walk around and check to make sure all students in the group are participating; make sure one person is not taking over and doing all the work. Taking the time to do this allows you to observe how your students are operating socially.

- If the students are working in small-cooperative groups, keep the groups small enough (2 or 3) so that all students in the group are involved in classifying the data

- Use of Numbered Heads to build in accountability is important.

- If you use Numbered Heads, don't identify who in the group is going to do the reporting until after they have done their classification.

Summary of Concept Formation

- Be careful about the size of the data set; especially if this is their first time or if the data set is more complex (e.g., a lot of reading).

- Leaving the data set open to the students' interpretation, with no right or wrong answer, or no right or wrong number of groups (as long as they could justify why they classified the way they did) is appreciated by the students and is more motivating. Students consistently report that it encouraged them to take more risks.

- Remind them before and during the activity not to label first and then try to fit examples in; this reduces the flexibility of their thinking.

- When doing this for the first time, take a few minutes to explain the strategy and why you are asking them to be involved in this type of process. Take the time at the end to ask them what they thought.

- When ever possible, design the data set so that the students can physically manipulate the data. Using 'stickies' allows the students to come back the next day and re-work the data.

- Make sure that students look over/read the data before beginning to classify the data.

- The 'reality' of the data set makes a difference; if using pictures, select pictures that are meaningful; use colour if possible.

- If it is the first time the students are doing an inductive lesson, have the students practice on less complex and fun data sets to get the idea of what it means to classify.

Chapter Ten

Complex Organizers: Mind Mapping and Concept Mapping

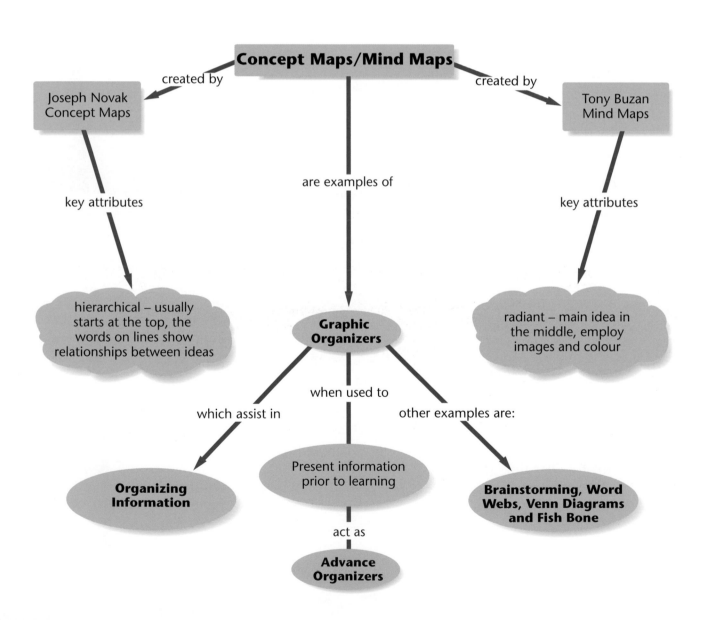

Concept Maps/Mind Maps

created by → Joseph Novak Concept Maps

created by → Tony Buzan Mind Maps

are examples of → Graphic Organizers

key attributes → hierarchical – usually starts at the top, the words on lines show relationships between ideas

key attributes → radiant – main idea in the middle, employ images and colour

which assist in → Organizing Information

when used to → Present information prior to learning

other examples are: → Brainstorming, Word Webs, Venn Diagrams and Fish Bone

act as → Advance Organizers

Chapter Ten

Complex Organizers: Mind Mapping and Concept Mapping

This chapter includes the following interconnected areas:

- Introduction and Rationale
- Concept Attainment Data Set on Mind Maps and Concept Maps
- Two Sample Lessons
- An Explanation of Mind Mapping
- Sample Rubric for evaluating a Mind Map
- A brief note on Word Webs
- An Explanation of Concept Mapping
- Sample Rubric for Evaluating a Concept Map
- Concept Maps – Exploring Linking Words
- Sample Lessons
- Summary – Final Thoughts

Key Questions

1. Thinking of Howard Gardner's work on multiple intelligences, how many intelligences are in play when students are working in small cooperative learning groups to construct a Mind Map or a Concept Map?
2. Does the research on the human brain justify the use of these two organizers?
3. Are Mind Mapping and Concept Mapping employed for the same or different outcomes?
4. What is the research on Mind Mapping and Concept Mapping?
   (For the research and resources, see Chapter 3.)

Remember this book is designed to illustrate how these two strategies can be integrated with other instructional processes to meet the diverse needs of the learner— not for an in-depth analysis of these two strategies. If you want to develop a more powerful understanding of these two strategies, consider the information in these two thoughtful books:

- *The Mind Map Book: Radiant Thinking* (Tony Buzan)
- *Learning, Creating, and Using Knowledge* (Joseph Novak)

Graphic Organizer for the Chapter
...a Flow Chart

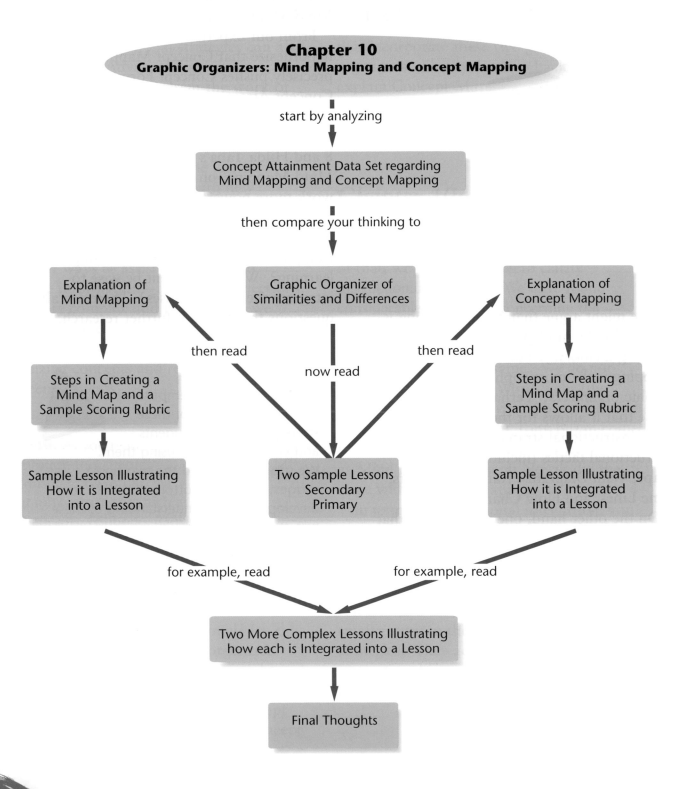

Chapter 10
Graphic Organizers: Mind Mapping and Concept Mapping

start by analyzing

Concept Attainment Data Set regarding
Mind Mapping and Concept Mapping

then compare your thinking to

| Explanation of Mind Mapping | Graphic Organizer of Similarities and Differences | Explanation of Concept Mapping |

then read   now read   then read

| Steps in Creating a Mind Map and a Sample Scoring Rubric | | Steps in Creating a Mind Map and a Sample Scoring Rubric |

| Sample Lesson Illustrating How it is Integrated into a Lesson | Two Sample Lessons Secondary Primary | Sample Lesson Illustrating How it is Integrated into a Lesson |

for example, read   for example, read

Two More Complex Lessons Illustrating
how each is Integrated into a Lesson

Final Thoughts

Concept Attainment Process: Mind Maps and Concept Maps

On this page and the next are four examples of Mind Maps. Following those are two pages containing four examples of Concept Maps. Compare and contrast each of the sets. Try to identify the essential characteristics or critical attributes of both Mind Maps and Concept Maps. On page 283 there are two testers and a place to write down your thinking. You can then turn to the section that describes each of the two processes to compare your thinking with that of Tony Buzan (Mind Mapping) and Joseph Novak (Concept Mapping).

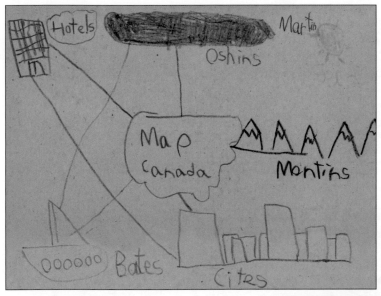

grade one's first attempt at Mind Mapping related to what information maps provide

university student's first attempt at Mind Mapping issues/topics related to water ecology

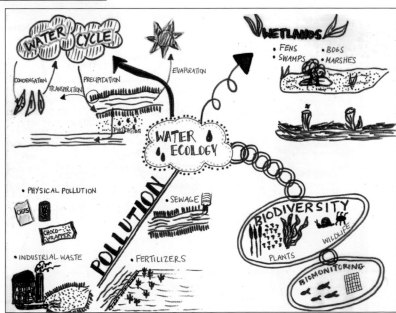

university student's second attempt at Mind Mapping

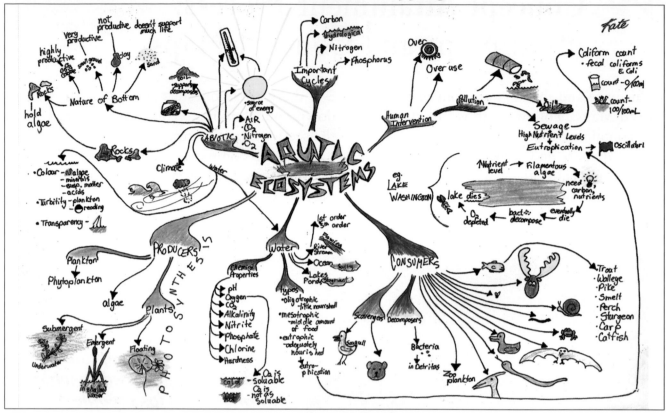

grade eight student's second attempt at Mind Mapping

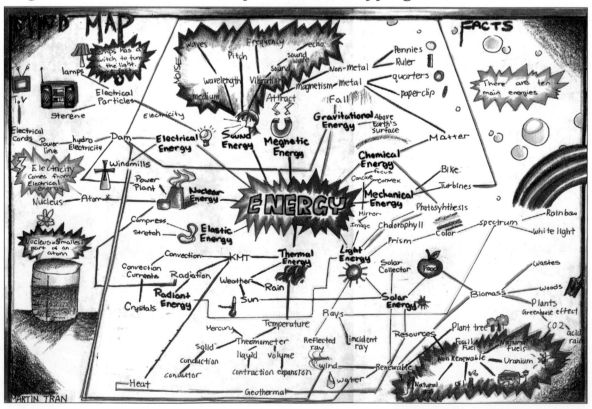

Concept Maps

university student's first attempt at a Concept Map

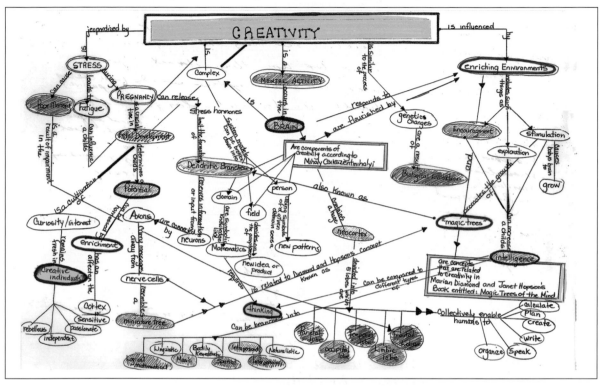

grade four's first attempt at a Concept Map

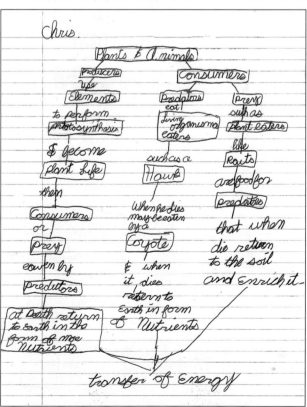

university student's first attempt at a Concept Map

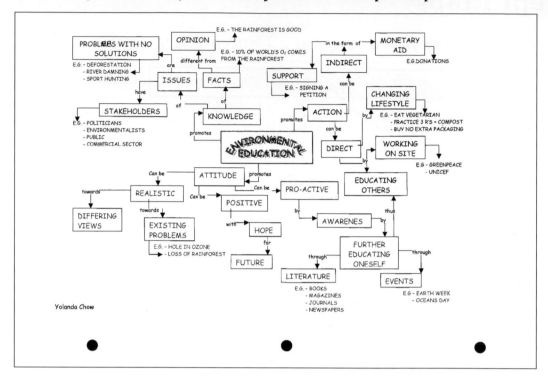

grade 11's first attempt at a Concept Map related to what he knew at the start of the unit

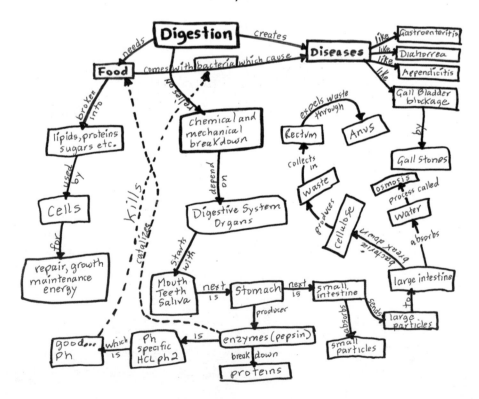

Testers: Concept Map(s) or Mind Map(s)?

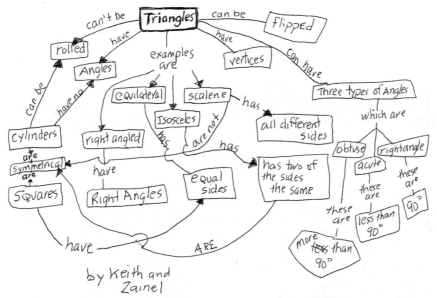

by Keith and Zainel

Your Thinking:

_____
_____
_____
_____

On the following page is an organizer that is neither a Concept Map nor a Mind Map but simply a graphic organizer that explores the similarities and differences between Mind Maps and Concept Maps.

A Brief Note on Word Webs

Below is a Word Web done by a grade nine student. He used the graphic program "Inspiration" to create the Word Web. Word Webs are easier to construct than Mind Maps and Concept Maps. It might be wise to have students start with Word Webbing and then move into Mind Mapping or Concept Mapping.

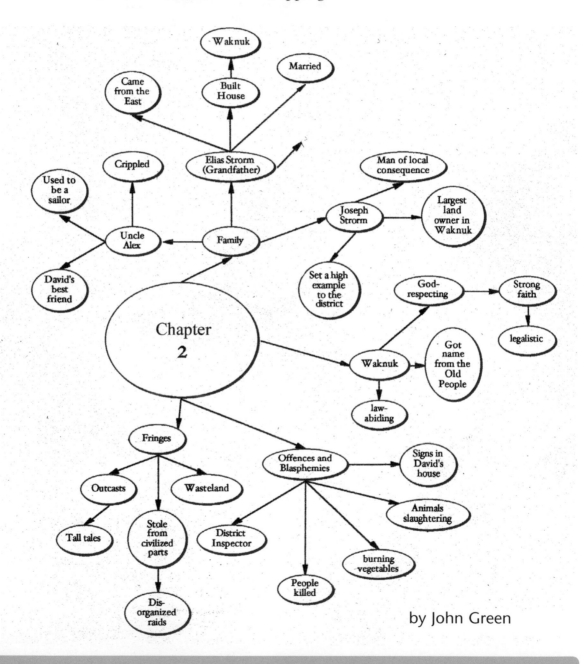

by John Green

Challenge: Is it possible to integrate Word Webs, Mind Maps, Concept Maps, Venn Diagrams, Fish Bone, Flow Charts etc., in the SAME graphic organizer to summarize a unit of study? We think so!

Mind Maps and Concept Maps: Similarities and Differences

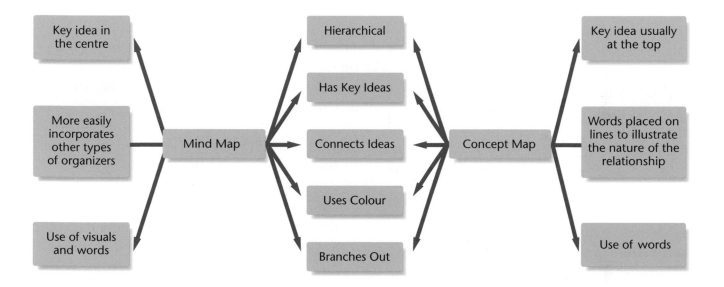

Key idea in the centre			Hierarchical			Key idea usually at the top
More easily incorporates other types of organizers	Mind Map		Has Key Ideas	Concept Map		Words placed on lines to illustrate the nature of the relationship
Use of visuals and words			Connects Ideas			Use of words
			Uses Colour			
			Branches Out			

On the following three pages are two lessons that incorporate one of each of these processes. You do not see the product; rather you see how the process is woven into the lesson.

Secondary Lesson: English Grade 11
Lesson Plan: Media Script Writing

MENTAL SET – CONNECTING TO THEIR EXPERIENCES:

Take a few moments and think to yourself please. What are the things that occur in a script that you don't see in the finished product? Students think to themselves, share with a partner and then discuss as a class. Their ideas are put on chart paper.

OBJECTIVES AND PURPOSE:

Today our focus is to have you apply your understanding of the concept of script writing by constructing a script.

Some of you may some day have the opportunity to do script writing in your careers. Connect to their ideas and discuss how scripts are used not just for movies, but also for radio and television commercials. *The purpose of this unit of study is to provide you with the opportunity to inquire into script writing. One process that assists in script writing is finding organizers to illustrate the connections between ideas. We will also be applying several conceptual organizers.*

INPUT: PART I

Employ Team Analysis (see Chapter Eleven for an in-depth explanation of Team Analysis) Students are placed in groups of four. (Number groups 1 to 7 and letter group members A,B,C, D)

Each person read through pages 88 and 89 in your text three times. It's important to read these pages three times for understanding.

Now that you've read this information three times your groups will have four minutes to pull out what you think are the critical attributes of script writing. What has to be in place for a script to be effective? Once Team Analysis is completed shift to Mind Mapping.

Mind Mapping: Large group Mind Map of the key features of a script.
Teacher constructs this on white board—call on students randomly to hold them accountable to think. Make sure you use different colours/draw images.

INPUT: PART II

Cooperative Learning Simulation Split students into pairs (A and B); Number groups 1, 2, 3 etc.

You are a television production company. You need a company name. Your first task is to give yourself a name that incorporates both your names or incorporates the idea of a parent company. You have one minute. After one minute have them share their company name.

Directions: Your tender for a contract to produce a script for a Short Subject (already covered) television program has been accepted. Your task is to adapt this famous poem by Raymond Souster (Yonge Street Saturday Night) into a script for television. The script has to have one or two scenes and the deadline for completion is by the end of the period tomorrow. You must use the proper formatting techniques already discussed. Other than those conditions, you can determine how to adapt this poem into a script.

Read the poem aloud to students (twice) as they follow along.

Connecting script format to the poem:
(Brainstorming in pairs)
Having looked at the critical aspects of a script's format, and having read the poem, what else will you have to consider in writing this script?

Process as a class: Return to the Mind Map on the white board and build out from it.

Now that we have all the parts, how are you going to sequence your script? Where will you start?

You and your partner have the rest of this class and all of the next to complete your script; that is, except for the last 15 minutes, which we will use to share our scripts with other pairs for editing. We will also take a few minutes to discuss your group's efforts at the end.

You have a budget of $10 000 to purchase assistance from a freelance consultant (me) or members of other production companies. The cost of support is 500 dollars per request.

MODELLING:
Occurs during Input stage.

CHECK FOR UNDERSTANDING:
The final script will be the check for understanding.

CLOSURE:
Take 5 minutes to talk about the process. Summarize key ideas. Make sure everyone's voice is heard.

Yonge Street Saturday Night

Except when the theatre crowds engulf
    the sidewalks
at nine, at eleven-thirty,
this street is lonely, and a thousand
    lights
in a thousand store windows
wouldn't break her lips into a smile.

There are a few bums out,
there are lovers with hands held tightly,
there are also the drunk ones
but they are princes among men, and are
    few.

And there are some like us,
just walking, making both feet move out
    ahead of us,
a little bored, a little lost, a little angry,

walking as though we were honestly going
    somewhere,
walking as if there was really something
    to see
at Adelaide or maybe on King,
something, no matter how little
that will give us some fair return
on our use of shoe-leather,

something perhaps that will make us
    smile
with a strange new happiness,
a lost but recovered joy.

—Raymond Souster

Elementary Lesson -
Grade Five: Introductory Lesson Biographies and Autobiographies.

OVERVIEW: In this grade five class, the teacher wanted the students to develop an introductory understanding of the meaning of biography and autobiography. They would be using biographies of people throughout the year. In addition, this was the second week of class, and the teacher wanted to employ this as another way to have the students get to know each other — to work at building a community of learners.

OBJECTIVE: Students will develop an introductory understanding of biographies and autobiographies by constructing and sharing a Concept Map that organizes the concepts that inform others about who they are. In addition, students will use the Concept Maps to extend their understanding of others in the class.

To introduce Concept Maps to the students, I provided ten YES examples of Concept Maps done the previous year by students and 10 other types of organizers, also done by students the previous year. These were put around the room. Beside each Concept Map was another type of organizer. These were the NO examples. The NO examples were three Mind Maps, two Visual Organizers, a Time Line, a Venn Diagram, a Ranking Ladder and a Fish Bone (also work samples from students from last year). The students had to work in pairs to identify what it was that all these Concept Maps had in common.

CHECK FOR UNDERSTANDING: I then put an overhead transparency on the overhead and they compared their thinking with what was on the overhead.

PRACTICE: The students then completed a Concept Map. They worked in pairs on one piece of chart paper that was folded in half. One person worked on one-half, the other person worked on the other. They had 20 minutes to complete their Concept Maps about themselves. They used their initial classification to get started with the most important ideas coming out first. When finished, person A shared their Map with person B. Then B shared with A (autobiography) . Next, they cut the paper along the fold, A gave his to B and B gave hers to A. They then had to find 3 other people and explain their partner to another person (biography).

CLOSURE: The students were put into pairs. Each pair was provided with an explanation of biography and autobiography. Each person read the sheet. They then met with one other person from another group who had the same sheet to discuss the major ideas on the sheet (a Jigsaw). They then returned to their partner and explained the key ideas. I randomly called on pairs to share their thinking. Last, the students used a Venn Diagram (they had used these previously) to illustrate the similarities and differences between biography and autobiography.

An Explanation of Mind Mapping

We strongly recommend Tony Buzan's (1993) book, *The Mind Map Book: Radiant Thinking*. It is an excellent and colourful resource for taking you deeper into the Mind Mapping process. It also provides numerous examples of Mind Maps. Buzan makes connections to the literature related to brain research and learning. He sees Mind Mapping as a natural function of the human brain.

Another useful book is Nancy Margulies' (1991) book, *Mapping Inner Space*. This book illustrates practical ways to get started. The ideas provided in both are essential - Buzan's book provides an in-depth explanation of the process while Marguiles' book provides a useful introduction regarding how to start.

Mind Mapping is an analytical process that involves creatively integrating a combination of visuals, colour, codes, words, and connectors. It can be employed as a method to take notes, to study before an exam, to brainstorm, or make connections between ideas. It can be extended with little effort to be an alternative way of applying Hilda Taba's Inductive Thinking model of teaching (see Chapter 9). Additionally, several high-school English teachers have students employ Mind Maps to collect and portray their arguments when involved in Academic Controversy (explained in Chapter 11).

Buzan states that Mind Maps have four essential characteristics and several non-essential characteristics. We would argue that colour is also a critical attribute rather than non-essential. Our rationale is the mind processes and is intrigued by colour.

ESSENTIAL:
1. a central image that represents the subject being mapped
2. main themes that radiate like branches from that central image
3. those branches have a key image or key word printed on an associated line
4. the branches have a connected structure

NON-ESSENTIAL:
1. colour
2. codes

RATIONALE: Mind Maps enhance the brain's capacity to store and recall information. Because it uses visuals and colours, it provides a novel and interesting way to make sense of something the student is learning. It can be a motivating way for students to summarize a unit on a Friday afternoon when things are dragging and a bit of a "pick-me-up" is required. One enjoyable example of integration is to weave the Johnsons' Cooperative Learning process (explained in Chapter 7) with Buzan's Mind Mapping process to have a small group create a Mind Map. The lesson on heroes later in this chapter illustrates this integration.

Also, students can employ Cooperative Learning structures such as Gallery Tour and Three-Step-Interview to explain the major messages in their Mind Map.

Steps in Creating a Basic Mind Map

MATERIALS: Each student or group of students will need a sheet of paper and coloured pens or crayons. The size of paper will depend on the topic, the time, the amount students know, and what you are going to do with the Mind Maps. You can also have students cut and paste pictures from magazines instead of (or along with) their drawings.

SIZE: If the Mind Map is to be a poster for sharing, the size will be different than if it is to serve as notes and placed in a binder for review before a test. We saw a Mind Map that took up the complete wall of the classroom and evolved over the year—it served as an ongoing summary of the students' learning in a middle-school English class.

The following steps are only suggestions; feel free to add, adapt, or extend to make it responsive to your students' needs. Remember that when you do this with a partner, you are attending to five of the eight intelligences identified by Howard Gardner, as well as the brain's propensity for creating patterns and its need for talk.

1. **Select a topic** (for example "the heart" or "factoring" or "poetry" or "democracy").
   - Think of a visual that captures the essence of that topic and place that visual in the centre of the paper using colours that will assist you to remember that idea. For example, in a kindergarten class, the students did a Mind Map of the story "The Billy Goats Gruff." They put a picture of the bridge in the middle.

Steps in Creating a Basic Mind Map:

2. **Brainstorm for the key ideas related to that topic.**
   - Record all the ideas that come to you - this can be personal or group brainstorming. Now you can simply pick out the most important ideas that will branch out first or you can group those ideas into common categories – give each of those categories a label and then those become the first key ideas.
   - Draw a picture or symbol that represents each of the key ideas you brainstormed. Then position those visuals that make sense to you around the outside of the visual you placed in the centre of the map. Put in the key word and then connect the key words to the centre topic with a line or bubbles.
   - Flow with ideas radiating out from each of those key ideas; again, think of visuals that capture the essence of that idea and place them in a way that makes sense to you. Then, place the word by the visual. Again, connect with lines.
   - Continue until you have exhausted the topic, the space, the time, or your patience.
3. **Reflect with a partner or with small groups or with the class —perhaps a Three-Step-Interview or Gallery Tour.**
   - In your mind or with a partner, talk through the journey you took to conceptualize the key ideas related to the topic. Explore the relationships between different aspects of the map.

Sample Rubric for Evaluating a Mind Map

Rubric for Mind Map Performance Levels

CRITERIA	PERFORMANCE INDICATORS (Observable descriptors indicating extent to which a criterion is met.)			
	Level1	Level 2	Level 3	Level 4
Central Image	Not clear; difficult to separate from other information	Present; not eye catching or memorable	Clear; use of picture or image that relates to key idea	Stands out; meaningfully grasps the key idea through metaphor or humour
Ideas radiate out from central image and from most to least complex	Little to no indication that ideas are connected to and radiating out from centre, from most to least complex	Ideas radiate out from centre, some confusion as you follow ideas moving from most to least complex	Ideas clearly connect to central image and ideas, and for the most part move from most to least complex	Ideas clearly connect to central image and ideas consistently and accurately shift from most to least complex
Ideas have key images or key words	Little to no evidence of key images. May have a few keywords or vice-versa	Images and keywords are evident, but either too few or imprecise	Images and key words clearly show an understanding of the content, although not that memorable	Dynamic use of images and keywords. They clearly connect to central image. See use of metaphor, humour, cut-outs from magazines, clipart, etc.
Colour or codes or links used to illustrate connections between ideas	Little to no use of colour, codes, or links to illustrate connections between ideas	Obvious attempt is made to use colour, codes or links to enhance clarity and memory. Still a bit confusing.	Clearly uses colour, codes, or links to clarify connections and to assist with memory for most aspects of Mind Map	Effectively uses colour, codes, or links to meaningfully clarify connections for all aspects of Mind Map
Depth of coverage	Insufficient coverage of content covered	Shows a basic level of coverage of key ideas but little extension of ideas	Shows a solid grasp of most of the content and shows extensions of most key ideas	Shows a solid grasp of all the content covered. Extensions of the key ideas show a deep understanding of that content

Note: this is one teacher's suggestion for evaluation – please feel free to design your own or adapt this one.

An Explanation of Concept Mapping

Although we provide you with an introduction to Concept Mapping, as stated previously, we recommend that you read Novak's and Gowan's (1984) book, *Learning How to Learn.* As well, you may want to read articles related to Concept Mapping to assist you in taking the process deeper. Chapter Two in the book *Probing for Understanding* by Richard White and Richard Gunstone (1992) provides a useful and detailed explanation of the process with a number of student examples of Concept Maps.

EXPLANATION: A Concept Map is a visual representation that illustrates how one understands relationships between concepts. Those concepts could be any combination of things, people, ideas, arguments, solutions, places, etc. Concept mapping serves to move the learner from simply recalling facts to making the linkages or relationships between those facts. It encourages more complex and meaningful thinking. Below are the essential characteristics of a Concept Map.

ESSENTIAL:
1. Start with a major term or idea from which the next term or idea extends either in a hierarchical or radiating format — Concept Maps usually start at the top.
2. Shift is from a more complex to less complex idea or major idea to minor idea. It often ends with an example.
2. Connecting line is drawn between concepts.
3. Linking words are placed on the lines stating the relationship between concepts
4. Cross links between one segment of the concept hierarchy or classification and another

NON-ESSENTIAL:
1. Colour to clarify segment areas or ideas that relate. This is useful when the use of connecting lines makes it confusing to follow the relationships.
2. Examples of the concept being presented. This adds meaning, communicates that the student understands the concept and aids in retention of the information.

Who can use Concept Maps? Like Mind Maps, Concept Maps can be used by students of all ages (kindergarten to adult learners – although younger students will need more help). For more in-depth information on younger students, see Stice (1987). This educator examined the potential of using Concept Maps with kindergarten to grade five students. With older students, teachers often employ Concept Maps as alternatives to essays or as organizers for essays.

Like Mind Maps, Concept Maps (often called semantic maps) increase students' abilities to organize and represent their thoughts. Initially, Concept Mapping was associated primarily with metacognition and science. More recently, it has been applied to reading comprehension as it helps the learner activate and retrieve prior knowledge. In one of our doctoral classes (a research colloquium on current brain research) large concept maps were created to facilitate the synthesis of each book and to find connections and patterns between books.

Jeni Wilson (1987) in her article on Concept Mapping, argues that although Concept Maps are personal, peer discussion is extremely worthwhile for assisting students to verify, clarify, and extend their graphic representation.

Steps in Creating a Basic Concept Map

The steps are similar to those of Mind Mapping. Before we describe the steps, we will review the four major differences between Mind Maps and Concept Maps.

First, Concept Maps usually start at the top, but can begin at the bottom or sides or in the centre; whereas Mind Maps begin in the middle and radiate out.

Second, Concept Maps employ words on the lines between concepts to illustrate the link between those concepts. Mind Maps usually do not.

Third, Concept Maps seldom employ colour; Minds Map usually employ colour.

Fourth, Concept Maps seldom employ visuals; Minds Maps employ visuals. You can see that these two processes can be easily integrated.

MATERIALS: Each student or group of students will need a sheet of paper and coloured pens or crayons. The size of paper will depend on the topic, the time, the amount you know, and what you are going to do with it.

SIZE: If the Concept Map is to be a poster to be shared, the size will be different than if it is to serve as notes and placed in a binder for a review before a test.

The following steps are only suggestions, feel free to add, adapt, or extend to make Concept Mapping responsive to the students' needs. Remember that when you do this with a partner, you are attending to five of the eight intelligences identified by Howard Gardner, as well as the brain's propensity for creating patterns and its need for talk.

Steps in Creating a Concept Map:

1. Brainstorm (individually or in a group) the key ideas. So if you are studying energy, you might introduce the unit by creating a class Concept Map of the students' current understanding of energy. The result might be items such as: solar energy, nuclear energy, electrical energy, nuclear waste, global warming, sun, solar heating, gas, oil, pollution, fossil fuel, etc.

2. Students put the ideas onto cards or post–it notes. (Students enjoy manipulating the data.) Once the ideas are on cards, they can begin to sort and classify these cards, looking for relationships between ideas. If working alone, they can work for a few minutes, and then do a Walk-About to see how others are sorting the cards.

3. The students can now paste or transfer the ideas onto a piece of paper. They then draw lines between the concepts and place words on the lines that illustrate their thinking about the relationships between the concepts. They will have to decide whether they want to create a hierarchical Concept Map or a more radiant Concept Map (similar to Mind Mapping).

4. Students also look for cross links between different concepts.

On the following page is a scoring rubric for Concept Maps.

Sample Rubric for Evaluating a Concept Map

Performance Levels

Performance Indicators	Level 1	Level 2	Level 3	Level 4
Concepts	• Insufficient number of concepts selected relating to topic • Arrangement of concepts illustrates no understanding of conceptual relationships	• Minimal but acceptable number of concepts selected, with some relationships to the topic • Arrangement of concepts demonstrates simple understanding of subordinate conceptual relationships	• Most concepts relating to topic were selected • Arrangement of concepts demonstrates an understanding of subordinate conceptual relationships	• Most concepts and all significant concepts selected and they clearly relate to the topic • Arrangement of concepts demonstrates complete understanding of subordinate conceptual relationships
Hierarchical Structure	• Concepts are displayed in a linear sequence. Little or no sense of hierarchical structure	• Limited hierarchical structure used	• Concepts connected in a hierarchical structure	• Concepts connected in a hierarchical structure leading to more specific concepts
Linkages	• Some basic relationships indicated by connected lines • Linking words are simple and repetitive	• Straightforward relationships connected with linking words • Linking words show variety	• Most relationships indicated with a connecting line and labeled with linking words • Linking words are accurate and varied	• All relationships indicated by a connecting line and accurately labeled with appropriate linking words • Linking words are expressive and purposeful
Cross Links	• Cross links not used	• Few cross links are used to illustrate minimal connections	• Cross links used to reflect straightforward connections	• Cross links show complex relationships between two or more distinct segments of the concept map

Designed by: Shirley Smith, Bev Elaschuk

Feel free to adapt this rubric or create your own.

Concept Maps: Moving to a More Complex Level-Exploring Linking Words

Once your students have an idea of how to construct Concept Maps, you may want to have them develop a deeper understanding of how to think in terms of linking words. The next few pages are intended to help you explore how to get students to be more consciously precise as they select connecting words.

In the box below is a collection of linking words. How would you classify them into groups based on how they represent the nature of relationships? (Note: This is Phase I of Hilda Taba's Inductive Thinking strategy – Chapter 9.)

Once you have determined two or more groups, compare your analysis with the data set on the following page.

On the following page is a data set of examples (Clear Ovals and Blue Ovals). They each present a linking word on the line between each oval. (Note that this data set is the start of a Bruner's Concept Attainment strategy – Chapter 8.) You may want to work with a partner — this brings in aspects of social theory (Cooperative Learning). If so, make sure you both get a chance to talk about your thinking.

After you've finished sharing your ideas, you might consider reflecting on the "trip" your mind went on as you explored the data set.

When analyzing the two data sets on the following page, remember that the linking words between the Clear Ovals have something that is the same. Likewise with the linking words between the Blue Ovals. On your own, see if you can determine how the linking words between the two sets of ovals are different.

When you think you have some ideas, try the testers on the following page.

is	part of	can be
can effect	detected by	follows
precedes	is like	similar to
includes		absorbed by
excluded from		example is
same as		eaten by
	destroyed by	
	causes	influences
is greater than		incorporated into
leads to		digested by
prevented through		connects
need	produces	have

Suggestion: With younger students you can provide a list of linking words. Then, once they have placed/pasted the ideas on the paper and drawn the lines, they can select words from the list.

Concept Attainment: Exploring Linking Words

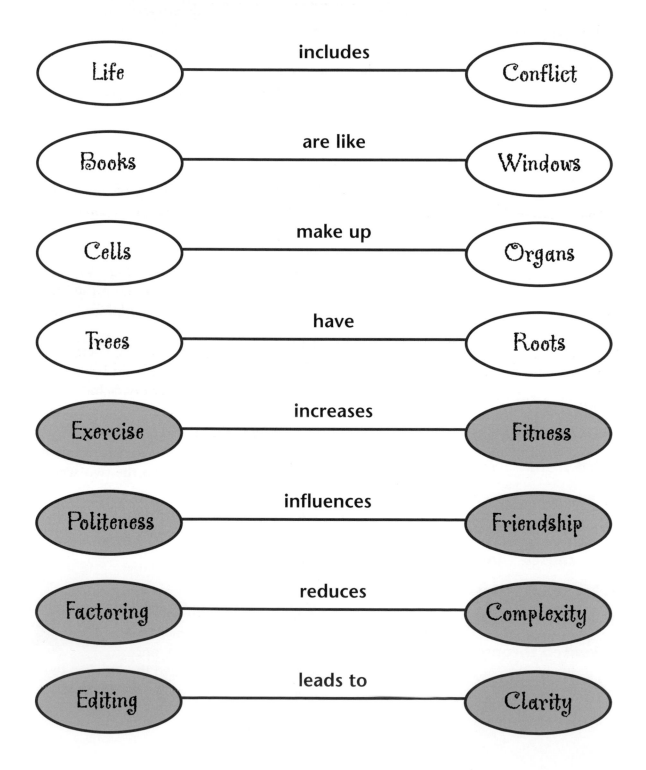

Life —— includes —— Conflict

Books —— are like —— Windows

Cells —— make up —— Organs

Trees —— have —— Roots

Exercise —— increases —— Fitness

Politeness —— influences —— Friendship

Factoring —— reduces —— Complexity

Editing —— leads to —— Clarity

Testers

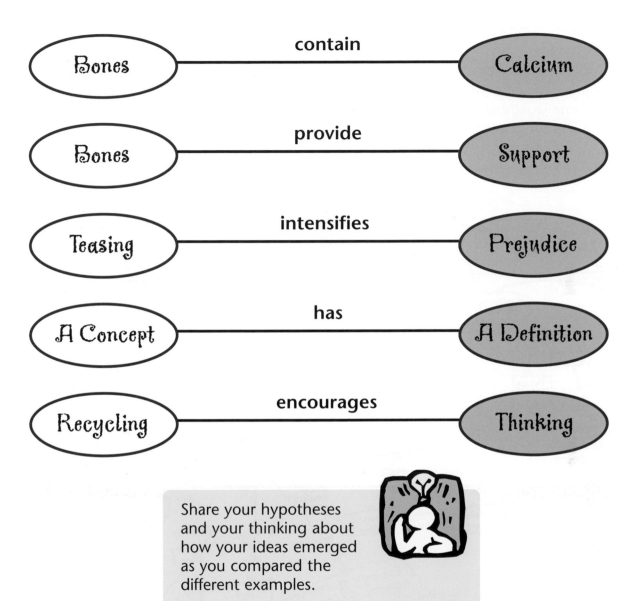

Bones —— contain —— Calcium

Bones —— provide —— Support

Teasing —— intensifies —— Prejudice

A Concept —— has —— A Definition

Recycling —— encourages —— Thinking

Share your hypotheses and your thinking about how your ideas emerged as you compared the different examples.

Concerning the Previous Page:

The Clear represent "Descriptive" or "Analogical" linking words. The Blue Ovals represent "Dynamic" or "Cause and Effect" linking words.

On the next page is a copy of part of a larger Concept Map. See if you can find examples of these two categories of words.

Sample from a Larger Concept Map

Below is a portion of a Concept Map related to the environment. Analyze the words used by this student. See if you can find examples of "Descriptive" and "Dynamic" words. Note that some words act as both Descriptive and Dynamic.

Most linking words can be placed in one of those two groups. The Descriptive tend to provide more information or push clarity — they are sensed as static. The Dynamic explore the effects that one thing has on another — they are about action.

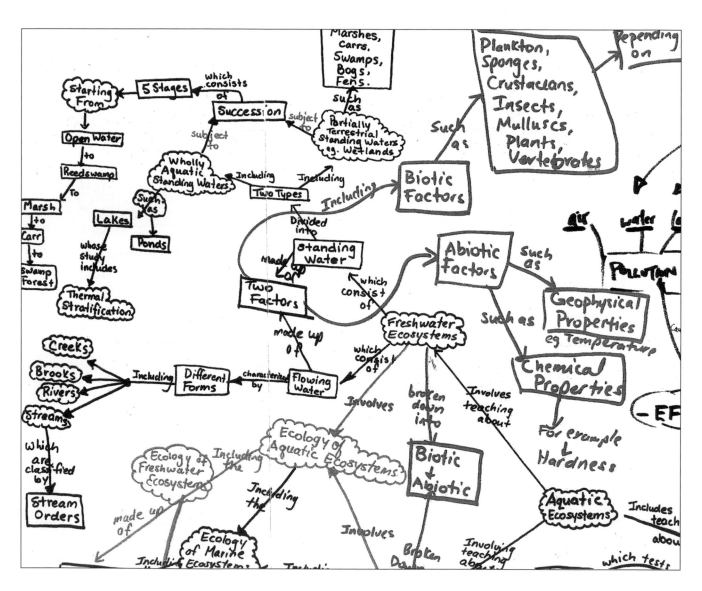

Applying Your Understanding

Practise with linking words. Try and develop different ways of using words to illustrate different types of relationships. Place one word in each oval and place a linking work that illustrates the relationship between the two words.

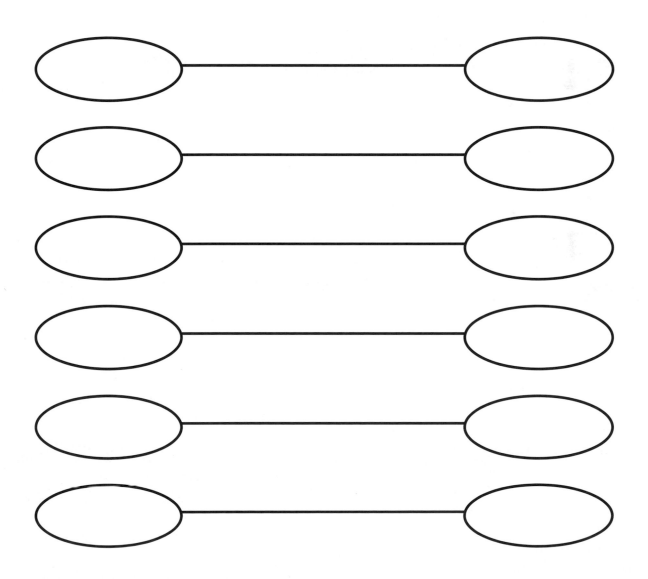

Concept Mapping: Dissecting Owl Pellets
Elementary Lesson - Grade 4/5 Split:
Integrating Concept Mapping and Cooperative Learning

OBJECTIVE

The students will further their understanding of the interdependency of all living things in an ecological system by analyzing owl pellets and mapping their findings to illustrate how living things are interdependent. The other objective is to have them apply their understanding of Concept Maps as a strategy to organize information—especially as a study technique.

> **Note:** The students are working on a unit related to the interdependency of living things. They recently observed a video that contained a segment related to owl pellets.

SET

Begin the lesson by asking everyone to think of a time when they were sick to their stomach. *Why do they think this happens?* (Wait 15 seconds and then have the students share their ideas.) Then ask them to think about the film we watched and recall the discussion about the owls regurgitating pellets and why this happens. We discussed the similarities between humans vomiting to get rid of something that is not being digested, and the owls regurgitating bones in the form of a pellet because they cannot digest them.

OBJECTIVE AND PURPOSE

Explain that they are going to be working in small groups to dissect owl pellets. They will be graphing the bones found onto the animal chart, classifying them according to the animal (i.e., mouse, shrew, vole, bird, etc.). And then, once they have completed that analysis, they will transfer their ideas into a Concept Map to illustrate the relationship between all living things. They will include the other areas they have already investigated—not just the owl pellet information.

MODELLING

The teacher first models how to go about dissecting the owl pellet, surgical gloves are put on and a demonstration is shown to the students on how to use the dissecting sticks and tweezers. The steps are reviewed and a recorded bone graph is shown. A large chart is hung up and the roles of each group member are discussed.

INPUT

The students work in cooperative small groups (3-4). They each take turns according to their assigned roles, rotating every 4 minutes. The children gently pick apart the pellet, finding various bones and grouping them according to their common attributes. Using a picture animal web and bone chart, they glue the bones, skulls, beaks, etc., onto black construction paper and classify them in animal groups and fill in the bone graph.

CHECK FOR UNDERSTANDING

Throughout the lesson the teacher interacts during the input time, asking relevant questions about their findings. Each student also hands in an individual bone graph and five answered questions about the lesson on dissecting pellets. (individual accountability)

PRACTICE

The students now apply their understanding of Concept Maps by interpreting the information from the pellet analysis and connecting to other information in this unit on the interdependency of living things. Here the objective is to get them to extend their ability to apply Concept Maps to organize information.

CLOSURE

After the students had completed the dissecting and had recorded their findings, the students gathered on the carpet to share with each other. They discussed what animal bones they found in their pellets. We then looked at the food web/chain we previously studied, and talked about the importance and interdependency the owl has on other animals to survive. All of the group's findings were displayed on a bulletin board.

REFLECTION

This lesson was taught in a grade 4/5 combined classroom as a culminating activity for an owl unit I had been working on with them. During this lesson I used the first four levels of Bloom's Taxonomy. The mental set asked for the students to recall information. The input stage asked for comprehension and application. The students had to dissect the pellet and match and group the bones according to their common attributes. They also had to classify and graph the bones according to which animal they belong. The closure stage asked for analysis from the students as they explained what animals their owl had consumed, and discussed the importance of the owl's interdependency on other animals.

The students were very excited about this activity—given the build-up to it during the previous week. Although the students had been given some prior knowledge about owls through other lessons, books, and a film, I knew I still had to come up with a mental set for this cooperative lesson. I thought about it for several days. I knew it had to be meaningful to the students and something that they could relate to. I finally came up with the concept of throwing up. I know it sounds awful, but boy, did it work. I had their full attention, and even though they were saying "gross, yuk" they were quite intrigued with the conversation and were able to make a connection between vomiting and the owl regurgitating a pellet.

I have really come to understand the importance of explaining and modelling to the students the steps and procedures they are to follow to carry-out the lesson.

Complex Lesson
Integrating Mind Mapping, Lesson Design, Five Elements of Cooperative small–group Learning, Think/Pair Share, Round Robin

Lesson Plan - Grade 10

OBJECTIVE

Students will extend their understanding of the concept of "hero" by inquiring into the characteristics of classical Greek heroes through first reading the mythology of Perseus, and second discussing the concept of hero as it applies to the reading. To summarize the key ideas, they will work in teams of 3 or 4 to Mind-Map Perseus' heroic qualities.

MENTAL SET

Before the students came into class, I had on the board the word "HERO" in scrambled form, "OERH." The letters were covered with a piece of paper to create suspense. Of course, the students wanted to know what was behind the paper and why it was covered.

When everyone was seated, I started the class this way: I held up pictures of Babe Ruth, Martin Luther King, Jr., Mother Teresa, Mahatma Gandhi, and Winston Churchill, and asked the students to identify a common quality shared by these people and to share their idea with a partner (Think/Pair/Share).

The students were quick to point out that these people were modern heroes. At this point, I uncovered the scrambled word and put the letters in order. Had the class shown difficulty in pinpointing the people as modern heroes, I would have uncovered the scrambled word and would have given it to them as a clue, making the students figure out the word themselves.

Next, I gave the students an opportunity to tell their peers what they knew about these people, the characteristics and/or achievements that made them heroes.

I also gave the students an opportunity to name some of their heroes and tell their peers why they admired these people. At the end of this brief mental set, I shared with my students the objective of the lesson.

INPUT

Photocopies of the story of Perseus were handed to each student. It was read as a class. Occasionally, I stopped the reading and asked students the meaning of certain words found in the text. I told them to write the meaning in the margin beside the text. Moreover, since the students had previously experienced an introduction to mythology in grade nine, I stimulated and maintained interest in Perseus' story, and kept the sleepy students on their toes by asking questions where they had to think back and recall what they had learned in grade nine. (e.g., Perseus steals the single eye shared by the three hags, the Graeeae, in order to get information about Medusa's lair. I asked the students, "What other mythological being have you met who had only one eye?" Answer: the Cyclops.)

The particular text they were reading was chosen because of its appropriateness for Grade 10. Unfortunately, it did not have pictures. So I brought along a pictorial depiction of the story found in another text to show the students. This was done in order to stimulate as many senses as possible and to facilitate auditory and visual learning. On the next page I briefly summarize what I did and what the students did.

Teacher Behaviour	Student Behaviour

Provided the reading material and Mind-Mapped the social skills seen and heard in a good working group.
 	
Allowed the students to form their own groups of 3 or 4, and monitored their behaviour to see if they were on task and were practicing the social skills.
 	
Randomly chose a student in each group to present the group's Mind-Map the next day.
 	
Rotated the assigned tasks e.g. timekeeper, etc., every 10 minutes.
	Students formed their groups and numbered themselves.
	   #1 = timekeeper
	   #2 = materials manager
	   #3 = drawer
	If there was a fourth person, he/she became the person who encouraged the group to stay on task
	
	Students Mind-Mapped their attributes of classical hero and presented it to the class the next day.
	
	Students evaluated themselves and their group on how well they participated equally and stayed on task.

Five Elements of Cooperative Small Group Learning

1) **Goal-Positive Interdependence** – Each group had to work together in order to finish the assignment in 30 minutes. There wasn't enough time for one person to do all the work and complete it. Each person was assigned a different responsibility, and all responsibilities were crucial to succeed. Moreover, since everyone in the group knew they could be given the same mark, each person felt obligated to participate, stay on-task, and do a good job. The good students didn't want a poor mark, and the average students were pressured to do their share of the work by the good ones.

2) **Individual Accountability** – Since the students were warned that I would be randomly calling out one person from each group the next day to present their Mind-Map, and that a mark would be given for the presentation, every person felt obligated to know their work.

3) **Face-to-Face Interaction** – The desks were arranged in clusters to promote cooperative work and learning.

4) **Social Skills** – The students were taught the two social skills I wanted them to practise: disagreeing in non-hurtful ways and expressing support/no put downs.

5) **Group Processing** – Students were given an evaluation sheet to rate themselves and their group on how well they participated and stayed on task and what they liked or disliked about the cooperative Mind-Mapping.

MODELLING

None of my students knew anything about Mind-Mapping, so it was necessary to model it for them. Since it was my intent to teach them two social skills—disagreeing in non-hurtful ways and expressing support/no put-downs, I Mind-Mapped the social skills one would find when one observes a group that is working effectively and efficiently together. Next is the mini–lesson that I then followed to teach the two social skills.

Social Skill–Mini Lesson
Mental Set

I started off with a mental set: "What is the major reason for getting fired on the job?" They had one minute to discuss in a Round Robin. Answer: the inability to respect and work collaboratively with fellow employees.

"Last week I heard several comments that convinced me that there are some people in this class who lack or need to refine the social skills needed to work in the real world. I heard comments such as,

> 'Shut up!'
> 'What a stupid question!'
> 'Do you want to be shorter than you already are?'
> 'You're going to get it after school!'

Since you will be working in small groups today, I thought it would be a good time to review a few things I would like to see and hear from groups that are working well together."

Input & Modelling

I asked the students to name the social skills practised in a group that was working effectively and Mind-Mapped them on the board.

I indicated that to put into practice all the items would be very difficult, so only two—disagreeing in non-hurtful ways and expressing support/no put-downs—would be practised that day.

I also indicated that this was a Mind-Map and went over its attributes with the class.

Drawing on the board in funny and innovative ways kept the students' attention.

Check for Understanding

I randomly picked students to tell me and the class what they were supposed to do for the rest of the period, how to Mind-Map, and what the responsibilities of the time keeper, materials manager, and drawer were.

In this way, a mini lesson on social skills was inserted within the framework of a larger lesson plan.

Whenever students left out any detail or gave the wrong information, I didn't correct them. I randomly chose another student to correct the former's answer. This kept the whole class alert. I could "hear their motors twirling."

Processing

In the last 10 minutes of the class, the students evaluated themselves and their group on how successfully they carried out the two social skills.

I ended the class by inviting the students to take what they had learned about classical Greek heroes and apply it to a different situation. "After having Mind-Mapped the attributes of a Greek hero, we are now fairly familiar with what it takes to be a hero. Let me give you a brain-teaser: how does Bilbo Baggins fare when you hold him up to the attributes you have listed today? You don't have to give me an answer now, but please think about it tonight because we will be taking up your opinions tomorrow." This closure invited the students to extend their thinking and to make connections to what I had them learn the next day.

Teacher's Comments:

Things That Went Particularly Well

Everything! The kids really enjoyed Mind-Mapping. It was a welcome learning tool. The following is a sample of student comments I received on the evaluation sheet. They were asked what was the best thing about working with their teammates:

> "Got to know each other."
> "I didn't have to get all the answers on my own; I had help."
> "It made doing the work faster."
> "When there was a problem with understanding something, we could talk it through."
> "Sharing ideas."

The only negative comment received was that I didn't give them enough time to relax and really enjoy doing this enjoyable task. The students felt rushed.

Things I Would Do Differently Next Time

I would make only two changes, if I had the chance to repeat the same lesson with another class.

1) The day before asking them to Mind-Map the attributes of a hero, I would teach the students how to Mind-Map using the social skills needed to work in groups.   This would give them more time to work on their assignment the next day.

2) I would ask them to practise only one social skill per lesson. I realized that learning social skills is not an easy process. Many students had difficulty enough trying to practise one skill, let alone two.

Applying the Mind Map Rubric

Using the Rubric from page 291, how would
you score this Mind Map designed by a
grade eight student? Note that this was a
grade eight's *first* attempt.

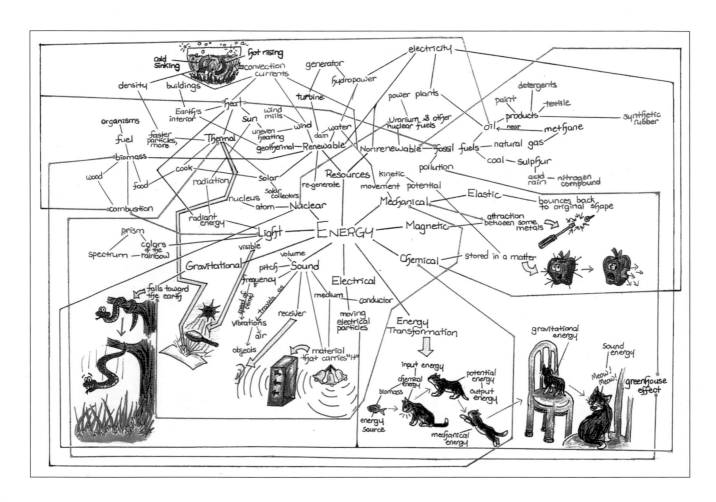

Final Thoughts

Of the two processes—Mind mapping and Concept Mapping—Concept Mapping is the more extensively researched. In an ERIC search, we found two meta-analyses on Concept Mapping and no such research summary on Mind Mapping.

Another issue to consider relates to the idea of WHEN to use one approach over another. For example, one small action research study involving 15 pre-service students compared the effects of using Mind Maps and Teams-Games-Tournament (TGT) as review processes before a science exam. The questions were mostly of the recall variety. The study favoured the students who were in the Teams-Games-Tournament by a mean score difference of 50% to 66% (an effect size of .46.) The instructor's comments were that if you are going to test students on recall type questions (multiple choice) then TGT is a more powerful process. If the exam was to explore relationships, she argued that Mind Mapping would be the more powerful process. The point made is that as educators we must think carefully about the decisions we make when designing learning environments. Our choices make a difference.

Below is a Mind Map that won joint first prize in a Mind Map competition. The judge was Tony Buzan.

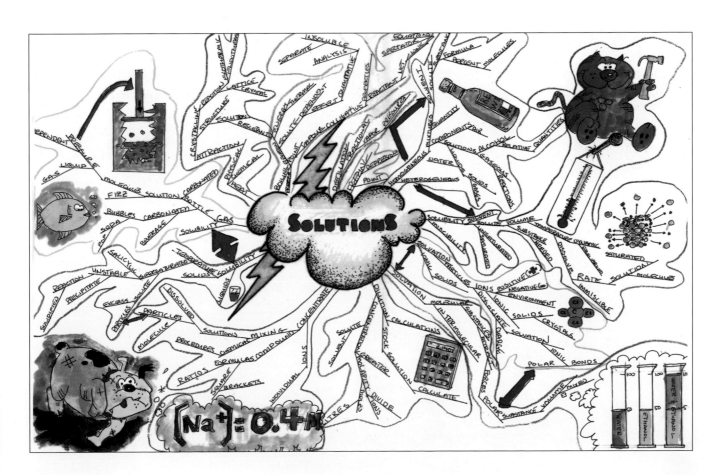

Chapter Eleven

Academic Controversy & Team Analysis

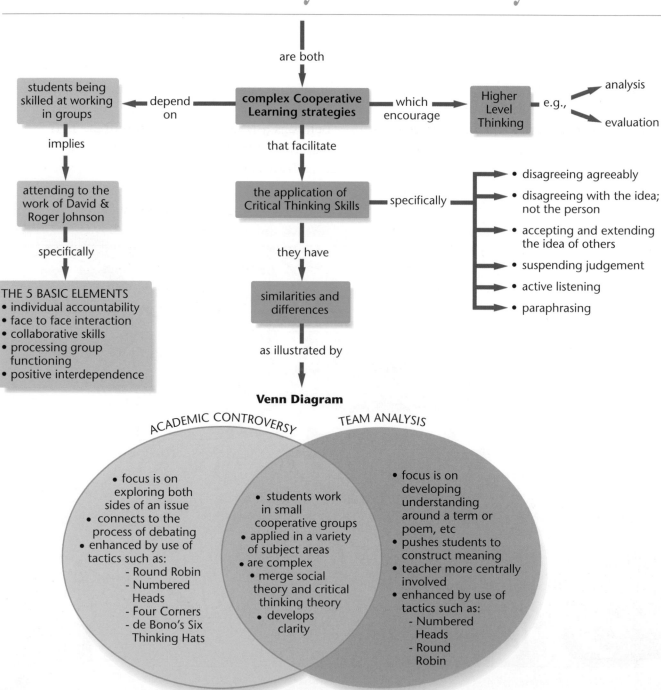

are both

students being skilled at working in groups ←**depend on**— complex **Cooperative Learning strategies** —**which encourage**→ Higher Level Thinking —**e.g.,**→ analysis / evaluation

implies ↓

attending to the work of David & Roger Johnson

specifically ↓

THE 5 BASIC ELEMENTS
- individual accountability
- face to face interaction
- collaborative skills
- processing group functioning
- positive interdependence

that facilitate ↓

the application of Critical Thinking Skills —**specifically**→
- disagreeing agreeably
- disagreeing with the idea; not the person
- accepting and extending the idea of others
- suspending judgement
- active listening
- paraphrasing

they have ↓

similarities and differences

as illustrated by ↓

Venn Diagram

ACADEMIC CONTROVERSY — TEAM ANALYSIS

- focus is on exploring both sides of an issue
- connects to the process of debating
- enhanced by use of tactics such as:
  - Round Robin
  - Numbered Heads
  - Four Corners
  - de Bono's Six Thinking Hats

- students work in small cooperative groups
- applied in a variety of subject areas
- are complex
- merge social theory and critical thinking theory
- develops clarity

- focus is on developing understanding around a term or poem, etc
- pushes students to construct meaning
- teacher more centrally involved
- enhanced by use of tactics such as:
  - Numbered Heads
  - Round Robin

Chapter Eleven

Academic Controversy & Team Analysis

Integrating Social Theory and Critical Thinking

This chapter is about heart and mind—the intersection of social and critical thinking theory through the integration of two complex Cooperative Learning strategies known as Academic Controversy and Team Analysis. Academic Controversy pushes dialectical thinking, that is, the flexibility/willingness to consider opposing perspectives. Academic Controversy is the work of David and Roger Johnson. It has a research base and is explained in depth in their book *Creative Controversy* (1992).

Team Analysis pushes clarity of thinking. It is the work of Richard Elson, who was a secondary English teacher with the Coquitlam School District in British Columbia. This is the only publication of his work.

Of critical importance to the successful implementation of both these strategies is the appreciation that both depend on students having the necessary social, communication, and critical thinking skills, as well as, the teacher having the skills to effectively structure group work. These two strategies are not for the weak of heart!

This chapter has eight interconnected areas:

1. Introduction and rationale for the chapter
2. An explanation of Academic Controversy followed by a sample lesson
3. An explanation of Team Analysis followed by a complex sample lesson
4. Introduction to Critical Thinking
5. Introduction to de Bono's Six Thinking Hats
6. Integration of Team Analysis and Academic Controversy with Critical Thinking
7. Concept Attainment lessons on two communication skills that enhance Team Analysis and Academic Controversy
8. Summary

Key Questions

What is the relationship between social theory and the search for truth?

Can students apply critical thinking skills if they cannot function effectively with other students (e.g., wisely apply appropriate social and communication skills)?

What is the interactive relationship between social skills, communication skills, and critical thinking skills?

Introduction and Rationale

The process of searching for ways to make the world a better place is a worthy task. Part of that search involves extending one's knowledge and sense of clarity around important issues. That implies that two or more perspectives exist. When those involved or affected by an issue can sit and discuss perspectives with a sense of humility, with a desire to search for truth and with the social, communication, and critical thinking skills that assist in pushing for clarity, then we increase the chances of making the classroom, school, community, and world a better place.

Not all countries, communities, schools, and classrooms encourage such exploration. Interestingly, a teacher recently mentioned to one of the authors that a student in his classroom asked that one of the rules in the classroom be "the right to disagree." The teacher said "yes, as long as the time, place, and approach is one that encourages discussion and makes people feel safe." That student's request is important. Of what value is democracy if those involved do not have a forum or opportunity to disagree? What chance do we have of resolving an issue if we fail to wisely disagree?

How democratic is your classroom, your school, your district? What would you see people doing and hear them saying that would tell you that they were or were not acting in a way that encourages a more democratic approach to life? For the authors, this is part of what it means to demonstrate intelligent behaviour, which connects to David Perkins's work in his book *Outsmarting IQ: The Science of Learnable Intelligence.*

Perkins argues that the brain is a pattern maker/seeker; an organ that integrates three types of intelligence: (1) neural power; (2) experiential knowledge/wisdom; and (3) reflective action (the thoughtful use of strategies). Team Analysis and Academic Controversy provide the process students need to integrate those intelligences—to demonstrate intelligent behaviour.

These two strategies provide a forum for the intersection of Cooperative Learning (social theory) and critical thinking.

De Bono's Six Thinking Hats is a useful tactic to support these strategies. De Bono introduces students to the dispositions we can take while exploring an issue—one way to attend to some of the recent work on our emotional brain by Joseph Le Doux and Daniel Goleman.

We start by providing an overview of each of the two strategies and a sample lesson that involves the strategies. That is followed by a brief explanation of critical thinking and the Six Thinking Hats. We then provide one more lesson that illustrates how the Six Thinking Hats can be woven into an Academic Controversy. Last we provide several data sets, one set as a complete lesson to illustrate how to introduce the social, communication, and critical thinking skills that are critical to the successful implementation of the two strategies.

Before reading about the application of Academic Controversy and Team Analysis, brainstorm for all the things that you think students must be skilled at before they can meaningfully engage in these two strategies.

Compare your answers with what teachers have told us on the next page.

Academic Controversy: The Essentials

Before you start: Students must be able to involve themselves in simpler group structures such as Think Pair Share, Place Mat and Three-Step Interview (see Chapters 6 and 7). Students must be able to demonstrate skill in the following Collaborative Skills:

- Taking Turns
- No Put Downs
- Suspending Judgement
- Actively Listening
- Paraphrasing
- Disagreeing in an Agreeable Way*
- Accepting and Extending the Ideas of Others*

(* see the end of chapter for sample lessons)

In addition, prior to doing Academic Controversy, students must have an understanding or experience with the topic being explored.

An Explanation of Academic Controversy

This strategy involves students sitting in small groups (usually four to six). Each group of four to six is then divided in half, with each half exploring opposite sides of an issue they have been studying. This process is similar to debating. As part of the process, they apply the social, communication, and critical thinking skills necessary to argue or present their case. Academic Controversy is one of the most complex of all cooperative small-group structures.

Importantly, students must first have the skills to work effectively in simple cooperative learning structures or they will not realize the benefit of these more complex group structures. From our experience with these two strategies, we would argue that Academic Controversy is a more complex process to implement than Team Analysis because the students must demonstrate a higher level of social, communication, and critical thinking skills. Team analysis lends itself to more subject areas and a wider variety of situations. In terms of research, Academic Controversy has an extensive literature and research base (see Johnson and Johnsons' 1992 book *Creative Controversy: Intellectual Challenge in the Classroom*). This strategy should be a precursor to student involvement in debating. You might consider beginning with Team Analysis as a skills development process for Academic Controversy—of course this all depends on your students and your relationship with them.

On the following page is a description of the eight steps of Academic Controversy.

Academic Controversy: A Description of the 8 Steps

1. Identify the Controversy
This is stated in the positive. For example, "Be it resolved that all vehicles should be RED." Note: when students first begin to play with this strategy, they are often disappointed that they cannot take the side that they are currently more excited about defending. You may want to explain that they will be exploring both sides of the issue so they don't have to worry about what side they are on initially.

2. Groups of 4 or 6 – Letter the Students AA/BB and assign PRO/CON Positions
Place students into groups of 4 or 6 and have them letter off. The A's sit on one side, the B's on the other. A's are PRO first; B's are CON first.

Be wise regarding who you place in the groups. Allowing friends to work together, especially if they have limited experience working in groups, is not wise. We also recommend that you then have the students number off as A1, A2, and B1, B2 (use of Numbered Heads). This allows you to increase accountability and participation. You can tell them during their planning phase that they must all be prepared to share; that you will call out "A1" or "B2" to start the discussion.

3. Time to Plan
The time given to plan is up to you. This depends on the complexity of the material. When doing the first controversy, do a simple one such as: "Be it resolved that all restaurants can serve only health food." This keeps planning to about 5 minutes.

4. Time for Each Group to Share
Again, the time you give depends on the material and the skill level of the students. We suggest you keep this time period short and be strict. The result is that students learn to present their ideas quickly and clearly. We often allow 60 to 90 seconds for each group, and we time them. Note, that the other group should be taking notes and demonstrating active listening skills. No one should be interrupting. When selecting who starts, Numbered Heads assists in increasing accountability.

5. Plan the Rebuttal
Students now push back and discuss what they consider are the flaws in the other group's presentation. This implies that they actively listened when the other group presented.

6. Present the Rebuttal
In this step, B's begin, then A's. Employ Numbered Heads to decide who speaks first. The time for this is usually around 60 to 90 seconds. Again, this depends on the complexity of the material and the skill level of the students.

7. Now Flip and Repeat Steps 3 to 6
We suggest that you have the students stand up and change seats.

8. End with a Round Robin
Here they discuss where they stand on the issue.

> On the next page is a simpler version you can copy for students.

Academic Controversy: Students' COPY

1. Groups of 4 or 6

2. Letter off AA(A) and BB(B)

3. Plan Opening Points

4. Present Opening Points

5. Exchange and Plan Disagreements

6. Present Disagreements Agreeably

7. Change Sides

8. Plan Opening Points (New Ideas or Extending Previous Ideas)

9. Present Opening Points

10. Exchange and Plan Disagreements

11. Present Disagreements Agreeably

12. Round Robin on Your Position

13. Attempt Consensus

14. Share Group's Thinking

General Comments on Academic Controversy

If your students have not worked extensively in groups, then this may not be the wisest place to start (unless you have a great class and you have few classroom management problems). We suggest you ensure the students are skilled in a number of simpler Cooperative Learning tactics such as Think Pair Share, Place Mat, Four Corners, etc., prior to moving to Academic Controversy—one of the most complex of all Cooperative Learning approaches.

Note that just before starting the Controversy you can begin with a simpler cooperative approach such as a Value Line. We often put a piece of tape across the room to represent the two extreme positions. The students are then provided with time to think and then they move and stand on the tape related to their position on the issue being discussed. (See the elementary lesson that follows.) Students can sign their name on the tape, and discuss with their nearest peer why they chose that spot. Next they move into the debate, and after the Round Robin in Step 8, they return to the tape and sign their name. They can then "measure" how far they moved from their initial position. This can be connected to math—graphing, averages, data management, etc.

We have found that treating Academic Controversy as if you are in a court of law (like a simulation) makes the process more manageable. The teacher is the judge who controls the time and process. The students are lawyers who listen intently to every word shared by the other side. This increases the chances that they do not get carried away during their time to present and to listen.

Connecting this to social theory and the research on Cooperative Learning (especially the work of David and Roger Johnson) we strongly encourage you to process the communication skills of active listening, accepting and extending the ideas of others, and disagreeing in an agreeable way. The more the students realize the importance of these skills, and become competent in applying them, the more they will benefit from the process.

You can see how this strategy allows for the intersection of the affective, macro and micro critical thinking skills presented later in this chapter. Without powerful strategies such as Academic Controversy, it becomes more difficult to meaningfully apply critical thinking skills.

Note: instead of employing Value Lines, you can use Four Corners. Here the issue is presented to the students and the students then move to one of four corners:
1. Strongly Agree
2. Somewhat Agree
3. Somewhat Disagree
4. Strongly Disagree
They discuss with a partner why they chose this position, then return for the controversy.

On the next page is a sample sheet to record students points for the controversy. That page is followed by a Team Assessment form (p. 316) which is followed by a sample lesson.

Academic Controversy: Recording Sheet

NAMES: _____

CONTROVERSY: Be it resolved _____

_____

_____

_____

PRO POINTS:
1. _____
2. _____
3. _____
4. _____
5. _____
6. _____
7. _____
8. _____

CON POINTS:
1. _____
2. _____
3. _____
4. _____
5. _____
6. _____
7. _____
8. _____

CONSENSUS: _____

_____

_____

_____

Team Assessment

Complete the following questions as a team.

	Low				High
1. Did all of the members of our group contribute ideas?	1	2	3	4	5
2. Did all of the members of our group listen carefully to the ideas of other group members?	1	2	3	4	5
3. Did all of the members of our group encourage other members to contribute their thoughts and opinions?	1	2	3	4	5

4. Three ways that we helped each other learn the material:

_____

_____

_____

5. **a)** One difficulty our group had was (explain fully):

_____

_____

_____

b) To resolve the difficulty we could:

_____

_____

_____

Group signatures: _____   _____

_____   _____

_____   _____

Academic Controversy: Grade Nine Nuclear Energy Unit

Note: These students are involved in a unit on Energy and have done several Academic Controversies.

Your Community

OBJECTIVE:
The students will apply their understanding of Academic Controversy related to whether or not a nuclear power plant should be relocated to their community. This implies their understanding of the components involved in arguing effectively.

TASK ANALYSIS:
1. Can the students apply the procedures involved in a debate?

2. Can the students operate in a way that disagrees with ideas, not people?

3. Do the students have relevant knowledge about the use of nuclear energy?

MENTAL SET:
"In your groups of four, please review the process of Academic Controversy. I will randomly call on one person from your group to share a few of the ideas."

INTRODUCE COMMUNICATION SKILL
(Use the Concept Attainment process to introduce the communication skill of "disagreeing with the idea, not the person.")

"I have an idea related to a communication skill that is important for you to focus on in this Academic Controversy. Last time when we worked on disagreeing agreeably, I noticed that some of you needed to focus on one other skill as well. I will not tell you what it is. I will show you YES and NO examples. Please keep your ideas to yourself for the first four YES and NO examples. I will ask you to share your hypotheses and your thinking with a partner after the fourth or fifth example." (I used a transparency with the following data on it.) The odd numbers are YES and the EVEN numbers are NO examples.

1. I see your point Eden, but the statistics you are presenting are generalizations.

2. Your idea of global warming is ludicrous John—open your eyes to the facts.

3. I had not thought of that idea Valisa; however, it doesn't solve the problem.

4. Yeh right! And if I follow that idea I will end up as smart as you.

5. Hmm. I think you need to go back and re-read the results. The calculations are incorrect.

6. Lawrence, I can't believe you think in such a shallow way—give your head a shake!

7. Okay, I will agree that it is costly, but the idea that cheaper is better is wrong.

8. When were you born? What about gender issues—does that ring a bell here?

"Take one minute to share your ideas concerning what you think 1, 3, 5, & 7 have in common—make sure everyone gets a turn. Okay, based on your discussion as a group decide where the four testers below would fit (A, B, C, & D). Each person takes one, takes a stand, and shares it with the group. The group tries to arrive at consensus. Then the next person goes, etc. In about two minutes, I will randomly call on one person from each group to share the group's thinking—be prepared to share."

TESTERS:

A. Well, finally, a good point. You're getting smarter.

B. That's fine for the contractor, but the homeowners have to deal with the noise.

C. The analysis isn't the problem. The issue concerns the long term effects.

D. Personally, I don't think you took enough time to think about it.

Randomly call on students to share their hypothesis and then discuss why the communication skill of disagreeing with the idea and not the person is important in a debate.

Share the Objective: "In a democratic society the people have the right to voice their opinions—to take action to support or prevent things from happening. Doing that in a fair-minded and reasonable way is not easy—that is why we completed the Concept Attainment process on disagreeing with the idea and not the person. Today we will take what we have gleaned from the reading, videos, and discussions, etc., and apply that communication skill. You will take a stand on an environmental issue related to energy. So, we are focusing on your ability to organize and present information and your ability to debate an issue in a way that disagrees with the idea, not the person."

Input: "This is the situation. The nuclear power station has reached a point that it can not be repaired. It is cheaper to move it to a nearby community … yours. The two A's represent the Nuclear Power Commission that has chosen this community. The B's represent the community. A's, you will argue in support of this statement (PRO); B's you will argue against it (CON): **Given the need for nuclear power to sustain a quality of life, the construction of the nuclear power plant in this community would be an overall asset to the community.**"

A1= Nuclear Engineer	B1= Parks Supervisor
A2= Director of Nuclear Power Plant	B2= Mayor

Directions:

1. 15 minutes to plan

2. A's present/B's take notes … THEN B's present/A's take notes (three minutes each)

3. Three minutes to analyze weaknesses

4. B's have one minute to share … THEN A's one minute to share

5. SWITCH ROLES and REPEAT process. Now you have to find new ideas or extend the ideas of the previous arguments—not repeat them.

6. Once finished steps 1–4 (exploring Both Sides of the Issue) do a Round Robin on where your group stands related to the issue—try to arrive at consensus. One person will be randomly called on to share from each group.

Remind students to be sensitive to the social skill of equal voice during the controversy.

Closure: Randomly call on one student to share the group's thinking. Then ask them to reflect on how effectively they disagreed with the idea, rather than the person.

An Explanation of Team Analysis

Richard Elson's interest as an educator was in integrating the social theory and critical thinking literatures. He argued that through their integration students could think more deeply and responsibly. A lot of Elson's Cooperative Learning work was based on the writing of Robert Slavin.

One of the authors sat down with Richard and he described his process. Since then we have used Team Analysis numerous times in almost every grade. Part of this chapter is a celebration of his thinking.

Elson's strategy allows the integration of cooperative learning and critical thinking skills while holding students accountable to be actively involved.

Perhaps the best way to describe this approach is to take you through the workshop that he created for us.

TEAM ANALYSIS WORKSHOP

Richard began by having us stand and robustly sing the national anthems of Canada and the United States—to the music. Next, he put us into groups of four, handed out copies of the two anthems and had us privately and quietly read over the complete anthem for both countries—four times. He then gave us four minutes to discuss in our groups and identify what we thought was the most important piece of information about

each country that emerged from singing and reading the anthems. He then randomly went around the room, and one person from a group was selected to report on what the group had decided. (When our group reported, we stated that for the first time, we understood why people at times burned the flag of the United States—the passion around the flag was intense.) He then gave us a grade (on a scale of 1-4) that represented the level of thinking he was encouraging us to achieve or the major message implied by the author(s). (Note: he often assigned marks of 1.25 or 3.75.) Then another group was selected and they had to disagree agreeably or accept and extend the thinking of the previous group. Again, a mark was provided.

After about three groups had shared, we had time (about two minutes) to rethink our original idea. Our goal was to re-examine our thoughts and merge it with the author's or teacher's thinking. Of course, we could challenge the mark, and challenge the Anthem author's or teacher's intentions. We had to provide a logical reason when we challenged.

What follows is a description of the Five Phases of Team Analysis.

Team Analysis:
A Description of the Five Phases

PHASE ONE:
Pre-reading and Reflection on the Issue

Students individually pre-read, reflect, and then in their group of 3-4 they have a brief discussion (4-5 minutes) on the issue to be discussed. It is imperative that the students have read and reflected individually. Richard Elson recommends the use of response journals as one tactic to prompt a personal relationship with the issue. Also, the presentation in Phase Two may be preceded by a quiz which tests recollection and general comprehension so that students will be successful with the demands of Team Analysis.

> Note, the individual pre-reading or reflection could occur the day before or be given as homework. It could also be done as part of the same class. The decision will depend on the time allocated for that class, the complexity or novelty of the material, and the students' skills in working collaboratively.
>
> Also, the teacher does not initially provide the criteria for assessing student responses in Phase Two. They must determine the criteria by the marks or grades the teacher provides. This encourages them to listen to one another.

PHASE TWO:
The Presentations on the Issue

The teams (or groups) are situated in the class in the form of a horseshoe. Although the horseshoe is not necessary, it facilitates the groups being able to listen to one another. The teacher sits in the middle of the horseshoe. One student from one group is selected to lead off with a presentation. The student can be selected randomly using Numbered Heads (each person in the group has a number 1, 2, 3, or 4) or the student can volunteer with the understanding that all students in the group will take a turn in rotation (Round Robin from Kagan's work on cooperative group structures). The presenter can request information from his or her group members during the presentation. (Note that you can have 2 or 3 groups present initially.)

Members of other teams make notes to help remember what was said in the presentations. These notes can be handed in at the end of the discussion or unit. The notes can be used later on for the student or the group to construct a brief summary or synthesis related to the issue.

For the first few times, or with younger students, we often put the students' responses in paraphrased form on the board or chart paper so that they have a map of their thinking. Recording their responses helps them track which comments are resulting in points.

PHASE THREE:
The Response to the Presentation

Remember that this phase is where the students apply the communication skills of Disagreeing Agreeably and Accepting and Extending the Ideas of Others. After the presentation or presentations, the teams are allowed 3-5 minutes to prepare a response to the presentation or the issue under examination. At this point, one of the teams is selected to reply critically to some aspect of the presentations or to extend the presentation by offering an insight or personal comment. The student who is selected or who volunteers stands. Note, although it rarely happens, there may be no reply to the presentation. If that occurs, you begin the process again with the next issue.

PHASE FOUR:
The Teacher's Response

Once the groups have responded to the initial presentation, the teacher immediately and publicly assigns a mark and rationale for that mark related to the quality of the contribution. The class can play a role in deciding how marks will be assigned, but generally, it is the teacher's job to exercise professional judgement and to explain the reason behind each assessment—students can appeal the mark. Marks of between 0 and 4 are awarded based on one or more of the following:

a. accuracy of the response
b. complexity of the response
c. originality of the insight

PHASE FIVE:
Responses by the Other Teams

Each team in turn adds to the developing communal interpretation, moving around the horseshoe in a clockwise direction. Once all the teams have responded, a second round begins. A different group will lead off and a different student will have to respond, and the cycle repeats itself until they've achieved a desired level of thinking or exhausted their thoughts. Richard asserted that all students on each team must make a comment before any team member can speak for a second time.

Adaptation: In phase Two, have several groups present initially and assign marks (PHASE 4) after each presentation. Then move into Phase 3 and provide time for all groups to rework their response. Then shift to Phase Five and have groups present. Again the teacher provides a mark... shifting back and forth between the last three phases.

Team Analysis:

PHASE ONE:
Pre-reading and Reflection on the Issue
Students individually pre-read, reflect, and then in their group have a brief discussion (4-5 minutes) on the issue to be discussed.

PHASE TWO:
The Presentations on the Issue
One student from one group is selected to lead off with a presentation.
The presenter can request information from his or her group members during the presentation.

Members on other teams make notes to help remember what was said in the presentations.

PHASE THREE:
The Response to the Presentation
The teams take 3-5 minutes to prepare a response to the presentation or to the issue under examination. At this point, one of the teams is selected to reply critically to some aspect of the presentation or to extend the presentation by offering an insight or personal comment. (Remember to apply the communication skills of Disagreeing Agreeably and Accepting and Extending the Ideas of Others.)

PHASE FOUR:
The Teacher's Response
The teacher assigns a mark and rationale for that mark related to the quality of the contribution.

PHASE FIVE:
Responses by the Other Teams
Each team in turn adds to the developing interpretation. Once all the teams have responded and the issue or topic is clarified and the assessment criteria are shared then a second round begins around a different topic/issue/poem, etc. Phase I starts, and a different group will lead off and a different student will have to respond, and the cycle repeats itself. All students on each team must make a comment before any team member can speak for a second time.

General Comments on Team Analysis

- In the original design of Team Analysis, students stand when they offer their teams' contributions, thus raising the level of individual accountability and combining a more formal speaking exercise with the informal talk of the group's ongoing discussion. You will have to decide if this idea works for you and your class.

- As the teacher, you must decide whether or not students who are randomly selected to respond have the right to pass. We initially allow the students to pass (in a clockwise direction); however, once they have had some experience, and feel comfortable with each other, we take away that right. The right to pass is one of the four norms established in Gibb's work *Tribes*. The other three are: attentive listening, appreciation statement, and mutual respect.

- The teacher assigns the mark and can accept and adjudicate appeals on the spot. The discussion of the value of any particular idea or insight is an important part of the process of analysis and evaluation. Richard was well aware of the need for the teacher to cultivate a high degree of trust in his or her classroom if this practice is to be successful.

- We have altered Richard's use of the process by not placing as much emphasis on the mark. For us, the mark provides the students with a mirror of how they thought relative to other groups and relative to the teacher's criteria. Richard, on the other hand, totals the marks, announces the marks, and awards prizes. Or, the marks earned are added as bonus

marks to the team members' records—this parallels the Student Team Learning process that Robert Slavin has researched and advocates. Again, you will have to decide how you want to approach this issue.

Remember the three underlying concepts of Student Team Learning
- individual accountability
- team rewards (be careful with this one)
- equal opportunities for success

We suggest you consider the pros and cons of employing the mark system when students are first learning the process. You might consider waiting until the students understand the skills they might employ and until they feel comfortable with the process and with each other. Please note that the students enjoyed Richard's class and looked forward to the use of prizes and bonus marks.

On the following page is a sample lesson that incorporates Team Analysis.

Team Analysis: Script Writing Grade 11 English/Media

Note that this lesson also involves: Mind Mapping, Cooperative Learning, and Simulation

MENTAL SET:

"Take a moment and reflect on what occurs in a script that you seldom and usually never see in the finished product (Wait about 15 seconds.) Discuss in your group. Use the Round Table format, start with the person wearing the most blue and move clockwise. If you are not sure, just say PASS. Thanks."

OBJECTIVE AND PURPOSE:

"Today we are going to take this idea of script writing a bit further. You are going to develop and apply your understanding of the process of script writing by creating a script."

INPUT/MODELLING:

Part 1 Team Analysis

Students are in groups of four (number groups and letter off in group ABCD). One group only has three. Each person reads through the two pages of a sample script three times. It is important that the students read it three times.

"Now, you have four minutes in your group to pull out what you think are the critical attributes or essential characteristics of script writing."

I then randomly call on the groups (group 2 person C) to identify the characteristics. I then give them a mark on a scale of 1 to 6. The next group is selected; again, I give them

a mark. After three groups have shared, they go back and re-assess their thinking. I again ask more groups—going back to earlier groups at times to reinforce the idea that lightning can strike the same place twice (accountability).

INPUT/CHECK FOR UNDERSTANDING:

Part 2 Mind Mapping

I then give them 15 minutes to work collectively to create a Mind Map on these characteristics. (They have done a number of Mind Maps—the art department got them going on them in grade 9.) When finished, they do a quick Gallery Tour to see what each group did (they take pride in this, they know I do this all the time, i.e., make public their work). I remind them that they have to make sure everyone is involved and that one person will have to stay with the Mind Map to explain it to others during the Gallery Tour. They do not know who, so they have to make sure everyone can explain it.

INPUT/PRACTICE:

Part 3 Simulation/Cooperative Learning

Students are placed into pairs (I decide who will work together). Some groups may have 3.

"You are a production company. You need a company name. Your task is to give yourself a name that incorporates two to three letters from either your first or last name (2 minutes)." Have them share the names.

"You were hired to produce a script for a television program that deals with interpreting famous poems. Your task is to adapt the poem "My Last Duchess" for a short screen play. It must contain at least two scenes. The deadline for completion is end of class tomorrow (two 70-minute periods). You must apply the formatting techniques discussed last class as well as the characteristics that tell you it is a script."

Before students begin working in groups read the poem through three times and ask them to identify the key ideas that might fit into the two scenes. Let them know they have all of this class and next class to finish. The last seven minutes of this class will involve a Gallery Tour to look at what others are doing.

"You and your partner(s) have a budget of 10 000 dollars. You can use it to ask for assistance from myself as a freelance consultant or from the members of another production group—at a cost of 500 dollars per request (hand out Monopoly money)."

CHECKING FOR UNDERSTANDING:
During the first working session, ask them to stop and take one minute of silence to look at the efforts of others (a scouting trip). The teacher also goes around and asks questions to refocus or encourage their efforts.

CLOSURE:
During the last 10 minutes of the last class, students do a Walk-About. One person from the group stays with the script to explain it while the other students move to another group to see what their "Production Company" has created.

Critical Thinking and deBono's Six Thinking Hats: How They Connect to Academic Controversy and Team Analysis

6

One of the necessary considerations when attempting to implement critical thinking is engaging students in meaningful and interesting content area. Another consideration is encouraging students to develop the skills and dispositions required to sustain critical thinking from multiple perspectives.

This section contains an introduction to the literature on critical thinking and the literature related to developing perspectives. To do this we will illustrate how the work of Richard Paul and associates at the Center for Critical Thinking and Moral Critique and the work of Edward de Bono can assist in developing the requisite critical thinking and disposition skills. Skills such as these are

necessary to effectively implement strategies such as Academic Controversy and Team Analysis. Note that many literatures exist in these areas including Lipman's *Philosophy for Children*, and Goleman's work on Emotional Intelligence.

Note that we are not providing an in-depth focus in these two areas. As stated above, we are simply illustrating how the literature related to critical thinking and thinking dispositions can be woven into more complex instructional processes. In terms of critical thinking, we encourage you to read books such as *Critical Thinking Handbook: K–3: A Guide for Remodelling Lesson Plans in Language Arts, Social Studies, & Science* (1987). This was written by Richard Paul,

A.J.A. Binker, and Marla Charbonneau. They also have two other similar books; one for grades four to six and one for high school. In terms of thinking dispositions, we recommend books such as the *Six Thinking Hats for Schools* (1991) by Edward de Bono. If you reflect back to Chapter 6 on Tactics you will remember that we also recommended another series related to critical thinking skills, also developed by de Bono. That program is CoRT and it contains 60 critical thinking skills. We use it extensively in our teacher-education program.

The literature on critical thinking suggests that integrating the teaching of critical thinking with the academic content extends learning in both areas—a synergistic effect. Integration allows the strategy of Team Analysis (a more complex Cooperative Learning strategy) to 'pick up' the critical thinking skills. The effectiveness of Team Analysis is determined by the extent to which the students learn to be fair minded and reasoning thinkers—ones who apply appropriate thinking skills. Once again, we see the benefit from the integration of skills and strategies.

"Critical" comes from the Greek word for "judge" (Kritikos). Its purpose is to increase the chances that we make wise decisions. From our understanding of the critical thinking literature, the purpose of critical thinking is the search for truth. In that sense, it assists us in finding weaknesses or flaws in our own and others' thinking and actions. It also assists us in planning and predicting appropriate courses of action. Books such as *With Good Reason* (1990) by S. Morris Engel provide specific examples of how to identify flaws in thinking such as the sweeping generalization, genetic fallacy, false

dilemma, and straw man.

Two volumes on thinking and learning skills *Thinking and Learning Skills: Volume 1* relating to instruction and research; *and Thinking and Learning Skills: Volume 2, Research and Open Questions* (1985) edited by Susan Chipman, Judith Segal, and Robert Glaser is one of the most in-depth syntheses of the "thinking' literatures".

A third resource, and perhaps the most easy to access is de Bono's CoRT program. This program provides teachers with extensive information on how to plan a lesson to apply one or more of the sixty thinking tactics that make up this program.

The challenge in the area of critical thinking is to make it come alive. From our experience, when educators do not have the powerful pedagogical processes into which they can integrate or enact the critical thinking skills, the result can be a superficial application of those skills.

Accordingly, we selected Academic Controversy and Team Analysis as examples of powerful strategies that facilitate the application of specific thinking skills. Other powerful strategies that would benefit from these skills would be Simulations, Group Investigation, and the Jurisprudential Model of Teaching (not presented in this book).

Another way of thinking about critical thinking are the dispositions that people assume to try and convince you to think or act in a specific way. For example, the words Ethos, Pathos, and Logos refer to ethics, emotions, and logic. These three concepts are the heart and soul of Socratic Dialogue. When you are in an argument with someone, you will experience one or more of these three. You can imagine that if you are arguing with emotions in the absence of logic and ethics (and the other person is doing the same) then you are not going to get very far in resolving an issue.

When discussing instruction we often hear people say they employ the Socratic approach in their classroom. Unfortunately what they do is usually not Socratic Dialogue; rather it is stand up recitation (I talk, you listen, I'll ask a few questions, some of you try to answer). Talking at kids and asking them questions is not Socratic Dialogue. We rarely see effective and

meaningful Socratic processes in classrooms. On the next page is a brief overview of Socratic Dialogue.

Below is a partial list of critical thinking skills that we can employ to more precisely pursue the search for truth. Some are more complex than others. As educators, we can select the ones that would enhance our students' abilities to more accurately and meaningfully engage in learning. (from Paul, R. et.al., *Critical Thinking Handbook: High School*)

15 Dimensions of Critical Thought

AFFECTIVE SKILLS

1. thinking independently
2. developing insight into egocentricity or sociocentricity
3. exercising fairmindedness
4. exploring thoughts underlying feelings and feelings underlying thoughts
5. developing intellectual humility and suspending judgement

COGNITIVE – MACRO-ABILITIES

6. clarifying issues, conclusions, or beliefs
7. clarifying and analyzing the meanings of words or phrases
8. developing criteria for evaluation: clarifying values and standards
9. evaluating the credibility of sources of information

10. analyzing or evaluating arguments, interpretations, beliefs, or theories
11. listening critically: the art of silent dialogue

COGNITIVE – MICRO-SKILLS

12. noting significant similarities and differences
13. distinguishing relevant from irrelevant facts
14. making plausible inferences, predictions, or interpretations
15. evaluating evidence and alleged facts

The challenge is:
How do we teach and enact these skills?

Socratic Dialogue: A Description

A philosophical discussion that is serious between two or more people is always more likely to yield the truth than a method of analysis practiced by a single person.

As Richard Paul et. al., (1990) state in their book on Critical Thinking, when invoking Socratic discussions, "the teacher is more of a questioner than a preacher" (p. 37). In Socratic discussions the teacher learns to ask questions that probe, clarify, and extend. The teacher learns to ask questions that request both reason and evidence. Obviously the teacher and students must be skilled in both inductive and deductive reasoning.

Socratic discussions allow students to develop and evaluate their thinking by making that thinking explicit, i.e., observably clear, and arguably defensible. Socrates's aim was to encourage others to search for their own truth, for goodness. For Socrates, being clear about what you were doing was closely linked to morality.

Richard Paul et. al., (1990) describe three general or loose categorizations of Socratic Discussion: the spontaneous, the exploratory, and the focused.

The Spontaneous: Here an event or question or statement immediately invites us to wonder how we might go about proving or disproving something, or what something means and how we can find out. For example, in a discussion someone might say "Women make better school administrators than men." What does that mean? Does it mean only women should be principals of schools?

The spontaneous form has no pre-planning or preparation.

The Exploratory: Here the teacher or someone wants to find out what students understand and believe about a specific issue or topic or comment. It could be used to assess student thinking on an issue or topic. Often it is used as an introduction to a unit, as a review, or as a check for understanding. Often it is employed through having students pick an issue or topic raised in a discussion and give their views, or having students form groups to discuss the issue or topic.

This form has some pre-planning or preparation—it deals with a broader range of interrelated issues, topics, and concepts. NOTE: The exploratory is the format we are integrating with Team Analysis.

The Focused: This is designed to inquire into an area in depth. Here the discussion by the students is more intensive and extensive: the students sort, classify, analyze, and evaluate thoughts and perspectives; distinguish known from unknown; synthesize, etc. The students pursue perspectives related to their most basic assumptions and through their furthest implications and consequences. (Note: this fits in perfectly with strategies such as Academic Controversy and Team Analysis.)

For example, one could use the Focused approach for a course of study and Group Investigation as the strategy to investigate issues related to equity, or the environment, or happenings such as the tearing down of the Berlin Wall.

de Bono's Six Thinking Hats

Rather than simply explain the Six Thinking Hats, we will employ Hilda Taba's Inductive Thinking strategy to assist our understanding of the different dispositions we can assume when interacting with information. Below is a set of data. On your own, read each item. Then, with a partner, classify these into the nature of thinking encouraged or represented. When finished, compare your thinking with the descriptions of Thinking Hats on the following page. Note that no right or wrong number of groups exists. Be prepared to share your justification as to why you put items into a specific group and your rationale for the use of them in a democratic classroom.

1. Whenever I think of math I get anxious.

2. The title of the poem is "My Last Duchess."

3. We need to make sure that both the male and female perspective is considered.

4. Maybe we need to go to another group to get additional ideas.

5. How long did it take you to complete the question?

6. It will work because of cost and it solves the problem.

7. I don't know. I just don't like the idea—I feel jittery.

8. Let's clarify what we now understand about the problem.

9. We do not have enough evidence to make that decision.

10. What are we trying to do? Let's lay out a plan of action.

11. Perhaps we could take this one idea and see if we can break it into simpler parts.

12. How old was this person when they discovered the idea?

13. What if we connected those three ideas? Would that be a possibility?

14. I appreciate everyone's input; however, the parents' response makes me nervous.

15. My insides are telling me this is going to make people angry.

16. Our reasons for making that decision are not going to pay off in the long term.

17. I like the ideas that all of you all have shared. This shows the power of collaboration.

18. Let's identify the benefits of taking turns.

19. Have you considered whether or not the weight will reduce its stability?

20. Suppose we made a mistake at step two; would this explain why we are stuck?

> Note: With Taba's strategy, the number of groups is not stated. So, in this case knowing ahead of time six groups exist is a modification and simplification of her strategy.

deBono's Six Thinking Hats: Six Possible Dispositions

Below is a brief explanation of each hat. Please understand that these hats represent thinking that is much more complex than illustrated below. We encourage you to read one of the books that de Bono has published related to hats and their use in schools. Our purpose here is to simply illustrate how the hats can be woven into the teaching and learning process.

White Hat: This hat represents information (white because of paper). It is applied to direct thinking into the area of attending to the information that is present and the information that is missing. Sharing statistics, or ideas, or asking for information is typical of this hat.

Red Hat: This hat deals with feelings, intuition, and emotions (red because it suggests fire and warmth). When red hat is in use, you share your feelings and intuitions without having to justify why. The red hat gives you permission to share those feelings.

Black Hat: This hat is used for caution (black because of a judge's robe). The black hat stops us from doing something because it may be wrong, harmful, too expensive, etc. It points out the risks, the hazards, the roadblocks—it explains why something will not work—shows weaknesses and makes assessments.

Green Hat: This hat suggests growth, energy, and life (green because it suggests vegetation—growth). When using this hat, you offer suggestions, make proposals, and explore alternatives. You look outside the box for elegant solutions. Here you would talk about how to add to something, or make modifications. With this hat, people are making an effort to be creative.

Blue Hat: This hat is at the centre of the thinking process (blue because it suggests the sky—above all else—thinking about our thinking). It is used to bring a sense of order and sequence to what is occurring. It is often used at the beginning and end of a discussion or when things are getting confused. It can be used to help decide the sequence of hats, or when to exchange hats, or how to summarize information.

Yellow Hat: This hat makes an effort to find the values and benefits in an idea or action—it seeks the good points (yellow suggesting sunshine and optimism). Here you would look for the good points even if you do not like the overall idea.

From the previous page:
RED: 1, 7, 14, 15; WHITE: 2, 5, 12; BLACK: 9, 16, 19; YELLOW: 6, 17, 18; GREEN: 4, 11, 13, 20; BLUE: 3, 8, 10 Sometimes they overlap—the hats can represent more than one disposition towards thinking.

Following are two Concept Attainment data sets illustrating how you could employ this strategy to facilitate students understanding of the Six Thinking Hats, two at a time. The first data set involve Red and White hat thinking; the second Green and Black.

Red Hat/White Hat: Concept Attainment Data Set

One way of initiating understanding of Six Hat Thinking is to employ Concept Attainment. Below are examples of Red Hat and White Hat thinking. How are ODD examples (Red Hat Thinking) different from the EVEN examples (White Hat Thinking)? Once you have an idea, find a partner and share your hypotheses. Then take turns deciding which testers would fit as Red Hat or White Hat Thinking.

1. I think it makes me feel sad.
2. Please tell me how much time you think we will save.
3. Your ideas make me laugh.
4. What are the reasons why we should recycle?
5. Your solution to the problem would make a lot of people happy.
6. I think the boy got into trouble for a couple of reasons.
7. Those actions make me feel angry!
8. We also recycle to save money.

TESTERS:

a. Some plants need water every day.
b. It's ridiculous, sorry.
c. I love it. It makes me feel smart.
d. It melted too soon, that's why it did not work.

Try this one: Green Hat and Black Hat Thinking

The ODD examples are Green Hat Thinking and the EVEN are Black Hat Thinking.

1. Let's find two more reasons before we decide.
2. If you continue to talk like that you will get in trouble.
3. Can anyone think of any other solutions?
4. If you use it that way someone may get hurt.
5. Those were great ideas! Any more?
6. You didn't study; that's why you didn't pass the test.
7. That's a good start. Who can take it one step further?
8. Could we sit down and try to find out what is wrong?

TESTERS:

a. So let's take a few minutes to brainstorm a few more ideas.
b. That puppy may have sharp teeth.
c. The iron was left on; it may be too hot to use.
d. Perhaps we could take the time to extend our thinking.

On the next page is a sample Academic Controversy lesson that weaves in the Six Thinking Hats.

Sample Lesson: Academic Controversy and Six Thinking Hats

Elementary:

BACKGROUND:

The students in this grade four class were studying the concept and process of quarantine. In this lesson, they were transferring the idea of quarantine to the idea of a student with AIDS being allowed into their classroom. The students had done a lot of work with Edward de Bono's Six Thinking Hats program.

OBJECTIVE:

To extend the students' understanding of the concept of quarantine by applying the process of Academic Controversy. The focus was on their feelings and thoughts of a student who was having difficulty being accepted into schools because he had AIDS. The idea being explored was that rejection can be a form of quarantine.

MENTAL SET:

The issue was brought to the students, and then they were asked to make a decision. Students formed themselves along a Value Line (like a continuum) with students who stood at one wall strongly believing students with AIDS should not be allowed into the classroom and those who stood at the other wall strongly believing they should be allowed into the classrooms. Students stood on a piece of tape that was on the floor, and they signed their name on the spot to indicate their current position.

DIRECTIONS:

- Students were then put into teams of four. The purpose was to Examine Both Sides of An Issue (EBS) and come up with what they throught were the Pluses, Minuses, and Most Interesting (PMI) things to consider re this issue. (PMI and EBS are from de Bono's CoRT program.)

- Students letter off A1, A2, and B1, B2.

- They are then informed that A's are in support (Pro), and B's are against (Con).

- They have 5 minutes to prepare.

- They come back together (like lawyers).

- A's present their case wearing Green and White Hats (2 minutes) (B's take notes).

- B's present their case wearing Green and White Hats (2 minutes) (A's take notes).

- Retire to Chambers to prepare an argument against what the other group presented (wearing Black & White hats).

- Students return and they have one minute to present the rebuttal (they apply previously learned skills of disagreeing in an agreeable way; and disagree with the idea, not the person).

- They now stand up, switch seats, and reverse the position.

  A's now argue against the issue, and B's argue in support of it.

- Repeat the process.

- At the end, the group attempts to come to a consensus. One person is randomly selected to present the group's response.

- Now repeat Value Line to "measure" their shift in thinking. Use Response Journals.

On the next 3 pages are two lessons: the first on how to 'Accept and Extend Ideas', the second on 'Disagreeing Agreeably'.

Accepting and Extending the Ideas of Others: Using Concept Attainment

Focus Statement: For each of the two data sets below, focus on the effect of each statement on social interaction. The statements on the left side represent a specific communication skill. Those on the right do not. We are not saying those on the right are wrong; rather, we are saying they do not represent this particular communication skill. Once you have an idea, try the testers.

1. We could take it one step further by....
2. To add to your idea, I'd say we could....
3. Let's piggy-back on that idea.
4. Along with that, we could say that....

5. All right, let's move on to the next issue.
6. That's ridiculous, it won't work.
7. We've wasted enough time, let's....
8. Sorry, but I disagree, you have not ....

TESTERS:

9. That is a wonderful idea!
10. Can you think of anything that we could add to that?
11. Connected to that is the idea that ....
12. I think that what we have done is perfect the way it is.

Note to teacher: this communication skill increases the students' ability to effectively apply Academic Controversy and Team Analysis

On the following page is another data set on the communication skill of **Disagreeing in an Agreeable Way.**

Sample Lessons on Teaching Social Skills: How to Disagree in an Agreeable Way

Note: this lesson integrates the processes of Lesson Design, Concept Attainment, and Cooperative Learning.

Lesson Design: provides the overall structure or flow of the lesson
Concept Attainment: provides the process to develop the concept
Cooperative Learning: provides the opportunity to dialogue

OBJECTIVE:

The students will understand what is meant by "disagreeing in an agreeable way" and the effect that has on resolving conflict. In addition, they understand that change is inevitable—we can only alter our stance towards both change and conflict.

MENTAL SET:

Place the students into groups of 2, 3, or 4 (whichever works best for your class). Ask the students to recall a conflict or disagreement that they witnessed or one in which they were involved. Ask them to share that conflict in the group—reminding them that they have to choose a conflict that might not be too personal. Now ask them to identify what the people involved did that prevented the conflict from being resolved (e.g., what they said, how it was said, how they acted, etc.). After 3 or 4 minutes, collect some of their responses. Now ask them to identify what the people involved did to help resolve the conflict or disagreement. Again, collect some of their responses after they have had sufficient time in their groups.

Sharing the Objective and Purpose:

"For the next half hour or so, I would like to have you develop a clearer understanding of a skill we can all use to help resolve a conflict or disagreement more quickly."

INPUT: (Using Concept Attainment)

Directions: On the next page is a data set of examples. Please work by yourself as you compare the ODD-numbered examples and contrast them with the EVEN-numbered examples. Although you are in groups, do the first 10 examples on your own. Then find a partner and share your hypotheses about what the ODD examples have in common and how they are different from the EVEN examples. Once you have shared your hypotheses, work with your partner on the testers listed near the bottom of that page and see if you can decide which examples are ODD and which are EVEN. Be prepared to share your hypotheses and your answers— anyone in your group can be selected to respond.

MODELLING: (THE DATA SET)

1. I don't think I agree with you; could you please explain it one more time to make sure I'm understanding you correctly?

2. I can't believe you think you're right—the idea is ridiculous!

3. You have explained it from your point of view; however, I think you need to see it from the point of view of the rest of the group.

4. No, I'm tired of considering other people's alternatives—we've wasted enough time talking; let's get on with what is really important.

5. That is a very good reason, Omar, but you have left out one very important point that you might want to consider, one that may cause you to change your mind.

6. Amanda, you're wrong. You simply didn't take enough time to do it properly.

7. You have presented some good arguments; nonetheless, I believe some of your arguments have flaws.

8. Get to bed now! I'm sick and tired of you telling me that everyone else gets to stay up late watching TV.

9. No, I am not saying your ideas are stupid. I am, however, saying that there might be a more effective way for us to solve the problem.

10. You will do your homework! I don't care whether or not you can already do all these types of problems. If the teacher assigned them, the teacher is right.

TESTERS

a. That is such a far-fetched idea; it will never work in reality.

b. Great idea, but I'm afraid it will not work. Let me explain why and see what you think.

c. Okay, I can see how you believe that this is a way to solve the problem. Would it be all right if I showed you why you might be wrong?

d. I'm not saying you're wrong; I'm simply saying you never see things from other people's perspective—you are so self-centred.

INPUT/CHECK FOR UNDERSTANDING:

Once students have had the chance to share their hypotheses with their partner, randomly call on students to discuss what they believe the ODD-numbered statements have in common and how they are different from EVEN-numbered statements. (Note: b & c are ODD)

CLOSURE/EXTENSION:

Give the students 3-4 minutes to come up with a statement about the effect disagreeing in an agreeable way would have on students and on the classroom learning environment related to resolving conflicts. Randomly select students to respond. Ask them to identify a situation that is free of conflict.

Don't Forget...

- Approximately 200 Cooperative Learning structures exist.

- Some are easy to apply others are more complex to apply.

- Academic Controversy and Team Analysis are two of the more complex structures.

- The Johnsons' Learning Together Model (the Five Basic Elements) presented in Chapter Seven enhances the use of all Cooperative Learning structures.

- If your students struggle with Think Pair Share and Round Robin (the least complex) then they are not ready for Three Step Interview and Four Corners (average complexity). If they struggle with any of these, they are not going to benefit from Academic Controversy and Team Analysis.

Chapter Summary

This was the last chapter in this book that deals specifically with instructional processes. The focus was on Academic Controversy and Team Analysis—two of the most complex of over 200 Cooperative Learning small-group structures. We classify these two structures as strategies because they are complex, driven by a theory, and provide theory-related results. Other cooperative learning strategies would be Teams-Games-Tournament (see Chapter Seven), Jigsaw and Group Investigation (not covered in this book).

In the case of Academic Controversy, research continues to evolve regarding the effect it has on student learning. That research is illustrated on our Web page and the address is provided in Chapter Three of this book. Team Analysis was designed by a teacher based on his research into Cooperative Learning and critical thinking. At this time, no research is available that explores the effect Team Analysis has on student learning. That said, our experience with this process tells us it has a lot of potential.

In terms of these two strategies, you can see how a variety of other instructional concepts, skills, and strategies can be integrated to enhance their effect.

Possibilities for integration include:

- Concepts: active participation, accountability, safety, success

- Skills: framing questions, wait time, responding to students' responses, checking for understanding

- Tactics: de Bono's Six Thinking Hats, de Bono's CoRT, Value Lines

- Strategies: Johnson's Five Basic Elements, Buzan's Mind Mapping, Hunter's Lesson Design, Concept Attainment

- Organizers: Brain Research, Critical Thinking, Multiple Intelligences

In the following and final chapter, we step away from the specific processes and focus on the lenses (Instructional Organizers) that assist teachers in wisely selecting and integrating specific processes from their instructional repertoire. Those organizers are Multiple Intelligence, the Human Brain, Emotional Intelligence, Learning Styles, Children at Risk, and Gender.

Chapter Twelve

Instructional Organizers

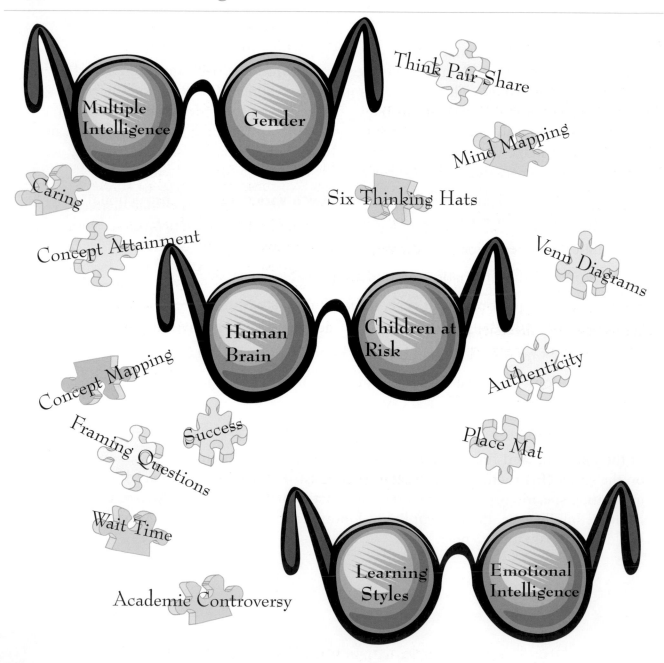

Think Pair Share

Mind Mapping

Six Thinking Hats

Multiple Intelligence

Gender

Caring

Concept Attainment

Venn Diagrams

Human Brain

Children at Risk

Concept Mapping

Authenticity

Framing Questions

Success

Place Mat

Wait Time

Academic Controversy

Learning Styles

Emotional Intelligence

Chapter Twelve

Instructional Organizers

This book's focus is instructional intelligence; and more specifically, on how teachers demonstrate expert behaviour in the design of powerful learning environments. This chapter takes us away from those instructional processes discussed in previous chapters and focuses more on the critical role that specific bodies of knowledge play in assisting educators to make wise decisions concerning the design of learning environments. Those bodies of knowledge ultimately help educators respond creatively to the complexity of teaching.

As stated throughout this book, no one knows the best way to teach. Rather, a teacher assesses the diversity and needs of the learners and, as things emerge over time (and more often in the moment) decisions are made. Importantly, so many instructional possibilities exist that a teacher could be effective and play with very little that is in this book.

The six Instructional Organizers or Conceptual Lenses we selected for this chapter are presented in an overview format. Each of these areas could be studied or researched for the rest of one's career. We are simply illustrating how these literatures inform instructional decisions.

A Question: What do the six bodies of knowledge below have in common in terms of how teachers make decisions about the design of learning environments?

1. Multiple Intelligences
2. Emotional Intelligence
3. Learning Styles
4. The Human Brain
5. Children at Risk
6. Gender

How are they different from these?

- Success
- Mind Mapping
- Concept Attainment
- Role Playing

- Academic Controversy
- Three Step Interview
- Providing Wait Time in Questioning

 More importantly, how do these two lists interact?

Instructional Organizers

This chapter clarifies the role that six bodies of knowledge play in the "informed" or "wise" selection and integration of instructional processes. Think of the relationships between the two lists on the previous page.

1 Multiple Intelligences
2 Emotional Intelligence
3 Learning Styles
4 Brain Research
5 Children at Risk
6 Gender

One way of approaching the list above is to consider these areas as lenses designed to extend teachers' understanding of how students learn, and from that understanding, to make decisions about how and when to select, integrate, and enact the items in the bottom list.

We have labelled these six conceptual lenses *Instructional Organizers*. We realize that many other lenses exist. Three additional lenses are: the literature on (1) Learning Disabilities, (2) Ethnicity and Culture; and (3) Child Development.

We encourage you to remember that knowledge in these six areas is constantly emerging. For example, **Multiple Intelligences** is a theory that assists in explaining and valuing different ways of thinking and acting. Tangentially, we are only recently reading research related to how it is affecting the teaching and learning process (Goodnough 2000). Likewise with **Brain Research** and **Emotional Intelligence**. The **Learning Styles** literature also lacks extensive long-term district-wide research. The message is that we must be critical consumers of our professional literature. The research on **Children at Risk** and on **Gender** is more extensive and provides a more solid grasp on what to do. That aside, if we select less effective instructional approaches and engage kids in non-meaningful activities in the name of Multiple Intelligences, or Children at Risk, etc., then we trivialize the importance of understanding the diverse ways of demonstrating intelligent behaviour.

Key Questions

1 What role do instructional organizers play in the teaching and learning process?

2. What might happen if a teacher is not knowledgeable in one or more of these organizers?

3. What would happen if teachers focused on Learning Styles or Multiple Intelligences but not on extending their instructional repertoire?

Lens#1: Multiple Intelligences Theory

The literature on Multiple Intelligences represents the thinking of Howard Gardner. He began his journey back in the 1960s, as he became increasingly concerned about the limitations of the existing perspectives on intelligence. The result of his inquiry was a theory that provides another lens for understanding the teaching and learning process. Gardner, however cautions us to be judicious in how we interpret and connect the theory of multiple intelligence to the teaching and learning process (Gardner & Hatch, 1989). Klein (1997) for example, reminds us to be careful in how we apply Gardner's theory on Multiple Intelligence. An excellent source for understanding Gardner's work in the classroom is Armstrong's 2000 book titled *Multiple Intelligences in the Classroom.*

The theory of Multiple Intelligences reminds teachers that students bring different strengths to a learning situation. Although you may appreciate and understand what each intelligence has to offer, educators are nonetheless influenced by an intense focus on the logical mathematical and verbal linguistic intelligences. Given the every-day challenges of classroom life and the pressures to cover curriculum (especially at the high-school level), educators are by default socialized into not responding to the reality that students have different creative and problem-solving strengths.

The question you might ask as an expert teacher is: "What instructional processes do I and my colleagues have in our repertories to respond to the student diversity that walks through our classroom doors?" As administrators or staff developers, you might ask: "How do we encourage teachers to respond to that diversity?"

Ignoring students' "clues" about how they learn is akin to a driver ignoring road conditions. We know that one of the dispositions and strengths of the human brain is its ability to search, interpret, and respond to patterns. The Multiple Intelligence literature provides teachers and students with one way of interpreting patterns.

Remember that Howard Gardner does not promote these intelligences as **"the"** list, rather they capture the kinds of abilities valued by a variety of cultures. Each person possesses each of the intelligences, and can develop each of the intelligences. The intelligences work together in complex ways, and each of the intelligences allows for a variety of ways to be intelligent within it:

- LINGUISTIC
- LOGICAL-MATHEMATICAL
- BODILY-KINESTHETIC
- INTRAPERSONAL
- MUSICAL
- SPATIAL
- INTERPERSONAL
- NATURALISTIC

With the intelligences we demonstrate the ability to resolve genuine problems or difficulties as well as the ability to find or create new ones, thus laying pathways for the continuous acquisition of knowledge.

> The following pages provide a quick introduction to the 7 intelligences, summarized from Gardner's 1983 book, **Frames of Mind.** (Note: we also include the Naturalistic Intelligence that he added later.)

Eight Intelligences: A One-Page Introduction

As Gardner asks in his 1993 book, *Multiple Intelligences: The Theory into Practice*, "What is the nature of the mind that can give rise to a plethora of possibilities that are meaningful to society?" Below are eight possibilities.

Intelligence	End-States	Core Components
Logical-mathematical	Computer Programmers Mathematicians Tax auditors	Ability to discern numerical patterns; to effectively think with numbers; classify information and make inferences/reason
Linguistic	Novelists Speech Pathologists Politicians	Ability to use words effectively when speaking and writing; being sensitive to the power, meaning, and flow of words
Musical	Composers Piano Tuners Music Teachers	Ability to appreciate and play with rhythm, pitch, and timbre; appreciation of musical form/expressiveness
Spatial	Architects Choreographers Athletes	Strength in visual spatial reasoning: sensing patterns and orienting oneself or thinking based on those patterns
Bodily-kinesthetic	Athletes Dancers Physiotherapists	Ability to sense, interpret, and create patterns involving the whole body
Interpersonal	Comedians Educators Social Workers	Ability to interpret and accurately respond to the moods/behaviours of others
Intrapersonal	Psychologists Counselors Monks/Nuns	Understanding one's own feelings (aware of personal strengths and weaknesses) and the ability to act on that understanding to guide behaviour
Naturalistic	Biologists Park Rangers Naturalists	Ability to make sense of nature's complexities, to classify aspects of nature and sense relationships within and between those patterns

LINGUISTIC INTELLIGENCE

This intelligence refers to the ability to use words orally or in writing. Of all the intelligences, linguistic intelligence is one of the most thoroughly studied (e.g., research related to the effects of brain damage on language).

While language can be conveyed through gesture, and through writing, the central core is the product of the vocal tract and a message to the human ear. Yet we are reminded that the deaf acquire a natural language and master gestural systems. That provides proof that linguistic intelligence is not simply a form of auditory intelligence. What implication does that have for teachers?

Although print is everywhere in our culture, our language is a sound-based system. Yet in the Orient, the emphasis is more graphic. For example, the Japanese have two systems: one processes linguistic forms and the other is ideographic which involves interpreting pictorial materials. So two mechanisms for reading are housed in the same individual. The benefit is that brain damage in one area will still allow the other to function effectively.

Certainly the previous information has pedagogical implications. For example, what about students who are struggling with the prevalent code of their culture or leave one culture and one language code and move to another culture and must learn in a different code? What are the implications for students who have neurolinguistic dysfunctions (e.g., dyslexia)?

Given the importance of this intelligence, think of the different ways we as educators can attend to this intelligence: prose, poetry, lectures, audio tapes, video tapes, word games, puppetry, Mind Mapping, Concept Mapping, Venn diagrams, Inductive Thinking, Concept Attainment, Cooperative Learning, word games, speeches, debates etc. Write down the ways you massage this intelligence in your classroom.

Gardner identifies four aspects of linguistic knowledge that have proven important in human society:

1. ability to use language to convince other individuals of a course of action; for example great speakers, lawyers, teachers
2. mnemonic (memory) potential to help one remember information
3. language's role in explanation; teaching, employing verse, etc.
4. language's ability to reflect upon itself; meta-linguistic analysis.

Gardner argues that syntax and phonology lie close to the core of linguistic intelligence, while semantics and the pragmatic include inputs from other intelligences such as logical-mathematical and personal intelligences.

Interestingly, he also argues that poetry is the highest form of this intelligence. Have you ever considered doing an Academic Controversy with your students on whether prose or poetry is the higher form of Linguistic Intelligence?

Linguistic Intelligence: Instructional Implications

Few educators would question the critical role of this intelligence in the teaching and learning process. Fundamentally, this intelligence is about speaking, reading, and writing. When we look at the literature on developing intelligent behaviour, the literature states that talk is critical to intellectual growth. It also tells us that reflection is critical for demonstrating intelligent behaviour. Reflection is the essence of reading and writing—we know that reflecting without acting and acting without reflecting are both untenable stances.

The information about this intelligence informs us that books, audio tapes, portfolios, diaries, discussions, debates, listening to lectures, and telling stories are all important. In addition, we could add the integrative application of specific instructional processes that are mentioned in this book: tactics such as Three Step Interviews, Think Pair Share, Round Robin, Place Mat; and strategies such as Academic Controversy, Team Analysis, Inductive Thinking, and Concept Attainment. Of course, the implementation of linguistic intelligence would depend on the extent to which the teacher can frame questions to engage all students and not just the few who choose to volunteer or who are consistently chosen to respond. Added to that would be the idea of feeling safe and knowing that one's voice will be respected. Of what value are portfolios and conferences if the student does not feel safe?

Another way to consider the role of intelligence is through linking linguistic intelligence with the role of semantic memory in terms of how the brain processes learning. The brain lays down information in different pathways or lanes. One of those lanes is known as semantic memory, as differentiated from procedural, emotional, episodic, and automatic memory lanes. This form of memory often employs words or symbols to do things like remembering dates, poems, and songs. Listening to a lecture would also weave into this semantic memory.

Importantly, this is a more difficult way of making meaning and retaining information. For example, to recall a poem, most of us have to work hard—practice. This is unlike the ease with which we recall a memorable moment or a face, where no rehearsal was needed. A musty smell and you recall images of the week you spent in Bali—no practice, no rehearsal. Connected to making meaning and retaining information is the need for the brain to find patterns, to make meaning. As educators we must access approaches that assist the learner in finding patterns and making meaning. And that implies encouraging the brain to work at more complex levels. When we can connect emotions and movement to words and speech we increase the chances that information is recalled.

Based on the above information and your experiences, what are the implications for educators regarding integrating linguistic intelligence into the curriculum?

MUSICAL INTELLIGENCE

This intelligence relates to the capacity to perceive, discriminate, transform, and express musical forms. Of all our genetic gifts, none emerges earlier than musical talent. Of interest is the varied nature of how it occurs. The student could be an exemplary violinist as a result of participation in the Suzuki Talent Education program and, through intensive practice, master the essential of the string instrument by the time he or she enters school. Another child could be autistic, a child who can barely communicate and who is severely disabled in affective and cognitive spheres. Yet, this child can flawlessly sing any piece he or she hears. And another child, one who is raised in a musical family, begins to pick out tunes on his or her own—like a Mozart.

So where does "music" fit? If you focus on composers, they indicate that composing is as basic for them as eating and sleeping. They have tones in their head. And for them, composing loses the character of a special virtue. Wagner stated he composed like a cow producing milk; Saint-Saens likened it to an apple tree producing apples. Yet there are many musicians whose musical strength was the result of intense study over years.

You might read *The Mozart Effect* by Don Campbell (1997). It provides an interesting intensification of Gardner's idea of musical intelligence. For example, one study from the centre for Neurobiology at the University of California (Rauscher & Shaw, 1993) found that students who listened to Mozart patterns had significant shifts in spatial temporal reasoning. Scientists are suggesting that listening to Mozart assists in organizing the neurons' firing patterns. Over the years we have met numerous special education teachers who played classical music—and other forms of music selected by students—in their classroom.

The position for educators to consider is that whether strength in music is an inherited gift or the result of hard work, the extent to which the talent is expressed publicly will depend on the specific circumstances experienced. Some children will achieve a high degree of musical competence, but importantly, many who could, will not.

Components of Musical Intelligence: Pitch, Rhythm, and Timbre.

Pitch (the melody) and rhythm are the most important aspects of music. In some cultures pitch is more central (Oriental societies) and in others like the sub-Saharan African societies, rhythm is most central. Timbre represents the characteristic qualities of a tone. Those 3 elements are the core of music. Yet, interestingly, the rhythmic organization of music can exist separate from the auditory sense—as evidenced by deaf individuals using rhythm as their entry point into music. And composers like Scriabin underscore the importance of seeing music performed, whether by an orchestra or a dance troupe. Stravinsky insisted that music must be seen to be properly assimilated. They argue a strong link to bodily or gestural language. Children find it virtually impossible to listen to music without some sort of bodily movement.

Interestingly, Stravinsky argued that music is closer to mathematics than to literature.

Musical Intelligence: Instructional Implications

Do your students use aspects of music (rap, playing instruments, singing, etc.) to interpret poems, to communicate meaning and emotions, or to interpret mood as background to a story? Can music be used to assist students to recall information—as a memory strategy? Do your students delve into music to aid in understanding history, for example, comparing the war songs of the First World War (e.g., "Over There," 1917) with the war songs of the Vietnam War (e.g., "Eve of Destruction," 1965)? Could you employ Concept Attainment to assist them to understand Baroque music or how Mozart was different from Beethoven or how Blues is different from Blue Grass? Gardner argues that music is the playful exploration of the other modes of intelligence.

How do you encourage students to select music to solve problems and to inquire into music to extend their understanding of other areas of study? What strategies do you employ as part of those actions?

Most fascinating are the emotional and social implications of music. We are often simultaneously found laughing, crying, pondering, questioning, challenging, hating, loving...all because of music. What effect is this having on the brain? How does music assist in laying down memory? Think of how rhythm assists in memory – how did you first learn the alphabet?

Unlike the continuing importance we place on extending our linguistic skills, music occupies a relatively low niche in the teaching and learning process, and so musical illiteracy is acceptable. Just as we can tease apart series of levels in language—from basic phonological level, through sensitivity to word order and word meaning, to the ability to appreciate larger entities, like stories—so too in the realm of music. One can examine sensitivity to individual tones or phrases and how these fit together into larger musical structures which exhibit their own rules of organization.

Did you see the movie *Mr Holland's Opus*? It shows some interesting and off-the-cuff attempts to encourage students to develop their musical abilities. Would it have helped if he had read the book *The Mozart Effect*? Would it have helped if he had other instructional skills, tactics, and strategies to provide the structure for musical inquiry? What happens to students when we don't? Below is a quote from *Frames of Mind*.

People like me are aware of their so-called genius at 10, 8, 9... I always wondered, *Why has nobody discovered me? In school, didn't they see that I'm more clever than anybody in this school? That the teachers are stupid, too? That all they had was information that I didn't need. It was obvious to me. Why didn't they put me in art school? Why didn't they train me? I was different, I was always different, Why didn't anybody notice me?* (p.115)

John Lennon.

Even though a student can lose linguistic abilities through damage or disease to one part of the brain (usually the left hemisphere in right-handed individuals), musical abilities usually remain intact.

Based on the above information and your experiences, what are the implications for educators regarding integrating musical intelligence into the curriculum?

LOGICAL-MATHEMATICAL INTELLIGENCE

If linguistic intelligence often refers to using words effectively, then the area of logical-mathematical intelligence often connects to using numbers effectively. Tangentially, logical-mathematical intelligence is responsive to patterns and relationships, to making hypotheses and predictions, and to sensing cause and effect. Instructional processes that involve classification, making generalizations, categorization, or the generating of hypotheses also relate to this intelligence. That said, one senses the role of Mind Mapping, Concept Mapping, Venn Diagrams, Fishbone, and Concept Attainment in encouraging logical-mathematical thinking.

Interestingly, Gardner writes that what characterizes those with mathematical gifts is that their powers in math rarely extend beyond the boundary of the discipline. Mathematicians are rarely talented in finance or the law. What does characterize mathematicians is a love of dealing with the abstract. As Hardy states: (quoted in Gardner's *Frames of Mind*)

> *It is undeniable that a gift for mathematics is one of the most specialized talents and that mathematicians as a class are not particularly distinguished for general ability or versatility.... If a man is in any sense a real mathematician, then it is a hundred to one that his mathematics will be far better than anything else he can do and ... he would be silly if he surrendered any decent opportunity of exercising his one talent in order to do any undistinguished work in other fields. (p. 139)*

The progress of science has been linked to the status of mathematics. Almost every mathematical invention has eventually proved useful within the scientific community. For example, George Friedrich Riemann's differential geometry proved basic for the theory of relativity. Indeed, the marked progress of Western science since the seventeenth century can be traced to a significant extent to the invention of differential and integral calculus. Piaget noted that the evolution of science displays certain intriguing parallels with the development in children of logical-mathematical thought.

Although we find correlations between science and math, in comparison with language and music, we know comparatively little about its organization in the brain. We do know that it is one of the loneliest of all the intelligences and the strength of the gift appears to lessen in the late twenties and early thirties.

Gardner describes the life of a mathematician as a world apart. The need to concentrate for hours without contact with other individuals is important. He also adds that language is not of much help during that "isolated" concentration.

How's your math anxiety? Have you ever had a math question to which you wanted a real life answer?

Logical-Mathematical Intelligence: Instructional Implications

In this section we will focus on specific instructional processes that encourage logical thinking—classifying, making inferences, and searching for cause and effect relationships (rather than on purely mathematical thinking). This implies a shift to the two sides of critical thinking: inductive (classifying all the plants in the jungle) and deductive (finding out why one particular animal is disappearing). Although inductive and deductive may appear to be different, they often play off one another. Once one has thought through things inductively—classified the information, explored relationships, etc.—one is often in a stronger position to think deductively, to play out the scientific method, to form and test hypotheses, to explore cause and effect relationships.

We will focus our discussion on Inductive Thinking as an example. One powerful inductive process to explore the logic within a set of data is Bruner's Concept Attainment process. By showing data (for example 10 problems that are all multiplication and 10 problems that are addition) and having the students compare how one set of problems is the same and how it is different from the another set of problems, encourages the brain to hunt for patterns, to understand relationships.

Another powerful inductive process is the classification of information (e.g., Taba's Inductive Thinking strategy). Taba's instructional strategy, like the instructional strategy of Concept Attainment, invites the learner to put things into groups based on common properties. The only difference is that with Concept Attainment, the examples are usually classified in advance and presented by the teacher.

What makes Concept Attainment and Inductive Thinking so powerful is that by shifting the data set to pictures, or music, or actions, etc., one can integrate the other intelligences. For example, if a teacher has students brainstorm their thinking around an issue—say pollution—then has them classify that information and then work in pairs to create a Mind Map or Concept Map – then the teacher is encouraging five different intelligences (Logical-Mathematical, Linguistic, Interpersonal, Intrapersonal, and Spatial). Of course students could act out the key ideas in their Mind Map or create a song or rap to assist in interpreting those ideas. That would bring in the Musical and Bodily-Kinesthetic intelligences.

If we shift the focus of classification to students who have autism, we find that one of the ways they make sense of the information in their world is through data analysis—concept formation. Although it may appear that they are just memorizing information, once they have enough they begin to organize it into categories. Often the word is only understood once an image is created. The more we as teachers understand the autistic child's thinking patterns, the more precisely we can arrange the learning environment. Two interesting books to read concerning autistic students are *Autism: The Facts* by Simon Baron-Cohen and Patrick Bolton, and *Thinking in Pictures and Other Reports from My Life with Autism* by Temple Grandin.

On the following page is a lesson on Baroque music employing Concept Attainment. It illustrates how to integrate logical-mathematical thinking into the curriculum.

Concept Attainment Data Set
BAROQUE MUSIC–MIDDLE SCHOOL TO ADULT

Mental Set:

As students enter the room, the teacher plays a CD of short excerpts from several styles of music: jazz, pop, Indian, Western classical, etc.

"Raise your hand if you know what "classical music" sounds like. Those of you who put up your hand, please turn to the person beside you and try to hum some of what you had in mind when I said "classical music." When you hear me begin to hum, that will be the signal that I need your attention and quiet. Thanks."

The teacher hums a "classical" (Baroque) melody, e.g., "Come Ye Sons of Art" (Purcell).

Statement of Objective and Purpose:

"Not all "classical music" is the same. Actually, when people say "classical music" they are usually referring to several different styles of music that started in Europe several centuries ago. In this class, you are going to gain a better understanding of one of those styles— Baroque music—so that you can enjoy it more as a listener and/or as a player. By the end of this session, you should be able to tell whether the music I was humming a moment ago is Baroque or not and explain why."

Focus Statement:

"In a moment I will play a CD. You will hear brief excerpts from various pieces of music—each lasts between 30 seconds and 1 minute. You will hear various combinations of instruments: solo voice and orchestra, violin and piano, solo piano, etc. These differences are NOT what you are listening for. Rather, please focus on musical style. Some of the selections are examples of the "Baroque" style; others are not. Your task is to define that "Baroque" style—i.e., decide what are its unique elements, characteristics, or attributes."

Directions:

"The first 10 pieces we will hear alternate between examples of Baroque music and examples that are not Baroque music (e.g., the first excerpt will be Baroque, the second not, the third Baroque, etc.). The CD will be stopped after each selection to give you time to think—to consider, compare, and contrast the Baroque and the non-Baroque styles that you've heard. After all ten selections are played, you will get together with a partner and share your hypotheses about what the Baroque style is."

Initial Data Set:

(Odd numbers are examples of Baroque music.)

1. Handel, George Friederic. Tanti strali al sen mi scocchi. (Vocal duet)
2. Prokofiev, Sergei. Sonata for violin and piano, op. 94. Moderato.
3. Bach, Johann Sebastian. Italian concerto. Presto. (Solo piano).
4. Ravel, Maurice. Jeux d'eau. (Solo piano).
5. Monteverdi, Claudio. Non si levana ancor l'alba. (Madrigal for 5 voices).
6. Tallis, Thomas. Salvator mundi. (Motet for 5 voices).
7. Corelli, Archangelo. Concerto no. 6 in f major – Allegro.
8. Beethoven, Ludwig Von. String quartet op. 59, no. 2 in e minor. Allegro.
9. Bach, Johann Sebastian. Concerto for 2 violins, strings and continuo in d minor, BWV 1043. Largo.
10. Schubert, Franz. Octet in f major. Sixth movement - Allegro.

"So, what do you and your partner think makes Baroque music different from other styles of music?"

Testers

"Next you will hear a dozen testers. Again, the CD will be stopped after each excerpt to allow you time for thinking and discussion. You and your partner will use your hypotheses to decide which of these excerpts represent Baroque music and which do not. Be prepared to share your decisions—anyone can be selected to explain their thinking to the larger group."

Testers Set:

(Teacher does not announce the composer or title of each piece at this time. Teacher monitors responses by use of thumbs up/thumbs down.)

(Y) Handel, George Friederic. Trio sonata in g major, op. 5 no. 4.
(Y) Bach, Johann Sebastian. Und ist ein kind geboren, BWV 142. (Cantata).
(N) Beethoven, Ludwig Von. Bagatelle, op. 33 no. 1.
(Y) Vivaldi, Antonio. Four seasons, no. 3: autumn.
(Y) Gabrieli, Giovanni. Buccinate in Neomenia. (Choir and brass orchestra).
(N) Mozart, Wolfgang Amadeus. Piano sonata in c major, K 279. Allegro.
(Y&N) Milan, Luis. Pavana IV del septimo y octavo tono. (Solo lute).

Summary:

The teacher poses the question, "So, what makes Baroque music different from other styles of music?" Students Think-Pair-Share, then return to home groups of 4. The teacher plays a selection from one of the above "yes" examples while the students complete a Place Mat to answer the question. Following this, the teacher and the class decide on a best possible hypothesis and record it on the chart below the question as a numerical list. Possible ideas for this list include:

Critical Attributes of Baroque Music:

- An underlying "low part" (bass part) that runs through the music (A number of different instruments can be used for this purpose);
- A very regular rhythm; rhythm doesn't change much within a section; one section will be almost uniformly fast, another almost uniformly slow;
- Very regular, predictable chord changes;
- The dynamics (loudness) of the music doesn't change much within a section; one section will be almost uniformly soft, another almost uniformly loud;
- Most of the music has complex melodies above the simpler chord changes in the bass part – lots of decoration and "frills" to the melodies;
- Sequencing of melody – moving the same idea through several successive pitch levels;
- Exaggerated emotions (in vocal music).

Extensions:

Next day, the students review the class hypothesis chart. Then, as they listen to an extended excerpt from one of the "yes" examples, they try to identify particular Baroque characteristics that they hear. Next, they listen to a non-Baroque excerpt (e.g., Schubert)—without being told that it is not Baroque—and try to identify in the music any of the characteristics listed in the hypothesis. This is done using Think-Pair-Share, then random call. Once told that the piece is not Baroque, the class decides if the hypothesis needs to be revised.

The class listens to a 2 or 3-minute excerpt of Baroque music. Then each home group of 4 creates a unique movement/gesture to represent each of the characteristics listed in the hypothesis. The excerpt is repeated and the students try to "map" their movements/gestures onto the music—i.e., they use movement and number signs (which correspond to the numbered items on the hypothesis chart) to identify the particular Baroque features that they hear. If desired, students can perform their choreographed music for the class.

In subsequent classes, repeat this exercise, but have each group select its own piece of Baroque music.

This lesson was designed by John Mazurek

SPATIAL INTELLIGENCE

This intelligence is sensitive to shapes, lines, colour, space, form, etc., and how they interact. One thinks of artists, architects, decorators, inventors, along with navigators and their ability to visualize and represent life's experiences graphically. As well, Michael Jordan's ability to orient himself within a matrix of movement and a grand master's moves on a chess board also illustrate spatial intelligence. Like the other intelligences, a number of ways exist to play out this intelligence.

One way to gain a feeling for the core of spatial intelligence is to attempt the tasks devised by investigators of that intelligence. In the figure at the bottom of the page, choose the form identical to the target item.

Central to spatial intelligence are the capacities to perceive the visual world accurately, to perform transformations and modifications upon one's initial perceptions, and to be able to re-create aspects of one's visual experience, even in the absence of relevant physical stimuli. The most elementary operation, upon which other aspects of spatial intelligence rest, is the ability to perceive a form or an object.

Although spatial intelligence is closely tied to and grows out of one's observation of the visual world, spatial intelligence can develop even in an individual who is blind.

THE CULTURAL PERSPECTIVE

Spatial acuity of the Inuit is legendary—for both men and women. This suggests that the spatial discrepancy reported in Western cultures can be overcome in some cultures or that the biases in our environments are producing apparent spatial deficits in females. At least 60 percent of Inuit youngsters reach as high a score on spatial ability as the top 10 percent of Caucasian children—this ability also generalizes to tests of conceptual ability and to tests measuring visual details.

Spatial intelligence entails a number of loosely related capacities:

1. the ability to recognize instances of the same element
2. the ability to transform or to recognize a transformation of one element to another
3. the capacity to conjure up mental imagery and then to transform that imagery
4. the capacity to produce graphic likeness of spatial information.

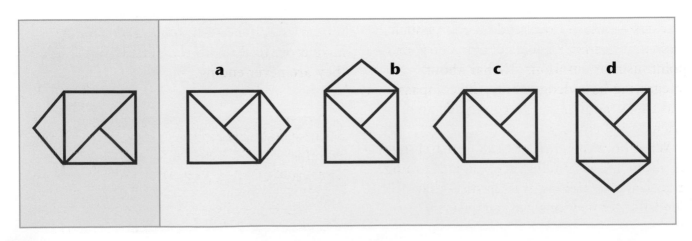

Spatial Intelligence: Instructional Implications

In relation to language, Rudolf Arnheim minimizes the role of language in productive thinking: he suggests that unless we can conjure up an image of some process or concept, we will be unable to think clearly about it. The consensus is that spatial and linguistic faculties seem able to proceed in relatively independent or complementary fashion. Perhaps read the book *Thinking in Pictures and Other Reports From My Life With Autism* by Temple Grandin (1995). For her, language was meaningless until she could create an image for the word. She now has a Ph.D. and has been a powerful re-designer of a number of industries. Her spatial skills are intriguing; her stories heart-warming and informative.

In terms of educational implications, how do you support this intelligence in your classroom? Think of the visual organizers such as **Mind Mapping**—where colour, lines, and shapes interact to organize information. What about the use of graphic organizers such as **Fish Bone, Venn Diagrams,** and **Ranking Ladders?** What about the use of charts, graphs, photography, videos, slides, puzzles, collage, painting, or the use of telescopes, microscopes, computer programs, and graphic calculators? How could **Concept Attainment** be employed using pictures to attain or extend a concept such as ionic architecture or lines of symmetry, or pointillism or emotions? What about integrating knowledge about the compass and topographical map to complete an orienteering course?

What does the current brain research tell us about spatial intelligence? For one thing, it is clear that the brain is plastic—that dendritic connections can increase throughout life. We hate to bring in the rats/research paradigm, but rats raised in stimulating environments (akin to Head Start for rats) have a thicker cerebral cortex (more neuronal connections) than rats in unenriched environments. So, we might think of what happens when logical-mathematical intelligence is massaged by spatial intelligence. Is there math in art; is there art in math? Consider fractals.

Another issue is that certain types of dementia destroy language regions of the brain and unmask art talent (e.g., what happened to stockbroker Bruce L. Miller, at the University of California). Autistic kids often perform well on tests of visual spatial ability such as jigsaw puzzles. Drawing is one of three areas that autistic children are often skilled at—way above normal. The other two are music and calendar calculation.

Interestingly, normal adults who are not spatially strong exhibit a falling off in their spatial performance, while those who are spatially gifted find that intelligence stays more robust as they age, while (as we stated earlier) those gifted with logical-mathematical intelligence become increasingly fragile. Artists do some of their greatest work as they get older. Henry Moore, a contemporary sculptor now in his 80s, argues that the reason is because the visual arts are more connected with actual human experience—painting and sculpture have more to do with the outside world and they are never-ending.

Based on the above information and your experiences, what are the implications for educators regarding integrating spatial intelligence into the curriculum?

BODILY-KINESTHETIC INTELLIGENCE

When we employ our body to express our thoughts and emotions, we are attending to the bodily-kinesthetic intelligence. Marcel Marceau exemplifies the talents of bodily-kinesthetic intelligence. Through mime he depicts the appearance of an object, a person, or an action; and this task requires artful caricature, an exaggeration of movements and reactions. Puppeteers must also sense action at a distance.

Characteristic of this intelligence is the ability to use the body in highly differentiated and skillful ways; as well, to do it with objects using both fine and gross motor skills. Gardner argues that control of the body and the skillful use of objects is at the core of this intelligence; an intelligence seen in swimmers, dancers, golfers, actors, inventors, etc. Related to language, Norman Mailer writes that boxing is a dialogue between bodies...a rapid debate between two sets of intelligences. Others may disagree.

Gardner argues that in our culture a gap exists between the mental and the physical. That separation has been coupled with the belief that what we do with our body is somehow less privileged, less special, than those problem-solving routines carried out chiefly through the use of language, logic, or some other relatively abstract symbolic system. The sharp distinction is not drawn in many other cultures. Psychologists have found strong links between the use of the body and the use of other intelligences. Interestingly, neurologists have found that those individuals who are physically fit have more support for brain activity. Recent research shows they have up to 40% more capillary support to supply oxygen and take away waste products. This means physically fit individuals do not get as tired and can sustain their focus.

Although we easily appreciate the history and importance of dance and acting, as educators we often forget the potential gift of the class clown. A number of comedians who later went on to achieve great success have indicated that their initial impetus for imitating (and making fun of) the teacher came from their genuine difficulties in understanding the point of lessons that they were supposed to be mastering. These comedians achieved their goals by filling in superficial outlines of a character; by developing the various situations in which the character customarily finds himself; and, by touching on the various abilities and deficits of that particular persona. Perhaps it was through this process that the great silent clowns of the past—Chaplin, Lloyd, and Keaton, and those of today—Lily Tomlin, or Seinfeld developed and honed their gift.

What about Wayne Gretzky? While many think Gretzky's achievements were effortlessly attained, he disagrees... *I've spent almost as much time studying hockey as a med student puts in studying medicine.*

Bodily-Kinesthetic Intelligence: Instructional Implications

We could enter into the discussion of bodily-kinesthetic intelligence in a number of ways. We are choosing a passageway from what is known about memory as it connects to what is known about the human brain. Again, one appreciates the connection between the two literatures of Brain Research and Multiple Intelligence. When we think of memory, we consider two issues: (1) information going in; and (2) information coming out. The more interesting though, is the way in which the memory goes in, how and when it is stored, and how we as teachers go about encouraging it to be retrieved and shared. We suggest you read Marilee Sprenger's (1999) book *Learning and Memory: The Brain in Action* for an easy-to-read introduction to memory, teaching, and learning.

Here is an example. What do you remember doing on August the 31, 1998 and on November 22, 1963? What do you remember doing when you heard about Princess Diana's death or John F. Kennedy's assassination? What is the difference? It seems that we have five ways or lanes of remembering:

- semantic
- episodic
- procedural
- automatic
- emotional

Below are two columns representing two of those five ways we retain information: what do the examples in each column have in common?

Column One	Column Two
• Venn Diagrams	• Role Playing the division of two numbers or an equation
• Fish Bone	• Practicing a process to gain mastery (making slides)
• Concept Mapping	• Dancing one's interpretation of a poem
• Word Webbing	• Playing games – bowling to learn addition
• Brainstorming	• Taking a field trip or even just walking and talking down the hall
• Time Lines	• Doing something novel while learning an idea
• Ranking Ladder	e.g., walk around with a shoe on their head while reciting

Column one affects semantic memory; Column two affects procedural memory.

What we see is that as educators we can be wise or not so wise in terms of how we choose to engage students in taking in information and in how we choose to assess its retrieval. If the students store information in one way and we are not wise in how we choose to assess it, we may not be accurately respecting what the students understand.

Role playing is one of the most researched of all the instructional approaches—with large effects on student learning. Your learning/teaching style may be inclined to talking more than the students need, or to putting students in groups to talk more than they need. You may have felt at risk at being invited to physically interpret something you were learning or had learned. Yet some kids need that opportunity. Such students are movement oriented. The literature on students with learning disabilities show that their performance IQ is noticeably larger than their verbal IQ.

Based on the above information and your experiences, what are the implications for educators regarding integrating bodily-kinesthetic intelligence into the curriculum?

THE PERSONAL INTELLIGENCES:
Inter and Intra

Knowing others and knowing oneself are the key words for **interpersonal** and **intrapersonal** intelligence. Think of the ability to interpret feelings, moods, to use humour, to laugh, to debate. When this is turned inward it is intrapersonal; when turned outward to others, interpersonal. Not wanting to gloss over the obvious, but intrapersonal definitely means that you understand yourself. Moreover, it also means that you appreciate that others may need to learn differently from you.

Most job ads in the paper, include a focus on interpersonal and communication skills and the ability to work as part of a team. We have seen none that ask for someone capable of sitting in a row, not talking, and willing to put up their hand and wait for the boss to come around and answer the question.

Freud was one of the first great psychologists to explore the *intrapersonal;* the location of the self as it exists in the individual's own knowledge of himself. Interest in others was used to better understand one's own problems, wishes, and anxieties. James, an older psychologist who travelled to hear the younger scholar from Austria, told Freud, "The future of psychology belongs to your work. There is no more dramatic moment in the intellectual history of our time." Yet James was from a different history and a different philosophy; he chose a more positively oriented form of psychology. James stressed the inter-personal...the importance of relationships with other individuals.

The *intrapersonal* intelligence is focused on access to one's feeling of life. This entails one's range of affects or emotions: the capacity to immediately effect discriminations among these feelings and to eventually label them; to draw upon them as a means of understanding and to guide one's behaviour. One finds this form of intelligence in the wise elder who draws upon a wealth of inner experiences in order to advise members of the community (for example, Chief Dan George). This intelligence is dealt with more specifically and at length in the literature on emotional intelligence (see Goleman, 1995). For a different research and analytical lens, see La Doux's book, *The Emotional Brain.*

The interpersonal intelligence turns outward, to other individuals. It refers to one's ability to notice and make distinctions among other individuals and, in particular, among their moods, motivations, and intentions. In its most elementary form, the interpersonal intelligence entails the capacity of the young child to discriminate among the individuals around him and to detect their various moods. In an advanced form, interpersonal knowledge permits a skilled adult to read the intentions and desires of many other individuals and, potentially, to act upon this knowledge. We see highly developed forms of interpersonal intelligences in religious leaders such as Mahatma Gandhi, in skilled teachers, and other individuals enrolled in the helping professions.

With autistic children and adults, we see examples of lower functioning regarding this intelligence. An inability to relate socially is the most important signal that a child has autism (see Baron-Cohen and Bolton, 1993). Autism is not about one social abnormality, but rather, a range of them. Likewise, those gifted with this intelligence have a range of abilities that allow them to effectively adapt to multiple situations (e.g., politicians and comedians). In our classrooms, they are usually the most popular students.

The Personal Intelligences: Instructional Implications

So how does this play out in the classroom? How do teachers value and act on extending their students' understanding of themselves and others? Consider that over 65 percent of all district school vision statements reflect the importance of these intelligences. Yet sadly, that is not what is seen in practice. The reality is an almost narrow and superficially shallow focus on the linguistic and mathematical intelligences. Sadly, individuals whose strengths lie in other areas, are often at a disadvantage.

One immediately senses that Cooperative Learning and all its variations represent a powerful lever into celebrating these intelligences. Given that interpersonal intelligence is one of the most powerful predictors of success in all cultures that Gardner studied, then one might argue that choosing not to invoke those practices that encourage interactions between students and among groups of students, would be unwise.

Focusing on the Cooperative Learning literature, we find over 300 group processes that support aspects of these two intelligences (e.g., Academic Controversy, Team Analysis, Teams-Games-Tournaments, Group Investigations, Three-Step Interview, Drama/Role Playing/Simulations, and Peer Tutoring). Note, though, that some of those 300 structures have little or no research base to support their use in the classroom. Only the more complex ones such as Jigsaw, Teams-Games-Tournaments, Academic Controversy, and Group Investigation have a literature that informs teachers about their classroom effects.

Of course to employ these structures effectively in the classroom, students must be progressively skilled in a variety of social, communication, and critical thinking skills.

For example, if students cannot be sensitive to equal voice and no put downs (social skills) then they are unlikely to employ communication skills such as active listening and checking for understanding, and critical thinking skills such as suspending judgement and examining both sides of an issue. Of course, one can quickly see that without those skills, it makes it less likely that students will effectively employ a tactic such as Three-Step Interview or a strategy such as Academic Controversy.

In terms of intrapersonal intelligence, the essence here is on reflection or metacognition or thinking about one's thinking. The use of portfolios, student self assessment, and role playing are three of many ways for students to better understand themselves. Of course, when students reflect and construct visual organizers such as Mind Maps or Graphic Organizers such as Concept Mapping they are also illustrating what is going on within their mind.

From our perspective, it would make sense for collective action to be taken in a school. Together teachers could identify specific skills for each grade level which are then reviewed the next year and integrated with additional skills. That would mean that students would have a repertoire of practiced skills that would enable them to more responsibly and meaningfully respond to life around them. We need to make the acquisition of interpersonal and intrapersonal skills valued by educators and students alike.

Based on the job ads on the following page, what are the implications for educators for integrating the personal intelligences into the curriculum?

CLIPS FROM THE EMPLOYMENT ADS

Below are statements concerning what employers are expecting of potential employees. What are the implications for us as educators concerning the design of our learning environments?

You may want to collect a few employment ads from your local papers or international papers and then give each group of three or four students about 9 to 12 ads (each student having 3 or 4). Perhaps use the Place Mat process described in the chapter on Cooperative Learning and have the students identity the most common expectations identified in their set of ads. Then, do a Round Robin and come to a consensus regarding the skills employers most value.

Programmer/Analyst

Qualifications: ...practical knowledge of system programming techniques; excellent analytical and problem-solving abilities; demonstrated ability to prepare estimates and perform multiple tasks concurrently; excellent customer service, interpersonal, consultation, and communication skills.

Environmental Management Specialist: Rural Groundwater

...demonstrated ability in technology transfer, including training techniques for agriculture sector: experience in program planning/evaluation, project management and team leadership; highly developed interpersonal and negotiation skills to develop effective relationships with clients and provincial and international experts; effective communication skills; ability to use computer applications; valid driver's license.

School Counselor: Secondary School

Your M.S.W., or Masters in Counselling and 5 years direct counselling experience, including experience with the target age group are further enhanced by your proven leadership abilities. As a strong team player, you are accomplished in team-based work in multidisciplinary settings and have an interest in generalist school-based practice.

Surgical Services: Clinical Educator, General Surgery

This role will see you join a dynamic, multidisciplinary team dedicated to the promotion of excellence in surgical care for our two 27-bed inpatient units which specialize in thoracic, abdominal, vascular, ENT, urology and plastic surgery. A superior communicator with excellent interpersonal abilities, you will bring strong leadership, clinical assessment and facilitation skills to our surgical team.

Translators

The applicant must have a perfect command of English and a command of two other official languages. Strong interpersonal and communication skills; self-motivation and the ability to work as part of a team in a multicultural environment are very important.

NATURALISTIC INTELLIGENCE

This is the intelligence that refers to the ability to solve problems based on one's knowledge/understanding of nature. For example, the Australian Aborigine, the Canadian Inuit, the North American Indian, have a sophisticated knowledge of nature. They have the ability to exist wisely with nature. You might also add Charles Darwin or those whose training or education involves outdoor education. One would hopefully expect that those who become Ministers of the Environment have naturalistic intelligence.

When we think of students who live their life in an urban or suburban environment and rarely, if ever, experience the country, we must worry about how they think concerning the environment. Do they know of ponds, lakes, streams, mountains, cliffs, valleys, acid rain, clear-cutting, oil spills, over-fishing? What do they care? Can we meaningfully engage students in science from within the walls of the classroom? One thinks of Peter Sellers in the movie *Being There*. In this movie we have a man whose life was what he gleaned from watching TV. Suddenly his life changes; he must leave this cloistered environment and exist in the real world.

When we think of how our actions affect systems, we realize that we have to have an intimate understanding of the system, not simply a labelled diagram of a water cycle. This intelligence represents the ability to understand who is affected by water pollution. This implies understanding that as water is polluted, fish become scarce, their price goes up, the restaurants charge more, the plumbers eating at the restaurant increase their fee to cover the increased cost of the

fish, the fishing industry pays more to have the plumber come and do repairs on the boat, and so forth. We see the emerging domino effect.

Naturalistic Intelligence also relates to recycling: Why are glass and plastic not recycled at most international airports? Even when we have recycling bins, why do people throw their juice glasses in a regular garbage bin? Ironically, they are drinking healthy (bodily-kinesthetic intelligence) but they are not thinking healthy related to solving problems concerning nature.

Naturalistic Intelligence: *Instructional Implications*

In this section we will simply tell a few stories. You most likely have your own.

Junior High: I wonder how many teachers who have worked with at-risk students would argue that Mother Nature is the best teacher. I know we would. One of the authors ran a special education program that involved getting the students out of the school. Outdoor education was a key approach in the design of the learning environments. This was based on a study done in Vanves, France, back in the 1960's where they cut the academic time in half and provided the students with an extensive outdoor education program. At the end of ten years, the students in the outdoor education/academic program did as well or better on the academic test as those students who had a more intensive academic program. In addition, the outdoor/academic students did significantly better on sociometric (interpersonal intelligence) and in overall fitness (bodily-kinesthetic intelligence). Returning to the action research study done collaboratively by one of the authors (Haug, Bennett, Jamieson &

Krause, 1977) when teaching junior high school in Edmonton Alberta Public Schools, the academic content was covered by December. In other words the academic content was covered in 1/4 of the time it usually took. Interestingly, the attendance rate rose from 78 percent to an average of 95 percent.

Elementary: In adapting the above process to an elementary school several years later, it meant that during October, the students spent their time outside the walls of the school. They spent time in swimming pools and on farms investigating the measurement of volume. They spent time at dump sites investigating issues related to pollution and recycling, at graveyards in the country discussing issues about subtraction, and at ponds studying animals using homemade periscopes and weaving together art projects using bullrushes collected from ponds. What was the pay-off? Thirteen of 15 special needs students had perfect attendance with most integrated partially or fully into the regular classroom during the year.

Survival Camps: For five days during the academic year, students went into the semi-wilderness with teachers—in minus 10 to 30 degree centigrade weather. They built simple shelters, cooked food, and completed explorations. In order to earn the right to take part in this program, students completed a manual that involved the identification of animals, their tracks and habits, as well as understanding environmental issues.

Relationship Camps: During the last month of school, sixty junior high boys and girls spent one week with about sixty Native American students at the Stoney Wilderness Centre near Banff, Alberta. They lived in real-sized teepees and for two days went on a trail ride up into the Rocky Mountains. Here the Native students taught the "city-slickers" how to catch and saddle a horse. The urban students hand-carved their own paddles out of a 2 x 10 piece of spruce lumber. They completed survival swimming classes and level one canoeing training—all of which was necessary in order to canoe and fish. The upshot—the city students cried when they had to return to the city. They had made such good friends with one another and with nature.

Based on the above information and your experiences, what are the implications for educators reintegrating the natural intelligence into the curriculum?

Lens#2: Emotional Intelligence

This section is designed around the work of Joseph LeDoux (1996): *The Emotional Brain: The Mysterious Underpinnings of Emotional Life*; Debra Niehoff (1999) *The Biology of Violence*; and Daniel Goleman (1994) *Emotional Intelligence*. Goleman's work more completely explains aspects of emotions and intelligence. Goleman's work also intentionally extends the work of Howard Gardner in the area of 'inter' and 'intra' personal intelligence and makes practical interpretations for educators. Perhaps we should say at the outset that no one brain system is responsible for the phantom-like phenomena of emotions; emotions arise in multiple areas and relate to our basic needs to eat, to be protected, and to procreate (fear, food, and sex). Note: think of the text and context of most movie and television programs or commercials. Media knows how to connect to our emotional brain—fear, food, sex.

Goleman argues that emotional intelligence may be more important than all other forms of intelligence. The neurologists inform us that we have more neurons from the emotional part of the brain connecting to the cerebral cortex than the reverse. The implication is that the emotions are capable of highjacking the cortex in less than a moment's notice.

Of course, the question is: What are the dimensions of emotional intelligence and what would we see in the classroom that supports the development of this intelligence?

Goleman presents the following focus areas for the development of Emotional Intelligence:

- Recognizing emotions – self awareness
- Managing Moods – self control
- Motivation   • Empathy   • Social Skills

Perhaps a key point for us as educators is how Emotional Intelligence relates to motivation and to stress. Important to both these areas is that emotions can have useful and pathological consequences. Fear is useful, but not when it turns to anxiety; pleasure encourages, unless it turns to addiction; love builds relationships, unless it turns into obsession; annoyance is a message—when not effectively dealt with it can turn to anger and hatred.

The Greeks talked of Ethos (ethics) Logos (logic) and Pathos. Pathos connects to emotions. All three are part of communication. We know that emotions arise involuntarily; that out-of-our-control, the emotional ball begins to roll. It appears. But critically, once it starts, and we are cerebrally aware of it, then we are in control—we can decide to hit or not to hit. Understanding emotions in order to increase our skills in interpreting and acting on them is wise. This implies that our cognitive resources be connected to that emotional information. As LeDoux points out, *"Surviving is not just something we do in the presence of a wild beast. Social situations are also survival situations."* The adolescent student certainly confirms that statement; for them, friends are everything. The at-risk students and the highly visible, yet unacknowledged homeless person, also provide an unacceptably rich backdrop of social survival.

Emotional Intelligence: Educational Implications

Think of a student who repeatedly fails in school. Not only does the learning process and the teacher become a negative learning force (conditioning) but the room itself becomes a conditioned stimulus towards failure. The fact that this at-risk student enters this box-like room mitigates learning. Now add to that "box" the stress of living in poverty, witnessing violence, being neglected, or being emotionally or sexually abused, and/or experiencing drugs and alcohol. In terms of learning, stressful life events can alter our hippocampus (an organ in the brain that is necessary for long term memory). With severe trauma, shrivelling of the dendrites occurs; with repeated stress (e.g., victims of repeated child abuse) that damage to the hippocampus can become permanent.

The implication is that we must create classrooms where students feel simultaneously challenged and safe. And we must realize that the idea of a safe and challenging classroom has different meanings for different students. What is challenging and safe for a bright or struggling confident student is not the same for a bright or struggling non-confident student. One's self concept (the extent you understand yourself) and self esteem (the value you place on what you know about yourself) plays a role in defining what is safe and challenging.

One program that is becoming increasingly popular is Jeanne Gibbs' *Tribes* program. This program is an intensive inquiry into creating a classroom of mutual respect, where students feel safe sharing their thoughts and emotions.

David and Roger Johnson, through their efforts in Cooperative Learning, argue from a research and theoretical perspective the importance of actively teaching and reflecting on social, communication, and critical thinking skills (see their 1989 book *Theory and Research in Cooperative Learning* for the research and theoretical development in this area). They argue that these skills are not going to occur by default. A quick reflection on recent staff meetings and relationships with family and friends often confirms our folly in the area of interpersonal intelligence.

Yet, even finer levels of creating a safe learning environment exist. Pick one area ... say, questions. Think of how you frame questions. Think of the time you give students to think. Teachers are often unskilled in the framing of questions. Are teachers sensitive to issues such as moving from covert to overt (e.g., asking students to think to themselves while providing, say 7 seconds, to think before they share with a partner)? Moreover, we are not always consciously skilled at why a student gave us a silly response, a no response, a partially correct response, a guess, a correct response, or a convoluted response (and those are about the only possibilities). What do you look for in a student's face that tells you "save me ... allow me to save face"? What skills can you share related to how you think and act when students respond to your questions?

Obviously, the issue of emotional intelligence is important and teachers are in a position to nurture its development.

Think back to a teacher that you had as a student: one who was effective; one who was not. What criteria did you use? Were they emotionally intelligent?

Lens#3: Learning Styles

CHECKLIST:

When you learn, do you prefer:

noise	silence
music playing	no music playing
group work	a lecture
low light	bright light
to work in the morning	to work at night
to read information	to act on information
to listen	to talk

Before you read any further:

Consider what Michael Fullan and Elliot Eisner stated about Bernice McCarthy's new book on learning styles titled *About Learning*.

This is a book for lovers of learning. Marvellously creative in ideas and format. Exciting, comprehensive and brimming with ideas and insights.

Michael Fullan, Dean, Ontario Institute for Studies in Education, University of Toronto.

Rarely in publications do form and content reinforce each other so well. About Learning is an exploration of ideas that afford the reader many opportunities to fashion their own ideational castles. It is intimate, charming and generative; quite an array of achievements.

Elliot Eisner, Professor of Education and Art, Stanford University.

Learning Styles is about extending our understanding and appreciation of how the learner approaches learning. It is not about intelligence or capacity to solve problems (Multiple Intelligence connects to that purpose). Nor is Learning Styles a specific strategy for solving problems. Rather, it is a lens that informs the teacher and the student about the differences in how individuals go about learning or go about solving problems. Importantly, though, in terms of Learning Styles, within each intelligence we have a variety of learning styles—with interesting patterns for higher-achieving students and those who are lower-achieving.

The learning styles literature encourages us as teachers to have a more extensive understanding of how students learn and a corresponding repertoire of ways to involve students in learning. It guides our thinking in terms of what processes to integrate to create meaningful and powerful learning environments. Our argument is that it increases our conceptual flexibility, i.e., it asks us to continue to learn, reflect, and connect information. We believe it makes us stronger critical thinkers because we clearly see the existence of multiple perspectives. For the authors, the Learning Styles lens is one of many (some of which are highlighted in this chapter) that informs the public that we as teachers understand diversity and we have approaches to respond to that diversity.

What becomes essential, then, is that extending your knowledge about Learning Styles without making the connection to your instructional practices, or extending your instructional practices without that Learning Styles knowledge, does not make much sense.

The Learning Styles literature is clearly illustrated in the work of Bernice McCarthy and Rita Dunn, and their work intimately connects to the teaching and learning process. McCarthy has produced several texts related to developing Learning Styles focused on classroom plans. Rita Dunn has completed extensive research related to Learning Styles and classroom practice. Other Learning Styles programs are also available (see the work of Anthony Gregoric, Pat Guild, and Ned Hermann). *True Colours*, a more recent program that has emerged on the market, is another perspective on Learning Styles. Although other programs exist, any one of the above programs will get you started.

In this section, we will briefly illustrate the work of Bernice McCarthy and Rita Dunn. This is NOT intended to provide you with an in-depth understanding of their work on Learning Styles. Rather, it invites you to place a higher value and critical eye on this literature, to understand the role it plays in teacher thinking, and to encourage you to explore this literature in more depth.

Bernice McCarthy:

Her latest book, *About Learning*, provides an interesting foray into appreciating how different we are and the implications that has for learning. Her presentation of Learning Styles is titled 4-MAT. She argues that it is based on her observations of diverse learners as they struggled to make sense of learning, and on the work of Lewin, Vygotsky, Dewey, Piaget, Bruner, and Kolb (note: Kolb is a brain researcher—she builds the emerging wisdom re brain research into her program).

For McCarthy, Learning Styles is a focus on a natural learning cycle (think of a circle with four quadrants that move from personal meaning in quadrant one to integration in quadrant four):

1. feeling/perceiving to find meaning
2. reflecting/processing to find conceptualization
3. thinking/perceiving to solve the problem
4. doing/processing to transform (see the diagram following).

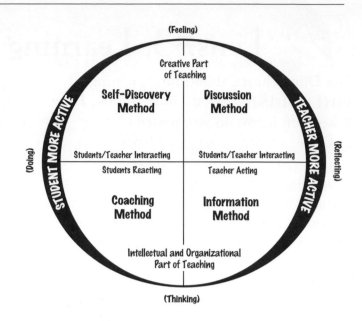

Based on: About Learning, (1996) p. 224

What jumps out at you when you read her book *About Learning*, is that 4 MAT has a logic. It asks us as educators to connect to the experience and feeling of the learner—to make what the students are learning of interest, authentic, and meaningful. Then the shift to problem solving is easy because the learner understands the concepts or ideas. Last, transforming or integrating ideas is the logical end point—the tapestry takes on a life of its own. Of course the flip side is that if we as teachers choose not to attend to those four areas, then we must ask why students would be interested in attending our classes. We know as professionals that when we attend a conference and the session we are in lacks meaning, interest, and engagement and does not connect to our efforts and goals, that we might leave. Of course our students do not have that luxury. That said, some students stick it out because they have to— someone is forcing them to go further. Or, they want to go to university and your class is a hoop. The result is that some make it, some choose to leave, some misbehave and some enact some combination of the three.

Rita Dunn

With this section, we will look at ideas that Rita Dunn shares about implementing a learning styles program. In her book, *How to Implement and Supervise a Learning Styles Program* (1996), she provides key information into a number of areas. Style implies things such as quiet or noisy backgrounds, low or bright lit surroundings, formal or casual seating, perceptual modes (visual, auditory, tactile, and kinesthetic) and so forth.

How Learning Styles Develop. Here Dunn discusses the connection between genetics and environment regarding the development of one's preferred Learning Style. She also mentions that Learning Style varies within a family.

One key piece of information from her research is that gifted students prefer kinesthetic (experiential and active) and tactile learning but can also learn auditorially and visually. Low-achieving students, however, who also prefer kinesthetic and tactile learning, can only master difficult information through those modalities.

She also found that few gifted students wanted to learn with their classmates—yet in Howard Gardner's work in the book, *Creating Minds*, he found that people like Picasso, Freud, and Graham did their best work while interacting with others. Of course, gifted in one area does not mean gifted in all. Just because an individual is strong in math does not mean she will be strong in music, or in getting along with others. The correlation between IQ and intelligent behaviour is around .07 percent.

IQ ≠ Intelligent Behaviour

Taking the First Steps. In this section Dunn discusses issues concerning "Finding Out Students' Learning Styles", and provides information on Learning Style Inventories and the research that supports them. In addition, she indicates key ideas related to how to "Introduce Learning Styles to Staff and Parents." The key idea here is being wise about when and how to go about initiating and implementing a Learning Styles program. The implication being that you had better understand the research on educational change if you are going to sustain and experience the benefits of Learning Styles.

Dunn's last two sections are **Stepping Into the Classroom** and **Personalizing Learning**. In these two sections she shares practical ideas and resources that relate to ways to attend to the different styles of learning. Although we agree that those approaches do relate to the different Learning Styles, there was little connection to the research on the more powerful instructional processes and the research that those processes had on student learning. The key message here is that we value the Learning Styles literature; however, it does not always provide a strong connection to instruction.

HERMAN®

"The capital of Holland is 'H'."

HERMAN© Jim Unger Reprinted with permission by Laughing Stock.

Educational Implications

Start with observing the students walking through your classroom door. Have a look at the "lesson" you have designed. Ask yourself: Is it meaningful? Are the students involved in processing and reflecting (metacognition)? Are they acting on what they know? Are they transferring this learning to the real world, and integrating it with what they know—creating a tapestry? If not, then McCarthy would most likely ask: What is the alternative: no meaning, no conceptual understanding, no reflecting, no connecting, no authenticity, and no transfer?

What instructional processes can we invoke to make those four areas of McCarthy's come alive? Where does Role Playing fit? Where does Mind Mapping fit? Where does Academic Controversy fit? Where does Cooperative Learning fit? Where does Inductive Thinking fit? Where does the lecture fit? Where does any of about 1000 plus instructional processes fit? Learning Styles provides a powerful lens to assist in explicating the messy world of motivation. It reminds us that not one of those 1000 plus instructional process is right or best for all kids.

If you understand and appreciate the Learning Styles literature, you immediately realize why teachers perpetually struggle to find ways to motivate the learner. What is interesting for one student is not interesting or meaningful for the other. One student wants to work cooperatively; the other does not. One wants quiet; another needs to talk. One wants hands-on—to learn experientially; another wants to read the directions first.

The gifted student who prefers to work on his or her own will say, "I don't want to work with anyone else!" In contrast, you know that the classified ads are asking for employees capable of working in teams, who can demonstrate strong interpersonal and communication skills. The day-in, day-out question that confronts teachers is: What do you do? Acting on this information is what describes and defines us as educators. Learning Styles literature is not a panacea—it is simply one additional lens to more deeply and precisely understand the learner.

When we take the time to discuss with students their Learning Styles and that of their classmates, we begin to develop empathy and respect for self and others. Students learn to stand up for their needs and recognize the importance of their needing to work outside their strengths— intelligent behaviour is the ability to integrate multiple domains of knowledge, identify patterns, and have a repertoire of responses to those patterns. If understanding Learning Styles is woven into the literature on Multiple Intelligences, Gender, Multi-Culturalism, etc., then students are more likely to become thoughtful citizens.

Once all is said and done, if you do not work at continually extending your instructional repertoire, do not select and integrate those processes that make a difference in student learning, then it is highly unlikely you will effectively attend to the demands of the Learning Styles literature.

Expecting Learning Styles literature to make a big difference in student learning without teachers employing powerful instructional processes is akin to expecting the blueprint to build your house. One's knowledge of the learner and instructional repertoire **interact**; they are **interdependent**.

The Implementation of Learning Styles

The Learning Styles literature was one of the first lines of inquiry that encouraged educators to see the differences between students concerning how they learned. Our concern is that it is not being implemented effectively. Our concern takes two forms: (1) how educators have failed to implement the knowledge base regarding Learning Styles; and (2), the failure of Learning Styles research to connect their discipline and their failure to connect to other related literatures. (We argue this concern is appropriate for the other topics in this chapter and especially appropriate for the literature on cooperative learning.)

1 The **first concern** relates to the idea that educators trivialize the implementation of this literature. This includes not understanding the role that Learning Styles play in the design of the teaching and learning process. Learning Styles (like Multiple Intelligences, Brain Research, Children at Risk Research, Gender and Multicultural Research) is not a tactic or skill or strategy—hence, it is not specifically designed to make a difference in student learning. The difference in student learning occurs when we do something about what we know. Learning Styles literature increases our conceptual flexibility about how to respond to the diverse ways students learn—how to structure the learning environment, how to present information, how to engage learners, etc. Conducting staff development on Learning Styles without making a corresponding link with how we teach and how we assess, is akin to building roads but never developing the vehicles to drive on the roads or the skills to actually drive the vehicles.

2 The **second area of concern** is the failure of many Learning Styles researchers to see a richer tapestry in this literature. This breaks into two areas: (1) a failure to assist educators implementing this literature to understand the different perspectives (e.g.,

you will not see McCarthy's ideas celebrated in Dunn's work; nor will you see Dunn's ideas celebrated in McCarthy's work); and (2) its failure to consistently and illustratively connect the reader to powerful instructional approaches that are crucial in wisely invoking Learning Styles.

Referring back to (1) above, this failure to connect other perspectives—to see the tapestry of the teaching and learning process—is common in many educational literatures. That failure is one reason for the lack of influence those literatures have on the design of powerful learning environments.

The failure to connect different voices is endemic in the educational literature. Teaching is too complex not to celebrate and act on the diverse efforts of many in the design of a learning environment. Yet in the throes of folly, we fail to connect.

Lens#4: Brain Research

This is becoming one of *the* hot areas for professional development. The literature is extensive and rich. It also cautions and guides us in our thinking and actions.

Below are key ideas from a number of researchers followed by a brief discussion of the implication this literature has for educators. The purpose is to illustrate how this literature can assist us in making wiser choices about how to create meaningful and powerful learning environments for students. Hopefully this will encourage you to extend your thinking in this area. The Web site lists some of the more current and thorough works related to the brain.

Brain Sensitive Teaching and Learning–What Does the Brain Research Tell Us?

1. The brain's goal is survival.

Implication: It does not like to be threatened; it functions more effectively in an environment where it is challenged, yet safe. This connects to interpersonal intelligence, to emotional intelligence, etc. Teachers need to focus on creating environments that provide students with opportunities to learn to disagree in an agreeable way, to take turns, to value equal voice, and not put each other down. If these are not part of the classroom and school norms, then the brain starts to shut down ... and when it is old enough, it escapes; it drops out of school.

> Remember, the emotional part of the brain can hijack the thinking part in a moment's notice.

2. Emotion is powerfully connected to thinking.

Implication: Emotions must be part of the teaching and learning process. When students are emotionally engaged they are more likely to retain the learning in long-term memory. Of course, we are more likely to be emotionally involved when we are successful and interested because the learning is meaningful, novel, and varied. Lecturing to students, having students sitting in desks and not interacting, and providing students with lacklustre topics is not a great way to engage their emotions or thinking.

3. The brain needs to make connections.

Implication: It needs to sense relationships and analyze. It is a pattern seeker. This is why Venn Diagrams, Mind Maps, Concept Maps, Word Webs, Time Lines, etc., are so valuable.

4. The brain is hard-wired for "Experience Expected" situations.

Implication: If those experiences do not occur during specific windows of opportunity, then those "wires" get pruned. Likewise, limiting one's instructional approaches is not going to provide a rich environment of experience.

5. The brain is also wired for "Experience Dependent" situations.

Implication: The brain is plastic, and the dendritic area increases throughout life (although more intensely when young). This means you can teach an old dog new tricks, but it is better to learn those tricks as early as you can. The well known saying, "use it or lose it" applies here.

6. **The brain is 'holistic'–although some areas have specific responsibilities, the areas are interdependent.**

   Implication: We do not teach to one side of the brain or one area of the brain—damage in one area that connects to another can affect functioning in that other area. Structuring activities to nurture the left or right side of the brain is not supported by neurologists.

7. **The brain remembers what is important.**

   Implication: If the learning is not meaningful, relevant, and authentic, the brain will get rid of it. How does this relate to Multiple Intelligences and Learning Styles?

8. **Intelligence is mediated/enhanced by social situations.**

   Implication: The brain needs to be in situations where it is allowed to experience talk. All aspects of Cooperative Learning would connect to this finding:

   - Think Pair Share
   - Inside/Outside Circles
   - Round Robin
   - Three-Step Interview
   - Team-Game-Tournament
   - Jigsaw
   - Academic Controversy
   - Team Analysis

9. **The human brain uses 25% of available metabolic energy at rest, It needs oxygen on demand—those who exercise increase the blood supply to the brain.**

   Implication: Don't be a couch potato. (Note: exercise does not increase brain cell connections, only the circulatory support systems for the brain.) Bodily-Kinesthetic Intelligence anyone?

10. **Brains that live in enriched environments have around 40% more neuron connections than brains that live in bland environments (research done with rats).**

    Implication: Put your rats in enriched environments if you want them to be better at destroying your property. That said, we can also assume that stimulating, challenging, and socially engaging environments for students would also affect the students' neuron connections.

11. **Dull, boring environments cause the loss of dendritic connection. These environments are more damaging than enriched environments are at enhancing brain development.**

    Implication: Students need to be actively and meaningfully engaged in relevant tasks.

Lens#5: Children at Risk

In this section we draw on the research literature from Canada related to students at risk and from the book *Reclaiming Youth At Risk* by Larry Brendtro, Martin Brokenleg, and Steve Van Bockern.

In Canada, approximately 1 in 5 students lives in an environment where they experience one or more of the following:

- physical abuse
- sexual abuse
- emotional abuse
- neglect
- drugs and alcohol
- witnessing violence
- living in poverty, single parent, on welfare, in subsidized housing
- divorce (and at times multiple divorce)

Add to that list the students who are at risk because we are not sensitive to their learning needs (for example the behaviourally challenged, the learning disabled, etc.).

The question that we ask as educators is what do we do when these students are in our classes? The literature explores "ideas"—not as panaceas—but as ways to increase the chances of creating a safe environment for these students. It also suggests how to respond to these students to restore social order so that learning can continue.

"Reclaiming Youth at Risk"...

is a gentle and thoughtful challenge to society and to the teachers who are part of that society.

Perhaps one of the most useful aspects of Brendtro etal's book is the attention the authors pay to connecting knowledge from a variety of areas such as:

- Emotions
- Gender
- Culture
- Brain Research
- Cooperative Learning.

Their book represents a rare effort at creating a tapestry of possibilities that make a difference for students. The ideas they share are just as salient for all students. They clearly state that the ideas are designed to prevent having to reclaim youth at risk. These youth are the ones who live in environments that foster discouragement— destructive relationships, climates of futility, loss of purpose and learned irresponsibility. Given those students walk through our doors and we are expected to demonstrate expert behaviour, then what should we do to extend the learning and life chances of these students?

KEY IDEAS FOR SCHOOLS

- The content must be integrated, meaningful and interesting, rather than fragmented and unauthentic.
- School staffs must be sensitive to students' natural desire to learn rather than for the sake of covering content or assessing in ways that are not in the best interests of kids.
- School staffs must act on the knowledge of cultural and individual differences.

KEY IDEAS FOR TEACHERS

- Work at creating successes and a respect for failure—both are useful.
- Design meaningful, realistic challenges.
- Structure opportunities for experiential and social learning.

KEY NEEDS OF STUDENTS

- to engage their brains with useful and meaningful experiences
- to master their social, physical, and emotional worlds
- to develop a "competence motivation" based on their natural inclination to learn

Interpretation and Implication of Their Work

The major medium in Brendtro et al's work on at-risk youth is the intersection of **Instructional Concepts (see Chapter 2)**. The book provides a delightfully thoughtful framework for thinking and guiding actions. That said, it does not provide the integration of powerful **Instructional Processes**. The actions are missing.

For example, as you read through the text, you will notice the use of words and phrases such as **"meaningful, competence motivation, courage, belonging, mastery," and "help them master their social, physical and emotional worlds."** The text identifies key concepts that we all must attend to, and from our perspectives as authors and teachers of at risk kids, the authors are right. For example, on page 72 they identify concepts and provide an explanation:

- **Affection:** Adult expressions of genuine interest, pleasure, and affection can increase measured achievement.
- **Expectations:** Low expectations and over-indulgence both lower achievement while realistic challenges with a high ratio of success to failure raises motivation.

These ideas are important—but what instructional actions does one take?

The one instructional area they touch on is the importance of Cooperative Learning. They connect this to the importance of brain friendly learning. They are very up front in challenging teachers to employ Cooperative Learning in the classroom. That comment aside, they did not convince us that they had a deep understanding of Brain Research or of Cooperative Learning in that they provide no insights into what it might look like or sound like if it was addressed. The dilemma for many educators reading this text, and other literatures that provide insights into students (such as the literature on Multiple Intelligences, Learning Styles and Emotional Intelligence) is that they rarely share HOW this plays out powerfully in the classroom. The key word here is POWERFULLY. Yes we see numerous books on activities and low-power processes, but few act in an intentionally integrative manner by weaving together multiple processes and, more importantly, providing illustrations of how this might play out in the classroom.

The issue for the teacher is, *Okay, so how am I going to act on what these at-risk students need?*

Please appreciate that the above comments are not meant to take away from the value of this literature; in fact, we have used their text in our university programs. Rather, our comments are a reminder that as teachers we must find the instructional skills, tactics, and strategies that will powerfully make those instructional concepts come to life. And speaking of coming to life, that is more likely to happen when, as teachers, we are kind, thoughtful, caring, and enthusiastic. Without those personal characteristics we can all pretty much kiss the instructional stuff goodbye.

Lens#6: Gender

The addition of Gender as a lens brings the moral issue of oppression (whether it be intentional or unintentional) to a central place in the design of learning environments. Some may think that oppression is too strong a word and may prefer "a lack of sensitivity." Whatever your preference, understanding this insensitivity through the lens of Gender brings specificity in analyzing the gap between the oppressed and those that oppress; between humanizing and dehumanizing. By selecting one view (Gender), we can focus on understanding those existing structures that encourage oppression and create new forms of relationships between people. Other lenses to understand oppression in education would be understanding those who live in poverty, who experience violence, and who live with mental illness.

Gender, then, is but one lens of understanding oppression. It refers to any situation where a person is dehumanized, marginalized, not encouraged to think, to dialogue, or to feel safe. This line of thinking related to the pedagogy of those oppressed was developed largely by the work of Paulo Freire. His work is translated in the book, *Pedagogy of the Oppressed* (1971) and relates to his work with the peasants in Brazil. Why the addition of the Gender lens is so important is that this literature (see Woyshner and Gelfond, 1998; and Weiler, 1991) extends Freire's ideas to a more focused understanding of humanization.

The Gender literature talks about the levels of dehumanization and asks us personally to understand that we may be simultaneously oppressed and the oppressor. As an example, this literature refers us to the feminist movement; a movement that positioned itself to counter patriarchy—historically, a movement about middle class white women—a movement that ironically marginalized black women (Maher, 1997).

In education, oppression may take the form of a female educator being oppressed by the existing promotion practices that favour males. Interestingly though, as a female teacher, you may marginalize at-risk students in the classroom by not acting on the literature and the parallel pedagogy to make the classroom more inclusive. For example, read about the struggle with boys and literacy (Alloway & Gilbert, 1997).

That said, and to keep this practical and focused on the classroom and how we make instructional decisions, we are going to explore two books, *Women's Ways of Knowing* and *Boys and Literacy*, to understand the messages and implications emerging from those literatures regarding the teaching and learning process.

Attending to Gender invites us to consider the idea of "methodology of positionality" employed by Francis Maher in her paper titled "*Learning in the Dark: How Assumptions of Whiteness Shape Classroom Knowledge.*" You might ask, how does your instructional repertoire relate to your position? Think of how we teach in kindergarten and in high schools and universities. Do we position our instruction to cover the curriculum or to assist the learner to meaningfully inquire? To what extent does your repertoire, or lack thereof, oppress learning?

This section introduces Gender as a lens through which we can understand how to more effectively respond to the needs of the learner. The information in this section applies to both men and women.

Women's Ways of Knowing

In this section, we present information from the book: *Women's Ways of Knowing: The Development of Self, Voice, and Mind* (Belenky, Clinchy, Goldberger, & Tarule, 1986). This is a report on how women view reality and draw conclusions about truth, knowledge, and authority. We picked this book because it has been around for awhile and provides an interesting path to begin exploring this literature.

Men designed most of the institutions of higher education in this country. Although changing, most continue to be run by men. In recent years feminist teachers and scholars have begun to question the structure, the curriculum, and the pedagogical practices of these institutions, and subsequently they have made proposals for change.

During the study of these 135 women, about 5000 pages of data were synthesized. Women's perspectives on their ways of knowing were grouped into five categories. As you read, think of how you teach, how your students see you, and where you (as male or female) might position yourself.

1. **Silence:** a position in which the learner finds herself as mindless and voiceless and subject to the whims of external authority

   Implication: What can we do to increase the chances students do not feel mindless and voiceless (powerless)? Certainly, attending to voice is critical; the brain research states that talk and socialization are critical to intellectual development. To operate a learning environment that does not nurture the invitation to learn is unethical. What does this say about Cooperative Learning, creating a safe classroom, or providing time to think and to share with a partner or in a group before sharing publicly? What does this say regarding how we as teachers respond to the efforts of the learner? If we cannot provide an escape route, to allow the student to save face, then are we guilty of silencing the learner? Does this connect to the research on emotion and the brain?

2. **Received Knowledge:** a perspective from which women conceive of themselves as capable of receiving, even reproducing knowledge from the all-knowing external authority, but not capable of creating knowledge on their own. Connect this to the idea of one's "methodology of position."

   Implication: This ties into Dale and Rath's work in 1945 and Goodlad's work in 1986. Dale and Raths found that the primary mode of instruction was stand-up recitation and little else. Goodlad's work in 1986 found that not much had changed since 1945. How do we move beyond the bland, the recall, or the meaningless? Of what value is learning if it is not transferable? If the learner does not understand the design of a concept or principle or idea, then they do not own it? Without owning an idea we reproduce and forget—we do not transfer and build. For example, how many of us "own" the concept of negative integers? Can we provide a real life example of solving a problem that involves the multiplication of two negative numbers? Well, it exists, and it is quite interesting, and many of us do not have a clue—including many math teachers.

Almost 80% of classroom questions are at the recall level of Bloom's Taxonomy. Interestingly, most students dislike recall questions. Their preference is Synthesis and Evaluation, followed by Analysis and Application. The implication of this is that our teaching needs to help learners create knowledge.

3. **Subjective Knowledge:** a perspective from which truth and knowledge are conceived of as personal, private, and subjectively known or intuited.

Implication: That learners will value learning that relates to personal experiences, but will not value the learning of others. We agree that the learning environment must encourage reflection and metacognition. Without interaction with others, however, we work against the development of intelligent or expert-like behaviour. This is argued in the work of David Perkins in the book, *Outsmarting IQ* and Carl Bereiter and Marlene Scardamalia's book, *Surpassing Ourselves*. Those authors argue the importance of personal knowing and reflection, but also argue the importance of integrating ideas from multiple domains, and of listening critically to the learning of others.

4. **Procedural Knowledge:** a position in which women are invested in learning and applying objective procedures for obtaining and communicating knowledge.

Implication: That learners are more focused on both acquiring and communicating knowledge, especially objective knowledge. They lack an appreciation of how the context or time or place, for example, can mitigate against the objective. They are not as flexible to explore both sides of an argument based on conflicting values (such as cutting down forests or the use of pesticides). The use of processes such as Academic Controversy, Team Analysis, Group Investigation, or Three-Step Interviews, or weaving in critical thinking tactics from de Bono's CoRT program (such as Examine Both Sides of an Issue, Consider all Factors, Examining the Aims, Goals, and Objectives of Others) would encourage students to move to the last category.

5. **Constructed Knowledge:** a position in which women are invested in learning and applying objective procedures for obtaining and communicating knowledge as contextual; they experience themselves as creators of knowledge. The women interviewed talked about constructed knowledge. They reclaimed personally important knowledge and integrated it with what they had learned from others; they talked of weaving the strands of rational and emotive thought. They rose to a new way of thinking. They let the inside out and the outside in.

Implication: Does this notion of constructed knowledge support students sitting and listening to someone lecture? Does this idea support sitting in rows and seldom discussing ideas with others? Or, does it imply the integrated use of a variety of instructional processes such as Group Investigation, or Role Playing, or Academic Controversy, or Team Analysis, or Mind Mapping, or Concept Mapping, or Inductive Thinking, or Concept Attainment? Does it also mean creating the inclusive classroom and school? Perhaps it also means field trips, guest speakers, videos, films, and puppet plays. If we as teachers do not extend our instructional repertoire to create learning environments that encourage and challenge students to construct knowledge, then how do we shift our focus to get to this level? These questions are targeted to all who teach, including university instructors who prepare teachers.

Boys and Literacy

This section introduces four findings and their implications from the research work by teachers in Australia who were part of the *Boys and Literacy Project*. As you read the findings, examine how these findings might affect your decisions and actions in the design of learning environments.

FINDINGS AND IMPLICATIONS 1:
Masculinity and literacy

Part A: We can't understand boys' literacy problems unless we understand boys' developing sense of masculinity and how literacy fits within this.
Special focus literacy programs for boys must provide more than functional literacy skills: they must also provide an examination of how constructions of gender affect literacy participation and performance.

Part B: The argument made here is that remediation programs that do not look at how issues of masculinity affect literacy

learning may often be inadequate. Boys' acceptance of various elements of socially constructed masculinity, and their desire to "do" masculinity effectively and successfully, may not be compatible with how literacy is taught and learned at school.

FINDINGS AND IMPLICATIONS 2:
Avoiding the "competing victim" syndrome

Part A: We can't solve boys' literacy problems just by "masculinizing" literacy— that will disadvantage girls.
Literacy programs tailored to boys' interests and focusing on boys' participation could easily silence and marginalize girls' interests and participation. Teaching strategies will need to focus on constructions of both masculinity and femininity, and on how these gender constructions affect literacy learning.

Part B: Boys are not having difficulties with literacy because teaching strategies and resources favour girls. Boys are having difficulties with literacy because of a complex interaction between masculinity and literacy—particularly the way literacy has been constructed at school.

FINDINGS AND IMPLICATIONS 3:
Foregrounding ideology at work in teaching and learning

Part A: We need to be more observant of the implicit and "commonsense" literacy teaching and assessment practices adopted in classrooms, in terms of how they advantage some groups rather than others, and how they obscure the textual construction of gender and gender relations.
Classroom work and assessment practices that emphasize and value personal and emotional disclosure may well disadvantage boys because such disclosure, potential vulnerability and surveillance is at odds with dominant ways of being male. In addition, classroom work and

assessment practices that do not foreground the textual, social construction of gender and relationships of power, disadvantage both boys and girls, by making such constructions and relationships appear natural and unproblematic.

Part B: Although we need to know more about how this relates specifically across groups of boys, it is possible to see how literacy strategies that expect boys to write personally in response to texts, to disclose their inner emotional worlds and fears, to empathize with female (as well as male) characters in fiction, and to participate in classroom oral work in sensitive and emotionally responsive ways, may be at odds with powerful and lived experiences of masculinity.

FINDINGS AND IMPLICATIONS 4:
The need for more research

We need more information and research on gender and literacy, particularly in terms of the connections between masculinity and literacy, and the impact of critical literacy approaches on improving the participation and performance of both boys and girls in language classrooms.

We need to know more about:

1. *cultural texts that preoccupy boys at home and at play, especially the electronic and visual texts that are targeted at boys and young men*

2. *boys' textual competence in literacy sites outside the school, especially in terms of how boys use language to construct themselves and their relationships with others*

3. *differences among boys, especially how constructs of ethnicity, sexuality or class affect the way boys take themselves up as masculine subjects in school institutions*

4. *boys' and girls' perceptions of critical literacy practices; are these practices more attractive to both groups because they work with real texts, in real ways, and position students as active and purposeful learners?*

GENERAL CONCLUSIONS

1. Boys are more likely to participate and achieve in school literacy work if they don't see participation and achievement in such work as being in conflict with desirable constructions of masculinity; if they can see, instead, how such work is relevant and useful

   • in understanding their lives
   • in making their lives richer and fuller
   • and in offering them new and different ways of remaking their lives.

2. Successful literacy classrooms provide such understandings and opportunities for all students by making critical readings of constructions of gender, ethnicity and socioeconomic class focal points for classroom literacy work. Successful literacy classrooms are also those in which teacher and student power is distributed more evenly, allowing students to be recognized and valued, and their knowledge and skills enfranchised and respected. This is important for all students but, given the connection between power and dominant forms of masculinity, it may be critical for boys.

Instructional Implications

One of the most obvious implications is that we all need to read and talk about Gender literature to more deeply understand the issues of masculinity and femininity.

Remember that the purpose of this chapter is to encourage a more focused inquiry in each of the areas presented. The bibliography of *Boys and Literacy: Professional Development Units* provides one of the most extensive reference lists we have seen related to gender. This text provides specific lessons that illustrate how to act on the current research to engage students in being more critically literate about how Gender plays out in the classroom and in classroom learning.

Whatever programs or texts you explore, it will still come back to the power of your instructional repertoire to make this information come alive. For example, in terms of Instructional Strategies like those found in the Cooperative Learning literature (Jigsaw, Academic Controversy, Group Investigation, etc.) we must be sensitive to the issue of boys and girls working with one another when we construct groups. How else will females and males come to appreciate and understand one another if they never interact? This implies taking time to talk about Gender and how it plays out in a variety of areas such as in children's literature (e.g., books like *The Paper Bag Princess, Dancing Bears, The Giving Tree, Crow Boy, and Beware of Boys*).

Using specific Instructional Tactics such as Three-Step Interview, Inside Outside Circles, Round Robin, Think-Pair-Share and so forth, provides structures to facilitate discussion around a question or issue or problem. Of course, this also implies that we have taken the time as teachers to put into place the students' use of social skills (such as taking turns and no put downs); communication skills (such as disagreeing in an agreeable way and accepting and extending the ideas of others); and critical thinking skills (such as examining both sides of an argument and suspending judgement).

When employing Instructional Skills such as framing questions, employing wait time, distributing responses, being able to respond to a variety of ways in which students respond, etc., we also communicate to our students our sensitivity to making sure they feel safe, challenged, and involved in their interactions with one another.

The message here is that it is one thing to understand the literature on Gender, while it is another thing to have an instructional repertoire that allows students to engage in thinking that is sensitive to Gender. Of course, that message applies equally to the literatures on Children at Risk, Multiple Intelligences, Learning Disabilities, Learning Disabilities, and Brain Research, etc.

Something to Consider:

One of the authors asked his niece (who is in grade 9) what she thought about attending an all girls public school. She stated she liked it. When asked why, she stated that she felt safe to talk.

What you should know is that she is a capable person, skilled athlete, captain of her ringette team, and an honour student. She has supportive, thoughtful parents. Makes you wonder how other girls feel?

More importantly though, if girls and boys learn in gender homogenous schools, then how do they come to understand each other; to value each other?

This is obviously a complex issue.

Final Thoughts

Again, we honor and appreciate the complexity of the teaching and learning process. When we return to the idea of demonstrating intelligent behaviour, and we connect that idea with the work of David Perkins (*Outsmarting IQ: The Art of Learnable Intelligence*) and the work of Bereiter and Scardamalia (*Surpassing Ourselves*) we understand the importance of Instructional Organizers.

For Perkins, the key factors of expertise are:
- intelligent behaviour depends more on knowledge than IQ
- expert behaviour is predominantly mediated by acquired complex skills
- the effects of extended deliberate practice with intentional reflection is critical
- through experience our brains become attuned to useful patterns that can be used efficiently and reflexively

He goes on to say that as you increase your repertoire of patterns through experience, you increase your intuitive abilities to select the strategies to demonstrate intelligent behaviour. However, for that to happen, one needs to self monitor (reflect). He states: "We do not always and automatically learn from experience, even extended experience. For instance, people play chess or bridge for years without getting much better at it" (p.109). Reflective intelligence functions as the leading edge of experiential intelligence; and importantly, neural intelligence is the hardware that supports these processes.

For Bereiter and Scardamalia, the key factors of expertise are:
- knowledge that can be adapted to task requirements
- thinking more about one's actions
- efficiency in recognizing configurations, patterns
- addressing and readdressing—development of cumulative wisdom
- progressively advancing on the problems constituting a field of work

They go on to state that this allows us to reduce the complexity through patterning and automaticity. Those automated skills becoming the building blocks of new skills not yet automated. As we learn more we can take on new challenges.

continued...

continued...

Take the preceding information in this chapter and connect it to the findings in Rosenholtz's study on teachers leaving the profession of teaching (20 to 30% after one year, another 20 to 30% at the end of 5 years). When asked why they left, the number one reason was no sense of efficacy around how to teach (not what to teach); having classroom management problems they could not resolve; and, being alone in the school culture.

The knowledge or wisdom gleaned from the integrating of multiple lenses or Instructional Organizers, while concomitantly being able to integrate an ever-increasing repertoire in response to that wisdom, is one component of expert behaviour.

Our Perspective on Instructional Organizers

In thinking back on what has been stated in this chapter, the key idea for all of us who are teachers is the idea of power or impact on student learning. Just because we address the needs of students in terms of their learning style or intelligences or gender or their being at risk etc., is not the key issue. The issue is whether or not we are impacting student learning in the most effective way possible. Remember that parents and students expect us to demonstrate expert thinking and behaviour – and to do that collectively within the school and district. Common sense tells us that we must consider the extent to which we are integrating our experience and the experience of others, with what the research is saying makes a difference in the life and learning chances of students. Ignoring any one of those three is unwise.

Too often we see activities done in the name of Learning Styles, Brain Research and Multiple Intelligences, but those activities, at best, are fun and, at worst, trivialize the value of these organizers in assisting educators to design powerful learning environments.

Consultants and teachers who run workshops on Brain-Friendly Learning or on Multiple Intelligences, etc., must be careful in how they are interpreting and connecting those literatures. The same holds true for those who run workshops on different instructional processes such as Graphic Organizers or specific approaches to Cooperative Learning. When we do the "once over easy" and fail to make those connections, then we are simply marketing ideas at the expense of what really makes a difference for students, it is both students and teachers who lose in the end.

Bibliography

Refer to the web site in Chapter Three for an update on the latest books and research related to instructional intelligence.

Adams, G., & Engelmann, S. (1996). *Research on direct instruction: 20 years beyond DISTAR.* Seattle, WA: Educational Achievement Systems.

Alloway, N., & Gibert, P. (1997). *Boys and literacy: Professional development units.* Carlton, Victoria, Australia: Curriculum Corporation.

Alloway, N., & Gilbert, P. (1997). Boys and literacy: Lessons from Australia. *Gender and Education*, 9(1), 49-59.

Alloway, N., & Gibert, P. (1997). Video game culture: Playing with masculinity, violence and pleasure. In S. Howard (ed.) *Wired-Up: Young people and the electronic media.* London: Taylor and Francis.

Arends, R. I. (1998). *Learning to teach.* New York: McGraw Hill.

Armstrong, T. (2000). *Multiple intelligences in the classroom.* Alexandria, VA: ASCD.

Aronson, E., & Patnoe, S. (1997). *The jigsaw classroom.* New York: Addison-Wesley Longman.

Ausabel, D. P. (1960). The use of advance organizers in the learning and retention of meaningful verbal material. *Journal of Educational Psychology*, 51, 267-272.

Barron-Cohen, S., & Bolton, P. (1993). *Autism: The facts.* New York: Oxford University Press.

Belenky, M. F., Clinchy, B. M., Goldberger, N. R. & Tarule, J. M. (1986). *Women's ways of knowing: The development of self, voice, and mind.* NY: Basic Books.

Bellanca, J. (1990). *The cooperative think tank: Graphic organizers to teach thinking in the cooperative classroom.* Palatine, IL: Skylight Publishing.

Bellanca, J. (1992). *The cooperative think tank II: Graphic organizers to teach thinking in the cooperative classroom.* Palatine, IL: Skylight Publishing.

Bennett, B. (1995). Th*e effects of integrating pedagogy on student learning: An experimental study.* Paper presented at the American Educational Research Association's annual conference.

Bennett, B., Anderson, S., & Evans, M. (1996). *Towards a theory of instructional acquisition.* Paper presented at the annual meeting of the American Educational Research Association, Chicago, 1997.

Bennett, B., Rolheiser, C., & Stevahn, L. (1991). *Cooperative learning: Where heart meets mind.* Toronto, ON: Educational Connections.

Bereiter, C., & Scardamalia, M. (1993). *Surpassing ourselves: An inquiry into the nature and implications of expertise.* Chicago: Open Court.

Blasé, (1985). The socialization of teachers: An ethnographic study of factors contributing to the rationalization of the teacher's instructional perspective. *Urban Education*, 20(3), 235-256.

Bloom, B. (1956). *Taxonomy of objectives: Cognitive domain.* New York: McKay.

Blumer, H. (1954). What is wrong with social theory? *American Sociological Review*, 19.

Brendtro, L. K., Brokenleg, M., & Van Bockern, S. (1990). *Reclaiming youth at risk: Our hope, our future.* Bloomington, IN: National Educational Service.

Britton, James. *Vygotsky's contribution to pedagogical theory.* English in Education.

Brophy, J. (1988). Research linking teacher behavior to student achievement: Potential implications for instruction of chapter 1 students. *Educational Psychology*, 23(3), 235-286.

Brown, A.L., & Palinscar, A.S. (1982). Inducing strategic learning from texts by means of informed, self controlled training. *Topics in Learning and Learning Disabilities*, 2(1), 1-18.

Brown, N, & Ross, R. (1995). Girl's stuff, boy's stuff: Young children talking and playing. In Holland & M. Blair with S. Sheldon (eds.) *Debates and issues in feminist research and pedagogy*. Clevedon: Open University Press.

Bruner, J. (1966). *Toward a theory of instruction*. Cambridge MA: Harvard University Press.

Bruner, J. S., Goodnow, J. J., & Austin, G. A. (1986). *A study of thinking*. New Brunswick, NJ: Transaction.

Buzan, T. (1993). *The mind map book*. Woodlands, London: BBC Books.

Buzan T. (1983). *Use both sides of your brain*. New York: E.P. Dutton.

Calvin, W. H. (1996). *How brains think: Evolving intelligence, then and now*. New York: Basic Books.

Campbell, D. (1997). *The mozart effect*. New York: Avon Books.

Clark, C. (1988). The necessity for curriculum objectives. *Journal of Curriculum Studies*, 20, 339-349.

Cohen, E. (1994). *Designing group work: Strategies for the heterogeneous classroom*. New York: Teachers College Press.

Collins, M. L. (1978). The effects of training for enthusiasm on the enthusiasm displayed by preservice elementary teachers. *Unpublished Doctoral Dissertation*, Syracuse University.

Cooper, J. M. (1986). *Classroom teaching skills*. Lexington MA: D. C. Heath.

Corno, L. (1996). Homework is a complicated thing. *Educational Researcher*, 25(8), 27-30.

Csikszentmihalyi, M. (1997). *Creativity*. New York: Harper Perennial.

Dale, E., & Raths, L. E. (1945). Discussion in the secondary school. *Education Research Bulletin*, 24, 1-6.

Darling Hammond (1998). Teachers and teaching: Testing policy hypotheses from a national commission report. *Educational Researcher*, 27(1), 5-15.

Darling-Hammond, L. & Sykes, G. (eds.). (1990). *Teaching as the learning profession: Handbook of policy and practice*. San Francisco, CA: Jossey-Bass.

De Bono, E. (1986). *CoRT thinking*. Advanced Practical Thinking and Training Inc.

De Bono, E. (1985). *Six thinking hats*. Toronto, ON: Little Brown and Company.

DeVries, D. L., Mescon, I. T., & Shackman, S. L. (1975). *Teams Games Tournament in the elementary classroom: A replication*. (Tech. Rep. No. 190). Baltimore: John Hopkins University.

DeVries, D. L., Edwards, K. J., & Wells, E. (1979). Biracial learning teams and race relations in the classroom: Four field experiments using teams games tournament. *Journal of Educational Psychology*, 70(3), 356-362.

Diamond, M., & Hopson, J. (1999). *Magic trees of the mind: How to nurture your child's creativity, and healthy emotions from birth through adolescence*. New York: Plume.

Dunn, R. (1996). *How to implement and supervise a learning styles program*. Alexandria, VA: ASCD.

Dunn, R., Griggs, S. A., Olson, J., Gorman, B., & Beasley, M. (1995). Meta analytic validation of the Dunn and Dunn learning styles model. *Journal of Educational Research*, 88(6), 353-361.

Dunn, R., & Dunn, K. (1993). *Teaching secondary students through their individual learning styles*. Boston: Allyn & Bacon.

Dunn, R., & Dunn, K. (1993). *Teaching elementary students through their individual learning styles.* Boston: Allyn & Bacon.

Dunn, R. (1990). Rita Dunn answers questions on learning styles. *Educational Leadership*, 48(2), 15-21.

Dunn, R., Beaudry, J., & Klavas, A. (1989). Survey of research on learning styles. *Educational Leadership*, 47(6), 50-58.

Egan, K. (1994). *Tools for enhancing imagination in teaching.* In Grimmet, P. P. & Neufeld, J. (1994). Teacher Development and the Struggle for Authenticity. New York: Teachers College Press.

Eggen, P. D., Kauchak, D. P. & Harder, R.J. (1979). *Strategies for teachers: Information processing models in the classroom.* Englewood Cliffs, NJ: Prentice-Hall.

Engelmann, S., Becker, W.C., Carnine, D., & Gersten, R. (1988). The direct instruction follow through model: Design and outcomes. *Education and Treatment of Children*, 11(4), 303-317.

Epstine, D. (1997). Boyz own stories: Masculinities and sexualities in school. *Gender and Education*, 9(1), 105-115.

Fogarty, R. (1991). *The mindful school: How to integrate the curricula.* Palatine, IL: Skylight Publishing.

Foster, J. R. (1995). Advocating a gender inclusive curriculum in the visual arts: Politics, pedagogy, and postmodernism. *Australian Art Education*, 18(2), Autumn, 17-27.

Fullan, M. (2001) The new meaning of educational change. New York: Teachers College Press.

Freire, P. (1971). *Pedagogy of the oppressed.* New York: Herder & Herder.

Frye, N. (1963). *The educated imagination.* Toronto, ON: CBC

Gage, N. (1963). *Handbook of research on teaching.* Chicago: Rand McNally

Garber, S. W., Garber, M. D., & Spizman, R. F., Spizman. (1997). *Beyond ritalin.* New York: Harper Perennial.

Gardner, H. (1999). *Intelligence reframed: Multiple intelligences for the 21st century.* New York: Basic Books.

Gardner, H. (1997). *Extraordinary minds.* (The CBC Massey Lecture Series). Toronto, ON: Canadian Broadcasting Corporation.

Gardner, H. (1993). *Creating minds: An anatomy of creativity seen through the lives of Freud, Einstein, Picasso, Stravinski, Eliot, Graham, and Gandhi.* New York: Basic Books.

Gardner, H. (1985). *Frames of mind.* New York: Basic Books.

Gardner, H. (1993). *Multiple intelligences: The theory in practice.* New York: Basic Books.

Gardner, H., & Hatch, T. (1989). Multiple intelligences go to school: Educational implications of the theory of multiple intelligences. *Educational Researcher*, 18 (8), pp., 4-10.

Gentile, R.J. (1993). *Instructional improvement: A summary and analysis of Madeline Hunter's essential elements of instruction and supervision.* Oxford, OH: National Staff Development Council.

Gibbs, J. (1995). *Tribes: A new way of learning together.* Sausalito, CA: Center Source Systems.

Gibboney, R. A. (1987). A critique of Madeline Hunter's teaching model from Dewey's perspective. *Educational Leadership*, 44(5), 46-50.

Goleman, D. (1998). *Working with emotional intelligence.* New York: Bantam Books.

Goleman, D. (1995). *Emotional intelligence.* New York: Bantam Books.

Guild, P. B., & Garger, S. (1985). *Marching to different drummers.* Alexandria, VA: Association for Supervision and Curriculum Development.

Good, T. L. & Brophy, J. E. (1994). *Looking in classrooms*. New York: Harper Collins.

Goodlad, J. (1992). *A place called school*. New York: McGraw-Hill.

Grandin, T. (1995). *Thinking in pictures and other reports from my life with autism*. New York: Doubleday.

Greenwald, R., Hedges, L. V. & Laine, R. D. (1996). The effect of school resources on student achievement. *Review of Educational Research*, 66, 361-396.

Hare, W. (1995). *What makes a good teacher: Reflections on some characteristics central to the educational enterprise*. London, ON: Althouse Press.

Haug, G., Bennett, B., Jamieson, A., Krause, G. (1977). *Vanves revisited*. Action research study completed with support from Edmonton Public Schools, Edmonton, Alberta, Canada.

Hunter, M. (1994). *Enhancing teaching*. New York: Macmillan College.

Hunter, M. (1991). Generic lesson design: The case for. *The Science Teacher*, 58(7), 26-32.

Hunter, M. (1987). Beyond rereading Dewey ... what's next? A response to Gibboney, *Educational Leadership*, 44(5), 51-53.

Hunter, M. (1990). Hunter lesson design helps achieve the goals of science instruction. *Educational Leadership*, 48(4), 79-84.

Johnson, D. W., & Johnson, R. T. (1994). *Learning together and alone: Cooperative, competitive, individualistic learning*. Boston MA: Allyn & Bacon.

Johnson, D., & Johnson, R. (1992). *Creative controversy: Intellectual challenge in the classroom*. Edina, MI: Interaction Book Company.

Johnson, D., & Johnson, R. (1989). *Cooperation and competition: Theory and research*. Edina, MI: Interaction Book Company.

Joyce, B., & Calhoun, E. (1996). *Creating learning experiences*. Alexandria, VA: Association for Supervision and Curriculum Development.

Joyce, B., & Weil, M. (2000). *Models of teaching*. New York: Allyn and Bacon.

Kagan, (1994). *Cooperative learning*. San Juan Capistrano: Kagan Cooperative Learning.

Kallison, J. M. (1986). Effects of lesson organization on achievement. *American Educational Research Journal*, 23(2), 337-347.

Kavale, K.A. and Forness, S.R. (1990). Substance over style: Assessing the efficacy of modality testing and teaching. *Exceptional Children*. 54(4), 228-239.

Klein, P. D. (1997). Multiplying the problems of intelligence by eight: A critique of Gardner's theory. *Canadian Journal of Education*, 22(4), 377-394.

Kounin, J. S. (1970). *Discipline and group management in classrooms*. New York: Holt, Rinehart & Winston.

Lang, H. R., McBeath, A., & Hebert, J. (1995). *Teaching: Strategies and methods for student-centered instruction*. New York: Harcourt Brace.

Lazear, D. (1991). *Seven ways of knowing*. Palatine, IL: Skylight Publishing.

LeDoux, J. (1996). *The emotional brain*. New York: Simon & Schuster.

Louis, K. S., & Miles, M. B. (1990). *Improving the urban high school: What works and why*. New York: Teachers College Press.

Macrorie, K. (1984). *20 teachers*. New York: Oxford University Press.

Madden, N. A., Slavin, R. E., & Stevens, R. J. (1986). *Cooperative integrated reading and comparison: Teachers's manual*. Baltimore: Johns Hopkins University, Center for Research on Elementary and Middle Schools.

Mager, R. F. (1962). *Planning objectives for programmed instruction*. Belmont, CA: Fearon Publishers.

Maher, F. A. (1997). Learning in the dark: How assumptions of whiteness shape classroom knowledge. *Harvard Educational Review*, 67(2), 321-349.

Marazano, R. (2001). *Classroom instruction that works*. Alexandria, VA: ASCD.

Marazano, R. (1998). *A theory-based meta-analysis of research on instruction*. Aurora, CO: Mid-continent Regional Educational Laboratory.

Marazano, R. J. (1992). *A different kind of classroom: Teaching with dimensions of learning*. Alexandria VA: ASCD.

Margulies, M. A. (1991). *Mapping inner space*. Tucson. AZ: Zephyr Press.

McCarthy, B. (1996). *About learning*. Barrington, IL: Excel.

McCarthy, B., & Morris, S. (1995). *4Mat in action, sample units for grades K-6*. Barrington, IL: Excel.

McCarthy, B., & Morris, S. (1995). *4Mat in action, sample units for grades 7-12*. Barrington, IL: Excel.

McCarthy, B. (1980). *The 4MAT system: Teaching to learning styles with right/left mode techniques*. Barrington, Illinois: EXCEL, Inc.

Millar, J. (1897). *School management*. Toronto, ON: William Briggs.

Millard, E. (1997). Differently literate: Gender identity and the construction of the developing reader. *Gender and Education*, 9(1), 31-38.

Mish, F. (Ed.). (1991). *Websters ninth new collegiate dictionary*. Markham, ON: Thomas Allen & Son.

Engel, S. M. (1990). *With good reason. An introduction to informal fallacies*. New York: St. Martin's Press.

Morgan, N., & Saxton, J. (1994). *Asking better questions*. Markham, ON: Pembroke Publishers.

Niehoff, D. (1999). *The biology of violence. How understanding the brain, behavior, and environment can break the vicious circle of aggressions*. New York: Free Press.

Novak, J. D., & Gowan, B. D. (1984). *Learning how to learn*. New York: Cambridge University Press.

O'Neil, J. (1990). Findings of styles research murky at best. *Educational Leadership*. 48(2), 7.

Ornstein, A. (1987). Emphasis on student outcomes focuses attention on quality of instruction. *NASSP Bulletin*, 71, 88-95.

Paul, R., Binker, A, Jensen, K., & Kreklau, H. (1990). *Critical thinking handbook: 4th-6th grades*. Rohnert Park, CA: Sonoma State University, Foundation for Critical Thinking. (Note that they also have a similar book for K-3, 6-9, and High School.)

Perkins, D. (1995). *Outsmarting IQ. The emerging science of learnable intelligence*. New York: Free Press.

Perkins, D. (1991). *Knowledge as design*. Hillsdale, NJ: Lawrence Erlbaum.

Phelan, P., Davidson, A. L., & Cao, H. T. (1992). Speaking up: Students' perspectives on school. *Phi Delta Kappan*, 73(9), 695-704.

Popham, W. J. (1987). Two-plus decades of educational objectives. *International Journal of Educational Research*, 11, 31-41.

Pratten, J., & Hates, L. W. (1985). The effects of active participation on student learning. *Journal of Educational Research*, 79, 210-215.

Pressley, M., Levin, J., & Miller, G. (1981). The keyword method and children's learning of foreign vocabulary with abstract meaning. *Canadian Psychology*, 35(3), 283-287.

Rolheiser, C. (Ed.). (1996). *Self-evaluation...helping students get better at it!* Ajax, ON: VISUTronX.

Rolheiser, C., Bower, B., & Stevahn, L. (2000). *The portfolio organizer*. Alexandria, VA: Association for Supervision and Curriculum Development.

Rolheiser-Bennett, C. (1986). Four models of teaching: A meta-analysis of student outcomes. *Doctoral Dissertation*, University of Oregon.

Rosenholtz, S. (1989). *The teachers' workplace: The social organization of schools*. New York: Longman.

Rosenshine, B. (1986). Synthesis of research on explicit teaching. *Educational Leadership*. 43(7), 60-69.

Rowe, M. B. (1974). Wait time and rewards as instructional variables, their influence on language, logic and fate control: Part 1. Wait-time. *Journal of Research in Science Teaching*, 11, 81-94.

Saphier, J., & Gower, R. (1987). *The skillful teacher: Building your teaching skills*. Carlisle, MA: Research for Better Teaching.

Saul, J. R. (1992). *Voltaire's bastards: The dictatorship of reason in the west*. New York: The Free Press.

Seigal, M. (1995). More than words: The generative power of transmediation for learning. *Canadian Journal of Education*, 20(4), 455 - 475.

Schmuck, R., & Schmuck, P. (1988). *Group processes in the classroom*. Dubuque: IA: Wm. C. Brown.

Schunk, D. H. (1981). Modeling and attributional effects on children's achievement: A self-efficacy analysis. *Journal of Educational Psychology*, 73, 93-105.

Seashore-Louis, K., & Miles, M. (1986). *Improving the urban high school: What works and why*. New York: Teacher College Press.

Sharan, Y., & Sharan, S. (1992). *Expanding cooperative learning through group investigation*. New York: Teachers College Press.

Sharan, S. (Ed.). (1990). *Cooperative learning: Theory and research*. New York: Praeger.

Sizer, T. (1984). *Horace's compromise. The dilemma of the American high school*. Boston, MA: Houghton Mifflin.

Slavin, R. E. (1995). *Cooperative learning*. Needham Heights, MA: Allyn & Bacon.

Slavin, R. E. (1986). *Using student team learning*. John Hopkins University: Center for Research on Elementary and Middle Schools.

Slavin, R. (1980). Cooperative learning. *Review of Educational Research*, 50, 315-342.

Snider, V.E. (1990). What we know about learning styles from research in special education. *Educational Leadership*, 48(2), 53.

Sprenger, M. (1999). *Learning and memory: The brain in action*. Alexandria, VA: ASCD.

Stelmaschuck, M. (1986). Identified and unidentified gifted: A comparative analysis. *Doctoral Dissertation*, University of Alberta.

Stice (1987). Hierarchical concept mapping in the early grades. *Childhood Education*, 64, December, 86-96.

Soar, R. S., & Soar, R. M. (1979). Emotional climate in management. In P. L. Peterson & H. J. Walberg (Eds.), *Research on Teaching*. Berkeley CA: McCutchan.

Sylwester, R. (1998). The brain and learning video: Part I. Alexandria VA: ASCD.

Taba, H. (1967). *Teachers' handbook for elementary social studies*. Reading, MA: Addison-Wesley.

Tobin, K. (1980). The effect of an extended teacher wait time on science achievement. *Journal of Research in Science Teaching*, 17, 469-475.

Tuchman, B.W. (1994). *March of folly: From Troy to Vietnam*. New York: A.A. Knopf.

Vance, C. M. (1981). The development and test of a prescriptive strategy for the use of incongruity humor in the design of instruction. (Doctoral dissertation, Syracuse University, 1981). *Dissertation Abstracts International*, 42, 1942A.

Wang, M.C., Haertel, G.D., & Walberg, H.J. (1994). Synthesis of Research: What helps students learn. *Educational Leadership*, 51(4), 74-79.

Wang, M. C., Haertel, G. D., & Walberg, H. J. (1994). Synthesis of research: What helps students learn. *Educational Leadership*, 51(4), 74-79.

Waxman, H. C., & Walberg, H. J. (Eds). (1991). *Effective teaching: Current research*. Berkeley, CA: McCuchan Publishing Corporation.

Weiler, K. (1991). Freire and a feminist pedagogy of difference. *Harvard Educational Review*, 61(4), 449-474.

Weinberg, M. D. (1974). The interactional effect of humor and anxiety on academic performance (Doctoral dissertation, Yeshiva University, 1973). *Dissertation Abstracts International*, 35, 492B-493B.

White R., & Gunstone, R. (1992). *Probing for understanding*. Basingstoke: Falmer Press.

White, W.A.T. (1988). A meta-analysis of the effects of direct instruction in special education. *Education and Treatment of Children*. 11(4), 364-374.

Wilson, J. (1991). *Concept mapping: What have you got in mind?* No. 4.

Wittrock, M. C. (Ed.). (1986). *Handbook of research on teaching* (3rd. ed.). New York: Macmillan.

Woyshner, C.A., & Gelfond, H. S. (1998). *Minding women: Reshaping the educational realm*. Cambridge, MA: Harvard Educational Review.

Index

Order Form

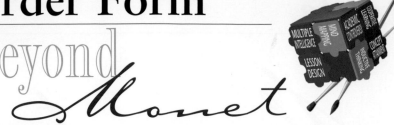

Beyond *Monet*

CENTER FOR DEVELOPMENT AND LEARNING (CDL)

208 S. Tyler Street
Covington, LA 70433
(985)893-7777 Fax: (985)893-5443
www.cdl.org   learn@cdl.org

Quantity	Title	Unit Price	Total
	Beyond Monet: *The Artful Science of Instructional Integration*	$38.95ᴜꜱ	$

(Price is subject to change without notice. Returns NOT accepted unless damaged in shipment.)

CREDIT CARD ORDERS:
Fax Order Form To:
(985)893-5443

ORDERS UTILIZING A PURCHASE ORDER OR PAYING BY CHECK:
Send Order Form To:
CDL
208 S. Tyler Street
Covington, LA 70433
Make check payable to: CDL

10% Discount for 50+ Copies   - $ _____

                                         Subtotal $ _____

Louisiana Orders: Add 4% of subtotal for state sales tax   + $ _____

US Shipping & Handling: $4.95 for one copy; for additional books ordered, add $3.00 each   + $ _____

For shipment outside of the US, please call for shipping and handling.

Total: $ _____

Receipt will be included in shipment.

Bill To:

Name _____ Organization _____
Address _____
City _____ State _____ ZIP _____
Phone (____) _____ Fax (____) _____
Email _____

Ship To (if different):

Name _____ Organization _____
Address _____
City _____ State _____ ZIP _____
Phone (____) _____ Fax (____) _____
Email _____

Credit Card Information:

❑ VISA/MC   ❑ AMEX   ❑ DISCOVER

Name As it Appears on Card _____
Card No. _____ Exp _____
Authorized Signature _____